Advanced Studies in Media

Joe Nicholas and John Price

Additional contributors:

Samantha Bakhurst
John Scotney
Andrew Webber

Thomas Nelson & Sons Ltd
Nelson House
Mayfield Road
Walton-on-Thames
Surrey KT12 5PL
United Kingdom

First published by Thomas Nelson & Sons Ltd 1998

ISBN 0-17-490047-3
9 8 7 6 5 4 3 2
02 01 00 99

Typeset in 9/12pt Palatino by Hardlines
Printed in China

Publication Team:
Acquisitions: Alex Bridgland, Steve Berry
Editorial Management: Simon Tanner-Tremaine
Freelance Editorial: Debbie Howard, Janice Baiton, Zeb Korycinska
Design and Illustration: Hardlines, Charlbury, Oxfordshire
Picture Research: Image Select International

Contents

Section 4: Toolkit

About the authors

Joe Nicholas has been teaching Media Studies and Communication Studies for more than ten years. He is Head of English and Communication at Oaklands College of Further Education, St Albans. He has lectured in Higher Education and is an honorary Research Fellow of the University of Reading. He is co-author of *Advanced GNVQ Media: Communication and Production*.

John Price has initiated and administered the Newspapers in Education department at the *Sunderland Echo* since 1986, which has enabled him to acquire inside knowledge of how a local newspaper operates. During this time he has been able to advise and help with the production of over 200 student newspapers. He began teaching Media Studies in 1972 and was Teacher Representative on the Board of Film and Television Studies at Bede College, Durham. His English department became a training ground for the first wave of specially trained Media Studies teachers. He has written or co-written several publications on print media, including *The Newspaper Study Pack, Headline News, Learning from Newspapers, Press Conference* and *Advanced GNVQ Media: Communication and Production*.

About the contributors

Samantha Bakhurst works as a writer, media projects consultant and educationalist. She has taught in France and England for eight years, mainly in the area of Media Studies and has contributed to several media textbooks. She is currently working on projects for radio and television.

John Scotney teaches a post-graduate course in Radio at West Herts College in Watford. He is a guest lecturer at the Central School of Drama and for BBC Staff Training. He has written over 50 radio programmes and produced over 300, including a period as Chief Producer of *The Archers* on BBC Radio 4.

Andrew Webber teaches Media Studies and English at Chatham Grammar School for Girls in Kent. He studied Film and Literature at Warwick University and Humanities at Christchurch College, Canterbury. He is undertaking a Doctorate in Education at the University of London.

Acknowledgements

The authors and publishers would like to thank the following people for their kind help with this project:

Samantha Bakhurst for her helpful and constructive advice as a media consultant and for her invaluable contribution to the Media Studies Toolkit in Chapter 19. Also for lending Activities 1 and 3 in Chapter 5.
John Scotney for his invaluable contribution to Radio in Chapter 11 and Audio Production in Chapter 17.
Andrew Webber for his invaluable contribution to Film Fiction in Chapter 9, Pop Music in Chapter 12 and Video Production in Chapter 18.
Also: John Holmes for lending Activity 10 in Chapter 5 which is based on one of his handouts; Tim Reeve for his concept design; and Richard Duszczak for the cartoons in Figures 13.7 and 18.5.

The authors and publishers would like to thank the following for permission to reproduce photographs:

Allsport: Figures 13.6 (Shaun Botterill), 13.9 (Adrian Murrell), 13.12 top, 13.12 middle (Shaun Botterill), 13.12 bottom (Richard Saker), 13.13 (Shaun Botterill), 17.5 (Phil Cole)
BBC News & Current Affairs: Figure 8.8
BBC Worldwide: Figures 3.1 (Stephen F Morley), 11.5, 11.7, 11.8, 11.12, 14.18, 17.1, 17.2, 17.3, 17.6, 17.7
BFI Stills, Posters and Designs: Figures 4.2, 4.3, 4.9, 6.4, 6.6, 9.2 left, 9.3 left & right, 9.5, 9.6, 9.7, 9.8 top & bottom, 9.10, 10.6, 10.7 left & right, 10.8, 10.9, 10.10 top, middle & bottom, 10.11 right, 12.5 left & right
Romano Cagnoni: photograph in Figure 10.5
Channel 4: Figures 2.4, 2.5 left & right, 2.6, 2.8, 10.4
Channel 5: Figure 8.1 right
Empics: photograph in advert on page 15
The Guardian: photograph on page 110
Hovis: photograph in Figure 14.3
Hulton Getty: Figures 6.5, 11.6
Image Select International: Figures 2.1, 10.2, 11.1, 11.4, 16.8, 17.8
The Independent: photograph in Figure 1.13 (Nicola Kurtz)
Independent Music Press: Figure 12.11 (Sharon Thornhill)
ITN: Figure 8.1 left
The Kobal Collection: Figure 9.9 top & bottom
LWT: Figures 3.3, 13.2
Mirror Syndication International: Figure 13.1
Andrea Norrington: photograph on page 14
Gail Olding: Figure 1.3
PA News: photograph in Figure 8.5 (Rebecca Naden)
PIX: Figure 8.6 (FPG/P & L Ambrose)
Polygram Filmed Entertainment: Figure 4.4 (Stephen Morley)
Popperfoto: photograph in Figure 8.4 (Ramesh Kumar)
Brenda Prince/Format: Figure 4.5,
Redferns: Figures 12.2 bottom (Mick Hutson), 12.3 bottom (H B), 12.6 top (Debbie Doss), 12.6 bottom (Mick Hutson), 17.4 left (Glenn A Baker Archives), 17.4 middle (Suzi Gibbons), 17.4 right (Mick Hutson)
Renault UK Ltd: Figure 14.17
Rex Features: Figures 3.4 (David Cairns/Today), 5.1 (Edward Hirst), 6.1 left (Brian Rasic), 6.3 (Juliet Coombe), 7.1 (Today), 7.3 (Today), 7.6 (Edward Webb), 8.7 (Alexandra Boulat), 10.1 bottom (Crispin Rodwell), 11.11, 12.2 top, 12.4 top (Sunshine/Grapevine), 12.4 bottom, 15.5 (Herbie Knott)
Howard Sooley: photographs in Figure 18.2, Figure 18.3
Stewart Bonney Agency: photograph in Figure 2.3
Sunderland Echo/Northeast Press Ltd: Figure 16.2
Today: photographs in Figure 7.5 (Steve Burton)
Tony Stone Images: Figures 15.6 (Zigy Kaluzny), 18.6 (Molinare/John Price), Cover (Tony Hutchings)
Trip: Figure 15.4 (H Rogers), 18.4 (Chris Parker)
Universal Pictures: Figure 10.1
John Walmsley: Figure 18.1
Warner Music UK Ltd: Figure 12.3 top (Steve Wright)
R Derek Wilbraham: Figure 7.7
Yorkshire Post Newspapers Ltd: Figure 16.3

The authors and publishers would like to thank the following for permission to reproduce copyright material:

Addison Wesley Longman Ltd for the illustration from *Communication Models, 2nd edition*, 1993, by Denis McQuail and Sven Windahl reproduced in Figure 5.9.

The Advertising Archives for the Guinness advert reproduced in Figure 14.5.

Glen Baxter (The Colonel) for his cartoon 'It was Tom's first brush with modernism' from *The Impending Gleam*, 1981, reproduced in Figure 1.2.

Steve Bell for his cartoon 'Lucky Beggars' from *Guardian*, 8 January 1997, reproduced in Activity 4 on page 16; and for his cartoon 'Lucky Beggars 2' from *Guardian*, 10 January 1997, reproduced in Figure 1.6.

BBC Worldwide Ltd and Hat Trick Productions Ltd for the cover from *Have I Got News For You*, 1994, reproduced in Figure 1.11; and for the text for the pages from *Have I Got News For You*, 1994, reproduced in Figure 3.5.

BIFF Products for their cartoon on media studies from *Guardian Weekend*, 31 August 1996, reproduced on page 235.

Bloomberg TV for the screen reproduced in Figure 8.2.

British Board of Film Classification for their certification symbols reproduced on page 31.

British Film Institute for the poster of *The War Game* reproduced in Figure 10.11.

British Telecommunications plc for the advert reproduced in Figure 14.10.

Broadcasters' Audience Research Board Ltd (BARB) for 'This Week's Viewing Summary', week ending 10 March 1997, reproduced in Figure 5.5; and for the graph reproduced in Figure 13.3.

Butterworth-Heinemann for the illustrations from *Radio Production, 3rd edition*, 1994, by Robert McLeish reproduced in Figures 11.2 and 11.3.

Camden Press Ltd for the text and illustrations from *Media & Power: from Marconi to Murdoch*, 1986, by Peter Lewis and Corinne Pearlman reproduced in Figure 5.6.

Campaign for Press and Broadcasting Freedom for the cartoons by John Morton reproduced in Figure 1.14.

Leanne Campbell for her singles and albums review page reproduced in Activity 1 on page 159.

Capital FM for their logo reproduced in Figure 11.9.

Channel 5 for the advert reproduced in Activity 3 on page 15.

Cherry Red Records for their logo reproduced in Figure 12.1.

Cinergi Pictures Entertainment for the poster of *Evita* reproduced in Figure 14.19.

Controller of Her Majesty's Stationery Office for the Official Secrets Act 1989 reproduced in Figure 3.6.

Tristan Davies for his article 'The heart of doorstepping' from 'Parish Pump', *Daily Telegraph*, 8 March 1997, reproduced in Figure 6.8.

Emi Records for the cover of *Dark Side of the Moon*, 1973, by Pink Floyd reproduced in Figure 12.10.

Factory Records for the cover of 'Blue Monday' by New Order reproduced in Figure 12.10.

4AD Records for their logo reproduced in Figure 12.1; for the covers of *Bossanova* by Pixies and *Last Splash* by The Breeders reproduced in Figure 12.7 top & bottom; for the covers of *Heidi Berry* by Heidi Berry and 'Aikea-Guinea' by Cocteau Twins reproduced in Figure 12.8 top & bottom; for the covers of *Monkey Gone to Heaven* by Pixies and *Down Colorful Hill* by Red House Painters reproduced in Figure 12.9 top & bottom; and for the covers of *Red House Painters* by Red House Painters and *Lush* by Lush reproduced in Activity 4 on page 160 left & right.

John Frost Newspapers for the pages from the *Radio Times*, 28 February 1936, reproduced in Figure 5.2.

Full Frequency Range Recordings for their logo reproduced in Figure 12.1

The Guardian for the article 'Protect this fragile heart' by Paula Milne from *Media Guardian*, 11 November 1996, reproduced on page 23; for the article 'Sam Peckinpah, Martin Scorsese – and me' by Bel Littlejohn from *Guardian*, 27 September 1996, reproduced in Activity 3 on page 39; for the article 'Modern recipes: No19: X-Files rip-offs' by David Bennum reproduced in Figure 6.10; for the extract from 'Wheen's World' by Francis Wheen from *Guardian*, 8 January 1997, reproduced in Figure 7.4; for the illustration from *Guardian*, 25 January 1997, reproduced in Figure 8.4; for the illustration from *Guardian*, 23 January 1997, reproduced in Figure 8.5; for the textual information from 'Murdoch's sporting empire' from *Guardian*, 26 July 1997, reproduced in Figure 13.4; and for the article 'Butties and Beer at No.10' by Trevor Beattie from *Media Guardian*, 19 May 1997, reproduced in Figure 14.3.

Haymarket Marketing Publications Ltd for the article 'The making of Cosmo Woman' by Dominic Mills from *Campaign*, 21 February 1997, reproduced in Figure 16.7.

House of Viz/John Brown Publishing Ltd for the comic strip 'The Modern Parents' by John Fardell from *Viz*, Issue 81, December 1996, reproduced in Figure 1.5; and for the article 'Elton and the general purpose builder' from *The Pan Handle*, Viz annual, 1994, reproduced in Activity 6 on page 108.

Icon Books Ltd for the text and illustrations from *Postmodernism for Beginners*, 1995, by Richard Appignanesi and Chris Garratt with Ziauddin Sardar and Patrick Curry reproduced in Figure 6.14.

The Independent for the text and illustrations from 'Men's glossies put Cosmo in slow lane' by Paul McCann from *Independent*, 15 August 1997, reproduced in Figure 1.8; for the illustration from *Independent*, 15 August 1997, reproduced in Figure 1.13; and for the article 'Health staff face widespread attacks surveys reveal' by Nicholas Timmins from *Independent*, 14 November 1986, reproduced in Activity 7 on page 109.

Institute of Practitioners in Advertising and NTC Publications Ltd for the graphs from MRSL/*Adworks* 9 reproduced in Figures 14.6, 14.7, 14.8 and 14.9; and for the graphs from BMRB/*Adworks* 9 reproduced in Figures 14.11, 14.12 and 14.13.

Island Records Ltd for their logo reproduced in Figure 12.1

Michael Jones for his project report on making a student video with John Sutherland reproduced on pages 221–225.

London Records Ltd for their logo reproduced in Figure 12.1

Macmillan General Books for the page from *The Unofficial X-Files Companion* by Ngaire Genge reproduced in Figure 6.15.

Methuen for the pages from *Oh What a Lovely War* by Joan Littlewood's Theatre Workshop reproduced in Figure 10.5.

The Mirror and Piers Morgan for the front page from *Mirror*, 24 June 1996, reproduced in Figure 3.2; and for the extract from the article 'I first had sex when I was 11' from *Mirror*, 4 January 1997, reproduced in Figure 8.3.

Murphy's and Bartle Bogart Hegerty for the advert reproduced in Figure 14.5.

National Readership Surveys Ltd (NRS) for Table 6, January to December 1996, reproduced in Figure 5.3.

Newcastle Chronicle and Journal Ltd for the article 'Newcastle United and *The Journal*' by Bill Bradshaw from *Newcastle Journal*, 7 October 1994, reproduced in Figure 7.2.

News International Newspapers Ltd for the extracts from the article 'We've Dan it!' by Martin Wallace and the editorial comment 'Dan finally...' from *Sun*, 20 November 1997, reproduced in Figure 5.7; for the article 'Ginny, Ginny, give us your answer do' by Adrian Lee from *Today*, 10 May 1995, reproduced in Figure 7.5; for the article 'Angels in Peril' by Fiona Webster from *Sun*, 26 November 1986, reproduced in Activity 7 on page 109; for the illustration 'How United will conquer the world' from *News of the World*, 12 January 1997, reproduced in Figure 13.5; and for the illustration of George Weah's great goal by Sian Frances from *The Times*, 16 September 1996, reproduced in Figure 13.10.

Nissan for the advert reproduced in Figure 14.2.

Northeast Press Ltd for the advertising rate card for *Sunderland Echo* reproduced in Figure 2.2; for the advertorial 'A fun-packed free-for-all' by Rob Freeth from *Sunderland Echo*, 9 October 1997, reproduced in Figure 2.3; and for the article 'Melville's big toe' from *Sunderland Echo*, 17 September 1996, reproduced in Figure 13.11.

Polygram Film International for the poster of *Four Weddings and a Funeral* reproduced in Figure 2.7.

Punch magazine for the 'Party Games' page from the issue of 22–28 March 1997 reproduced in Figure 16.6.

Radio Joint Audience Research Ltd (RAJAR) for 'Quarterly Summary of Radio Listening', 23 September–22 December 1996, reproduced in Figure 5.4.

Dave Raymond for the copy of *Just Seventeen*, 19 January 1994, reproduced in Figure 4.1.

Rough Trade Records Ltd for the cover of 'Hand in Glove', 1984, by The Smiths with Sandie Shaw reproduced in Figure 12.10; and for the cover of 'This Charming Man', 1983, by The Smiths reproduced in Figure 12.10.

SCOPE for the front cover of *Disability Now*, February 1998, reproduced in Figure 4.11; and for the advert reproduced in Figure 4.6.

Secker & Warburg for the extract from *Nice Work*, 1988, by David Lodge reproduced in Figure 1.7.

Donna Sheffield for her project report on producing 'Donna's Directory' reproduced on pages 199–200; for the page from 'Donna's Directory' reproduced in Figure 16.4; and for the advert for 'Donna's Directory' reproduced in Figure 16.5.

Sky Sports for the screen reproduced in Figure 13.8.

Sugar magazine for the 'Earth Alert' page from Issue 21, July 1996, reproduced in Figure 16.6.

John Sutherland for his project report on making a student video with Michael Jones reproduced on pages 221–225.

Thames and Hudson for the pages from *Derek Jarman's Garden*, 1995, by Derek Jarman with photographs by Howard Sooley reproduced in Figure 18.2.

Ian Turner for the text of the Andy's Records radio advert reproduced in Activity 2 on page 146.

Turner Entertainment Company/MGM for the poster of *2001: A Space Odyssey* reproduced in Figure 6.1.

Twentieth Century Fox Film Corporation for the images from *The X-Files*, 1996, reproduced in Figures 6.7, 6.9 left, middle & right, 6.11 left & right, 6.12 and 6.13; for the page from the web site www.thex-files.com reproduced in Figure 6.15; and for the poster of *A Walk in the Clouds*, 1995, reproduced on page 233.

Universal City Studios Inc for the poster of *Babe*, 1995, reproduced in Figure 1.12.

Rose Veitch for her project report on planning and making a children's radio programme reproduced on pages 192–194 and 214–216.

Walt Disney Pictures for the poster of *101 Dalmations* reproduced in Figure 3.8.

Warner Brothers for the poster of *Unforgiven*, 1992, reproduced in Figure 9.11.

Wonderbra and Jackie Cooper Public Relations for the advert reproduced in Figure 14.1.

Every effort has been made to trace all the copyright holders, but if any have been inadvertently overlooked the publishers will be pleased to make the necessary arrangements at the first opportunity.

CHAPTER 1

Analysing media texts

Introduction

This chapter looks at how to analyse media products, including:

- why and how media texts are analysed
- image analysis
- verbal language
- semiotics
- codes and conventions
- genre
- intertextuality
- narrative
- representation
- bias and ideology.

It covers a lot of ground, and is meant to be both introductory and a source of reference for you to return to. You may go into some sections in detail, working through the related activities thoroughly, while others you may read through and decide to come back to later. It is up to you to develop your understanding of the textual analysis categories and concepts introduced here, and to 'crack the codes' in the media products you read, hear, view and analyse.

Why analyse media products?

Often the output of the media seems 'natural' and just 'there'. Turning on the television can seem like turning on a tap. This is an illusion which conceals the amount of work which goes into media products and the choices that are made in putting them together. Analysis puts media products under a magnifying glass and 'reveals the joins'.

From your experience as a consumer, you already possess a multitude of skills in understanding media products, their language and signs. To study the media at advanced level you will have to develop this understanding and demonstrate it in written analysis. You will also need to become more aware of how you and others make meanings out of the media. This chapter explores how other people have increased their understanding and how the terminology of media studies has developed.

Understanding the language of media studies

Like any other subject studied at advanced level, media studies has its own language, or jargon, in which theories and methods are expressed. The word 'jargon' can be negative, but here it is used neutrally. Within a subject like media studies, jargon words are used because they have special meanings and can save time. They are tools which people use to summarise ideas and techniques.

Like other subject jargons, the terminology of media studies can be divided into:

- everyday words which have a special meaning
- terms specific to the subject.

If you look at the list in the introduction of areas covered in this chapter, you will see examples of both of these types of word. For example, in everyday language the word 'text' refers to a piece of writing such as a book. However, a 'media text' is the material which makes up a complete media product, including form, language, images, sounds and so on. The Spice Girls as people are not texts, but most people only know them through the texts in which they feature.

Figure 1.1 Images of the Spice Girls are at least as important as words in Spice Girls texts

You will also find words which are not usual in everyday language and which are probably new to you, such as:

- 'genre' (type) – Figure 1.1 is in the genre of the pop star poster found in magazines and on walls
- 'semiotics' (the study of how signs work in communication) – a semiotic analysis of the poster would involve identifying all the signs within it, including clothes, hair, facial expressions and postures
- 'intertextuality' (links between texts) – the Spice Girls poster has intertextual links with other texts such as their songs, videos and television advertisements.

Another word on the list is 'code'. A secret code can only be understood by people who have access to the rules which enable them to decode it into everyday language, and this is a good way to explain what this chapter is about. The codes in media studies are the patterns which rule how the contents of media products are selected and combined. When you look at how a media product works and how the text is put together, you are decoding it. Studying and analysing media texts can be compared to a detective cracking a code.

IT WAS TOM'S FIRST BRUSH WITH MODERNISM

Figure 1.2

All advanced media syllabuses cover the various concepts and theories which have been used to decode and understand media products. These come under the umbrella heading of text analysis.

Text analysis

Text analysis is the taking apart of a media product. As already explained, the complete pieces of communication which media organisations package and produce as programmes, features and publications are all known as 'media texts'. Text analysis involves asking questions about a media text and trying to find answers from within it.

For example, when carrying out text analysis you might ask the following questions:

1. What is the content of the text? What images does it contain? What do those images contain? What kinds of written and/or spoken language (verbal language) are used? What relationships are there between the verbal language and the images? What relationships are there between the forms in the text and its meaning? What conventions does the text use or fall under? Is there any part of the text which seems new or 'alternative'?
2. What type of product/text is it? Does it use any recognised types (genres)? What links does it have with other texts inside or outside the genres it fits into?
3. What is the overall shape of the text? What story or stories does it tell? What is the relationship between the story and the overall shape (structure) of the text?
4. How are groups of people referred to in the text and how are issues portrayed? Are issues of ethnicity, gender, class, or disability represented, and if so, how? (This is referred to briefly in this chapter, but is treated more fully in chapter 4.)
5. What is (are) the dominant message(s) in the text? What points of view are represented? What is apparent in terms of any political or other bias (ideology)?
6. Who produced the text? For whom was it produced (audience)? What is its intended outcome? How was it financed? (This is dealt with in chapters 2, 3 and 5.)

This chapter introduces and explains questions 1 to 5, all of which can be answered simply or mainly by close attention to the media text itself. These questions are also dealt with and developed in analyses of media texts elsewhere in the book.

Image analysis

All visual and print media draw heavily upon images in order to put across what they want to say. In fact, media products are often packed with images; a simple count of the images in one edition of the teenage football magazine *Match* (6 May 1996) showed that 56 pages contained 198 complete images (Nicholas, Price and Moore, 1996).

Content analysis of different categories of images (counting of categories) is also important. In the analysis of *Match*, for example, there was only one image including females, underlining the male orientation of the magazine.

Image analysis usually refers to the detailed analysis of an individual image, covering everything which can be identified in the image. For a photograph this would include:

- the positioning of the camera
- lighting
- composition
- framing
- focusing
- objects and people and their placing
- the meanings which result.

▶◀ *See page 233 for an example of a full image analysis*

Denotation and connotation

Image analysis can be broken down using two terms which originate from semiotics: denotation and connotation.

Two simple instructions can help you to organise and develop an individual image analysis:

1 Describe simply what the image contains within its frame.
2 Keep the interpretation of the picture separate from the description of its contents.

These stages can be described as:

1 Denotation – what is literally 'in the picture', such as colours or shades of black and white.
2 Connotation – the different interpretations which might be associated with a picture. For example, a colour has a number of possible connotations (green may be associated with envy, nature, fertility and eco-friendliness).

Figure 1.3

The *denotation* of the image above is the interior of a 'polytunnel', with polythene stretched over a frame with low walls and a curving roofline. The image is in black and white. The floor of the polytunnel is bare earth apart from a slab. In the background is the entrance to the polytunnel with fencing beyond. In the foreground of the image are two men. The one on the left holds the shafts of a wheelbarrow, and the one on the right is standing on the slab holding a shovel over the barrow. Both men have similar close-cropped hair, naked torsos, and are wearing tracksuit bottoms, heavy socks and boots. Both have tattoos and appear to be looking into the barrow. The man on the left is wearing a watch with a square face. The one on the right has a neck chain and appears to be wearing gloves, although only his left gloved hand can be seen.

The *connotation* of the image is of a male workplace. The appearance of the men strongly connotes traditional masculinity in their hair, tattoos and boots. This links with the activities of manual labour; the photographer appears to have caught the men in the middle of loading a barrow. The photograph has a documentary style indicated by the use of black and white, and the apparent use of natural light. It appears to have recorded actuality rather than a constructed fiction, since the two men do not look like actors.

◀ *See Activity 1, page 14*

Verbal language

An awareness of verbal language is important for the analysis of media texts. To meet the requirements of advanced media studies you will need to be aware of vocabulary and grammar at a basic level.

One way to look at media 'languages' is to begin with the language of words and their grammatical patterns. The language, or languages, in which you speak and write fall under the heading of verbal language ('verbal' here means 'of words', not 'of verbs').

Vo'cabulary *n* stock of words in a language or in a person's knowledge; stock of words peculiar to a particular profession etc; (book containing) a list of words in alphabetical order, with translations

Word (wœd) *n* smallest meaningful spoken or written unit; promise; news; conversation; message, order; (with **the** and *cap*) writings of the Bible

Figure 1.4 Dictionary definitions of 'word' and 'vocabulary'

Verbal language can be divided into:

- the 'signs' which it is made up of (i.e. words). A language's stock of signs is called the 'vocabulary', and it is useful to analyse how words from this vocabulary are selected and used in a text. Some media texts are characterised by unusual vocabulary. For example, stories involving sports stars, especially footballers, often use nicknames ('Giggsy' for Ryan Giggs, 'Gazza' for Paul Gascoigne, and so on)
- the patterns in which these signs are put together in order to convey more complex messages. These patterns are known as the 'code' or 'grammar'. When the structural pattern of words in a sentence is interesting or unusual, the grammar is worthy of comment. So, for example, tabloid newspapers use short sentences with short phrases such as 'up yours!', rather than 'disagree' or 'beg to differ'.

Let's begin an analysis of verbal language by looking at the vocabulary and grammar in one media text: 'The Modern Parents', a comic strip from *Viz* magazine (December 1996).

Figure 1.5 'The Modern Parents', Viz, December 1996

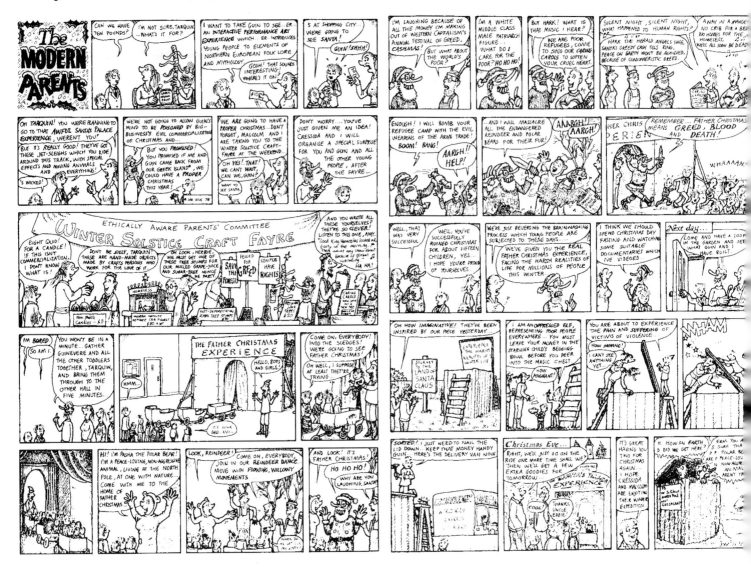

Vocabulary

One way to analyse the vocabulary selected and used in this text is to find groups of words which have a theme or area of meaning in common. These include:

- vocabulary associated with Christmas – Santa, Santa Claus, Father Christmas, Xmas, Nativity, North Pole, reindeer, Good King Wenceslas, Hark!, crib, manger, sledges, carols, party, Christmas Day
- vocabulary for gifts – presents, goodies, special surprise
- vocabulary for money and commerce – ten pounds, £8, £20, £80, money, big business, commercialisation, cash tills, consumeristic, begging bowl, western capitalism
- vocabulary of ethics – evil, greed, ethically aware, peace loving, rights, human rights

- ecological vocabulary – anti-deforestation, at one with nature, endangered reindeer, global warming, green, organic, recycled, save the forests
- political vocabulary – arms trade, brainwashing process, homeless, refugees
- vocabulary of gender – craftspersons, non-phallic.

Guinevere, the daughter, uses a vocabulary group associated with youth culture. She uses words with recent changes in meaning, such as 'wicked' and 'cool'. Tarquin also uses 'sorted'. Words are used to represent noises such as 'shhh!', 'ho ho', 'boom', 'bang', 'aargh!', 'whaah!', and 'wham'. This sort of vocabulary is strongly associated with comic strip conventions. The words are said to be 'onomatopoeic', because they sound like the noises they describe.

Code or grammar

The code into which verbal language is organised is called grammar. In grammar, small patterns of words are built up into larger patterns. So, for example, words are built up into phrases, which are then built up into sentences. The organisation of a phrase makes up a phrase structure, and the organisation of a sentence makes up a sentence structure.

Many of the sentences in 'The Modern Parents' comic strip dialogue are short and simple. There are also words and phrases without verbs which are punctuated as sentences, such as 'Hmm.', 'Into the sledges!', 'Enough!', 'Cool!'. These mimic the structure of real utterances.

In contrast with the simplicity of much of the grammar in the comic strip, there are also patterns like the following:

Group A

1 'that awful santa's palace **experience**'
2 'ethically aware parents' **committee**'
3 'winter solstice craft **fayre**'
4 'our mulled grape juice and sugar free mince pie **party**'
5 'white middle class patriarch **figure**'.

Group B

1 'an interactive performance art **experience**... which introduces young people'
2 'big business's evil **commercialisation** of Christmas'
3 'hand made **objects** made by craftspersons for the love of it'
4 'a peace loving, non aggressive **animal**, living at the north pole, at one with nature'
5 'western capitalism's annual **festival** of greed'
6 'the evil **weapons** of the arms trade'
7 'the brainwashing **process** which young people are subjected to these days'
8 'an oppressed **elf** representing starving peoples everywhere'
9 'the **pain** and **suffering** of victims of violence'.

These patterns of words are in groups which would make up part of a sentence, but would not normally stand alone as written sentences in their own right. They are strings of long complex phrases or groups of words built up around the words in bold (all nouns). Group A has a lot of descriptive words in front of the bold headword. Group B has descriptive words both in front of and following the headword.

There is a contrast between the simpler structures used in the rest of the comic strip and these long strings or phrase structures. These complex phrases are mostly used to mock Malcolm and Cressida's pompous use of the English language. They are couched in the language of new age, leftish anti-establishment ideologies which Malcolm and Cressida seem to love more than they love their children.

▶◀ *See Activity 2, page 15*

The relationship between verbal language and images

Language and images are combined in media texts, and verbal language tends to restrict the many possible meanings which images can have. For example, the commentary on a news film tends to add information which explains the images presented to the viewer. A frequently used image from a photo library may have many different uses over the years. The capacity of language to 'tie down' particular meanings connoted by images is referred to as 'anchorage'. For example, a photo of Tony Blair could have many different captions and anchors: 'father-of-three Tony Blair', 'the Prime Minister', 'New Labour leader', 'phony Tony' etc.

▶◀ *See Activity 3, page 15*

Semiotics and media languages

In media studies the term 'language' often refers to more than just verbal language. Looking at language may involve looking at every method of communication, not just those using words. Language in media studies may include images, for example.

This idea of language involving all systems of communication is associated with the modern study of language as proposed by the French theorist, Ferdinand de Saussure. He believed that all the ways in which humans communicate, such as through flags, smoke signals, religious ceremonies and clothes, could be looked at and analysed as if they were languages. In his book *Course in General Linguistics*, de Saussure called this method of studying all signs as language 'semiotics':

> ❛ *Language is a system of signs that express ideas and is thus comparable to the system of writing, to the alphabet of deaf-mutes, to symbolic rituals, to forms of etiquette, to military signals, etc. It is but the most important of these systems. We can therefore imagine a science which would study the life of signs within society... We call it semiotics, from the Greek semeion ('sign'). It would teach us what signs consist of, what laws govern them.* ❜

De Saussure regarded words as simply one system of signs among many. The word 'dog' has no resemblance to the four-legged animal that goes 'woof!'. We learn this connection between the form of the sign and its meaning as young children: it is a symbol.

Images can also be symbols in the sense that we may learn that a shot of a flag means 'patriotism'. However, unlike words, images can work through resemblance. The image of a star resembles the actor with that star career. When an image communicates information through resemblance it is referred to as an 'icon'. Likewise, sweat used in a film to communicate the idea of heat draws upon the power of the image to communicate non-visual information through a causal link or symptom. This type of sign is referred to as an 'index'.

▶◀ *See Activity 4, page 16*

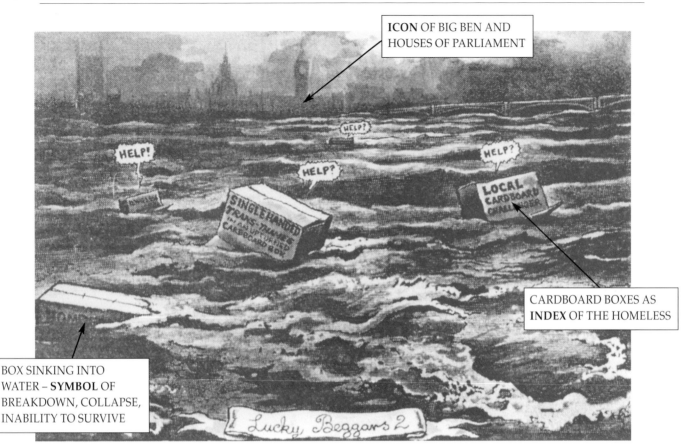

ICON OF BIG BEN AND HOUSES OF PARLIAMENT

CARDBOARD BOXES AS **INDEX** OF THE HOMELESS

BOX SINKING INTO WATER – **SYMBOL** OF BREAKDOWN, COLLAPSE, INABILITY TO SURVIVE

Figure 1.6 'Lucky Beggars 2' is a Steve Bell cartoon from the Guardian on 10 January 1997. The cartoon plays on two events in the news at that time: the rescue of lone yachtsman Tony Bullimore from the Exide Challenger capsized in the Southern Ocean and the plight of the homeless following Tony Blair's criticism of homeless beggars. In iconic terms, the cartoon shows cardboard boxes floating in the Thames

One way of classifying signs is to divide them up into:

- those which are learned (arbitrary signs, such as words)
- those which work through resemblance (photographs)
- those which work through a causal link or symptom (e.g. smoke as an index of fire).

It is sometimes difficult to classify a sign as just one of these, and the divisions are not always clear. Take as an example Mr Spock's pointed ears in *Star Trek*. The ears are:

- iconic of the difference between Mr Spock and other humans
- an index of the fact that Mr Spock is of mixed human and alien parentage (they are human ears with a difference)
- a symbol of Mr Spock's nature; his great intelligence and super logical mode of thought.

De Saussure made an important distinction between two sides of a sign:

- The physical form of the sign, which he referred to as the 'signifier'. For example, in spoken language the sound of the word 'dog' is the signifying part of the sign.
- The meaning or meanings the sign evokes, which he referred to as the 'signified'. For example, the four-legged hairy animal that goes 'woof!' is the signified.

In the case of Spock, the signifier is the physical appearance of his ears, presumably constructed by the make-up department.

◄◄ *See Activity 5, page 16*

Codes and conventions

Codes and conventions govern the way in which signs are chosen and combined.

For example, newsreaders sitting behind a desk as part of the set is a 'convention' of TV news. The choice of desks available, the meanings they create for viewers, and the way they fit in with other choices in the programme are all part of a 'code'. Conventions are the rules which describe predictable patterns. They govern which patterns are normally appropriate, and can also predict the meanings which the patterns convey. A code is the meaningful pattern into which signs are combined.

Consider as an example the filming of interviews. The traditional code of a TV or documentary film interview is to combine shots of the interviewee with occasional cutaways to the interviewer. The convention is that the shots of the interviewer show the putting of questions and the listening role the interviewer plays for the viewer. Behind the scenes in production, the interviewer shots are usually filmed separately, often after the interview has finished. The listening shots are called 'noddy shots' and are used to disguise edits.

Conventions can be broken and new or alternative codes set up. Recently some documentary film-makers have been making interviews breaking the traditional rules above. For example, they have been keeping the interviewee in shot throughout the interview and asking questions from behind the camera. This offers an alternative to the traditional interview code, and is developing its own conventional meaning as a new documentary technique.

A typical instance of this was the furious argument they had about the Silk Cut advertisement. They were returning in his car from visiting a foundry in Derby. ... Every few miles, it seemed, they passed the same huge poster on roadside hoardings, a photographic depiction of a rippling expanse of purple silk in which there was a single slit, as if the material had been slashed with a razor. There were no words on the advertisement, except for the Government Health Warning about smoking. This ubiquitous image, flashing past at regular intervals, both irritated and intrigued Robyn, and she began to do her semiotic stuff on the deep structure hidden beneath its bland surface.

It was in the first instance a kind of riddle. That is to say, in order to decode it, you had to know that there was a brand of cigarettes called Silk Cut. The poster was the iconic representation of a missing name, like a rebus. But the icon was also a metaphor. The shimmering silk, with its voluptuous curves and sensuous texture, obviously symbolized the female body, and the elliptical slit, foregrounded by a lighter colour showing through, was still more obviously a vagina. The advert thus appealed to both sensual and sadistic impulses, the desire to mutilate as well as penetrate the female body.

Vic Wilcox spluttered with outraged derision as she expounded this interpretation. He smoked a different brand, himself, but it was as if he felt his whole philosophy of life was threatened by Robyn's analysis of the advert. 'You must have a twisted mind to see all that in a perfectly harmless bit of cloth,' he said.

'What's the point of it, then?' Robyn challenged him. 'Why use cloth to advertise cigarettes?'

'Well, that's the name of 'em, isn't it? Silk Cut. It's a picture of the name. Nothing more or less.'

'Suppose they'd used a picture of a roll of silk cut in half – would that do just as well?'

'I suppose so. Yes, why not?'

'Because it would look like a penis cut in half, that's why.'

He forced a laugh to cover his embarrassment. 'Why can't you people take things at their face value?'

'What people are you referring to?'

'Highbrows. Intellectuals. You're always trying to find hidden meanings in things. Why? A cigarette is a cigarette. A piece of silk is a piece of silk. Why not leave it at that?'

'When they're represented they acquire additional meanings,' said Robyn. 'Signs are never innocent. Semiotics teaches us that.'

'Semi-what?'

'Semiotics. The study of signs.'

'It teaches us to have dirty minds, if you ask me.'

'Why d'you think the wretched cigarettes were called Silk Cut in the first place?'

'I dunno. It's just a name, as good as any other.'

' "Cut" has something to do with the tobacco, doesn't it? The way the tobacco leaf is cut. Like "Player's Navy Cut" – my uncle Walter used to smoke them.'

'Well, what if it does?' Vic said warily.

'But silk has nothing to do with tobacco. It's a metaphor, a metaphor that means something like, "smooth as silk". Somebody in an advertising agency dreamt up the name "Silk Cut" to suggest a cigarette that wouldn't give you a sore throat or a hacking cough or lung cancer. But after a while the public got used to the name, the word "Silk" ceased to signify, so they decided to have an advertising campaign to give the brand a high profile again. Some bright spark in the agency came up with the idea of rippling silk with a cut in it. The original metaphor is now represented literally. But new metaphorical connotations accrue – sexual ones. Whether they were consciously intended or not doesn't really matter. It's a good example of the perpetual sliding of the signified under the signifier, actually.'

Wilcox chewed on this for a while, then said, 'Why do women smoke them, then, eh?' His triumphant expression showed that he thought this was a knock-down argument. 'If smoking Silk Cut is a form of aggravated rape, as you try to make out, how come women smoke 'em too?'

'Many women are masochistic by temperament,' said Robyn. 'They've learned what's expected of them in a patriarchal society.'

'Ha!' Wilcox exclaimed, tossing back his head. 'I might have known you'd have some daft answer.'

'I don't know why you're so worked up,' said Robyn. 'It's not as if you smoke Silk Cut yourself.'

'No, I smoke Marlboros. Funnily enough, I smoke them because I like the taste.'

'They're the ones that have the lone cowboy ads, aren't they?'

'I suppose that makes me a repressed homosexual, does it?'

'No, it's a very straightforward metonymic message.'

'Metowhat?'

'Metonymic. One of the fundamental tools of semiotics is the distinction between metaphor and metonymy. D'you want me to explain it to you?'

'It'll pass the time,' he said.

'Metaphor is a figure of speech based on similarity, whereas metonymy is based on contiguity. In metaphor you substitute something like the thing you mean for the thing itself, whereas in metonymy you substitute some attribute or cause or effect of the thing for the thing itself.'

'I don't understand a word you're saying.'

'Well, take one of your moulds. The bottom bit is called the drag because it's dragged across the floor and the top bit is called the cope because it covers the bottom bit.'

'I told you that.'

'Yes, I know. What you didn't tell me was that "drag" is a metonymy and "cope" is a metaphor.'

Vic grunted. 'What difference does it make?'

'It's just a question of understanding how language works. I thought you were interested in how things work.'

'I don't see what it's got to do with cigarettes.'

'In the case of the Silk Cut poster, the picture signifies the female body metaphorically: the slit in the silk is like a vagina –'

Vic flinched at the word. 'So you say.'

'All holes, hollow spaces, fissures and folds represent the female genitals.'

'Prove it.'

'Freud proved it, by his successful analysis of dreams,' said Robyn. 'But the Marlboro ads don't use any metaphors. That's probably why you smoke them, actually.'

'What d'you mean?' he said suspiciously.

'You don't have any sympathy with the metaphorical way of looking at things. A cigarette is a cigarette as far as you are concerned.'

'Right.'

'The Marlboro ad doesn't disturb that naive faith in the stability of the signified. It establishes a metonymic connection – completely spurious of course, but realistically plausible – between smoking that particular brand and the healthy, heroic, outdoor life of the cowboy. Buy the cigarette and you buy the life-style, or the fantasy of living it.'

'Rubbish!' said Wilcox. 'I hate the country and the open air. I'm scared to go into a field with a cow in it.'

'Well then, maybe it's the solitariness of the cowboy in the ads that appeals to you. Self-reliant, independent, very macho.'

'I've never heard such a lot of balls in all my life,' said Vic Wilcox, which was strong language coming from him.

'Balls – now that's an interesting expression...' Robyn mused.

'Oh no!' he groaned.

'When you say a man "has balls" approvingly, it's a metonymy, whereas if you say something is a "lot of balls", or "a balls-up", it's a sort of metaphor. The metonymy attributes value to the testicles whereas the metaphor uses them to degrade something else.'

'I can't take any more of this,' said Vic. 'D'you mind if I smoke? Just a plain, ordinary cigarette?'

'If I can have Radio Three on,' said Robyn.

Figure 1.7 In this extract from Nice Work, a novel by David Lodge, lecturer Robyn Penrose gives a semiotic analysis of an advertising poster for Silk Cut cigarettes. She is talking to a businessman, Vic Wilcox, who responds with bewilderment

Figure 1.8 This pastiche reveals the codes and conventions of magazine front pages, and the different use of these codes by lads' and women's magazines

Each medium in the mass media has its own kinds of language, characteristic signs and sign systems.

Newspapers use signs such as words, diagrams, illustrations and photographs, structured by systems such as layout, typography, format and composition. A simple example of a newspaper code is the headline, which conventionally has its own 'telegram' grammar using short verb forms and missing out unnecessary grammatical words.

> FAN KILLS WIFE
> FUEL PRICES SOAR
> PRINCE SEEKS BRIDE
> POLICE WARN OVER DRINK RISKS
> UNION ISSUES CHALLENGE

Figure 1.9 Newspaper headlines using 'telegram' grammar

Television programmes use spoken and written language, graphics and images. One television convention is the opening credit sequence, which introduces the show with a brief collage of music, images and text giving information on actors, characters and/or the subject of the programme.

Radio programmes obviously depend upon sound: spoken verbal language, music and effects are edited together in the form required. Sound effects are conventionally used in radio to do more work than in visual media; they often set the scene and atmosphere, for example. Another radio code is the 'sound picture', where language, music and effects give the listener information to help them imagine a scene. This has led to the saying that radio is superior to other media 'because the pictures are better'.

Genre analysis

Genre – which originates from a French word meaning 'type' – has always been a powerful idea in the making and analysis of feature films. During the 1930s and 1940s Hollywood made many films in assembly line fashion in classic genres, such as Westerns, gangster films, musicals, horror films, war films, screwball comedies and romantic melodramas.

The genre of a media product is important:

- for production – the genre is like a toolbox which the film-maker can draw on
- for the audience – the genre allows the prospective audience to predict and choose which products they will enjoy
- for the analyst or critic – who can investigate the choices made in the production from the range of choices the genre offers, and comment on any variations or novel developments in the product.

Genre analysis was first used with fiction. This is reflected in the way a description of genre is traditionally organised around headings such as setting, character, storyline, key signs, message, and so on.

Analysing the Western genre

Here is a starting point for analysing the genre of the Western. How much are you able to add to this analysis?

Setting(s)
1. Place – the western states of America.
2. Location – e.g. the frontier town in the wilderness.
3. Time – within or around the period 1840–90.

Character(s)
Examples: the gunfighter, town drunk, saloon hooker with a heart.

Stars
Tend to be male with a macho, 'man of few words' characterisation which is in danger of becoming a cliché. Examples: John Wayne, Clint Eastwood.

Storyline(s)
Revenge.

Typical story situation/climax
The 'shoot out' in and around a main street or buildings.

Key signs
Guns worn openly by males.

Music
Orchestral (sometimes with a military feel), or US country music.

Message(s)
A typical message is that heroic individuals have integrity, whereas the community tends to compromise.

Example
High Noon, directed by Zinneman, 1952.

This analysis may over-generalise in places. For example, spaghetti Westerns made in Spain and Italy have landscapes which are not necessarily American. Nor are all Westerns so male-orientated.

Figure 1.10 Gary Cooper in High Noon

Analysing the TV soap opera genre

Although this analysis of a Western provides a useful set of headings, a genre analysis does not have to follow a headed format. Here is a somewhat different analysis of the television 'soap opera' genre.

Each television channel has its shop-window soap: the BBC has *EastEnders*; ITV has *Coronation Street*. In these soap operas, an assortment of characters grapple with crises and events, or simply talk about them, and attract audiences of millions for reasons which are (at least partly) analysed here.

Soap operas maintain the illusion that the slices of life they dramatise extend beyond the time slot the programme goes out in. One way in which they do this is by staying close to 'real time', so that the progress of the storylines over a week's episodes would more or less take one week. Time is not compressed or distorted as much as in other genres.

Soaps use, and constantly switch between, multiple plots. These plot lines are presented in parallel, and may merge or split to form new plot lines. Soap operas are indefinite serials; they are not building towards a final episode. A distinguishing feature is that scenes and episodes do not end with resolutions, or 'closure'. Scenes and episodes finish at climactic points where questions or action are typically unresolved, so that the audience is left in suspense, trying to second guess the progress of the plot and its characters. These 'non-endings' and their lack of closure are called 'cliffhangers'.

Soap titles usually refer in some way to a place. A soap will be set around a particular community and common locations so that the same sets continually reappear. Sets featuring interiors, usually including homes, are more in evidence than exteriors. Within these locations there are meeting places where characters can gather. One particular meeting place may be central, affording an opportunity for any or all characters to meet. This has been called the 'forum' setting.

For various reasons, many commentators have pointed out the 'feminine' nature of the soap genre (Glaessner, 1990). Soaps were originally built upon female audiences, and the female audience remains important to their success. Female characters in soaps are important and they often possess strong personal characteristics which are driving forces in plots. For example, soaps are remarkable in that older female characters are shown as sexually active.

Soaps draw upon two media styles. One is that of social realism: soaps usually have some reference to the everyday and to experiences which are close to those of the 'ordinary people' in their audiences. The other is melodrama: the over-the-top style which dramatises emotional crises.

▶◀ *See Activity 6, page 16*

Comment on genre

Genres are flexible and do not stand still. A genre will evolve and change over time. For example, recent films in the science fiction genre have taken to self-mockery: *Men in Black* (1997) and *Mars Attacks* (1996) are both tongue-in-cheek science fiction, as if studios and audiences have lost faith in the genre.

Westerns have also evolved over the years. Wright (1975) classifies:
- the Westerns of 1920–49 as 'classic' Westerns
- Westerns of the 1950s, such as *High Noon* (in which the hero is in conflict with the community), as 'transitional' Westerns
- Westerns where the protagonists are increasingly outside civilised society and associated with crime and/or professional violence, such as *Butch Cassidy and the Sundance Kid* (1970), as 'professional' Westerns.

More recently there also seems to be a more 'politically-correct' type of Western, such as *Unforgiven* (1992), which includes Westerns with ethnic and environmental themes, such as *Dances with Wolves* (1990). Nevertheless, it is difficult to describe the changes in Westerns over the years because many of the themes which have developed still seem to have their roots in 'classic' Westerns.

The boundaries between genre and other ways of talking about types of media product are not always clear. Genre as a theory began as a way of investigating film and TV fiction, but it is now applied to all kinds of media product. As a result, the meaning of the term has become general and vague. Is a magazine or a type of magazine a genre? Are documentary and comedy genres? Genre has a more definite and precise meaning if we say *no*. Magazines in general are a type or mode of publication containing texts with different generic characteristics. Documentary and comedy are general groupings of specific genres.

However, genre is still a useful way of looking at the media as it brings out interactions between the product being studied and other texts. It can show how the text uses and differs from previous examples in the genre.

Nowadays, however, media products tend to use more than one genre in a mix-and-match way. Most fiction today seems to be cross-generic, so that the single genre concept is often not applicable.

Intertextuality

Intertextuality is the term used to describe the almost bewildering sets of tie-ins, influences and other links which we find between different media texts. Different texts may have intertextual links through stars, characters, settings, language, images, storylines and so on.

Texts in the same genre are linked intertextually, but genre is just one set of intertextual links. For example, the Western is intertextual with many other aspects of American popular culture, including the road movie, space cowboy science fiction, cowboy novels, clothes, country music and tourism. Texts in different media channels and forms are often inter-related. For example, many BBC programmes have accompanying BBC magazines.

One media form in which intertextuality is of particular importance is advertising (McArthur, 1984). For example, there are often intertextual links between TV adverts and the programmes they break up. Television companies use the possibility of such links to sell advertising slots; and advertisers exploit them to enhance the advertisement's influence or effect.

The following case study explores the links between the media product *Have I Got News For You* and its intertextual companions.

Figure 1.11 An intertextual reference: the TV show Have I Got News For You and the 'shameless cash-in book' from the series

CASE ▼ STUDY

THE INTERTEXTUALITY OF
HAVE I GOT NEWS FOR YOU

GENRE

Have I Got News For You is a variant on the celebrity quiz show. The quiz show is close to the genres of the chat show and the game show. In turn, quizzes have links with the quizzes, board games and parlour games which people play in 'real life', outside media settings. *Have I Got News for You* is also comedy with a satirical side, and thus it is intertextual with satire such as *Spitting Image* and *Rory Bremner*.

GENRE AND SUBJECT MATTER

Although *Have I Got News for You* is a quiz show, its subject matter has links with news and current affairs. The show often features journalists and people in the news, and it quotes from the news in all forms (spoken, written, photography and film). The questions often involve press headlines.

Have I Got News For You reworks the news genre into humorous material. It plays significantly upon the news values of unexpectedness, and plays up the surprise value and oddity of selected news stories to humorous effect. It is a text which encourages people to talk about its content, and has links with gossip columns and showbiz gossip.

INFLUENCE

The radio celebrity quiz show *The News Quiz* is the forerunner of its television counterpart. It is broadcast on Radio 4 on Saturdays and Wednesdays. *Have I Got News For You* is very similar in concept and format.

STARS AND CELEBRITIES

The celebrities who appear on *Have I Got News For You* reinforce links with the genres of comedy. For example Angus Deayton, who currently plays the host role, has appeared in the sitcom *One Foot in the Grave*. The show also draws upon media personalities from categories such as politics and newspaper columnists.

SPIN-OFFS

Have I Got News For You is commercially reproduced, mainly in the form of videos and humorous book publications.

▶◀ *See Activity 7, page 16*

Narrative

Narrative is just another word for story. All media products contain stories. Stories are combinations of characters, action, settings, atmosphere, imagery and themes. Each of these aspects of story has a life of its own. In semiotic terms, they are sets of meanings with their own conventions and sets of possible combinations. In other words they work as codes.

We will classify three types of narrative code here:

1 A code of 'dimensions', which includes setting, time, imagery and atmosphere.

2 A code of action and change, which includes plot, sub-plot and turning points in plot.

3 A code of character.

A code of dimensions

Settings, imagery and atmosphere work in similar ways and often come together. For example, a churchyard at night gives images such as tombstones, a moonlit sky and the outline of a gothic building, and may evoke an atmosphere of the irrational, the eerie and life after death.

A code of action and change

Action is the progress of the story in terms of happenings, events, turning points and so on. It is not the same as what happens in the real world. Story action is compressed, dramatic and moves between phases such as build-up, climax and relief. However, action must make sense, and therefore it relates to the ways things happen in the real world in terms of verisimilitude, believability, and cause and effect. Action codes can be seen to relate to plans of action in the real world. For example, if a story recounts a journey it may relate to stages in a real journey such as preparation, departure, travelling and arrival.

The action and change in a story is organised into a plot or set of plots. In the so-called classic narrative, the protagonist is at the centre of a main plot which is only resolved or brought to a head at the end of the story. Around the main plot there may be less important plots concerning other characters. These are called sub-plots.

There are exceptions to this, as in multiple plot narratives where the status of the different plots is more equal. Soap operas, as already discussed, set up multiple plot narratives.

A code of character

We are interested in characters because of their relation to real people, but characters are not people. Characters are part of the stories they inhabit.

The main character with whom the audience identifies is the protagonist. In a classic narrative the main plot concerns a single protagonist and the story is driven by various forces, including the protagonist's desires. A central question in any story is what does the protagonist want? The protagonist will be driven by at least two desires: a conscious desire and an unconscious desire.

The links between narrative codes in Babe

The main setting of the film *Babe* is a farm. The atmosphere is that of a children's story with a fairy story reality, talking animals and camera shots which occasionally mimic storybook illustrations. The imagery is predominantly agricultural. However, within that agricultural imagery is a set of images linked to the theme of slaughter and death, which symbolise the central dilemma of Babe's existence.

The film *Babe* is a classic narrative. The main plot concerns the pig, Babe, and his struggle to find his purpose in life. This must be qualified. Babe's conscious desire is to please others; this becomes translated into a desire to become a special kind of sheepdog. His instinctive desire is to survive. In order to achieve this he must remedy the separation from his mother, who fed and protected him, and at the same time evade the purpose of a pig: to be slaughtered.

There are various sub-plots concerning other characters: a duck that wants to be a rooster for similar reasons to Babe; a cat that Babe offends and who tells him the purpose of pigs; the flock of sheep he saves from rustlers and worrying dogs; and the family of the farmer's son who visit.

In the climax of the film, in which Babe wins the sheepdog trials for Farmer Hoggett, he achieves all that he wants both consciously and instinctively. He pleases the farmer, he finds the place he lost when he was separated from his mother, he becomes a pig version of a sheepdog, and he finds an alternative purpose to being slaughtered for pork.

▶◀   See Activity 8, page 17

Representation

Representation is concerned with the way in which the world, or some part of it, is portrayed in a media product. This is an enormous area of discussion and argument in media studies, and is dealt with more fully in chapter 4.

▶◀   For more on representation, see page 43

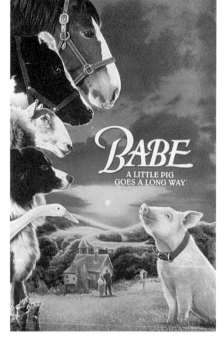

Figure 1.12 Babe – a story with talking animals

Yes we've done it: Scramble intensifies for last free places

Earlier this week, Mrs Clare Cooper wrote to us, pointing out quite correctly that 'Each year, on publication of the A-level results, the front page of every broadsheet pictures jubilant young women laughing and hugging each other. While of course they look beautiful, we've had this each year for about a decade. As concern grows about the decline in young men's school achievement and motivation, could we, this year, have some photos of young men similarly celebrating?' Fair dos. But it hasn't been easy. First, as the writer pointed out, young men often have less to celebrate. And second, when they do, a modest shrug, a glare at the ground and the ghost of a smirk is all you mostly get. But we've done our best, Mrs Cooper. These young men were receiving their results at Parliament Hill School, north London, yesterday.

Figure 1.13 The stereotype is to show female students' emotions on receiving exam results. On its front page of 15 August 1997 the Independent drew attention to this by showing the responses of male students

The representation debate focuses repeatedly on certain questions, including:

- What are the representations of a subject that are repeated in different products? What is the truth or otherwise of these clichés? What are their effects, if any? Does the audience see through them? What are the factors which 'explain' the representations which are selected and how they are put together?
- How are people portrayed in large social groupings (e.g. by gender, ethnicity and socio-economic class)? Where are you represented in media products in terms of the type of person you are?

Studies of representation which deal with the selective portrayal of people in terms of character 'types' usually lead on to the theory of 'stereotypes'. A stereotype is the selection of certain characteristics to define a subject or a person, although the selection simplifies and/or distorts, and falls far short of a complete or true picture. This selective picture is repeated in many media texts, and thus becomes instantly recognisable to audiences. It should be emphasised that stereotyping is a theory, not a fact, and that it can only be used to describe *part* of how representation may work.

An example of a stereotype is that of the disabled person as evil (see chapter 4). This stereotype appears in all sorts of media product, including films ranging from *Frankenstein* and *Hook* to *Dr No*. This stereotype tells us more about the fears of able-bodied people and the way that they project their fears onto disabled people than it does about the reality of being a disabled person.

Media representations change over time. For example, you may find representations of working-class people in older films patronising and stereotypical in ways that would no longer be 'allowed' today. If you look at representations of gender you will still find traditional stereotypes such as the 'dumb blonde'. However, pressures of changing social attitudes and feminism mean that representations of the female gender are more diverse than they used to be, and are avoiding or reworking some of the traditional stereotypes.

◀◀ *See Activities 9 and 10, page 17*

Bias and ideology

Bias is the term used to describe the slanting of media coverage and portrayal towards a certain point of view. Any close text analysis is bound to come to conclusions which indicate bias. The bias you find may tend towards your own views or you may disagree with it. You do not have to disagree with bias in order to identify it.

Some bias is obvious. All media texts show bias towards their intended audiences, for example. There is bias which we take for granted, such as the bias in news coverage towards parliamentary democracy and against criminal activity.

There is also bias which many people may be surprised by and object to, such as the bias in news coverage against unions and working people in industrial disputes with their employers (Glasgow University Media Group, 1982).

Bias may be found in all categories of media text. If photographs are taken from behind police lines during demonstrations or industrial action, bias will result. Language is not a neutral medium. If workers on strike are said to 'reject', 'demand' and 'threaten', whereas employers 'offer' or 'promise', the language used is loaded against the workers. News as a genre and in its methods of storytelling can be loaded against anyone who protests or takes action against those in power and authority. For example, news stories often represent the protester or striker as someone who is 'against the norm' and disruptive, so that the resolution to the story is the restoration of the power of the government and industrial bosses.

Ideology

As these examples show, studies of bias tend to involve politics. The media studies term which is close to the everyday word 'politics' is 'ideology'. The Glasgow Media Group claims to have found evidence that mainstream news has an ideological slant towards powerful and dominant groups in society, such as employers.

The reason for introducing the term 'ideology' from the language of media studies is that it goes beyond what is

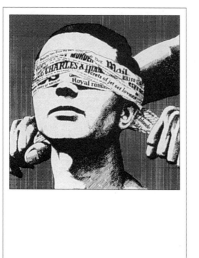

Figure 1.14 The Campaign for Press and Broadcasting Freedom use these images on postcards to encourage awareness of press news selection and bias, criticising tabloid news values in particular

commonly thought of as 'political'. Ideology is about politics with a capital 'P', as in political parties and government, but it is also about other ideas which shape people's lives. It includes views of the world and religious ideologies, such as Christianity and Buddhism. It includes other 'isms', such as feminism, pacifism and racism. It covers politics with a small 'p', as in the politics of everyday family values, sexuality and gender. Ideology is about the ideas surrounding how we live: from global issues such as Americanisation to local issues such as litter, from religion to atheism, from social issues to personal choices.

Stories show ideology. For example, the narrative of the Irish joke interacts with stereotypes of Irish identity and can be used to express, or unconsciously reinforce, racist attitudes. The narrative of the Western interacts with ideology about gender and tends to portray male and female roles in a traditional polarisation (it is often said that the classic Western is sexist). The narrative of the soap opera has a feminine bias, and may support feminist ideology by bringing strong female characters of all ages to the fore.

Analysing bias and ideology

When you are working on a text analysis you should be aware of issues of bias and ideology in the media, for example equal opportunities for women and men, different ethnic groups,

people from different class backgrounds and people with disabilities. These issues are particularly relevant to target audience and the inclusion or exclusion of different audiences. Some media products are freer to show bias than others. For example, national television channels are under an obligation to be impartial in their news coverage of mainstream political parties, whereas newspapers are free to show their own bias, particularly in opinion columns.

Here are some questions to use when carrying out text analysis, in order to look at the broad spread of bias and ideology:

- What points of view are represented in the text?
- What evidence is there in the text of balance between opposing views?
- What is missing from the text?
- How is bias shown in the selection and presentation of language and images?
- Is any opinion or point of view given preference in the text?
- What kinds of ideology are relevant to the text (e.g. political bias, religious and moral issues, pressure groups, equality of opportunity)?

◄◄ *See Activities 11, 12 and 13, pages 17 and 18*

ACTIVITIES

Activity 1

Conduct an image analysis of the image above, including and using the terms denotation and connotation.

Activity 2

Find a suitable comic strip from *Viz* and analyse the verbal language and its role in the text and story. Use the section on verbal language (page 3) as the basis of your analysis. You may find another suitable example in the 'Modern Parents' series.

Activity 3

Analyse the relationship between written text and image in the advertisement above, using the term 'anchorage'. You are free to describe different relationships of meaning, not just simple anchorage.

Activity 4

What signs does Steve Bell use in the cartoon below? Identify and label signs in the cartoon which are:

- icons   • indexes   • symbols.

Activity 5

View an episode of *Star Trek*. Make a list of all the physical signs (i.e. the signifiers which are significant in the *Star Trek* setting and 'world').

Once you have completed the list, start to make a list of the meanings which link to the signs (i.e. the signifieds). What does the list in total lead you to conclude about the overall meaning and/or message of *Star Trek*? (See Berger, 1982, pages 20–21.)

Activity 6

1 Reorganise the soap opera analysis in the genre section (see page 9) under appropriate headings.
2 Develop the account in more detail. In particular, include examples of each point from the characters and storylines of a current soap.
3 If you wish, develop this into practical work by writing your own outline proposal for a new serial in the soap opera genre.

Activity 7

Choose a broadcast soap opera and investigate its links with other texts. For example, soap operas are intertextual with newspapers in the sense that their storylines change and that stars' lives frequently make the news. Collect titles and write short summaries of the links between your chosen soap and the linked texts.

Present your findings in the form of a spider diagram on poster paper, and exhibit the results under a title such as 'Case Study of Intertextuality'.

Activity 8

Watch the film *Babe*. Map out the three codes of dimension, character and action as they are realised in the film.

Alternatively, choose a number of texts with storylines of different kinds and identify the three narrative codes of dimension, action and character as they appear in each.

Activity 9

A genre such as horror tends to represent the world as a place of hidden horrors, where irrational and dream-like fears can take real shape.

Science fiction suggests that there are possible happenings in the future which we cannot predict. These future worlds challenge the narrow views of what is possible which we hold in the present.

Take other genres and discuss their representations, and summarise in one or two sentences their representation of the world.

Activity 10

Take a social group of your own choice and discuss its representation in a specific area of the media. When you are ready to move on, put together your ideas into a hypothesis of what you would expect to find in an examination of the representation of this group in a chosen group of media texts.

Conduct a survey of your own design, looking at the texts chosen.

Present a report of your findings, with relevant illustrations.

Activity 11
Matching exercise

This activity enables you to check your understanding of the terms used and explained in this chapter. The terms are listed on the left, but the definitions on the right are mixed up. Can you match the term with the correct definition? For example, the first term, 'code', matches up to definition 'f'.

1	Code	a. The study of signs and codes in communication
2	Connotation	b. The telling of a story
3	Convention	c. Links between different texts
4	Denotation	d. The associations and interpretations we make from the content of images and signs
5	Icon	e. The form and meaning of a communicative sound, word or picture
6	Intertextuality	f. The patterns into which signs can be combined
7	Genre	g. The construction and portrayal of an aspect of the world in a media text
8	Language	h. The content of a picture or photograph; what it shows
9	Narrative	i. The accepted rules which govern codes and their meanings
10	Representation	j. A system of verbal communication
11	Semiotics	k. A sign which has the meaning of what it resembles
12	Sign	l. A pre-existing type of media product

Activity 12

Conduct a survey of national British daily newspapers. Look at their editorial columns on the same day of the week, with the aim of finding the political bias of each paper.

Is there any difference between the ideological style and bias of the tabloid press and the broadsheet press?

Activity 13

Choose a media text for investigation.

Using this chapter to guide you, write an analysis of the text. Use some of the terms given in Activity 11 as headings, and make sure that you use all of the terms at some point in your analysis (remember that the terms are not matched with the correct definitions). You will have to decide how to organise the analysis and its writing up.

BIBLIOGRAPHY ▼

Berger, A, *Media Analysis Techniques*, Sage, 1982

Glaessner, V, 'Gendered Fictions', in Goodwin, A, and Whannel, G (eds), *Understanding Television*, Routledge, 1990

Glasgow University Media Group, *Really Bad News*, Writers and Readers, 1982

McArthur, C, 'TV Commercials and Old Movies', in Masterman, L (ed.), *Television Mythologies*, Comedia, 1984

Nicholas, J, Price, J, and Moore, B, *Advanced GNVQ Media: Communication & Production*, Nelson, 1996

De Saussure, F, *Course in General Linguistics*, tr. R Harris, Duckworth, 1983

Wright, W, *Six Guns and Society: a Structural Study of the Western*, University of California Press, 1975

CHAPTER 2

Media institutions: local and national

Introduction

This chapter and the next focus on media institutions with the aim of showing you how to investigate the way media products are produced. To do this you will need to:

- become more aware of the economic, institutional and legal frameworks which surround media production
- find out about the ownership and control of media organisations
- understand the different ways of financing media products and the effects these have on the products themselves
- understand the ways in which media products are determined by both external laws and internal codes of practice.

The important thing is to be able to understand the concepts so that you can apply them in your own analysis of media texts. Above all, you should avoid simply learning lots of facts and then regurgitating them to impress an examiner. Ideally you should study 'institutions' through discussing contemporary issues, investigating media organisations themselves and by using particular media texts as your starting point.

The first part of this chapter gives advice on how to investigate a local media organisation. The second part takes a close look at Channel 4, showing you one approach to studying a media institution.

Studying a local media organisation

One of the best ways to develop your understanding of the concept of 'media institutions' is to study the organisation and practices of a local media organisation, such as a local newspaper, radio station or TV station.

Figure 2.1 A local newspaper office: accessible to its community

To do this effectively you need a clear idea of how to approach an organisation for help. As a starting point, try to obtain as much public relations material from the organisation as possible. Please note that it is best if the company has to deal with just one request per school or college. Several individual requests can lead to an organisation 'shutting up shop' or becoming less co-operative. Media companies usually produce packs of information for potential advertisers and many have their own promotional videos and packs. Some companies have education liaison staff, but if they don't a marketing department might help you.

Ideally, try to talk to a representative of the company who can provide you with up-to-date information and inside knowledge. If you do manage to speak to someone, it is helpful if you set the agenda.

The following sections outline some of the areas you could decide to investigate.

The company's ownership

You can find out who owns the organisation by consulting its annual report, which will list major shareholders and the board of directors.

It is more difficult to find out what effect its ownership has on the organisation, as this is often indirect and long term. Some indication can be found in items such as mission statements and comments in reports. Influences such as reasons for appointment of senior staff, which affect the content and style of the organisation's products, are more obscure. A common argument from owners is that ultimately it is the consumers who determine the nature of media products.

The company's history

This should be explored briefly rather than exhaustively. If you know about the media organisation's origins it might help you to understand its current practices. Some newspapers, for instance, were set up by individuals seeking political influence in their communities. It would be relevant to find out if this is still the case; and if not, why not.

How has the organisation changed? Has it grown or declined? Has it been taken over by another company, and if so why? If a company's profit margins are not high enough it becomes vulnerable to take-over by other companies with bigger profit margins. Thompson regional newspapers were taken over by Trinity holdings (originally the *Liverpool Echo*) in the early 1990s in these circumstances. Take-overs like this can lead to significant changes in staffing and editorial policy.

Have there been any major technological changes, such as the introduction of full page make up in print media organisations, or digital editing in broadcasting? What effect might these changes have had on the way news is processed? Have reporters become their own sub-editors, for instance?

Involvement with the local community

A local media organisation has to identify with its region very strongly. Its staff live in the area and have to meet with their public. A national media organisation can upset the odd local community or two and still survive. When the *Sun* printed its story about the behaviour of Liverpool fans during the Hillsborough disaster under the headline 'The Truth' (19 April 1989), it risked alienating people on Merseyside. The story was never substantiated and the people of Liverpool showed their feelings by boycotting the paper. If the same thing had happened to the *Liverpool Echo*, it would probably have gone bust.

You can find out how an organisation determines its region by looking at its advertising rate cards, which show maps of the area covered by the broadcast or publication. Regional or local identity can also be indicated by titles and images: the *Hull Daily Mail* sounds as if it is less interested in appealing to readers in Grimsby than the *Humberside Herald*. In 1997 BBC's *Look North* news programme had fixed cameras continuously transmitting pictures of the Tyne Bridge, the Middlesbrough Transporter Bridge and Carlisle Castle. This reflected the programme's Newcastle headquarters, its desire to appeal to viewers in the south and west of the region, and also implied that in general it had little interest in nearby Sunderland or Wearside.

Other evidence of an organisation's local identity can be:
- coverage of sports teams
- campaigns for local issues
- selection of news stories
- public relations activities
- public access (e.g. phone-ins, letters pages).

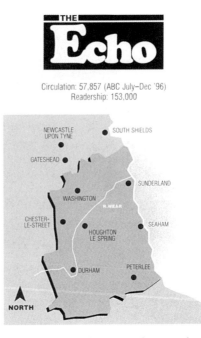

Circulation: 57,857 (ABC July–Dec '96)
Readership: 153,000

Figure 2.2 Regional coverage shown on the advertising rate card for the Sunderland Echo

Competition

All media organisations have a clear idea of their competitors. The normal practice is to conduct market tracking, which means being aware of the performance and character of competing products. A media organisation is usually competing for audience (listeners, viewers or readers) and for advertising revenue.

For example, in the case of a local evening newspaper:
- the competition for readers could be with other local papers based in neighbouring towns, other forms of news media (local radio and television), and national news media (newspapers and broadcasts)
- the competition for advertising revenue could be with freesheets, other local or regional papers and magazines, other local and regional media (especially radio), and occasionally national media.

Advertising

How does advertising affect the organisation's media product?

Some television programmes have to be constructed so that peaks of interest occur just before commercial breaks. Half-time breaks in sports contests have to be extended to fit with scheduled advertising slots during live transmissions. Local newspapers are usually bigger on Fridays, because they carry extra advertising (especially property and classifieds) and the news expands to fill the extra pages. There is often a close link between articles and advertisements. A travel feature, for instance, may attract readers interested in holidays, who then read the travel agents' ads. These are the kinds of things you should look out for and ask about.

Figure 2.3 A local newspaper advertorial

A media organisation's critical independence can sometimes be affected by its relationship with other organisations which need publicity. For instance, a local theatre manager will want as many positive reviews of performances as possible. The fact that she not only gives newspapers and broadcasters free tickets for performances, but also arranges access to performers for interviews, means that there is some pressure on journalists to keep good relations.

Product costs

Hard economic facts may be difficult for you to find, as they are often sensitive. However, an awareness of the economic determinants of media texts is important.

Television needs programmes which are cheap to produce but attract big audiences. This is why game shows are so important, as they need just one set which can be used again and again. A single drama requiring several sets and perhaps some location work is much more expensive to produce, and does not have the advantage of building up an audience.

It is much more expensive for a British TV company to develop its own shows than to import American and Australian shows. New ideas for a game show, for instance, have to be produced, piloted, refined and may not then be accepted, so that all the expenses are lost. A tried and tested import can be bought in much more cheaply. Sometimes just an idea is bought, which is then adapted for British TV.

Newspapers have to bear in mind economic considerations such as the price of newsprint, the threat of having VAT imposed on the industry, and the health of the national economy (which affects major advertising such as motoring and property).

Staffing

Try to find out the occupational structures within the organisation. What separate departments are there and what functions do they perform? How do they communicate with each other? Who has the real power and how is it exercised?

Depending on the type of organisation you are investigating, this might involve finding out:

- how radio phone-ins are organised
- who chooses the records on a music programme
- who is in charge of scheduling TV programmes
- how many staff are involved in a live TV broadcast and what they do
- who writes a newspaper's editorial.

This type of investigation will help you to understand how things work behind the scenes of a media organisation. It will give you insight into the pressures, motivations, fears and hopes which affect the way media products are presented to the public.

Studying Channel 4

Charting and discussing the development of Channel 4 television is an interesting way to study the notions of ownership, public service broadcasting, commercialism and independence. This is because Channel 4 is so distinctive and unusual. In 1995 its chairman, Sir Michael Bishop, claimed that Channel 4 was unique as a broadcasting organisation because it combines the responsibilities of a public service broadcaster exclusively funded by commercial airtime sales.

The organisation has to survive without public subsidy (unlike the BBC, which depends on the licence fee) and has to provide for minority interests yet still appeal to advertisers. It has been owned by the government since the 1990 Broadcasting Act, when its shares were handed over by the Independent Television Commission.

Channel 4's remit

In 1982, when Channel 4 began transmissions, its remit was to:
- appeal to tastes and interests not generally catered for by ITV
- encourage innovation and experiment
- be distinctive
- maintain a high general standard and a wide range
- include a proportion of programmes which are educational
- provide high-quality news and current affairs
- include programmes which are European and are supplied by independent producers.

▶◀ *See Activity 1, page 26*

Channel 4 aims to make itself attractive to advertisers, who provide almost all its revenue, by appealing to the younger, more up-market and lighter viewing groups. These groups are of particular interest to advertisers as they have high levels of disposable income. But the revenue from advertising is insecure and Channel 4 faces increasing competition for it from Channel 5 and the cable and satellite companies. You can find out how well it is coping with this competition from its annual report or from figures produced by BARB, Glenthorne House, Hammersmith Grove, London, W6 0ND.

Marketing information from Channel 4 can be obtained from Channel 4, 124 Horseferry Road, London SW1P 2TX (one request per school or college, please). This shows the types of advertising which the company seeks to attract.

The marketing department can supply prospective advertisers with a detailed breakdown of its viewers' buying habits and attitudes. An advertiser can find out, for instance, what proportion of the audience that watches *Friends* is between 16 and 34, and of this group what proportion attend rock concerts four or more times a year, how many take slimming foods, and what proportion definitely agree that it is important to keep looking young. Advertisers might find that although more people watch ITV, there are more of the kinds of people likely to buy their products in a smaller Channel 4 audience.

Providing for minorities

The balance between raising revenue and providing for minority interests is crucial and interesting. As Michael Grade, Channel 4's former chief executive, put it in 1995: 'In the commercial sector, increasing competition for revenue always carries a threat of a reduction in innovation and risk taking, as predictability of audiences and revenues assumes greater significance.'

If Channel 4 was required to maximise audience potential at every single point in the schedule, it would be impossible for it to provide programmes for minority audiences. Unlike other commercial broadcasters, because of its public service remit Channel 4 has to broaden the programme choices available. This could have been achieved by producing programmes for middle-aged, middle-range, middle-class taste, but as Michael Grade explained, it was decided to 'represent those (sometimes large) minorities, who by reason of age, culture or disposition fall outside the familiar, comfortable, consensual middle ground'. This kind of philosophy produces conflict, as individuals and groups from the 'consensual middle ground'

Figure 2.4 Former chief executive of Channel 4, Michael Grade

are disturbed by the unconventional. The *Daily Mail* in particular led a crusade against Michael Grade when he was in charge of Channel 4's programming. However, as Grade said in the 1995 Annual Report:

> ❛ The Channel 4 programme remit has been a durable and effective formulation. It has thus far ensured that the widest range of viewer interests has been provided on British television, discovering new audiences, and bringing new interests to the public. ❜

When Michael Grade left Channel 4 in 1997, the organisation was at a crossroads. Its funding was at the mercy of the fickle audience-driven advertising industry. Its share of net advertising revenue stood at a healthy 21 per cent, but this was threatened by the introduction of more competition (especially from the new Channel 5). The decision that had to be made was, as Emily Bell said in the *Observer*, whether 'to compete as a more mainstream broadcaster, or go down the route of being a more exotic, exclusive channel in the hope of keeping its young up-market audience'. She went on to express concern about Channel 4's future as a 'licensed, publicly owned broadcaster in a den of hungry politicians'. In 1997 the company was valued at about £3 billion, which, as Bell remarks, 'would rebuild a flotilla of *Britannias*, equip a dozen hospitals and even buy a few schoolbooks'.

Privatisation, however, would change Channel 4's character and would erode the protection given to non-profitable programming. Sir George Russell, former chairman of the ITC, argued in January 1997 that Channel 4's integrity could best be preserved if it was turned into a trust in the way that the *Guardian* newspaper is owned by the Scott Trust. 'It doesn't stop you doing normal commercial things, but you preserve the core,' Russell argued.

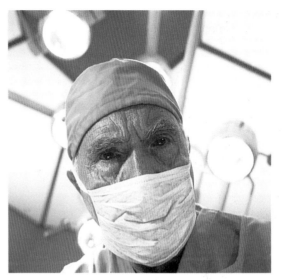

How institutional characteristics affect programmes

The differences that the style of a company's organisation, economics and philosophy can make on its products are vividly illustrated by Paula Milne, writer of successful Channel 4 drama productions *The Politician's Wife* and *The Fragile Heart*.

Figure 2.5 Drama productions from Channel 4, The Politician's Wife and The Fragile Heart

'The Government has mostly ensured that television, like the NHS, is now predominantly governed by marketing forces. The Broadcasting Act in 1990 was the first step. John Birt's recent structural upheaval at the BBC is the latest manifestation. The BBC is covertly privatising itself while overtly protesting that it is merely trying to prepare for the digital/telecommunications revolution. John Birt knows that mass audience appeal is ultimately the BBC's safeguard in an unpredictable future.

But Channel 4 makes no such claims because its remit protects it from the mercenary incentives which now govern the rest of our broadcasting system. If you like the remit provides Channel 4 with a flak jacket for the telecommunications revolution which is to come. The diversity and distinctiveness of Channel 4, catering for minority tastes, will continue to give it the necessary viewer identity it needs to survive a bloody revolution.

As a screenwriter I will tell you how I see the creative implications of privatising Channel 4. Take *The Politician's Wife* as an example. The ITV network was quick to say, after its transmission, that it too would have made the drama. Certainly, it might have commissioned a drama about a revengeful politician's wife, but the content, the behind-the-scenes Whitehall intrigue, the brutal and complex sex scenes, would have made them acutely nervous, lest they alienate or shock their audience. They would have sanitised it.

Each episode filled a 75 minute slot. How would they schedule such a beast?

If I'd taken the same idea to BBC2, I doubt if I would have had a problem with the content of the piece. But as anyone in TV will tell you, the BBC now epitomises 'manana' decision making. I needed a quick commitment to the idea if it was to retain its contemporary edge. Channel 4 saw it had to be made and transmitted quickly and put the necessary cogs in motion while I set about writing it.

This is where the remit bit comes in. It imbues the whole infrastructure and ecology of the place. For example, in a television climate where the writer's voice is being eroded by market researchers and the need to comply to populist demands, Channel 4 creates an arena where writers are positively encouraged to be individualistic. We are also uniquely empowered in the production process to ensure our ideas emerge from the assault course of production intact. We are consulted and involved in casting, on the choice of director, on the music, rather than being marginalised as happens on other channels. Equally importantly, the writer's original con-

cept is respected. I was never, for example, told how many episodes the drama should be composed of, as is the case with ITV and, increasingly, with the BBC, where they talk as if you are supplying them standard eggs to go in their prepacked scheduling carton.

I knew from the start that this story would only stretch to three episodes. This was never questioned either creatively or for financial reasons. The financial investment of making a three part drama serial with heavyweight actors is pretty hefty. You are not going to see a return on that investment in viewing figures alone, because three weeks is not enough time to build a mass audience...

I don't believe that *The Politician's Wife* would have been made if Channel 4 had been privatised. A plc based company could not have sanctioned the budget, for a start. They would ensure that it was the accountants, not the commissioning editors, who were in the driving seat. They would inexorably lean towards the long-strand, 'safe bet' dramas to maximise their financial investment.

The building blocks of TV scheduling are long-running dramas and comedies. They are the high audience shows, around which a constellation of lower audience programmes and – as importantly to the broadcasters – their trailers can orbit.

I recently counted around 14 UK crime or crime-related drama series on ITV and the BBC within a year. In the same period there have been precisely none on Channel 4. Just one long strand, high octane crime series could deliver the viewers in their millions. The *Radio Times* could sport supine nude pictures of its stars on the cover. Tabloids could devote columns to titillating behind-the-scenes stories. But Channel 4 does not take this obvious commercial route because it relies on the audience seeking it out... They recognise that the viewer, whether consciously or not, is seeking originality and diversity. It is precisely the diverse appetite of the audience, and their proven initiative with the remote controls, which demonstrates the continuing need for the remit...

...the public broadcasting remit protects innovation, and innovation means ideas, and it's ideas which enrich and inform our culture.'

Paula Milne, *Media Guardian*, 11 November 1996

> ❛ *They [the BBC] talk as if you are supplying them standard eggs to go in their prepacked scheduling carton.* ❜
> Paula Milne

CHANNEL 4'S HISTORY

Key moments

1955   BBC's monopoly was broken with the launch of ITV, which was financed by advertising.

1962   The Pilkington Report criticised ITV and recommended that a third TV channel be given to BBC. BBC2 began broadcasting in 1964.
Pilkington also suggested the need for a fourth channel, which should be given to ITV but should provide different types of programmes.

1971   The TV4 Campaign (a coalition of academics, journalists, advertisers, politicians, producers and trade unionists) argued that the fourth channel should not be allocated to 'the present independent television contractors'.

1972   Government decided not to proceed with the allocation of a fourth television licence.
Anthony Smith, director of the British Film Institute and later on the first board of Channel 4, proposed a National Television Foundation which would act as a publishing house of the air, buying in programmes from independent programme makers and being accessible to minority groups with something to communicate. He argued for a different broadcasting culture from that established by BBC and ITV. He wanted openness rather than balance and expression rather than neutralisation. He wanted the channel to break away from the stifling effects of bureaucracy and to be able to say new things in new ways.

1977   The Annan Report argued for a 'third force' in British broadcasting to challenge the control of ITV and BBC. It argued that: 'There are enough programmes for the majority... What is needed now is programmes for the different minorities.'
It saw the fourth channel as a 'test bed for experiment' and said that it should be about 'new initiatives, practices and liberties which could inspire broadcasters'.

1979   The incoming Conservative government's intention to proceed with a fourth TV channel was announced in the Queen's Speech. The fourth channel was to be developed under the aegis of the Independent Broadcasting Authority (which had replaced the ITA in 1972). This was meant to keep it independent of ITV and therefore less likely to use programmes produced by ITV companies.

1980   The Broadcasting Act established that Channel 4 should appeal to tastes not generally catered for by ITV (see page 22 for Channel 4's remit). The IBA decided to allow Channel 4 to collect an annual subscription from ITV companies to meet its costs. In return, ITV companies sold advertising time on the new channel in their own areas.

1982   Channel 4 began transmitting programmes in November.

1990   The Broadcasting Act. Channel 4 became an independent trust and had to sell its own advertising. A funding formula was established which required Channel 4 to pay half of its advertising revenue over a set benchmark to ITV. In return, ITV agreed to help to subsidise any losses incurred by Channel 4.

1994   Michael Grade protested about the unfairness of the funding formula in the annual report. The report showed that Channel 4 paid £57.3 million to ITV companies in 1994. In 1995 this figure rose to £74 million. Grade and others argued that this money would be better used to finance British-made programmes, and that this would create over 1000 new jobs.

Programming and scheduling

How far does Channel 4 'encourage innovation and experiment in the form and content of programmes'? Will this remit remain unchanged? Can Channel 4 continue to serve 'all of the people some of the time'? These are the kinds of question you could be discussing as part of your study of 'institutions'.

Programming and scheduling are always closely connected with economic and political issues. This could be seen in 1986, for instance, when the Peacock Report recommended that Channel 4 be given the option of selling its own airtime (to advertisers). This resulted in a reconstruction of the schedule under the guidance of Michael Grade. It became more commercial and more popular. It bought in high-quality American comedy shows such as *Cheers*, *The Cosby Show* and *The Golden Girls*, all of which attracted loyal, young audiences. There is some argument about whether Channel 4 was losing its way under Michael Grade by striving after popularity. Did its current affairs programmes lose some of their bite? Were regional and class voices less varied than they had been in the early eighties?

Figure 2.6 The American sitcom Cheers attracted a young audience to Channel 4

The following sections summarise some of the different aspects of programming and scheduling on Channel 4 which you can investigate.

Seasons of programmes

Channel 4 sometimes broadcasts 'seasons' or 'clusters' of programmes. For example, in 1994 there was a week of documentaries about Northern Ireland to mark the 25th anniversary of the 'troubles'. In the weeks before Christmas 1995 a cluster of programmes provided an alternative to the normal festive viewing by examining man's inhumanity to animals, particularly graphically in *The Turkey Business*.

According to John Willis, Director of Programmes, seasons both 'refresh the schedule and deepen our treatment of a particular subject'. They also, of course, attract particular audiences which can be sold to advertisers. The Friday night *Comedy Zone*, which grouped sitcoms and light entertainment programmes after the watershed, was aimed principally at the 16 to 34-year-old audience.

Film on 4

How has *Film on 4* flourished? The aim behind this strand was to reinvigorate the British film industry by putting television money into it in the form of co-productions. In 1982, its first year of operation, there was enough funding to support 20 films with an average of £300,000 per film.

By 1995 the budget for *Film on 4* and drama was almost £45 million, which produced 599 hours of broadcasting. *Film on 4* helped to produce the most commercially successful British film of all time, *Four Weddings and a Funeral*. The film's first showing on TV, on Channel 4 of course, attracted an audience of 12 million.

Figure 2.7 A Film on 4 commercial success

Factual programming

How effectively does Channel 4 provide for 'complementary scheduling' of factual programmes? As ITV has virtually no factual programmes in peak-time viewing, does Channel 4 give viewers an alternative by showing documentaries such as the *Cutting Edge* strand at peak times?

Minority programming

How well do Channel 4 programmes present minority and challenging points of view? One way to determine how effectively Channel 4 is fulfilling its remit is by watching responses to its programming in the comfortable middle England newspapers. It could be argued that the more protests there are about Channel 4 in the *Daily Mail*, the better it is doing its job. The Black Christmas special of 1993 presented 20 hours of programmes celebrating black life, music and culture, and provoked much press hostility. Similar antagonism is caused by gay and lesbian programmes such as *Dyke TV*.

Innovation and experimentation

How well does Channel 4 innovate and experiment? In 1995 it received two awards for innovation in light entertainment – for Chris Evans' zany game show *Don't Forget Your Toothbrush* and for Spitting Image's scatological soap spoof *Crapston Villas*. In the same year *The Real Holiday Show* used holidaymakers' own camcorder footage together with interviews by Gaby Roslin.

Figure 2.8 Chris Evans remembering his toothbrush

In 1995 *Undercover Britain* used hidden lightweight cameras in an investigation of activities which were legally dubious – badger baiting and child labour, for instance. In 1995 the *People First* strand of documentaries about disabilities was shown at peak time.

Educational programmes

Channel 4 spends four times more on educational programmes than it does on feature films, although they fill a roughly equal amount of programming time. It took over the ITV schools service in 1993, and funds and commissions educational programmes covering the range from infants to A-level. Does Channel 4 still have these educational responsibilities and how well do the programmes serve their audiences? You can conduct some audience research of your own in local schools to help answer this question.

▶◀   *See Activity 2, page 26*

Advertising revenue

Various factors affect the amount of revenue earned by television commercials, in particular:

- Length of time – a 30-second commercial (the commonest length) costs twice as much as a 10-second commercial and half as much as one lasting a minute.
- Size of audience and its composition – the larger the audience, the more can be charged for time. Difficult to reach audiences, such as the young and the affluent, are more expensive to advertisers.

- Time of day – peak-time advertising (between 6 p.m. and 10.30 p.m.) is the most expensive because this is when most people watch TV. Peak-time advertising costs twice as much as off-peak. There are special rates for particular programmes which are expected to attract an unusually large audience.
- Region – advertising charges vary from region to region, with London being the most expensive.
- Time of year – the run-up to Christmas is the most expensive time to advertise. The cheapest times are January to March and in August.

▶◀ *See Activity 3, below*

The audience

How well is Channel 4 preserving or developing its 'reach'? (Reach refers to the proportion of people who watch a channel at some time or other.) Without a wide audience, Channel 4 could become a minority ghetto.

In 1994 Channel 4's reach was over 80 per cent. In 1995 it was the third most-watched channel, after BBC1 and ITV. However, in the late nineties Channel 4 has been developing a strong following among the young and affluent. As this audience has a strong appeal to advertisers, it will be interesting to see if efforts will be made to increase this following.

▶◀ *See Activity 4, page 27*

ACTIVITIES

Activity 1

The Channel 4 remit in 1995 laid down a minimum number of hours per week, on average, which should be allocated to the following categories:

- Education – 7
- Current affairs – 4
- News – 4
- Religion – 1.

(Changes to these requirements should be noted in the annual report, available from Channel 4, 124 Horseferry Road, London SW1P 2TX.)

Calculate the actual amount of time devoted this week to each of these categories.

Calculate what percentage of programmes carried subtitles for the deaf and hard of hearing. (The ITC set a target of 50 per cent by 1998.)

Activity 2

Conduct a survey in a local school which uses Channel 4 educational programmes to find out what teachers and pupils think of them.

Some of your research should be quantitative; for instance you could ask teachers and pupils to record their opinions of the programmes on a scale from very satisfied to very dissatisfied. Some of your research should be qualitative; you could talk to teachers and pupils in depth about what they liked and disliked about a particular programme.

Send a copy of your findings to Channel 4's viewer response department.

Activity 3

You have been given a £100,000 budget to buy advertising space on Channel 4 for a week. You have two commercials: one lasting 30 seconds and one lasting 10 seconds. Assume that peak-time advertising space costs £14,000 per minute and off-peak half that.

Study this week's programming for Channel 4 and decide how you can most effectively spend the budget to reach an audience of 16 to 25-year-olds who are interested in popular sports, action films, light entertainment, health issues, popular music and fashion. Produce a laydown schedule using the following format:

- Day
- Time
- Length of commercial
- Programme
- Cost

Explain in writing the thinking behind your schedule to the company whose product you are advertising.

Activity 4

Use these statements to prepare for a class or group discussion on the topic: 'Public service broadcasting is an outmoded ideal for which there is no place in today's commercially oriented world.'

Broadcasting as a business

- Broadcasting is essentially a business in which people should be allowed to make profits with the minimum of interference from the government.
- TV should be provided free to people by selling their attention to advertisers who pay for the privilege of trying to sell their goods to them. This system keeps everyone happy – the viewers by having good quality programmes at no cost to themselves, the advertiser by being able to maintain or increase sales, the TV company by making profits for its shareholders.
- There is no 'public', only individuals who must be enticed to part with their money.
- 'Anybody who, within the law of the land, provides a service which the public wants at a price it can afford is providing a public service.' Rupert Murdoch.
- 'Programmes will not survive in the new ITV [post-1990 Broadcasting Act] if they do not pay their way.' Paul Jackson, director of programmes for Carlton Television
- Audiences today are increasingly fragmented because they want to be. General interest programmes are giving way to minority interest programmes because that's what people want.
- 'Broadcasting is like any other economic activity. It should be provided competitively unless there are compelling reasons for not doing so.' Cento Veljanovski, 1989.
- With the proliferation of new TV channels from the late nineties onwards, the BBC's share of the total TV audience will decline. Viewers will grow increasingly resistant to paying a licence fee, especially if they tend not to watch BBC programmes. This will put pressure on the BBC to make itself more commercial.

Broadcasting as a service

- Broadcasting 'is not a business trying to distribute dosh to its shareholders... but something held in trust and in law for every citizen'. Dennis Potter.
- Audiences should not be thought of as consumers but as citizens. Broadcasting should be about developing and refining a mass culture. The programmes should be free from the influence of both advertisers and government.
- Only a public service broadcaster can provide for informed national debate on questions of morality and politics by being freed from commercial pressures. People have the right to be given disinterested information about those agencies with power over their lives.
- In his essay 'Money Talks' (in Hood, 1994), Graham Murdock argues that broadcasters should provide the right to speak as well as be spoken to, and that for this to happen broadcasting should not be in the hands of any one power group. He also argues that broadcasting should 'promote diversity... offering the widest possible range of view-points, perspectives and expressive forms, rather than a restricted choice in a variety of packages. And it must be available to everyone at a minimal feasible cost.'
- 'All citizens have the right of equal access to the BBC's service of information, education and entertainment provided they are prepared to pay their licence fees.' BBC's evidence to the Hunt Committee (quoted in Hood, 1994).
- When commercial considerations prevail over public service ideals, broadcasters will deliver a service only to the most profitable markets, which are in densely populated urban areas.
- 'By placing political, religious, civic cultural and entertainments in a common domain, public life was equalised... Consider the FA Cup Final, the Grand National or Wimbledon. All these existed before broadcasting, but whereas previously they existed only for their particular sporting publics they became, through radio and television, something more... The events became, and have remained, punctual moments in a shared national life... The BBC calendar became the expressive register of a common, corporate public life.' Paddy Whannel.

BIBLIOGRAPHY ▼

Annan, *Report of the Committee on the Future of Broadcasting*, HMSO, 1977

Curran, J, and Gurevitch, M (eds), *Mass Media and Society*, Arnold, 1991

Curran, J, and Seaton, J, *Power Without Responsibility*, Routledge, 1991

Hood, S (ed.), *Behind the Screens*, Lawrence and Wishart, 1994

Milne, P, 'Protect this fragile heart', in *Media Guardian*, 11 November 1996

CHAPTER 3

Media institutions: freedom and controls

3

Introduction

This chapter introduces you to some of the issues you need to consider when thinking about how much freedom the media should have.

It includes:

- common attitudes to media freedom and control
- a case study of the film *Crash*, which explores the question of censorship by analysing different attitudes to the film

- information on the work of some of the self-regulatory bodies that influence the media, in particular the British Board of Film Classification, the Broadcasting Standards Council and the Press Complaints Commission
- a brief summary of legal controls on the media.

Having read this chapter, you should apply what you learn to contemporary examples of the media freedom debate.

Attitudes to media freedom

The following sections summarise common attitudes to the media. Try to find examples of each of these attitudes in your own reading, viewing and listening.

There is too much violence in the media

Concern about the amount of violence in the media is partly because of the belief that it can incite people to copy what they see. For example, journalist Natasha Walter sees danger in the *Sport* newspaper, which she thinks encourages male violence by filling its pages with stories of violence against women. She argues that the paper should be classed as pornography and treated as such. She is offended by the fact that the 'abuse of women is so mainstream that we can happily call it "sport" and see children laughing over it as they buy their ice creams'.

> ❝ The British do have strange attitudes to sex. Teenage girls' magazines that provide sex education are rebuked by MPs; British adults are not allowed to watch people making love on television; women are not allowed to dream over the picture of an erect penis. And yet we accept that a publication mainly dedicated to the abuse of women is a newspaper. Does it have to be like this? ❞
> Natasha Walter, 1996

People are concerned that the amount of violence in the media increases the fear of crime which many feel. The cumulative effects of the portrayal of violence can lead to a distorted sense of the dangers of the world we live in. There is also a danger that programmes involving re-enactments of crime can turn violence into entertainment.

There is too much sex on television

Many people feel that television can encourage promiscuity. Some pressure groups, such as the National Viewers and Listeners Association (founded by Mary Whitehouse), argue that this is the case. It believes, among other things, that 'sexual innuendo and explicit sex [on television] trivialise and cheapen human relationships whilst undermining marriage and family life'. The Association also argues that 'taste and decency should be better defined and better enforced to bring about general improvements of moral tone in programmes'.

The BBC issues guidelines to producers about the portrayal of this 'most delicate of subjects', and while recognising that 'over the years popular taste has accepted a more explicit treatment of sex' notes that 'there are many outstanding examples of the precise portrayal of sexual relationships achieved without explicit scenes'.

Too much regulation damages artists' creativity

In 1996 writer Alan Plater described the changing face of institutional control at the BBC. He recalled how in the 1960s, when he was writing the police series *Z Cars*, the average time for an episode from desk to audience was six weeks. He usually had to negotiate with just one person, who acted as producer, director, script editor and 'guide and mentor'.

After the BBC's management revolution in the 1990s Plater found that he had to deal with a host of different departments, which slowed the process down considerably. One of the departments which Plater found particularly bizarre was the swearing department. He had to submit scripts for a police drama called *Dalziel and Pascoe* based on characters in Reginald Hill's novels. Dalziel was an old-style copper who swore like an

29

old-style copper. To remain true to the original stories, Plater lightly garnished the scripts with 'buggers' and 'sods'. He took out the 'fucks' because 'fuck' was forbidden on BBC1 'unless you are Billy Connolly'. Each script had to be sent to the Head of Buggery and Blasphemy (Plater's term) with all swear words highlighted. They were then returned with alternatives: 'Delete "wankers" – insert "tossers"; delete "Jesus Christ" – insert "bloody hell"; delete "cobblers" – insert "crap" ', and so on.

Figure 3.1 Dalziel and Pascoe from the eponymous BBC police drama – Dalziel's language posed Plater a problem

Freedom of expression should take precedence over everything else

When she was director of programmes at Channel 4, Liz Forgan made an impassioned plea for freedom of expression. She said it should be enshrined in law and that it should be a clear and unequivocal and prevail over all other interests.

She argued against arbitrating quangos, such as the self-regulatory bodies described later in this chapter, saying that they should not be allowed to erode the freedom of expression which belongs to us all. The more watchdogs there are the more difficult it is to get anything even slightly controversial broadcast. 'Who is going to try to get difficult programmes on the air if you have to go through an assault course before you can even start?', she asks.

The danger of prohibition

The columnist and broadcaster Bernard Levin, as a self-appointed guardian of freedoms, often attacked people who 'want to make us good against our will'. As an example he wrote witheringly about the Council of Europe committee which recommended a ban on all television alcohol advertising in order to cut alcohol abuse among the young and 'the human damage of excessive drinking'.

He saw such proposals as the work of instinctive prohibitionists who are always trying to protect other people from themselves, not from outside forces. These prohibitionists see themselves as immune from dangers and think that they should have the power to control the conduct of the rest of us. Levin argued that references to protecting the young are used as a kind of blackmail and that what these people want is to ban all alcohol.

He sees the prohibitionist mentality as more dangerous than the attitudes of the National Viewers and Listeners Association, which he parodies as believing that 'you can catch Aids off a television screen, so that nothing naughtier than Donald Duck (not Mickey Mouse because he once used Minnie's bra as a hammock) should ever be seen'. Such people want to censor television, according to Levin, but the totalitarians want to control it. And that is much more dangerous.

Some sections of society need protection

Richard Hoggart expressed this belief in his book *The Way We Live Now*.

He argued that in democratic societies all freedoms will be exploited and that we must tolerate a large amount of exploitation. However, he asked at what point society should say 'Enough: this is where we should exercise our freedom to limit our common freedoms'. The answer he gave was when there is risk of damaging vulnerable groups such as children, the very old and the mentally ill.

▶◀   *See Activity 1, page 39*

The media cause and exacerbate social and behavioural problems

Many people express a fear of copycat crimes similar to those shown on the screen. Evidence that such things happen is often anecdotal, as in the following news story from October 1996 about a woman who had to move house eleven times in ten years because of the behaviour of her eight children. As reported in the *Guardian*, she gave this explanation of why she could not control them:

'When they watched *Rambo* they became fascinated by knives and guns and put them in their socks. They have thrown knives at each other. I decided violent films were not a good idea so I hired *Mary Poppins*. They next day they were running over the roofs of houses. They watched the musical *Oliver* and started pick-pocketing and when they saw the Mutant Ninja Turtles they went out and managed to lift up a drain. I got to them just as they were beginning to climb down the drain to meet the turtles.'

The media's attempts to control excesses

In 1989 Britain's first woman national newspaper editor was 'sacked' by two newspaper proprietors. Rupert Murdoch replaced her as editor of the *News of the World* after she published a series of photographs of freakish children and very fat women. Robert Maxwell then sacked her from her next job as editor of the *People* because she printed pictures of Prince William having a 'pee in the park', a dying Sammy Davis Junior and some horrific images of air-crash casualties. Maxwell said that she was a very talented journalist, 'but she does like to shock'.

Voluntary controls

This section looks at some of the most active regulatory bodies connected with the media. They have been set up by the media industries themselves in an attempt to dissuade governments from passing more laws to control the media.

British Board of Film Classification

The British Board of Film Classification awards certificates for film and video.

In 1997 the categories were:

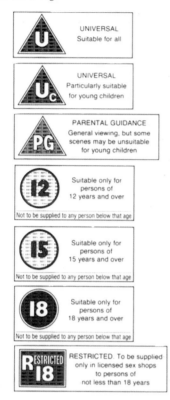

The Board is organised by a director, three vice-chairmen (all appointed by the Home Secretary) and a full-time management team of three. The examiners who watch the films and make judgements have been full-time professionals since 1993. It is the job of the Board members to decide what the public should be allowed to watch both in the cinema and at home.

The Board is very secretive. It does not give reasons for what it allows and doesn't allow. It does not explain the cuts it makes. It won't even let its staff or former staff talk about their work. It can do this because it is a private company, paid for by the film industry. It was set up by the industry because of fear of government interference and control. The censorship it exerts is not usually based on legal requirements, but on what the examiners think will or will not offend audiences. The power in the system lies very much with the director and the full-time managers, who lay down guidelines which the examiners have to follow. If examiners disagree with the guidelines they are usually overruled. The three vice-chairmen are known informally as the three blind mice.

Apart from judging individual films and videos, the Board tries to come to conclusions about matters of sex, violence and swearing. It debates questions such as the distinction between soft porn and sex education, taboos about aroused male genitalia, and possible links between video violence and crime. The Board carries out extensive research on such matters.

▶◀ *See Activities 2 and 3, page 39*

Press Complaints Commission

In 1991 the Press Complaints Commission replaced the Press Council, which had tried to maintain high ethical standards of journalism for nearly 40 years. It was set up after the Calcutt Committee's report (1990), which looked at the question of press intrusion into the private lives of individuals.

The Press Complaints Commission is essentially a committee of national and regional newspaper editors. In 1997 it was composed of 16 people: a chairman, eight members of the public and seven senior editors. Its Code of Practice is accepted by all publishers and editors, partly because the industry prefers self-regulation to regulation by law.

The Code of Practice covers:

- the need for accuracy
- giving people the right of reply
- distinguishing clearly between opinion and fact
- respecting privacy
- the use of listening devices
- not approaching people in places such as hospitals and schools without permission
- not obtaining material by misrepresentation or subterfuge
- not intimidating or harassing people
- not paying witnesses in current court cases
- not identifying relatives of criminals
- not interviewing under-16s on personal welfare matters without parental consent
- not publishing details about a person's race, colour, religion, sex or sexual orientation
- not identifying victims of sexual assault.

A copy of the Code can be obtained from The Press Complaints Commission, 1 Salisbury Square, London EC4Y 8AE. Tel: 0171-353 1248. Fax: 0171-353 8355.

The Commission meets monthly and considers complaints about the press which suggest there may have been a breach of the Code of Practice. It begins by trying to get the editor of the publication against which the complaint has been made to sort out the problem directly with the complainant. Only about 15 per cent of complaints have to go to the next stage of an adjudication. Problems are normally resolved in the form of a published apology, correction or letter to the complainant.

Most complaints are about inaccurate reporting, which can be resolved by corrections or apologies. Cases involving intrusion of privacy are usually more difficult. The Code of Practice stipulates that intrusions into an individual's private life without his or her consent are only justified when it is in the public interest. The Commission defines public interest as: 'detecting or exposing a crime or serious misdemeanour, protecting public health and safety, preventing the public from being misled by some statement or action of an individual or organisation'.

Complaints against newspapers

Some newspapers seem to attract more complaints than others. In 1994 the *Sun* topped the complaints league with 167 complaints, the *Daily Mail* came second with 89, while the *Financial Times* had only 2. The *Sunday Sport* was the second least complained against publication with only 7 complaints.

An example of the kind of adjudication the Commission has to make occurred in June 1996, when the European Football Championship was held in England. England played Germany in the semifinal. The *Daily Mirror* ran a series of articles, which were meant to be humorous, attacking Germany and the Germans. The front page had a faked picture of two English footballers wearing army helmets and apparently shouting 'Achtung! Surrender. For you Fritz, ze Euro 96 Championship is over.'

Figure 3.2 Controversial front page of the Daily Mirror on 24 June 1996

An editorial announced 'Mirror declares football war on Germany' and was written in the style of the Prime Minister's declaration of the Second World War. Articles inside the paper made predictable anti-German jokes mixed with petty insults:

> ❛ *The Germans hate being reminded of their failures. Like eating well matured cheese for breakfast. Or nicking all the sun-loungers in the Mediterranean. But what they hate most is being reminded of that glorious day in 1966 when England made them the sourest of sour-krauts.* ❜

The PCC received 300 complaints about these stories and similar ones in the *Star* and the *Sun*.

The *Mirror* and the other papers were told of the complaints and asked to respond. The *Mirror* pointed out that it had realised a number of people were offended and had published an apology for any offence caused. It agreed that it had tried to be humorous but had failed because the material was 'offensive and over jingoistic'. The *Mirror* and the other papers denied that they had breached clause 15 of the Code of Practice:

> ❛ *The press should avoid prejudicial or pejorative reference to a person's race, colour, religion, sex or sexual orientation or to any physical or mental illness or handicap.* ❜

The Council found that the coverage was 'shrill and poorly judged', but because it was reflecting partisan national support and was not intended to 'incite prejudice directed at specific individuals on the grounds of their race' there was no breach of clause 15.

However, the Council did regret 'lapses in editorial judgment' and recognised that the proud tradition of supporting British sportsmen and women while at the same time reporting tolerance and fair play towards others had not been maintained.

▶◀   *See Activity 4, page 40*

Broadcasting Standards Council

The Broadcasting Standards Council looks at complaints made by the public about radio and television programmes. It deals with about 500 complaints a year, which are mainly about taste, decency and sex, though there are some about violence. Typical concerns are:

* a complaint about Dr David Starkey, presenter of a Talk Radio UK programme, who referred to a woman who died while protesting against the export of veal calves as 'a silly cow who died for some silly veal calves' (complaint upheld)
* the use of the word 'pissed' during a GMTV programme when young children might be watching (not upheld)
* a complaint that Michael Barrymore was mocking one of his guests, an Elvis impersonator (not upheld)
* a complaint about a sketch where Mr Bean had his shirt-tail protruding from the front of his trousers when standing in a presentation line awaiting the arrival of a royal personage (not upheld)
* a complaint about Blind Date encouraging a sexual relationship between contestants (not upheld)
* a complaint that a Colgate toothpaste advertisement during early morning children's television showed people kissing (not upheld)
* a complaint about a reference to showjumping being 'better than sex' in a trail for *Cutting Edge* (not upheld)
* several complaints about an edition of Channel 4's *The Word* which featured a report on John Bobbit whose penis was cut off by his wife and subsequently restored by surgery. Pictures of the restored, flaccid penis were shown, as was a false phallus used by Mr Bobbit during a stage show (complaint upheld).

Figure 3.3 Does Cilla Black encourage sexual relationships on Blind Date? The Broadcasting Standards Council did not uphold just such a complaint

The Council was established at the end of the 1980s in response to concerns about violence, sex and bad language on television. The rise in violent behaviour in society at the time was the main reason for the public's concerns.

The Council's research consistently showed that in the early 1990s there were twice as many people who thought that there was too much violence on television than thought that 'it was about right'. Just over half the population thought that the amount of sex on television was 'about right', with just under half thinking there was too much. The proportion of people who thought that there was too much bad language on television was decreasing by the mid-1990s, although it was still over 50 per cent.

The Council published a Code of Practice in 1994. Any regulations have to take into account a variety of factors, such as the channel, the time of day, minority interests and the nature of the programme. There also needs to be some place where broadcasters can challenge conventions and explore contemporary realities.

Broadcasters have accepted the idea that after a certain time in the evening, made known to parents, programmes could contain material which might be considered unsuitable for children. This is known as the watershed. This could be seen as infringing the liberties of the high proportion of households with no children who are denied, at the time of writing, material which is considered unsuitable for children between 5.30 a.m. and 9.00 p.m.

Broadcasting Standards Council's views on violence

In news, real-life violence such as terrorist killings should be portrayed because 'any shrinking from the retelling of savage and bitter truths about the world does the audience a disservice'.

Figure 3.4 Broadcasters seek to find a balance between portraying the real truth of tragedies, such as the detention camps in Bosnia, and causing distress to viewers

However, broadcasters are urged not to linger on pictures of casualties or on 'the bloody evidence of violence'. Only in the rarest circumstances should broadcasting dwell on the moment of death itself. Programme makers are also warned about using film of former disasters to illustrate current news stories. They need to bear in mind the distress which such pictures could cause survivors and relatives of victims, especially if they are shown, as would almost inevitably be the case, without warning. The portrayal of violence is likely to be less visually explicit in news programmes shown during the day, when children could be watching.

Care must be taken not to glamorise or soften the image of criminals, nor should there be personal financial gain for them if they tell their stories.

Violence in fictional programmes can help audiences come to terms with the world by helping them understand the situations and dilemmas which people face in their lives. There is a danger, however, that an audience repeatedly exposed to violence could become desensitised, or that people could become unreasonably fearful in their own surroundings, damaging the quality of their lives.

The Council is particularly concerned about violence which shows villains taking pleasure in inflicting pain on victims in case this encourages feelings of pleasure in the audience, and about the use of weapons which are readily available in homes, such as kitchen knives. It emphasises the importance of not glossing over the serious consequences of violent actions.

The Council warns programme makers about the dangers of combining sex and violence, in case the violence is made erotic. In particular, women should not be degraded by being shown as objects of male violence: 'Rape, in particular, should never be presented in a way which might give the impression that its occurrence was anything other than a tragedy.'

Broadcasting Standards Council's views on sex

The Council gives advice on the portrayal of sex, arguing for 'sensitive scheduling and labelling' so that the sensibilities of minority groups can be respected. Its research in 1992 showed that there was a high degree of tolerance towards the depiction of sex on television, even among those who did not want to watch it themselves. However, there was still a 'substantial minority' which felt that there was too much sex on television. Among parents in particular there was a strong feeling that sex in fiction programmes should take place 'in a meaningful relationship'.

The Council says that the degree of explicitness about sex should take into account the context in which it occurs. It forbids actual sexual intercourse being shown and any 'overt sexual conduct between adults and children'. The 1992 research showed that most people accepted the showing of female nudity and some male nudity, but not of full-frontal male nudity.

Comedy which relies on sexual references to women causes offence to a growing number of people and 'its justification becomes increasingly difficult'.

News stories involving sexual relations should not exploit their sexual aspects and the explicitness of the stories should take into account the time of the broadcast.

Documentaries on sexual themes should consider the borderline between sensitive observation for the purposes of information and spectacle for the purposes of sensation.

Broadcasting Standards Council's views on swearing

The Council receives more complaints about swearing than anything else, especially swearing involving expletives of the Christian holy names.

It recognises that this is a particularly difficult area because of the different attitudes to swearing, and indeed specific swear words, across different cultures, age groups, social classes and even geographical areas. It recognises that swearing provides us with a means of giving emphasis and relieving tension, but argues that 'in constant use, expletives represent an impoverishment of language and a barrier to communication. Their prevalence in broadcasting could, in time, erode the relatively high standing among the public of the radio and television services'. The Council is particularly concerned about swear words which refer to genital organs and 'fuck' and its derivatives. Such words should never be used before the watershed and only after the watershed following 'discussion at the most senior levels of control'.

Other controlling bodies

Other controlling bodies which you could study include:

* The Advertising Standards Authority. This tries to ensure that all advertisements in print and in the cinema are legal, decent, honest and truthful and gives advice to advertisers, agencies and publishers.
* The Broadcasting Complaints Commission. This investigates complaints against broadcasters of unjust or unfair treatment in programmes. It is also concerned with any unfair infringements of privacy.
* The Independent Television Commission. This is a statutory body which was appointed after the 1990 Broadcasting Act to replace the Independent Broadcasting Authority. It grants licences to commercial television services in the UK, regulates the services, and issues guidelines and codes of practice. It tries to ensure that there is a wide range of television services of high quality.
* The Radio Authority. This a statutory body which licenses and regulates all independent radio broadcasting.

Organisations which deal with censorship

Organisations with a special interest in matters of censorship include:

* The National Viewers and Listeners Association, which seeks to uphold high moral standards in radio and TV programmes
* Article 19, which is a human rights organisation helping to defend media threatened with censorship
* The Campaign for Freedom of Information, which tries to get better access to public sector information and to privately held information which may be in the public interest
* The Campaign for Press and Broadcasting Freedom, which campaigns for democratic and accountable media accessible to all.

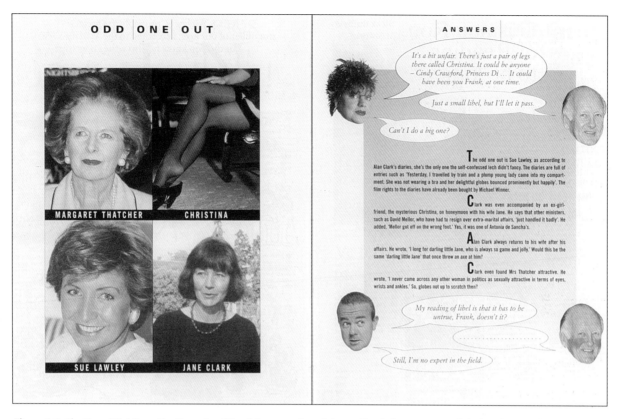

Figure 3.5 The Have I Got News For You spin-off book humorously points out that it is very aware of the legal constraints that satire operates under

Legal constraints

Knowing something about the legal constraints on the media can help you make informed judgements about media texts. The laws themselves are complex, and the details are of interest only to media professionals and lawyers. However, it is useful to know some of the general restrictions the law imposes on the media.

Defamation

Defamation is the legal word for libel. The Broadcasting Act of 1990 defined defamation as something that:

• unjustifiably exposes someone to public hatred or ridicule
• causes a person to be shunned or avoided
• lowers public estimation of a person
• disparages the business or professional capacity of a person.

This can also apply to organisations. In 1997, for instance, a libel case was taken out against the BBC by the Outward Bound Trust. The BBC had portrayed a course instructor as a 'deranged sexual pervert' in the Rowan Atkinson sitcom *The Thin Blue Line*. The Trust argued that the allegations were without foundation and had caused massive damage to its reputation. The BBC recognised its 'grave error' and settled out of court for undisclosed damages.

In another example, a character's death in a radio play was blamed on the tannoy not working. 'Tannoy' is in fact a brand name, and the company complained that the play defamed their product. Again money was paid in compensation and the BBC had to broadcast an apology.

The 1996 Defamation Act allows you the defence that if you do not intend to defame someone you can offer to apologise. However, you must publish the apology and pay compensation for your opponent's costs. In practice, producers need to know when to pass a matter to a company lawyer before going ahead with the broadcast or publication. Some sensitive programmes like *Have I Got News For You*, a satirical current affairs programme, have a legal expert on hand during the editing process.

One issue for debate surrounding defamation concerns the cost of taking out libel actions. Wealthy people can take the risk of losing a libel action and having to pay the legal costs, whereas poor people are not able to do that. This means that personal attacks on those who do not have the means to take a newspaper to court remain unpunished.

Official Secrets Act

Until 1989, no crown servants or government contractors could divulge any information which they had learned while doing their job. It was also an offence to receive information from such people. Ridiculous as it may seem, it was a crime for someone working in a government department to report, for instance, how many cups of tea a minister drank in a week, or to divulge the pattern on a new carpet in a minister's room.

The 1989 Official Secrets Act changed this 'catch-all' law by defining six classes of information which were secret:

1 Security and intelligence.
2 Defence (e.g. locations of weapons, state of readiness and training of armed forces).
3 International relations.

4 Crime (e.g. anything which impedes the prosecution of suspected offenders).

5 Information on government phone tapping and interception of communications.

6 Information entrusted in confidence to other states or international organisations.

The Act was aimed at gagging members of the security services, crown servants and government contractors. An offence would be committed if the disclosure of information by a journalist was damaging (for instance to the work of the secret services) and was intended to damage.

Official Secrets Act 1989

Figure 3.6

Potential conflicts arise if government officials are likely to be embarrassed by the release of information. They could be tempted to use the Act to block reporters, whose job is to question, probe and see if there has been an abuse of power. Reporters are not doing the job of a 'free' press if they simply accept handouts from people in high places and churn out what they are told to say.

There are many situations where there could be conflicts of interest. You should be able to find some contemporary stories to study, but here are a few examples:

- A policeman (a crown servant) gives information to a journalist that a senior opposition MP's phone is being tapped for dubious reasons.
- A journalist receives information from a member of the security services about the illegal activities of other members of the service.
- A fishing boat gets its nets tangled with a Royal Navy submarine. The boat sinks with loss of life. The reporter discloses the position of the submarine, having found out from a coastguard (a crown servant). The submarine was on secret manoeuvres.

Contempt of court

This law prevents the media publishing or broadcasting anything which might prejudice a fair trial. Anything which is 'sub judice' cannot be reported. In criminal cases this process starts as soon as someone is arrested. In civil cases it begins as soon as arrangements are made for a hearing. Sometimes this can give opportunities to people or organisations who want to hide something to take things to court where they can be argued over for months until the fuss has died down.

Another issue which can occur in high-profile criminal cases is the payment of witnesses for their stories. This is likely to influence the evidence given, and can even lead to guilty people going free if a case has to be dropped because of the possible manipulation of witnesses.

Race relations

The Public Order Act of 1986 makes it an offence to publish anything which stirs up racial hatred, whether or not it is intended to. This means, for example, that a newspaper could not report an inflammatory speech by an extremist politician at the time of an election. Nor can editors print readers' letters which are inflammatory, even if they balance them with a different point of view.

▶◀ *See Activity 5, page 41*

Military conflict

In times of war or limited 'armed conflict' (e.g. the Falklands campaign), the State can exercise strict control of the media.

Some journalists, like John Pilger, object to this on the grounds that the State then encourages people to support armed conflict and denies them knowledge of its horrors. Pilger's experience of war reporting led him to believe that journalists seldom question the assumptions behind wars. He believed that the role of the journalist as the teller of truths unpalatable to those in power was almost impossible to perform because the military has most of the information that journalists need. If their reporting does not reflect 'the national interest', journalists risk losing access to the information.

There are many other legal restrictions on what journalists can and can't do. If you want to study this in more depth, consult *McNae's Essential Law for Journalists* (Welsh and Greenwood, 1995).

The effect of new technology

Arguments about censorship have to take into account the effects of new technology. The notion of the watershed on television is affected by children's freedom to take control of their own viewing choices by having their own televisions in their bedrooms and by the use of video recorders. At the time of writing the V chip was being tested. This is a device which, when installed in televisions, will scramble programmes coded as containing any sex or violence. In the USA, it was government policy to have a V chip installed in every television set by 1997. The chip gives parents the power to 'protect' their children from watching 'unsuitable' programmes.

In the UK, satellites and modems give people the opportunity to call up programmes into their homes from countries with more liberal attitudes to censorship.

C A S E ▼ S T U D Y

DAVID CRONENBERG'S FILM *CRASH*

This case study shows how you can study a debate over the 'suitability' of a media text by trying to discern a pattern in the media coverage of the controversial film *Crash*. The categories below are not definitive. They are a personal summary of the debate at the time (1997). You should use them as a starting point, but question them as you try to apply them to whatever current dispute you are looking at.

Figure 3.7 Rosanna Arquette in Crash

THE MORAL OUTRAGE ARGUMENT

There is almost always an expression of moral outrage. Alexander Walker of the *Evening Standard* wrote that David Cronenberg's film *Crash* contained 'some of the most perverted acts and theories of sexual deviance I have ever seen propagated in mainline cinema'. The film was, according to a sub-editor's headline for Walker's review, 'a movie beyond the bounds of depravity'. Walker saw the film at the Cannes festival, but there was not much reaction until months later when it emerged that the British Board of Film Classification (BBFC) was considering granting the film a certificate.

The *Daily Telegraph* then ran a front-page story under the headline ' "Depraved" film to be released in Britain'. The next day the *Daily Mail* expressed its disquiet with another front-page story under the headline 'Ban this car crash sex film'. Other pro-censorship voices added to the expressions of outrage. The Heritage Secretary, Virginia

Bottomley, urged local authorities to refuse to screen the film if the BBFC decided to give it a certificate. A few did. Mary Whitehouse of the National Viewers and Listeners Association urged Michael Howard, the Home Secretary, to overrule the BBFC. Groups of young Christian evangelists prepared to stage protests wherever the film was shown.

The *Daily Mail*'s film critic, Christopher Tookey, urged his readers to attack the film's distributors, Columbia Tristar, a subsidiary of Sony, by boycotting all Sony electrical goods at Christmas. The *Mail* investigated the private lives of the film's British distributors and tried to show that the BBFC's examiners were non-family people. It also demanded that the BBFC, a voluntary body established by the film industry, should be disbanded and its job done by the state.

The copycat effect

The arguments for banning the film concerned the 'copycat effect'. The basic belief is that certain material is likely to induce or uncover criminal tendencies in the susceptible user. Tookey argued that people who saw *Crash*, especially those who derived 'satisfaction from perpetrating and witnessing sadistic and masochistic acts' would be encouraged to behave that way by what they saw. He saw the main thesis of the film as being 'car crashes can be used to promote sexual pleasure'. The film was simply a succession of sex scenes relieved by minimal characterisation, he maintained.

Those who believe in the copycat effect seek to link major crimes to television and film viewing. They point out that the child killers in the James Bulger case had seen *Child's Play 3*; that the man responsible for the Hungerford shootings was influenced by *Rambo* films; that Stanley Kubrick chose to withdraw *A Clockwork Orange* because it was inspiring vicious hooliganism in the 1970s.

◄ *See Activity 6, page 41*

Personal attacks

Having accused the film of being a corrupting influence, Tookey went on to mount personal attacks on people connected with the film. He criticised the director, Cronenberg, for being obsessed with horrifying his audiences by filming 'exploding heads, psychotic baby-killers, gory amputations'. Tookey also demanded the resignation of the director of the BBFC, James Ferman, wondering if 'anything can appal this man'. Ferman is described as 'a moral watchdog without the will to bite'. Tookey also argued for the abolition of the BBFC itself, claiming that it was secretive, staffed by people from 'the public sector', and financed by the film industry.

RESPONSES TO THE MORAL OUTRAGE ARGUMENT

Responses to these arguments fall into four categories:
1 What's all the fuss about?
2 There's no evidence that films and television programmes produce the damaging effects that people claim.
3 Anti-nannyism.
4 Censorship doesn't work.

What's all the fuss about?

The director of *Crash* wondered why people who had accepted *Braveheart*, a popular and violent Oscar-winning film of the time, objected to *Crash*. 'Would it have been all right if all the actors had worn kilts?', he asked.

Some critics expressed surprise at people's reactions. One said that the film was less scary than *101 Dalmations*. Another said, tongue in cheek, that the *Wizard of Oz* was more dangerous, with its violent attack by Miss Gulch (who becomes the Wicked Witch) on Dorothy's dog, and three of the characters going into an opium-induced dream in the poppy field before being revived by the Good Witch who showers them with white powder she calls, slangily, 'snow':

> ❛ In short, the film [Wizard of Oz] is a non-stop orgy of drugs and violence; and yet its video is still certified as "U – Suitable for all". Will no one – not even the Daily Mail – protect us from this filth? ❜
> Francis Wheen, 1996

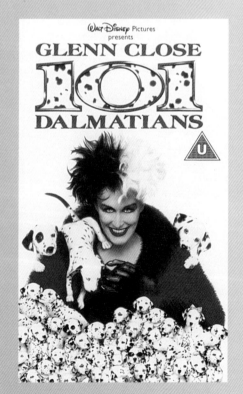

Figure 3.8 Can 101 Dalmations really be more frightening than Crash?

Another variation of 'what's the fuss about?' is to dismiss the film as tedious. Alistair Dalton, film critic of the *Scotsman* began his review: 'Without the hype, *Crash* would be a low-key art-house film that few people would recommend to their friends.' He goes on to say that it is 'boring' and 'instantly forgettable'. He saw the film in a Belgian cinema and said that 'the unfamiliar Belgian cinema advertisements which preceded it were more memorable'. He concludes: 'The film appeared to make no big statement about society's obsession with sex and car crashes. It certainly will not entice people to go out crashing cars for sexual gratification. I don't think audiences will empathise with the characters – or want to go out and emulate them.'

Figure 3.9 Natural Born Killers – police found no links to actual crimes

There's no evidence of damaging effect

Francis Wheen argued that there is no evidence to support copycat theories. He responded to Tookey's claim that, '*Natural Born Killers* triggered a string of crimes including a murder and a near-fatal shooting' by saying that the BBFC conducted an investigation into every single case of alleged copycat crimes in both the USA and France. In no instance were the police prepared to attribute any crimes to this film or any other film.

Anti-nannyism

Others oppose censorship because it represents the 'nanny state' and infringes personal liberty. During the *Crash* controversy film producer Stephen Woolley argued that: 'If you are going to expand people's minds, you are going to need to be a bit dangerous. It is difficult enough for producers to make films that are not simply cynical exercises in making money. And people with the intelligence of David Cronenberg and British producer Jeremy Thomas make films that need to be subversive.'

He argued that *Crash* encourages serious debate about the connection between sex and death and about why we are fascinated with car crashes and speed. He said that film-makers should be allowed to film whatever they want to film as long as people want to see their work. He objects to people such as politicians 'mouthing off about a film [they have] not even seen and probably would not understand'.

Censorship doesn't work

The anti-censorship argument maintains that censors are like fascists who want to tidy up the world and that they use any controversial production as an opportunity to clean up the media. The censors are portrayed as hating any new medium which has mass appeal and is best understood by the young. As the *Daily Mail* expressed it in its headlines:

CURB THE DARK AND BRUTAL SIDE OF TV
TOUGH NEW PACKAGE WILL PROTECT CHILDREN FROM SQUALID AND SEAMY PROGRAMMES

' As always with censorship debates, the Crash controversy reveals the patronising attitude the middle-class has towards popular audiences, which are thought incapable of understanding or evaluating what they see, hear and read. The Westminster licensing subcommittee, in its published statement, claims "the West End is the entertainment heart of London and it is likely that many young people who drift into London will visit the cinema without planning which film to see". Unlike, presumably, a district such as Kensington or Barnet, where the citizens double check the newspaper reviews against Ceefax before going to the pictures. '
Philip French, 1997

ACTIVITIES

Activity 1

'We have to recognise this terribly unpalatable truth in a democracy: that care has to be taken, even to the extent of limiting our own freedoms, on behalf of some others not so fortunate.' Richard Hoggart, 1995

How far do the young, the old, the frightened and the mentally ill need protecting? Discuss this with reference to specific contemporary media products.

Activity 2

The British Board of Film and Video Classification makes a distinction between 'manners and morals'. Issues such as whether a woman's naked breasts should be shown on television are a question of manners. Moral questions are more fundamental, such as whether to show a humiliating rape scene. This distinction is used to clear away narrow-minded, custom-bound objections, so that more important and difficult questions can be dealt with.

Collect examples of manners and morals from current censorship issues, both in the media and from your own personal experience.

Activity 3

Would you ban this film?

'There is a truly memorable scene in Sam Peckinpah's new movie *Now Take It Away Again*, the little known sequel to *Bring Me The Head Of Alfredo Garcia*, in which an old man, his ears and hands and most of his right leg blown off by a sawn-off Colt .44 triple action repeater, crawls away to the shelter of a tub of water, only to find that his left leg, what remains of both arms and a good percentage of his head are all shot off by a man with a machine-gun.

Violent? Well maybe to the squeamish. Yet it is a scene which is strangely compassionate, even poignant; the anti-hero of the movie, the unnamed X, is so enraged by this ruthless act that he takes out his machete and slices the heads off over 80 Mexican bandits in less than 35 marvellous screen seconds. The rest, of course, is one of the most gentle and profound moments in cinematic history; in a stunning sequence, one of these heads rolls down a slope, knocking over a can of oil. The oil is set alight by a smouldering match and within the next 17 screen seconds a further 328 men, women and children are burnt to death. The director's use of the telling close-up is particularly noteworthy in some of the reaction shots (surprised, outraged, bemused, resigned) of the blazing victims.

Happily, salvation – a kind of Biblical salvation, at once primitive yet strangely up to date – is at hand in the shape of Maria Schneider, who has tragically lost all her clothes in an earlier accident involving a misplaced safety pin. After taking a well-earned break from her responsibilities as Avenging Angel by soundlessly consenting to 16 screen minutes of sexual intercourse with X, the Schneider character murders a further 148 bandits before fellating the dying X, thus injecting a much-needed note of optimism into this otherwise bleak yet strangely cathartic slice of life.

In my opinion, *Now Take It Away Again* – allusive, plangent, supple – amounts to one of the 17 greatest Peckinpah movies of all time. Yet there are still those who, from their towers of ignorance, stand in judgement on the so-called 'harmful effects' of violence on the screen. Do they not realise that movies such as *Now Take It Away Again* and Tarantino's brilliant *Reservoir Dogs* do not create violence but merely reflect the violence in our society?' Bel Littlejohn, 1996

Activity 4

If you were serving on the Press Complaints Commission how would you adjudicate on this complaint?

A headteacher has complained that two reporters visited his school and in the course of their enquiries harassed a member of staff (in breach of clause 8 of the Commission's Code of Practice) and approached pupils without permission of the authorities (in breach of clause 12).

The reporters went to the school because there had been allegations that a teacher had taken drugs into school. They asked to see the head, but were told that he was busy and were asked to leave the premises. They returned by a back entrance and tried to see another member of staff. They were asked to stay where they were but refused. A teacher who confronted them later said that their behaviour amounted to harassment because of their 'confrontational body language' and the pressure they put on him for an answer.

The head also complained that one of the reporters approached a pupil in the school without permission and asked him if a photograph he showed him was in fact a picture of the teacher about whom the allegations were being made.

The editor of the paper said that his reporters had been very rudely treated on their first visit. They did not believe that the head was too busy to see them, but thought he was refusing to help. They denied being threatening in any way except through persistent questioning, which was part of their professional training. With regard to getting confirmation concerning the photograph, his reporters had first asked the school secretary about the picture, but she refused to answer. One reporter had then asked a pupil on the way out of school. No pressure was put on the pupil to answer.

Clause 8

'Journalists should neither obtain nor seek to obtain information or pictures through intimidation or harassment... should not persist in telephoning or questioning individuals after being asked to desist; should not remain on property after being asked to leave.'

Clause 12

'Journalists should not normally interview or photograph children under the age of 16 on subjects involving the personal welfare of the child, in the absence of or without the consent of a parent or other adult who is responsible for the children. Children should not be approached or photographed while at school without the permission of the school authorities.'

Activity 5

Would you give publicity to a racist organisation like the British National Party? Discuss this question with others in your group. These are some of the points that you might consider.

- If the media treat fascist and racist organisations like any other organisation, is this dangerous? If you give freedom of speech to a group that advocates the forcible deportation of millions of black and Asian Britons, are you restricting the freedoms of those groups?
- Is providing a platform for fascist ideas really an incitement to fear and violence?
- Can people in the media be neutral about malignant social forces?
- Free speech cannot be absolute. We are not free to libel others, hurl racial abuse or incite people to violence.
- On the other hand if you ban media access to an extreme organisation does this not mean you have to ban others? The BNP today, the Socialist Workers tomorrow.
- Their own words condemn them and we have nothing to fear from hearing them. There should be no argument we are afraid to face head on.
- If you value freedom of speech you have to listen to people who are dangerous and despicable. Do you retreat into authoritarian bans or do you let ridicule, contempt and simply letting people speak do the job?

Activity 6

Martin Bryant killed 34 people at a tourist attraction in Tasmania in April 1996. A week later the *Daily Mail* in Britain reported that the Australian Prime Minister had called for a ban on certain weapons, and also 'tighter restrictions on violent videos and on the broadcasting of horror films on TV'. The latter was because Bryant was reported to be an avid fan of Chucky, the evil doll in the *Child's Play* video films. The Prime Minister is reported as saying: 'It is hard to believe that the repetitive, mind-numbing violence seen on television does not have a serious effect on some people.'

The *Mail* goes on to quote 'one military psychologist' who said that ' "kill the enemy" video games closely resemble training methods for desensitising soldiers to killing'.

Discuss the tendency for people to make cause and effect links without evidence and to make sweeping generalisations based on personal hunches. What can be done to counter such thinking? Or is this 'gut reaction' approach both understandable and acceptable?

BIBLIOGRAPHY ▼

Forgan, L, 'The right we have wronged', in *Guardian*, 26 March 1990

French, P, 'Crash, there goes the censors' Berlin Wall', in *Observer*, 25 May 1997

Hoggart, R, *The Way We Live Now*, Chatto and Windus, 1995

Littlejohn, B, 'Sam Peckinpah, Martin Scorcese – and me', in *Guardian*, 27 September 1996

Masterman, L, *Teaching the Media*, Routledge, 1985

Matthews, T D, *Censored: The Story Of Film Censorship in Britain*, Chatto and Windus, 1996

Plater, A, 'How BBC drama is being neutered', in *Guardian*, 16 November 1996

Walter, N, 'The sport of misogyny', in *Guardian*, 16 October 1996

Welsh, T, and Greenwood, W, *McNae's Essential Law for Journalists*, Butterworths, 1995

Wheen, F, 'Wheen's World', in *Guardian*, 27 November 1996

Williams, G, *Britain's Media – How They are Related*, Campaign for Press and Broadcasting Freedom, 1996

Woolley, S, 'Head-on collision', in *Guardian*, 16 November 1996

CHAPTER 4

Representation

Introduction

This chapter provides:
- a brief explanation of the meaning of 'representation' in media studies
- an introduction to the way studies of representation have developed, from straightforward content analysis to looking

at how audiences make different meanings from what they see, read and hear
- examples of how representations of gender have been studied
- advice on how to study representations of disability.

What is representation?

Representation is about:
- how social groups, different subcultures, occupations, ages, social classes and places are portrayed in the media
- how audiences interpret these portrayals.

Most academic work on representation has focused on gender and race, but you should be aware that there are many other possibilities for your own investigative work based on your particular interests.

▶◀ See Activity 1, page 53

The word 'representation' implies that people are being re-presented by the media to others and to themselves. So in the case of women, for example, some argue that if images presented by the media concentrate on physical attractiveness, this reinforces sexism by encouraging us to think that the way women look is more important than what they do. This affects our attitudes to others and how we think of our own bodies and personalities.

The way we think of ourselves as individuals and how we relate to each other is continually being modified by our experiences. A child reared by animals behaves like an animal (as in the film *L'Enfant Sauvage* (1970)), but can learn to become 'human' if offered human company. In the film *The Elephant Man* (1980), with the help of a sympathetic medical specialist, John Merrick learns to think of himself not as a freak, but as a human being. When he is chased and cornered in an underground lavatory by a vindictive mob, he asserts with as much dignity as he can summon 'I am not an animal'.

The media play a part in this constant development of our identities. Our experience of the media offers us a wide range of models of behaviour and attitudes which we can copy or reject. We can become imaginatively involved in characters in a broadcast drama so that we understand their thoughts, actions and points of view. We can identify with famous people portrayed in the press and want to be more like them. We can recognise certain social or group characteristics and want to adopt or modify them.

In order to start examining representations, you need to ask these questions:
- Who is presenting the images and why?
- How do the people receiving the images, including your-self, react to what they see, read and hear?
- Over a period of time, what do the images suggest about certain groups in society?
- What points of view are neglected or ignored?

▶◀ See Activity 2, page 53

The best way to see how this works in practice is to look at various problems that critics have dealt with.

Representing gender

Some critics argue that the articles and advertising which dominate women's magazines help to reinforce the notion that women are passive bodies to be looked at. Women are encouraged to believe that each part of their bodies needs careful attention to make it attractive to the male gaze. Because most cannot match the images of beautiful models, they feel they cannot attain the ideals before them. This can lead to feelings of self-disgust and helplessness.

To investigate these issues in more detail, critics carry out a content analysis of different media.

▶◀ See Activity 3, page 53

Content analysis and stereotypes

Gillian Murphy gives a good example of the effectiveness and limitations of content analysis in her essay 'Media Influence on the Socialisation of Teenage Girls'. She argues that the media exert a strong influence on the gender-related behaviour of teenagers. She says that from the age of 11 or 12 youngsters begin to break away from the main sources of authority such as the family, and start looking to their peer group and the media for ideas about how they should behave and what their roles and aspirations should be.

Her research involved analysing the content of romantic magazines popular with working-class girls from the 1920s up to the end of the 1970s. She looked specifically at the use of adjectives in descriptions of males and females. In the case of the magazine *Jackie*, she also investigated the values, roles and aspirations of male and female characters.

What she found was a flourishing of 'sexist ideas' such as:

- females don't take the initiative
- girls are almost always depicted looking for or keeping a boyfriend
- the hero initiates, the heroine follows
- girls are depicted in nurturing roles – looking after small children or old people, for instance
- girls' work and hobbies are of little importance
- women are seen primarily as home-makers
- the boy-meets-girl happy ending (leading presumably to marriage) is seen as part of the escapism from work (equated with drudgery).

Murphy believes that these ideas become stereotypes which are 'unrealistic' and 'unsatisfactory'. In particular she complains about the teenage magazine *Jackie*, which shows 'girls as having an overwhelming need to find a man', saying that this is 'counter to all notions of Women's Liberation'.

Murphy goes on to complain about the 'depoliticisation' of girls' magazines, saying that they neglect things like 'unjust management, fair pay for women workers, the power of the unions, and political parties and leaders'.

There are three main problems with this kind of approach to representation. First, there is a danger of the critic wanting to impose her own agenda on the media. Murphy criticises magazines for not doing what she wants them to do. She wants to force women to free themselves from romance and become 'politicised'. She also criticises romantic magazines for concentrating on romance, which is rather like criticising detective novels for concentrating on crime.

The second problem relates to stereotyping. Stereotypers tend to be élitist. As educated critics, they see their duty as being able to spot stereotypes and then protect the uneducated from their harmful influence. Implicit in this is the tendency to believe that audiences are passive, unthinking and easily duped.

This leads to the third problem, which is that Gillian Murphy does not seem to have researched the meanings which readers of romance magazines make of the material they read. Analysis of the content of media products needs to be accompanied by analysis of how people interpret what they read, see and hear.

▶◀ *See Activities 4, 5 and 6, pages 53 and 54*

The importance of the audience

Angela McRobbie, however, in her book *Feminism and Youth Culture* explores the pleasures that working-class young women find in magazines such as *Just Seventeen*. She considers the changing images of women represented by teenage magazines from the 1950s to the present day, and finds more than the simple stereotypes described in Gillian Murphy's analysis.

McRobbie's analysis is not limited to the media text, but also looks at the social situation in which magazines are consumed. She believes that young working-class women who live with inequality on a day-to-day basis have, in magazines such as *Just Seventeen*, an outlet for resistance to their situation. Firstly the magazines make young women visible where they are so often invisible. Secondly, the notion of femininity offered is not negative, but is a source of pleasure and self-reliance.

> ❝ McRobbie considers how the representations of women within the magazines have changed over the years, so that simple stereotypes no longer exist in the way they once did. She notes that: 'In girls' magazines in the 1980s romance no longer occupies the place it once did.' She affirms that magazines like Mizz and Just Seventeen respect the female readership, considering their readers to be intelligent and discerning ❞

The emphasis on the importance of the reader to these magazines reflects McRobbie's own position. Unlike Murphy, she concentrates on the way young women use teenage magazines for their own gratification and to negotiate socially imposed situations (such as inequality), rather than on the stereotypes of femininity offered in the media text itself.

Figure 4.1

Differing interpretations

In his essay 'Restyling Masculinity: the Impact of *Boys from the Blackstuff*' (in Curran, Smith and Wingate, 1987), Richard Paterson argues that:

> ❛ *To understand the effect of television programmes on an audience is much more complicated than either survey methods or textual analysis would indicate, though both of course have much to contribute.* ❜

He believes that there is no automatic link between intended meanings and 'any particular viewer's attitude at the moment of viewing', and that there is a 'secondary discussion' when the programme is talked about by those who have seen it. He describes the 'public after-life of the series', which includes reviews, newspaper stories, studies of the series in education, and informal conversation.

In his discussion of *Boys from the Blackstuff*, Paterson shows how the series, which was about the effects of unemployment on working-class Liverpudlians, became part of everyday life. Lines from the series were incorporated in football crowd chants at Liverpool games. The series was endorsed by Liverpool City Council and used by trade union groups. It became a 'symbol within the national culture differently appropriated by different groups' because 'it touched common sense understandings about the life of unemployed men and their families in the 1980s'.

Paterson's textual analysis of the series shows that by focusing on characters in their domestic and working lives it dealt with the problem of what it is to be male, with particular reference to the conventional role as breadwinner. The stories dealt with ways of trying to resist increasing disillusionment because men could no longer earn enough to support their families.

Figure 4.2 Yosser Hughes in Boys from the Blackstuff

Paterson interviewed a number of people to find what the series meant to them and found that people's reactions varied according to region, experience of unemployment, class, race and gender. Some readings were very personal: 'I've been at some time or another as desperate as Yosser, or feeling stripped of dignity as Chrissie... he's given us words to communicate with each other about our own experiences.' Some were political: 'He took the lid off the box, and then he wants you to know what the bloody hell is going on in this town.' Some were about taking action: 'The series left me with... more determination to change things.' Some saw it simply as a nostalgic fighting for lost causes.

▶◀ *See Activity 7, page 54*

Boys and masculinity

In his essay 'Boys' Talk: Television and the Policing of Masculinity' (in Buckingham, 1993), David Buckingham argues strongly for studying how audiences play an active part in constructing meaning.

He argues against the kind of research which sees the media 'as an extremely powerful source of stereotyped role models which children simply absorb and internalise'. Children are seen as 'bombarded by stereotypes and as effectively helpless in the face of the onslaught. Media messages are typically conceived as uniformly sexist, and thus as inevitably producing sexist attitudes.' But he believes that children are not 'television zombies' passively absorbing everything they see. To teach people simply to analyse media stereotypes in the hope of 'liberating' them from false ideologies both overestimates the power of the media and underestimates the ways in which children make their own meanings from what they absorb.

His own research involved studying how young boys made sense of what it means to be male or masculine, partly from the ways they talked about television programmes and videos. He analysed the way a group of 7 to 8-year-old boys reacted to watching *Thundercats*, and argued that ideas of masculinity are not fixed, but are constantly being negotiated and redefined. Being masculine is not simply about fitting into an existing role, but is an ongoing struggle. This struggle is partly concerned with denying feminine characteristics or any behaviour which has effeminate connotations, and is especially important in talk with other males. This can involve, for example, denying liking what are seen as girls' programmes, or refusing to admit to identifying with female characters.

According to Buckingham, young boys and probably most men fear being labelled as homosexual or effeminate. The pressure to conform to male codes is often exerted in male banter and repartee. Buckingham found that in talk about television there was much more pressure on boys than on girls to avoid being ridiculed or humiliated by peers. As Antony Easthope put it in his book *What A Man's Gotta Do*: 'Within, femininity and male homosexual desire must be denied; without, women and the feminine must be subordinated and held in place.'

Buckingham found that boys are reluctant to admit that they are scared by films: 'learning to watch horror was very much a matter of learning not to display their own fear'. They do not like admitting that their viewing is censored by their parents. In the conversations which Buckingham analysed, he discerned that boys constantly put themselves at risk, primarily of humiliation or ridicule by each other, and then rapidly withdraw:

> ❛ RIK (watching television): War, war, bloody war. Why can't they have stories about love and peace? VYVYAN: Because it's cissy, you girlie. ❜
> The Young Ones (quoted in Easthope, 1986)

Social context

The work of David Morley, described in his book *Family Television*, makes an important contribution to the debate about gender and representation. He looks at the social dimensions of viewing and interpretation, and shows that people don't just absorb messages passively but produce 'readings' of what they see. These readings are affected by the social context, often the family at home, in which they are made. Gender turns out to be one of the most important principles which shape these readings.

Morley's main findings were:

- men define home, where television is mainly watched, as a place of leisure, whereas women see it as a place of work where they have domestic responsibilities
- because of this women tend to watch television distractedly and guiltily
- men prefer to watch television silently 'in order not to miss anything'
- women are more likely to talk as they watch and more likely to be doing something else, like ironing (this is more through their domestic circumstances rather than choice)
- television is used as a conversational device by women more than by men
- the only television that men will readily admit to talking about are sports programmes
- as meanings are not made simply at the moment of viewing but in the subsequent social processes of discussion, this reluctance to talk about television on men's part means that their experience of television is of a quite different kind from women's
- men, by strategies like controlling the remote control and the video and by ridiculing certain types of programme such as soaps, tend to define what is serious and what is silly viewing, leaving women feeling that their pleasures are downgraded and that they have to watch the programmes they like almost in secret
- men have a strong preference for factual programmes such as news, current affairs and documentaries, whereas women tend to prefer fictional programmes (Morley points out that his findings were partly due to the fact that he was measuring 'attentive and enjoyable viewing'. Research into more casual viewing found more overlap between the categories.)
- women who occupy the traditional feminine position in the home tend to disapprove strongly of anarchic humour (the example most cited in the research was *The Young Ones*).

◄◀ *See Activity 8, page 54*

Figure 4.3 *The Young Ones*

CASE ▼ STUDY

DISABILITY

This case study looks at the way in which disabled people are represented in the media. It draws upon research which relies heavily on the term 'stereotype' to describe categories of portrayal. These categories of portrayal have been found to occur frequently when the content of media products featuring disabled people has been analysed (Barnes, 1992). However powerful a case these categories make, as already explained in this chapter, stereotyping is a theory, not a fact. You should not necessarily assume that stereotypes have simple effects, for example.

This case study begins with an overview of the topic before moving on to look at representations of disability in cinema, television and the press. It concentrates solely on disability, but it is important to emphasise that other aspects of representation cut across the subject. For example, representations of gender, social class and ethnicity are also relevant to the portrayal of disabled people.

DISABILITY IN THE MEDIA: AN OVERVIEW

Some representations of disabled people are both positive and non-stereotypical. In the romantic film comedy *Four Weddings and a Funeral*, the brother of Charles, the hero of the story, has a hearing impairment. David's deafness is not a big issue, but it does play a role in the plot. When Charles is about to wed a woman for the wrong reasons, they conduct a conversation with each other in sign language which helps Charles to decide to withdraw from the wedding ceremony. David is played by a deaf actor and the words are not 'interpreted' by someone else speaking, they are written in subtitles.

It should not be exceptional for a disabled character to be played by an actor with a disability. Nor should it be remarkable that the portrayal does not include the disabled character as the butt of humour, an object of violence, or superhuman in some way. However, the portrayal has been much appreciated by those who have, or who are interested in, disability. The character is cast appropriately, and is positive without being patronising or stereotypical.

Figure 4.4 David signing to Charles in Four Weddings and a Funeral

Negative portrayals

Whatever you call the hackneyed and negative portrayals of disability which are so common – stereotypes, archetypes, habits of mind, clichés, prejudices – they put obstacles in the

way of disabled people. They also seem to have deep roots not just in media culture, but also in Western culture, and possibly even psychology. Representations which reinforce a world view that impairment of ability and/or lack of 'wholeness' in a person are socially unacceptable pre-date Christianity, going back even to the theatre of Ancient Greece.

In simplest terms, most portrayals of people with disabilities in the media are not truly representative of people with disabilities in the real world. They convey messages about people with disabilities which distort the picture. Most portrayals of disabled people in 'non-specialist' media products originate from so-called able-bodied people, and seem to reflect able-bodied people's attitudes towards those with disabilities. If you decide to investigate the portrayal of people with disabilities and associated issues, you will soon find that representation is bound up with attitudes and values. Relationships between people with disabilities and society involve political/ideological issues such as access, rights and power. Representation always involves ideology.

The categories of representation which researchers examining the portrayal of disability have identified and criticised as stereotypes say more about the attitudes with which people, particularly the able-bodied, regard disability than they do about the disabled people they are supposed to portray. They project fears and other negative attitudes on to disabled people.

Figure 4.5 A demonstration against the negative portrayal of wheelchair users

Forces for change

The portrayal in the media of people with disabilities is not only debated in media studies and by media industries, but also by organisations concerned with disability. Disabled people and their organisations have scrutinised portrayals of disability in the media and have put forward powerful critical arguments against the omissions and distortions they have found. Representation does not stand still, and if you investigate images and portrayals of people with disabilities in the past you may find change, or even 'progress' of a kind, has taken place. The portrayal of people with disabilities will continue to change, and various forces, including organisations representing disabled people, are trying to influence the nature of such change.

You can find many examples of change in the kinds of language used to talk about disability. Terms such as 'spastic', 'cripple', 'retard' and 'handicapped', which once might have been used freely and without question, are now associated with negative attitudes to disability and are not acceptable descriptions to most progressively minded people. However, you still hear people use terms like this, some in ignorance, others as 'everyday' insults. There are many expressions in English which show inbuilt prejudice against disability, such as 'lame duck', 'deaf to reason', 'blind stupidity'.

Language is not neutral and is a powerful component of portrayal. It is also an area of debate. There are strong arguments for using the term 'disabled people' rather than 'people with disabilities':

' "People with disabilities" assumes that disability is the property of the individual and not of society.' Barnes, 1992

There is an even stronger argument that the term 'the disabled' is a label which is dehumanising and offensive. In this case study the terms 'disabled people' and 'people with disabilities' are used. 'The disabled' is avoided.

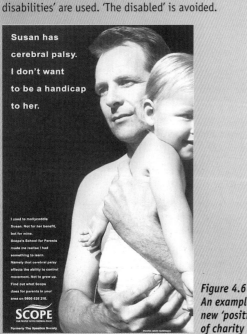

Figure 4.6
An example of the new 'positive' style of charity advert

The lack of representation of disability

More than one in ten of the UK population is disabled (government evidence indicates 12 per cent). This leads on to perhaps the most significant feature of representation of disability in the media: the *absence* of representation of disabled people and disability issues. In mainstream TV fiction, for example, disabled people represent less than 1.5 per cent of all characters portrayed according to one study (Cumberbatch and Negrine, 1992). In many cases disabled people are invisible, disregarded, marginalised or simply excluded. This makes the categories which portrayals tend to fall into even more significant, since on the few occasions disabled people do appear, labelling usually takes place.

Charity appeals

One media area which does feature representations of disabled people is that of the charity advertisement or appeal. These advertisements often feature a disabled person as 'suffering' from the disability concerned; someone to feel sorry for and an object of pity. These representations are very much resented by disabled people. Organisations run by disabled people have put forward criticisms of such portrayals as perpetuating stereotypes of disabled people as 'victims' and 'pitiable'.

CINEMA REPRESENTATIONS

This section concentrates on 'sampling' Hollywood and British cinema. For a long time the cinema has been dominated by representations of disability associated symbolically with the villainous. The use of some form of disability as a 'sign' of evil seems so deeply rooted in culture that it may be a deep psychological habit: what the psycho-analyst Carl Jung called 'an archetype'.

The cinema is linked historically with older forms of popular culture such as the fairground and circus, where disabled people were exhibited as freaks or curiosities. The disabled face and body was exhibited as part of the eye-grabbing spectacle of cinema. This was associated with the horror genre and even particular stars, such as Lon Chaney.

Figure 4.7 Lon Chaney made a career out of the portrayal of 'freaks' and monsters, including the 1925 film of Phantom of the Opera

Figure 4.8 John Merrick benefitting from the 'benelovence' of able-bodied people in The Elephant Man

This freakish strain has continued, as in the film of *The Elephant Man*, although this also includes newer 'enlightened' attitudes. The film tells the tale of John Merrick, an intelligent man with very 'abnormal' physical features, who is rescued from a fairground freak show by an able-bodied man, Sir Frederick Treves. The story reinforces the negative view that disabled people must depend on the benevolence of able-bodied people. These portrayals are frequently linked with other recurring representations, such as the disabled person as the object of violence.

After the Second World War, many films were made with plots revolving around the rehabilitation of disabled people, in particular disabled war veterans (*The Best Years of Our Lives*, 1946; *Reach for the Sky*, 1956).

These portrayals underline the point that so-called stereotypical representations are not always simply negative. *Reach for the Sky* is the biographical story of Douglas Bader, a pilot who lost both his legs as a result of a crash but returned to become a successful fighter ace and war hero. Its portrayal of the disabled hero fits into the category of the 'supercripple', where the disabled person is given superhuman qualities. One of the problems of this kind of portrayal is that it implies that disabled people must have 'super' qualities in order to earn respect from the able-bodied.

Horror films, such as those made by the British Hammer studio, kept on the tradition of the disabled person as monstrous freak and villain. The James Bond spy thrillers of the 1960s and 1970s portrayed disabled characters as villains, such as the megalomaniac Blofield in *Goldfinger* (1964), and the superhuman Jaws in *The Spy Who Loved Me* (1977) and *Moonraker* (1979).

In his essay 'Everywhere: Disability on Film' (in Pointon and Davies, 1997), Paul Darke argues that cinema portrayals of disability are partly 'explained' by stories in which disabled characters are exploited for their entertainment value. In these narratives, problems are made for people to solve as individuals (marginalising the roles of groups and society): 'Consequently, society is absolved of any responsibility while at the same time it is left unchallenged and unaffected.'

Thus there is the plot formula in which the disabled person has an attitudinal problem, as in *The Raging Moon* (1970). This is sometimes referred to as 'the disabled person as their own worst and only enemy'. This is also a component of the film *Born on the Fourth of July* (1989), which is based on the true story of a war veteran who becomes an activist against the US war in Vietnam. Although in this film the disabled hero is part of a social movement for change, the narrative concentrates on his personal struggle.

TELEVISION REPRESENTATIONS

The first thing to say about television is that there is a relative absence of disabled people. Many programmes do not feature disabled people. Where disability issues are central, the material is often in specialist programming set apart from the 'mainstream'. In comparison with gender and ethnicity, there is also a lack of media studies research into the representation of disabled people on television.

Chris Davies, who writes a television column for the monthly newspaper *Disability Now*, has produced an overview of examples of disabled people represented on television over the decades (in Pointon and Davies, 1997). His survey includes the following 'milestones' from the 1950s to the 1970s:

- In the 1950s Michael Flanders, a wheelchair user, appeared on television as one of a comedy pair, Flanders and Swan, whose main performance was comic songs.
- In 1964 a programme of equal access to hearing impaired and hearing children, *Vision On*, appeared on children's television. Children's TV programmes like *Blue Peter* have a tradition of including disability, even if this is frequently in the context of supporting charities.
- In the same year the soap *Crossroads*, based on a fictional hotel in the Midlands, began. Over the years, this soap featured a wheelchair user (Sandy), a character with Down's syndrome, and Benny, a character who was 'slow'.
- In the late 1960s a detective series called *Ironside* featured a wheelchair user played by an able-bodied actor as its hero.
- In 1974 *Joey*, a drama-documentary about a real person with cerebral palsy, was broadcast in the BBC Horizon series.
- In 1976 the only regular disability strand programme on the ITV network, *Link*, began. The programme is now made by disabled people through an independent company for Carlton Television.
- The BBC's Education Department has made many specialist programmes about disability, beginning with a series of ten programmes called *Contact* in 1976.

At the time of writing there are a number of specialist programmes focusing on disability. Channel 4 has several programmes which target disabled viewers, including *People First* (since 1992) and *Inside Out* (1995). *Sign On* (since 1992) targets hearing impaired viewers. The BBC produces specialist programmes through its Disability Programmes Unit, including *From the Edge* and *See Hear*.

The problem with specialist programmes is that disabled viewers sometimes complain about being isolated from the rest of society in a 'ghetto'. The showing of specialist programmes in 'mainstream' evening slots on Channel 4 is a move towards a wider audience, which may take off.

In the meantime, you will continue to find many examples of stereotyping on mainstream television. Research has shown that disabled characters in TV fiction are three times more likely than non-disabled characters to be dead by the end of the show. More than half of these deaths were the result of violence (Cumberbatch and Negrine, 1992). This

Figure 4.9 *Ironside as played by the able-bodied Raymond Burr*

'object of violence' stereotype is linked with other categories of representation, such as the representation of the disabled person as an evil person or criminal.

If disabled people appear in the news media they are often negatively represented as pitiable: 'Pictures of disabled individuals, frequently children, in hospitals or nursing homes are repeatedly flashed across our TV screens perpetuating the myth that disability is synonymous with illness and suffering' (Barnes, 1992).

Research has also shown that in 'factual' news and documentary programmes portrayals of disabled people are most often linked to medical treatments and 'miracle cures' (Cumberbatch and Negrine, 1992).

Another particular target for criticism has been the television charity 'telethon', such as BBC *Children in Need*. Telethons as a genre originate from America. They typically involve heart-tugging appeals and fund-raising as a celebration of giving, with the whole affair packaged into a kind of variety show.

The receiving organisations can use more funds, and are pleased to receive the sums raised. However, disabled people do not have to be represented only by 'cute' children and the television equivalent of the begging bowl. As Anne Karpf asks in her book *Doctoring the Media*:

'Could telethons be different? In 1979 United Cerebral Palsy (UCP), an American organisation known for its "look we're walking" telethons, decided to change them. They wrote up the speeches the celebrities were supposed to make, asked people with disabilities to monitor the telethon, and set out guidelines stressing that telethons should show both adults and children and should reflect the degrees of difficulty typical among people with cerebral palsy. Celebrities were to be thoroughly informed about the condition and use appropriate terminology, avoiding terms like victim, poor, cripple, unfortunate, tragedy and other words arousing pity rather than respect. They were also to avoid asking viewers to give out of thankfulness that their own children were born healthy... They also wanted to draw attention to the organisation's advocacy role in helping people with disabilities realise their own desires and needs, like gaining access to public education, barrier-free buildings and transport, housing and jobs.'

The view that disability is something to laugh at and be mocked is often reinforced through television comedy. The old American cartoon *Mr Magoo* portrays an elderly man with a visual impairment as a 'hapless fool' (Barnes, 1992). The cult comedy series *Monty Python's Flying Circus* famously found ways to laugh at people who have difficulty walking in 'The Ministry of Funny Walks'. You will still find that when disabled people appear in television comedy they are often the butt of the humour.

Many people try to laugh off the serious implications of such humorous portrayals. However, psychologists have pointed out that humour is a way of expressing deeply held attitudes which are normally censored from consciousness. The 'disabled person as the object of ridicule' is a representation which very clearly tells us more about attitudes towards disability than about the reality of disabled people's lives.

THE PRESS

Newspapers tend to feature disabled people in stories which include the stereotypical portrayals already described. Some reporters use neutral terminology such as 'disabled person' or 'people with disabilities'. However, sentimental language such as 'unfortunate', 'victim', 'courageous' and 'heroic' often distorts the portrayal of disability in news stories. One study found that over half the news stories featuring individuals with learning difficulties portrayed them as victims (Wertheimer, 1988).

Mainstream leisure magazines tend to select representations of the face and body which only feature glamorous able-bodied people. They have been criticised for encouraging people to view a restricted range of characteristics and body shapes as desirable or even acceptable. The same criticisms are relevant where the absence of people with disabilities in mainstream magazines is concerned. 'The disabled person as sexually abnormal' is another stereotypical category of representation, and exclusion supports the attitudes it represents.

One way to increase your awareness of the narrow way that disabled people are portrayed in the press is to look at a publication written by disabled people about disability issues, such as the monthly *Disability Now*, 'the award-winning newspaper for everyone with an interest in disability'.

◀ *See Activity 9, page 55*

**Figure 4.10 John Cleese in 'The Ministry of Funny Walks'
– an example of disabled people as the butt of humour?**

Figure 4.11

CONCLUSION

The following list summarises 11 stereotypical categories in the representation of disabled people. These categories are the result of media research undertaken by the British Council of Organisations of Disabled People in 1991 (in Barnes, 1992).

A list of commonly recurring portrayals of disabled people

1 The object of pity
2 The object of violence
3 The disabled person as sinister and/or evil
4 The disabled person as atmosphere or curio (e.g. 'blind man with stick' used as an extra)
5 The 'supercripple'
6 The object of ridicule
7 'Their own worst and only enemy'
8 A burden on society and others
9 Sexually incapable or abnormal
10 Incapable of full participation in community life
11 'As normal' (i.e. oversimplified, one-dimensional portrayals which ignore the experience of disability).

◄ *See Activities 10 and 11, page 55*

> ❢ Disabling stereotypes which medicalise, patronise, criminalise and dehumanise disabled people abound in books, films, on television, and in the press... They are fundamental to the discrimination and exploitation which disabled people encounter daily, and contribute significantly to their systematic exclusion from mainstream community life. ❟
> Barnes, 1992

What would acknowledge the complexities and the realities of disability and a disabled identity? What is your reaction to the case put forward here?

For more information on disability issues and particularly on the reporting of disability, the Disabled Members Council produces a disability pack. Contact: Disabled Members Council, National Union of Journalists, 314 Grays Inn Road, London WC1X 8DP. Tel 0171 278 7916, Fax 0171 837 8143.

◄ *See Activities 12 and 13, page 55*

> ❢ POSITIVE ASPECTS OF BEING DISABLED
> You can park on a double yellow line if you have an orange badge.
> No one expects you to be clever.
> If you can't visit someone you can say, "Sorry, I can't come because I can't get transport."
> Doctors are struck dumb when faced with your very different body to examine.
> You can wear funny clothes because people don't like to comment.
> People move aside and apologise when you run them over with your wheelchair.
> Social workers give up on you.
> If you spill your food when you are in a restaurant, everyone ignores it because people expect it of you.
> No one expects you to be rich.
> You can have sex any time you like because no one thinks you can do it. ❟
> Jacqueline Rodgers, *Disability Now*, 1997

Portrayal

It is important to realise when you are writing about representation that media producers are often, although not always, aware of their responsibilities when portraying social groups. In its guidelines the BBC warns producers, for instance, about perpetuating myths, reinforcing stereotypes and causing offence to minority groups. They are specifically advised to:

> ❢ draw participants or casts from a broad range and not concentrate unreasonably on white, able-bodied men... It is important that BBC programmes should not regularly categorise black people as criminals, women as housewives, disabled people as victims, gay people as ineffectual, old people as incapable, or people of any particular profession, vocation or walk of life as inevitable figures of fun... We must be careful not to perpetuate stereotypes by thoughtless use of material which associates groups with particular patterns of behaviour.
> Repeated use of pictures of immigrants at an airport to illustrate the theme of drugs, or of women in supermarkets to illustrate food prices, or of transvestites to illustrate gay issues – all serve to reinforce images which are of dubious validity. ❟

However, the recommendations do go on to say that in trying to avoid offending people the BBC must not end up portraying a society which does not exist, as this could ignore important issues such as prejudice and disadvantage. Again the guidelines say that while sexist terms should be avoided, there is also a danger of using 'politically correct' terms which can be equally annoying.

There may also be sound commercial reasons for particular representations or non-representations. It would be pointless criticising a teenage magazine for not having enough positive images of old people, as this is not what the magazine's audience is interested in. Public service broadcasters and national newspapers may have a duty to present a balanced overview of society, but individual programmes and titles aimed at small sections of society have more urgent commercial considerations, and cannot be pilloried because they don't portray an accurate cross-section of society.

ACTIVITIES ▼

Activity 1

Choose a topic which you are interested in and carry out your own investigation of representation. Possible topics you could consider include:

- how the media portray pop festivals and whether there are any differences between the mainstream media and the specialist pop media
- the portrayal of environmental protestors, such as those who try to halt the building of roads and airport runways by direct action
- the way single mothers are depicted in the press
- how the media see teachers and how teachers react to the way they are portrayed
- how teenagers are depicted on comedy television shows compared with the way they are represented in magazines aimed at the teenage market
- whether women tennis players are portrayed differently from men tennis players during reporting of Wimbledon
- the way your local media represent 'problem' places and how the people in those 'problem' areas react to stories about where and how they live.

Activity 2

'There is a TV tradition of portraying newspaper reporters as dodgy people you are better off keeping at arm's length.

From the trilby-wearing pigs in *Spitting Image* to the polarised BBC drama *Casualty*, reporters are portrayed as leeches, only interested in getting the story.

Now we have *Staying Alive* which seems to be peddling the same inaccurate image.' Editor of a regional newspaper

Discuss the image of newspaper reporters in current or recent TV fictional programmes. How far are they represented in the way described by the editor? What other portrayals are there? Try to interview local journalists to see how they react to the portrayals.

Activity 3

To check out the representation of women in magazines and its effects, carry out a content analysis of a selection of contemporary women's magazines to see what kinds of female images they contain. It is very important not to have preconceptions about the images you expect to find, as this might prevent you from noticing images which do not fit in with your expectations.

Remember that the audience can make its own interpretation of the images and content. They are not necessarily passive victims of sexist representations. Once you have done the content analysis, organise some in-depth discussions with regular readers of the magazines to see how far they identify with the contents and modify their behaviour, and how far they reject or reinterpret the messages.

Activity 4

With help from the rest of your group, collect examples from current magazines for teenage girls which either support or contradict the following 'sexist ideas':

- females don't take the initiative
- girls are almost always depicted looking for or keeping a boyfriend
- the hero initiates, the heroine follows

- girls are depicted in nurturing roles – looking after small children or old people, for instance
- girls' work and hobbies are of little importance
- women are seen primarily as home-makers
- the boy-meets-girl happy ending (leading presumably to marriage) is seen as part of the escapism from work (equated with drudgery).

Refer to these examples in an essay about sexism in modern teenage magazines.

Activity 5

'The whole stereotyping edifice depends on hostility to thinking in group terms... but it is open to me to argue that working-class people [who are more prone to categorical thinking] are in general more accurately aware that the social world is really divided into categories. If they have a stereotype of managers... as exploitative, greedy, selfish... that is not a false generalisation. It is an accurate summary of their experience of the inherent tendencies that arise from occupying a concrete social position.' Martin Barker, 1989

Discuss these statements in the light of Barker's opinion:

- 'Never trust second-hand car salesmen. They are all out to cheat you.'
- 'We are told by our superiors not to stereotype people when we are on the lookout for car thieves, but we always watch out for boys in their late teens wearing leisure clothes and trainers and baseball caps. We'd be wasting our time watching out for middle-aged women pushing shopping trollies or young mums with babies in their arms.' (An undercover policeman)
- 'If it's a shop run by Asians it's more likely to be open all hours, but watch out because if you're a young kid they'll try to make you spend all you've got.'
- 'If he's been to public school he'll have super confidence and talk convincingly even if he knows nothing.'
- 'People with strong regional accents are less likely to get jobs and will never get into really powerful positions.'

Activity 6

'Advertising... simplifies and typifies... rarely picturing individuals, it shows people only as incarnations of larger social categories.' Michael Schudson, 1993

Look at current TV and print advertising and find examples of images of people who represent social categories. Why do you think advertisers use this technique? Discuss the difference (if any) between 'incarnations of larger social categories' and 'stereotypes'.

Activity 7

Find two people who have very different reactions to a current drama series (e.g. someone who is 'in trouble with the law' and a police officer reacting to a crime series). Interview them in depth (for at least an hour each) to find out their reactions to the way the police are portrayed. Write about how they make different meanings out of the same material.

Activity 8

Here are some examples of comments from David Morley's book *Family Television*:

- 'What was our favourite one? Dell Boy in Only Fools and Horses. He's a great character that bloke. Because we go to the East End quite a lot. We go to the market... Seeing Dell Boy, it's like meeting up with characters you meet when you go over there... Eastenders is nothing like it is in real life.' (Woman)

- At work we constantly talk about Dallas and Dynasty. We run them down, pick out who we like and who we don't like... who is good looking and who do you fancy, and if they should be paired with each other.' (Woman)
- 'I won't talk about television at work unless there'd be something like boxing on. I wouldn't talk about Coronation Street.' (Man)

Conduct your own investigation into how people talk about what they see on television, concentrating on how they react to images of their own social class or occupation.

Activity 9

Find a news story which is covered both in a publication produced by disabled people, such as *Disability Now*, and in the mainstream press. Compare the representations you find.

Activity 10

Conduct a content analysis of coverage of disability in a media area, using the categories listed on page 52 as an aid to categorisation. You might decide to look at local or national newspaper coverage over the course of one week. Or you might look at the weekly terrestrial television schedule, using a listings magazine as an aid.

Activity 11

Prepare a profile of a character with a disability to be included in a fictional television programme of your choice. Include some sample storylines. Try to avoid the categories listed on page 52. Write an evaluation of what you have achieved.

Activity 12

Find an audience and a need for a media product which includes disability issues, either in your school or college, or in the local community.

For example, you might identify a need for:

- information on a local topic on audio cassette for people with sight impairment
- a campaigning video documentary about a building which it is difficult for wheelchair users to access
- a poster campaign to discourage misuse of disabled parking spaces by able-bodied drivers.

At the end of the production and distribution process, evaluate how you have represented people with disabilities. Include an audience questionnaire if appropriate.

Activity 13

If, during your work in this area, you find matters worthy of complaint, write to the media organisation concerned or the relevant media industry regulatory body.

Alternatively, you could look at representations nearer to hand. You might, for example, have a look at your school or college library and see how positive it is in representing disability issues and disabled people.

BIBLIOGRAPHY ▼

Barker, M, *Comics: Ideology, Power and the Critics*, Manchester University Press, 1989

Barnes, C, *Disabling Imagery and the Media*, British Council of Organisations of Disabled People, 1992

Buckingham, D (ed.), *Reading Audiences*, Manchester University Press, 1993

Cumberbatch, G, and Negrine, R, *Images of Disability on Television*, Routledge, 1992

Curran, J, Smith, A, and Wingate, P (eds), *Impacts and Influences*, Methuen, 1987

Easthope, A, *What A Man's Gotta Do*, Paladin, 1986

Karpf, A, *Doctoring the Media*, Routledge, 1988

McRobbie, A, *Feminism and Youth Culture*, Macmillan, 1991

Morley, D, *Family Television*, Routledge, 1986

Murphy, G, 'Media Influence on the Socialisation of Teenage Girls', in Curran, J, Smith, A, and Wingate, P (eds), *Impacts and Influences*, Methuen, 1987

Norden, M F, *The Cinema of Isolation*, Rutgers University Press, 1994

Pointon, A, with Davies, C, *Framed: Interrogating Disability in the Media*, BFI Publishing, 1997

Schudson, M, *Advertising: the Uneasy Persuasion*, Routledge, 1993

Wertheimer, A, *According to the Papers: Press Reporting on People with Learning Difficulties*, Values into Action, 1988

CHAPTER 5

Audition

Introduction

The people who consume media products are referred to as the 'audience', just as you are part of this book's audience. Audience is a topic you will need to think about when you analyse the media and make your own media products. This chapter looks at the following areas:

- what is meant by audience and how it fits into the communication process

- how the media industries, their clients and audience research services go about measuring audiences
- academic research into audience, including concepts and debates raised by media studies students and teachers in the past.

Who is the audience?

To most people, 'audience' suggests its original meaning of a theatre audience which gathers together with the main, perhaps sole, intention of watching something acted out for its interest and entertainment. This is not its true meaning in the context of the media.

If some of the larger media audiences actually did this it would be like hundreds of Wembley crowds all put together. The meaning of such an event would be staggering. Media audiences do not gather like this. They sit in groups or alone; next door to one another or spread across cities, towns and the countryside; and often consume the same product at different times or dates.

There are different types or categories of audience, for example:

- an audience for a particular product (e.g. Channel 4's Brookside)
- an audience for a type of product (e.g. the audience for the mainstream soap opera genre)
- an audience at a certain time slot (e.g. the early evening audience from 6 p.m. to 9 p.m.)
- an audience which belongs to a group described by characteristics such as age, gender and class (e.g. working-class males aged 20–40).

The term audience refers to many things. It involves not only measurements of actual audiences, but also how audiences behave and interpret what they watch. It brings in the question of the role of the audience in the making of media products. As you read through this chapter you will see that there are many different ways of thinking about audience and many different theories about how audiences behave.

The audience and media producers

During the crucial early stages of a media product, when it is being decided whether or how the product will be made, the makers and writers have ideas about who will buy, consume and/or use the product, and what they will get out of it. 'What's in it for Ms or Mr so-and-so?' is an important question.

However, even when products are market tested by asking

potential audience members, the final decisions are made by those controlling production. If the most popular choice among those asked about a new BBC soap had been used, *EastEnders* would have been located in Manchester. London was chosen as the least unpopular choice among those asked (Buckingham, 1987).

Figure 5.1 The London setting of EastEnders is part of its relationship to its audiences and its popularity

How media producers think about their audience, and the relationship between the two, plays an important part in determining what is made and how it is made. In their dictionary, Watson and Hill (1997) distinguish between ideas of the audience as 'public' and ideas of the audience as 'market'. Thinking about the audience as public means considering what people need in terms of values such as 'education' and 'community'. This used to be the case at the BBC, where it was felt that only the 'best' plays, music, talks and light entertainment should be produced. If you look at any edition of the *Radio Times* before 1940, you should be able to see the effect of this.

Technological change can have a major effect on the relationship between the making of media products and the

Figure 5.2 Pages from the Radio Times in 1936

audience. Consider, for example, the effect of television technologies such as cable, satellite and personal video. Cable television allows for local programming. At the other end of the scale, satellite television is beamed over continents and around the globe. And how has the availability of relatively cheap video cameras changed the relationship between TV and its audience?

◀◀ See Activity 1, page 68

Communication models

The language that people use to describe audiences often reveals the way that they are picturing or imagining how audiences work. For example, people use metaphors such as 'market', talking about audience in terms of something else. The phrase 'couch potato' describes heavy television viewing through a vegetable model of inactivity.

A concise example of a media or communication model is Lasswell's formula (Lasswell, 1948). This states that a mass communication process consists of 'who; says what; to whom; through which channel; with what effect(s)':

- 'Who' refers to the producer/media industry.
- 'Says what' refers to the media text, its content and message.
- 'To whom' refers to the audience.
- 'Through which channel' refers to the form in which the text is conveyed to the audience (e.g. broadcast, television, BBC1).

- 'With what effects' refers to any effects the media product may have on members of the audience (e.g. an advertisement might have the effect of persuading someone to buy a product).

The Lasswell model is useful for considering how the audience interrelates with all aspects of communication as a process. The producers of a media product tailor the text to fit the intended audience and gather information about the audience they get. The audience interprets the content and message, and reacts in various ways such as laughing, crying or falling asleep.

A communication model consists of the following:

1 A model classifies media and/or communication processes by breaking them down into categories. A label is then attached to each category. For example, Lasswell's model is a variation on one of the most basic communication models, which consists of the labels 'sender', 'channel', 'message' and 'receiver'.

2 A model combines a set of categories in a relationship. For example, in Lasswell's model the way in which categories are put into a logical order by a sequence of questions places them in a relationship.

Often, but not always:

3 The model is also given a graphic dimension, with a diagram or illustration which shows the labels and their relationships. Lasswell's model can be explained with the help of a diagram, however, it can function effectively simply in words (as a 'verbal model').

◀◀ See Activity 2, page 68

A model always underlies some kind of theory and description about how the media and/or communication works. It has the power to simplify, organise, generalise, explain and predict (McQuail and Windahl, 1981). All models have their strengths and weaknesses, although these may be a matter of opinion and discussion. You may find that some models are more 'true' or useful than others, so always view a model critically.

The language of media industry research reveals the models which underlie researchers' work. For example, producers 'aim' their product at a 'target'. Talk about 'competing' in 'markets' reveals the economic and commercial model which drives media industry audience research. They work within a 'selling' model. It is bound to be so because they sell research as a service to media organisations, which buy the information for financial reasons.

Measuring media audiences

You are a member of various audiences which media producers who make programmes, magazines and music products can 'target'. You may think of yourself as a unique individual, but this is not how media industries think of you. As far as they are concerned, you belong to various categories which you share with other people, and you have money in your pocket which they would like to know how you spend.

▶◀ *See Activity 3, page 68*

This section looks at how the industry goes about measuring its audiences. In doing so, it uses approaches to, and knowledge about, media audiences which are very different from the 'academic' approach (Kent, 1994). Academic critics often tend to be critical of media processes. For example, the Canadian media economist Dallas Smythe has theorised that the major commodities in the media trade are not the textual products or their messages, but the audiences which are 'sold' to advertisers. As he said in an interview in 1984:

> ❛ *Are there any precedents for this particular commodity? Yes, there is a precedent, but it is an ugly one which we thought had been eliminated. I refer, of course, to slavery... The slave works but does not sell his/her labour. But someone else does – the slave owner.* ❜

▶◀ *See Activity 4, page 69*

The industry measures audiences in order to succeed or survive. It is not seeking 'pure', academic knowledge. Instead, it wants information about the audience and its behaviour in order to make some kind of return from the media product which has attracted the audience.

Most media industries in Britain have to survive on a commercial basis, which means making money and profit from the audiences they attract. Commercial media products depend on the money they can make from an audience in terms of:
- 'direct' returns, such as subscriptions and cover prices
- the advertising market – selling opportunities to advertisers to communicate with potential purchasers of the products advertised.

The main alternative to this commercial approach is public service, where the business of attracting audiences follows the purpose of serving the public. Public service media products, such as those produced by the main corporation of the BBC, depend on:
- their ability to compete with commercial producers for audiences
- state revenue, which must be justified not only in terms of competitiveness, but also in terms of meeting audience needs which would not be met by competitors.

What does audience research involve?

Audience research involves the use of three main instruments, either on their own or in combination:
- questionnaires
- diaries
- electronic recording devices.

There are other possibilities, such as audience observation and recordings of group discussions (usually called 'focus groups'), but these are used less often and tend to concentrate on specific issues and products.

The audience research which different companies and organisations undertake for media producers falls into two main types:
- Quantitative research. In very simple terms, this is research which requires counting (for example audience numbers). It means measuring audience activity in terms which are of statistical significance. In the media industry, samples are used which are large enough to predict or estimate activity among the total viewing population.
- Qualitative research. This involves a more personal approach to members of the audience through interviews, discussions and so on. This type of research is used to discover the quality of the audience experience and responses which are often difficult to measure in large statistical samples.

Quantitative research

Quantitative research aims to measure the activity of entire audiences by measuring a sample. The use of a sample involves conducting research with groups of people who make a population which, although small, is representative of the entire audience under study. There are two basic methods:

1 Random methods rely on the fact that if people are picked for a sample using a procedure which excludes human judgement then human bias is excluded. It is like sticking a pin into a list without looking. Random sampling has to be balanced by methods which ensure that the sample includes all types of people represented in the population as a whole.

2 Quota methods simply ask that the sample includes a fixed number of people from the types represented in the population as a whole. This can be easier than random sampling, but opens up more possibilities for human bias in the sample.

In practice, random and quota methods may be combined. Statistical measures are also used to calculate how representative the sample will be and how far it may stray from the perfect measure (this is called the 'margin of error').

It is important to remember that all audience figures are estimates. Those which rely on investigation of samples are estimates weighted or extrapolated on the basis of the results from the sample investigated.

Qualitative research

Qualitative research is like the research carried out by journalists. When journalists look for information through observation, recording, questions and interviews, they investigate a subject in depth. They are not concerned with whether the people and sources they investigate are representative in terms of quantitative samples or statistics.

Qualitative research into audience attempts to develop an in-depth understanding of who is consuming media products and their responses:

'Qualitative research talks to people in much greater depth, exploring topics freely and without specifying the form of answer required; but it can only be handled on a small scale, rarely on samples big enough for statistical analysis.' McDonald and Monkman, 1995.

Diaries are used in both quantitative and qualitative audience research, and are a good illustration of the difference between the two. The diaries used for quantitative research are surveying documents, with columns and rows which record times and viewing in such a way that they specify what the respondent must write in answer. In qualitative research, a group of people would be asked to keep their own diaries about their viewing, deciding for themselves what to write.

Audience research organisations

The following list gives examples of some of the many services, companies and organisations in the UK which undertake audience research:

- ABC (Audit Bureau of Circulations) measures audiences for the publishing industry and gives circulation figures for newspapers and magazines.
- BARB (Broadcasters' Audience Research Board) contracts out research programmes which measure audiences for television channels.
- CAVIAR (Cinema and Video Industry Audience Research) is commissioned by the CAA (Cinema Advertising Association).
- JICREG (Joint Industry Committee for Regional Press Research) organises research into audiences for regional and local newspapers.
- National Readership Survey Ltd (NRS) is a private research company which provides information about the readers of national newspapers and several hundred magazines. It measures average issue readership. This helps advertisers to choose publications and helps publications to market their advertising space.
- RAJAR (Radio Joint Audience Research) is an organisation which supervises research into radio audiences for both the BBC and commercial radio. It issues a set of specifications which are put out to a contractor.
- TGI (the Target Group Index) provides information about a sample of 25,000 adults, their exposure to media output and their use of some 3000 branded products. The information is sold in various forms to media companies, advertising agencies and client companies who buy advertising. TGI is owned by BRMB International.

For addresses of audience research organisations, see page 72.

Print media: audience research

Readership surveys have been carried out in Britain for over 60 years. The earliest surveys, however, were concerned with the number of copies bought (circulation), rather than with readership by individuals.

NRS (National Readership Surveys Ltd) surveys the readership of newspapers and magazines by interviewing samples of adults aged over 15, representative of the adult population as a whole. Using a questionnaire with a sample size of about 40,000, NRS asks:

- which newspapers and magazines people have read in the past year
- which titles they have read recently
- which products people own or use.

NRS interviewers use booklets of mastheads and title blocks from publications as question prompts.

	TOTAL		15-17		18-24		15-24		25-34		35-44		45-54		55-64		65+	
	000	%	000	%	000	%	000	%	000	%	000	%	000	%	000	%	000	%
UNWEIGHTED SAMPLE	38143		1555		3329		4884		6825		6258		6083		5028		9065	
EST.POPULATION 15+(000'S)	46100		2122		4951		7072		9087		7855		7400		5611		9074	
Daily Newspapers- 6 Day AIR																		
The Sun Q	10211	22	566	27	1487	30	2053	29	2455	27	1699	22	1509	20	1046	19	1449	16
The Mirror/Record. Q MD	8250	18	370	17	881	18	1251	18	1480	16	1314	17	1341	18	1163	21	1701	19
The Mirror Q D	6389	14	291	14	678	14	969	14	1109	12	973	12	1032	14	919	16	1387	15
Daily Record Q	1931	4	84	4	208	4	292	4	386	4	359	5	323	4	251	4	321	4
Daily Mail Q	5159	11	224	11	413	8	637	9	719	8	867	11	1031	14	775	14	1130	12
The Express Q	2878	6	97	5	215	4	312	4	395	4	454	6	537	7	421	7	760	8
The Daily Telegraph Q	2542	6	72	3	175	4	247	3	288	3	381	5	513	7	440	8	873	7
Daily Star Q	2089	5	135	6	372	8	507	7	523	6	457	6	275	4	183	3	138	2
The Times Q	1904	4	77	4	178	4	253	4	357	4	388	5	362	5	261	5	282	3
The Guardian Q	1274	3	38	2	149	3	187	3	269	3	300	4	257	3	124	2	138	1
The Independent Q	867	2	35	2	88	2	123	2	214	2	196	2	183	2	87	2	64	1
Financial Times Q A	717	2	11	1	75	2	87	1	181	2	185	2	145	2	90	2	30	*
The Sporting Life Y	252	1	13	1	25	1	39	1	44	*	61	1	47	1	31	1	31	*
Racing Post Q	223	*	7	*	25	1	33	*	39	*	57	1	38	1	19	*	36	*
The Herald Y R	328	1	6	*	20	*	26	*	57	1	63	1	71	1	49	1	83	1
Dundee Cour & Adtsr Y R	787	1	10	*	23	*	33	*	42	*	40	1	44	1	47	1	80	1
The Scotsman Y R	221	*	5	*	16	*	21	*	37	*	51	1	40	1	38	1	33	*
Yorkshire Post Y R	217	*	4	*	15	*	19	*	21	*	29	*	42	1	49	1	58	1
Wales Western Mail Y R	135	*	1	*	8	*	9	*	12	*	33	*	27	*	23	*	31	*
London Ev. Standard Q L	1123	2	25	1	149	3	174	2	364	4	225	3	198	3	79	1	83	1
W'ton ExStar/ShrStar Y R	743	2	36	2	77	2	113	2	110	1	127	2	119	2	119	2	154	2
Manchester Ev. News Y R	429	1	20	1	48	1	68	1	88	1	71	1	81	1	56	1	66	1
Liverpool Echo Y R	408	1	14	1	51	1	66	1	84	1	61	1	64	1	63	1	70	1
Birmingham Eve Mail Y R	375	1	15	1	32	1	48	1	59	1	69	1	63	1	49	1	87	1
Glasgow Evening Times Y R	324	1	10	*	35	1	45	1	78	1	56	1	62	1	38	1	46	1
Leeds Yorks Ev. Post Y R	292	1	10	*	28	1	48	1	52	1	64	1	42	1	40	1	46	1
N'castle Ev.Chronicle Y R	284	1	18	1	33	1	52	1	55	1	56	1	35	1	26	*	50	1
Ed'brgh Evening News Y R	250	1	11	1	21	*	31	*	43	*	48	1	40	1	37	1	53	1
Dundee Evening Tele. Y R	90	*	4	*	10	*	14	*	12	*	16	*	15	*	17	*	17	*
Any national morning Q P	26616	58	1132	53	2711	55	3843	54	4785	53	4362	56	4538	61	3576	64	5513	61
Any reg morn/eveng. H J	12877	28	490	23	1268	26	1758	25	2326	26	2155	27	2297	31	1815	32	2526	28
Any regional evening H J	10842	24	440	21	1155	23	1595	23	2071	23	1863	24	1907	26	1450	26	1956	22
Sunday Newspapers																		
News of the World Q	11884	26	592	28	1668	34	2260	32	3017	33	1999	25	1752	24	1207	22	1629	18
Sunday Mirror Q	7207	16	358	17	915	18	1273	18	1383	15	1175	15	1198	16	927	17	1250	14
The Mail on Sunday Q	6294	14	278	13	806	12	884	13	1060	12	1179	15	1233	17	888	16	1050	12
The People Q	5286	11	230	11	579	12	809	11	973	11	860	11	891	12	700	12	1053	12
The Sunday Times Q	3873	8	194	9	442	9	636	9	845	9	811	10	766	10	423	8	392	4
The Express on Sun. Q D	3365	7	115	5	274	6	390	6	513	6	448	6	619	8	541	10	855	9
The Sunday Post Q	2410	5	56	3	178	4	234	3	323	4	324	4	324	4	401	7	743	8
Sunday Mail Q	2151	5	94	4	308	4	302	4	422	5	413	5	389	5	300	5	346	4
The Sunday Telegraph Q	2007	4	74	3	192	4	266	4	308	3	297	4	357	5	302	5	477	5
The Observer Q	1295	3	52	2	130	3	192	3	275	3	271	3	260	4	161	3	156	2
Independnt on Sunday Q	941	2	45	2	116	2	161	2	233	3	185	2	192	3	82	1	87	1
Sunday Sport Q	858	2	72	3	210	4	282	4	302	3	144	2	72	1	40	1	18	*
Scotland on Sunday Y	290	1	13	1	23	*	36	1	68	1	77	1	57	1	30	1	22	*
N'castle Sunday Sun. Y	419	1	22	1	74	1	96	1	86	1	70	1	66	1	45	1	57	1
B'ham Sund Mercury. Y	375	1	11	1	26	1	37	1	48	1	73	1	54	1	57	1	109	1
Any national Sunday Q P	29889	65	1266	60	3228	65	4491	64	5782	64	4963	63	5028	68	3915	70	5711	63
Any natn/reg Sunday Q P	30117	65	1272	60	3244	66	4516	64	5805	64	4994	64	5060	68	3944	70	5796	64
Any regional Sunday. H S	900	2	35	2	108	2	142	2	142	2	161	2	144	2	120	2	190	2
Newspaper Colour Magazines *																		
(W) Telegraph Mag... Q T	2853	6	74	3	212	4	286	4	370	4	434	6	581	8	479	9	704	8
(W) ES Magazine.... H T	1477	3	32	2	207	4	240	3	160	2	254	3	220	3	98	2	106	1
(W) Independent Mag Q	938	2	20	1	109	2	128	2	228	3	203	3	211	3	47	1	78	1
(W) Sunday Magazine. Q T	11465	25	528	25	1614	33	2142	30	2956	33	1959	25	1693	23	1165	21	1550	17
(W) Personal...... Q TD	6854	15	322	15	864	17	1186	17	1299	14	1120	14	1166	16	880	16	1199	13
(W) You Magazine.. Q T	6042	13	257	12	587	12	845	12	1040	11	1126	14	1170	16	865	16	1000	11
(W) Yes! Magazine.. Q T	5129	11	206	10	568	11	773	11	982	11	845	11	855	12	686	12	1005	11
(W) Sunday Times Mag Q T	3679	8	168	8	403	8	571	8	779	9	777	10	739	10	426	8	373	4
(W) Sunday Post Mag. Q T	2531	5	66	3	182	4	248	4	340	4	376	5	409	6	417	7	741	8

All Adults - TABLE 6

* NEWSPAPER COLOUR MAGAZINES' DATA FOR JULY TO DECEMBER 1996 INCLUDE DATA ASCRIBED TO THE TEST SAMPLE. FOR DETAILS SEE APPENDIX G OF VOLUME 2, 1996.

FOR SYMBOLS SEE APPENDIX B   JANUARY TO DECEMBER 1996   NRS LTD.

Figure 5.3 Sample reader information from the NRS

Radio: audience research

The early history of the measurement of radio audiences was dominated by the BBC. In recent years the situation has become more complicated, with the huge growth in commercial local and national radio stations. Radio Joint Audience Research, or RAJAR, now puts out to tender the task of measuring these audiences.

The radio measurement system used today is complex. Samples are based not on individuals but on households, and all members of the household participate. The method of measurement uses diaries over one week, with a time grid and named stations as headings. The national sample includes 2400 children aged 4 to 14, and 14,500 adults aged 15 and over.

This national radio survey is dogged by problems. Perhaps the most tricky of these is station coverage and identification. There is now a large number of stations for which audiences need to be measured, including local stations, and respondents filling out the diaries often have problems remembering or identifying stations and their names. In this way audience research is related to how well stations identify and market themselves. The needs of research put pressure on stations to convey their identities as 'brands', to differentiate themselves, to get noticed, and to do this frequently.

QUARTERLY SUMMARY OF RADIO LISTENING

Rajar Radio Joint Audience Research Limited

QUARTER 4/96   23 September - 22 December 1996

PART 1 - UNITED KINGDOM
Adults aged 15 and over: population 47,320,000

	Weekly Reach '000	%	Average Hours per head	per listener	Total Hours '000	Share of Listening %
ALL RADIO	40197	85	17.2	20.2	813114	100.0
ALL BBC	27103	57	8.5	14.9	403127	49.6
All BBC Network Radio	23773	50	6.9	13.8	327475	40.3
BBC Radio 1	10648	23	2.1	9.5	100974	12.4
BBC Radio 2	8819	19	2.2	11.8	104427	12.8
BBC Radio 3	2581	5	0.2	3.8	9919	1.2
BBC Radio 4	8333	18	1.8	10.4	87051	10.7
BBC Radio 5 Live	4953	10	0.5	5.1	25105	3.1
BBC Local/Regional	8653	18	1.6	8.7	75651	9.3
ALL COMMERCIAL	27885	59	8.3	14.1	392597	48.3
All National Commercial	11423	24	1.7	7.2	82288	10.1
Atlantic 252 *	3621	8	0.5	6.0	21904	2.7
Classic FM	4712	10	0.5	5.5	25849	3.2
Talk Radio 1053/1089 AM	2338	5	0.3	6.5	15213	1.9
Virgin Radio (AM only)	2924	6	0.4	6.6	19322	2.4
All Local Commercial	23099	49	6.6	13.4	310309	38.2
Other Listening	2774	6	0.4	6.3	17390	2.1

Source: RAJAR/IC

For definitions please see back cover.
*See notes on back cover.
Enquiries to: RAJAR, Collier House, 163-169 Brompton Road, London SW3 1PY
Telephone: 0171-584 3003 Facsimile: 0171-589 4004
©RAJAR. Any use of information in this press release must acknowledge the source as "RAJAR/RSL."

Embargoed until 17.00 hrs
Friday 7 February 1997

Figure 5.4 Sample issue of a quarterly summary of radio listening from RAJAR

Television: audience research

For some reason, measurements of television audiences are more widely available than those for radio or the print media. You may know these television figures as 'the ratings'. In the audience research industry, 'television ratings' is a technical term which refers to the size of the audience expressed as a proportion of all the people in that category in a given area. For example, the ratings of a television programme shown in the East Anglia television area could be the actual audience expressed as a percentage of the total population in that area, or it could be adults watching as a percentage of all the adults in the area, and so on.

In the UK, the measurement of television audiences has been dominated by BARB (the Broadcasters' Audience Research Board) since 1981. BARB is owned by two shareholders: the BBC and the ITVA (Independent Television Authority). BARB levies charges on those using the research it manages. It draws up a description or specification for the research needed, contracts the actual research out, and oversees the contractors' work.

Television audience research measures the viewing of a carefully selected sample of households. BARB-supervised research relies in the first instance on electronic devices, or 'meters', which monitor television viewing and VCR use. These devices log and store information about viewing in the sample households, which is then fed back to a central computer via modem and telephone lines. Each member of the household has a remote control, which is monitored as part of the information collected. Viewing by guests and visitors is recorded separately, using buttons on the handsets.

The meters simply record actual viewing. Audience reaction is measured in separate research.

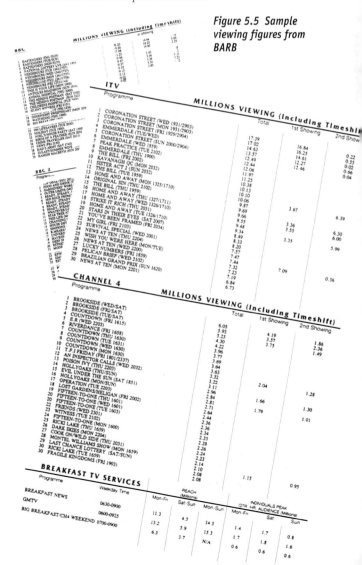

Figure 5.5 Sample viewing figures from BARB

Cinema: audience research

Attendance and ticket-buying at cinemas are more easily measured and monitored than the choices of broadcast radio and television audiences. A number of different organisations are involved in carrying out surveys.

The Cinema Advertising Association commissions Gallup to monitor cinema admissions on a weekly basis. They do this by contacting the head offices of nine major cinema chains: Apollo, Associated Tower, Cannon/MGM, Caledonian, Curzon, Odeon, Showcase, UCI and Warner. They also conduct a weekly survey of a representative sample of cinemas across the country, including a panel of independent cinemas.

In addition, two other surveys of media consumption give information about these audiences: the NRS (National Readership Survey) and the TGI (Target Group Index). Their investigations include who is going to the cinema, how often, and other characteristics of the audience which are relevant to advertisers and marketing people interested in film. The TGI also includes information on cinemagoers' product purchasing habits.

CAVIAR (Cinema and Video Industry Audience Research) is funded by a consortium of interested parties across the industry, including advertisers, distributors, exhibitors and video retailers. It contracts out two types of research:

- One research contractor (at present BMRB International) conducts a yearly survey on a quota sample of about 2800 respondents from age 7 upwards, using market research interviews based on a questionnaire. The survey looks at cinema visits, including details such as film titles, source of information about the film, size of party and transport. There are also questions about other media consumption.
- A second contractor (at present Carrick James Market Research) conducts a quarterly survey which questions a sample of 4000 people from age 7 upwards on attendance at 24 current release films.

BARB, CAVIAR and TGI also include video audiences in their investigations.

▶◀   See Activities 5 and 6, page 69

Studying media in terms of audience

Studying media audiences for its own sake (academic study) is different from studying audiences to meet the needs of the media industries (carrying out market or industrial research). The subject of audience is very large and whole books have been written about audience, sometimes just looking at the audience for one product.

Thinking about audiences

When you start talking about or researching audiences, people's attitudes will start to enter the picture. Many people who study and write about the media get their attitudes to real and imagined audiences entangled. There are critics writing in the press who seem to believe that they themselves are critical of what they see, but others are not.

For example, there is a tradition among certain male critics to patronise female audiences of soap operas as undiscriminating and passive. To quote the flavour of such judgements, soap audiences have been described as 'housewives lapping up soft core emotional porn'. Many of these critics are arrogant, particularly in their assumption that everyone else is vulnerable to brainwashing by media products but they are not. As Sam Bakhurst explained in a lecture on the media in 1996:

'It's like saying "I don't think you should be allowed to go on holiday because you never know what you may end up getting involved in. I know that I'm reliable and can therefore go on holiday when and if I choose to." '

Views on mass audiences

Many critics seem to assume that if you look at a fine art painting or a literary book you are automatically part of a more intelligent and critical audience than if you are consuming a media product as part of a mass audience. Mass audiences are thought of in a different way from minority audiences, such as theatregoers. Mass audiences are felt to be more unpredictable than smaller audiences. But why should the fact that an audience is large mean that the effect of consuming a piece of entertainment should be potentially so much more dangerous?

The concepts and descriptions of media audiences can be thought of in relation to points of view, with extremes at either end. At one end is the view of media audiences as a homogenous mass, passive and easily manipulated. This sees audiences as wanting to be the same, simply accepting the messages beamed out to them without thinking too much about recognising or challenging bias or omission. At the other end is the view of media audiences as a variety of different groups composed of thinking individuals. This sees audiences as active, interpreting media products in different ways, debating with others about them, and not easily manipulated.

▶◀   See Activity 7, page 69

The first view of audience – as a passive, easily manipulated mass – is particularly influential. You will often find it used when the audiences for popular products such as soap operas and quiz shows are discussed. It is linked to phrases such as 'couch potatoes' and 'the lowest common denominator'.

The history of this view of society, and a fear of human beings acting as a homogenous mass under evil influences, goes back a long way. In the twentieth century you can find it in the writings and views of sociologists of the Frankfurt School, notably Herbert Marcuse. They were influenced by the example that Nazi Germany had shown of the majority of a population being manipulated as a mass by propaganda and media. Marcuse wrote a book called *One Dimensional Man* (1964), in which he argued that the masses were hoodwinked by the media into a blind alley of 'false consciousness' so that they were easily manipulated by the powers that be. If you study English literature you can find nineteenth-century versions of this idea in a fear of mobs and crowd behaviour, as expressed by George Eliot in her novel *Felix Holt* (1886). In the eighteenth century a link between mass culture and mass stupidity was apparent in the fear of hack writing and 'Grub Street journalism' and its effect on the people, as expressed by writers such as Jonathan Swift.

More recently, researchers, teachers and students of the media have seen audiences as active in their consumption of the media, responding in different ways to media output. This view is expressed in the following cartoons from *Media & Power* (Lewis and Pearlman, 1986).

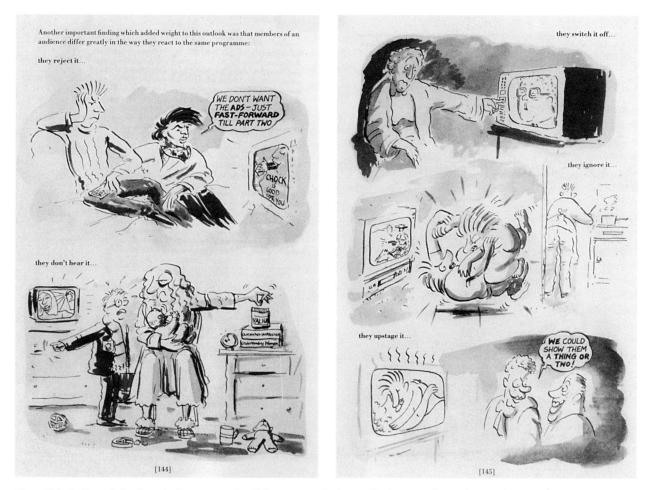

Figure 5.6 *Audience behaviour studies suggest that 'it's not so much what media do to people as what people do with media' that counts*

CASE  STUDY

THE *SUN* READER

'That tawdry little journal, the *Sun*, written for morons by morons.' *Sunday Express*

Have you ever read the *Sun*? If you answer yes, but have a low opinion of 'the *Sun* reader', it is likely that you do not include yourself in this category when you read the paper.

'The *Sun* reader' is an interesting example of an audience which has been subject to patronising and negative views by critics of popular media. The *Sun*, with a circulation (sales) of around 4 million, has about 10 million readers. 10 million people is a huge slice of the population. Yet the *Sun*'s audience has been portrayed as if this was a ready-made group of people, and as if it is only natural that a newspaper of the *Sun*'s type should be manufactured to find this audience. This is also part of the market forces argument that the *Sun* is only 'giving the punters what they want'.

THE *SUN* READERS AS PASSIVE

The view of *Sun* readers as passive sees the audience as receiving the content of the newspaper, and its political bias, in a relatively uncritical and accepting manner. The contents and political bias are determined by the newspaper's producers and writers. They then put this into the newspaper (or 'encode' it), so that these are the 'preferred readings' which support the political views or 'dominant ideologies' which the *Sun* carries and promotes. The assumption is that the overwhelming majority of *Sun* readers either agree with these readings and ideologies, or are swayed by the persuasive bias which leans towards them: 'Those ideas which were associated with Fascism of the 1920s and 1930s are now appearing every day in the *Sun*.' Tony Benn, 1990.

These pictures of the *Sun* audience are powerful, and when you look at the persuasive and propagandist nature of the *Sun* in its stories and editorial, you seem to see a mass of people who might well be swayed in this manner. However...

THE *SUN* READERS AS ACTIVE

The view of the readers of the *Sun* as active sees the readers as heterogenous (i.e. as individuals who fall into a great variety of categories and groups). Thus *Sun* readers are not all the same, nor do most of them fall into a convenient category such as 'the overwhelming majority' who fall in with 'preferred readings' and 'dominant ideologies'.

The *Sun* may be a 'conservative' paper in terms of the political party and views supported in the bias of its stories and its editorial line. However, it is not true that most of its readers vote Tory; its readership profile includes a substantial proportion of Labour supporters. At the 1997 election the *Sun* switched allegiance from its traditional endorsement of the Tory party, and (grudgingly) advised readers to vote Labour.

The *Sun* has slightly more male readers than female, but in number it still has more female readers than the *Daily Mail*. Research has shown that 70 per cent of the *Sun*'s readers are in the C2/D/E social groupings; 30 per cent are in the A/B/C1 demographic groups. More than 3 million A/B/C1 readers take the *Sun*. This means that more readers in the A/B/C1 groupings read the *Sun* than read the *Daily Telegraph*, the most popular broadsheet paper.

It has been argued that the sensationalist and humorous aspects of news stories found in tabloid papers like the *Sun* actually encourage a more subversive approach to news and its 'factuality' than the 'serious' tone of most broadsheet stories. This could suggest that tabloid audiences

We've DAN it

SUN LURES HERO BACK TO DANDY

By MARTIN WALLACE

COMIC book hero Desperate Dan last night agreed a sensational return to The Dandy – thanks to a massive campaign by The Sun.

The bristle-chinned cowpoke was persuaded to make a Cactusville comeback after our heartbroken readers demanded: 'Dan must ride again.'

Bosses at the 60-year-old comic, forced to publish their first-ever issue without him last week, were delighted by his decision. Editor Morris Heggie said: 'Desperate Dan is back for good – and it's all down to Sun readers.

'The Sun has saved Dan and I'm glad because my life has been made hell since he left. Some fans have stopped only just short of death threats.

'I've been stunned by the response to the campaign . It's made me realise he's a national institution.'

THE SUN SAYS

Dan finally...

BREAK open a case of owl hoot juice. Cook a cow pie or two.

Let's have a dandy of a party – Desperate Dan is coming back.

The Sun's campaign to persuade our favorite comic strip character not to quit has done the trick. Aunt Aggie will be delighted. And so will million of Dan's fans.

Life would have been desperate without you, Dan.

Figure 5.7 The Sun constructs a campaign in which it 'saves' Desperate Dan on behalf of his fans and Sun readers

have a more sceptical view of news, the way it is produced and its factual nature. If you actually question *Sun* readers, they often remark on the paper's lack of seriousness and show scepticism about the truth of what they read.

There are many obvious shortcomings of the view of the *Sun* readership as a passive and unthinking mass with the same views. When you actually ask *Sun* readers what they think about the paper and its views, they often say that it provokes them and that they question much of what it says.

▶️ *See Activity 8, page 69*

Academic research methods and studies

In this section you will take a closer look at how academic researchers investigate media audience and find out about some famous studies.

Both industry and academic researchers gather information and base what they say about audiences on evidence. Whereas commercial research projects are usually concerned with finding out information which will enable those who back them to make money using the results, academic research investigates wider questions. Academic researchers use their research to test out ideas or assumptions, and to generate new theories.

The academic research field tends to use a wider range of research methods than media industry researchers. If you decide to carry out some academic research, you may use the diaries and questionnaires explained in the section on industry research. However, you may also draw on other methods, such as experiments and observation studies.

Experiments

In order to set up an experiment you need a hypothesis describing what you expect to find. If your experiment is to

have quantitative significance, you need a research design which tests your expectations on a sample of significant size. You also need co-operative subjects to experiment on.

A famous example of an experiment carried out to examine the effect of propaganda films was the so-called 'Yale Studies' (Hovland, Lumsdaine and Sheffield, 1949). Hundreds of army recruits were given a questionnaire which was 'disguised' so that it would not alert them to its real purpose: to investigate and measure knowledge and attitudes in relation to the war effort. Control groups who did not see the propaganda film were matched against experimental groups who did, so that they resembled one another in sampling terms. Some matched groups did the questionnaire only once; the experimental group having seen the film, the control group having not. Others did the questionnaire twice over the same period; the experimental group having seen the film before answering the questionnaire for a second time. Both experimental designs showed similar results. General morale and motivation showed no change as a result of the film. However, certain areas of knowledge and specific opinions had changed in the direction of the propaganda among soldiers who had seen the film.

A recent example of a more qualitative experiment was carried out by Greg Philo of the Glasgow University Media Group. He showed groups of people photographs associated with the 1984–5 miners' strike in Britain and asked them to write about them. Participants in the experiment seemed to show the influence of news reports in their accounts and the language they used. There was a tendency to exaggerate the violence and to blame the strikers. Philo went on to give evidence that this was the result of media coverage (Philo, 1990).

Observation studies

You can use observation as a method of research in two ways:
- by observing 'directly' as an outside observer
- by observing as a participant.

There are studies of audience both as observers and participants. The examples chosen here are from observation studies of child audiences.

It is perhaps not surprising that observation studies of child audiences are overwhelmingly from the outside. Audience research on children is interesting for all sorts of reasons, not least because child audiences are often patronised and seen as 'more vulnerable'. However, studies which actually pay attention to what children do with media products challenge the adult knee-jerk reaction that child audiences are dominated by the media products they consume.

In his report 'Favourite TV Programmes' (1983), Palmer included the findings of observational studies of children watching television. Children were found to be anything but passive in these studies. They enjoyed turning the TV on and playing with the controls. They would make personal choices from the selection available. The content of television programmes did affect the children in their talk and acting out.

In another experiment, half the child sample under study were allowed to watch *Sesame Street* without toys, and half with. The children with toys were found to make active choices, selecting what for them were the more informative parts of the programme (Anderson and Lorch, 1983).

▶◀ *See Activity 9, page 70*

Figure 5.8 The hypodermic syringe model (also known as the 'effects model')

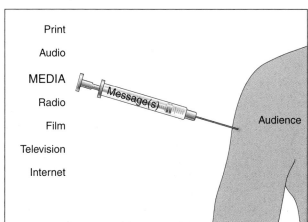

An interesting question?

The Dutch academic Ien Ang put the following advertisement in *Viva*, a Dutch women's magazine:

❛ *I like watching the TV serial Dallas, but often get odd reactions to it. Would anyone like to write and tell me why you like watching it too, or dislike it? I should like to assimilate these reactions in my university thesis. Please write to...* ❜

Although you could call this a form of open questionnaire, it is original research following a qualitative research design. It has the potential to go into depth with individuals. The research is not standardised since each letter-writer can set his or her own agenda. Although a random sample results (Ang actually received 42 replies), there is no way that the sample is representative or quantitatively significant. You can read the results in Ien Ang's book, *Watching Dallas* (1986).

The debate about effects and ideology

'Effects' are concerned with what the media 'do to you'; what you 'act out' as a result of your exposure to media texts and messages. 'Ideology' is concerned with politics; from personal and family, to regional, national and global.

In the minds of commentators, politicians and the rest of us, the media have become strongly linked with power. The success of Hitler's propaganda machine in the 1930s convinced many that media propaganda had the power to bend the masses to one political point of view. The war with Iraq in 1991 over the occupation of Kuwait was widely seen as a media war in which the USA and its allies (including Britain) manipulated media coverage and used lies and propaganda to win public support (Glasgow University Media Group, 1993). Closer to home, British broadcasting has a public service tradition in which it has a role in representing and even 'holding together' the nation. For example, the media are seen to have a powerful role in shaping how the British public views the royal family (Eldridge, Kitzinger and Williams, 1997).

There is a long history of academic theorisation about the effects of media content, as in debates about the influence of the portrayal of sex and violence in the media. Whether, how and how much the media affect audiences is an old and continuing obsession, despite the fact that it seems to be a maze in which academics make slow progress, and sometimes seem to be lost (Barker and Petley, 1997).

The idea that there is a simple cause and effect relationship between media content and audience behaviour is often called the 'effects model'. When people talk about more of something in the media causing more of the same in society, they are thinking in the way described by this model.

❛ *The term model (in this context at any rate) refers to a way of imagining a complex area. Often an underlying model is revealed by the use of particular metaphors – such as "inject", "bombard", "manipulate", "copycat" or "drug" for the effects model.* ❜
Branston and Stafford, 1996

In many ways, the language used to name this model is more exciting and interesting than the rather dull way of thinking about the media it represents. The effects model has also been called the 'silver bullet model' and the 'hypodermic syringe'. The effects which are supposed to be induced include:

• inactivity (the 'couch potato')
• manic activity (such as performing sexual or violent acts because of a movie containing the same).

Certain groups are considered more vulnerable than the rest, including:

• women (who are 'fed' soap operas and daytime TV)
• children (who are parked in front of the TV by their parents whether they like it or not)
• the working classes (who mindlessly consume popular culture)
• people who are mentally ill or have learning difficulties.

As I'm sure you'll realise, the comments in brackets are meant ironically.

Views which follow this model are often expressed around the time of media and moral panics, when everything is blamed on the media. The sad affair of the killing of a child by other children, as in the case of Jamie Bulger, is an example of this type of media panic.

Methods of media analysis such as content analysis, where categories of portrayal are counted over a large area of media space, seem to imply thinking along these simple effects lines. Theories such as stereotyping, which depends upon the repetition of a hackneyed category of portrayal having some kind of brainwashing effect, also seem to depend on the hypodermic syringe.

How can media effects be classified?

It is useful to be able to distinguish between the different media effects that are possible. If you hear a traffic report while driving from A to B and change your route as a result, this is one type of effect. It is short term, based on information, and does not change your views. If you follow a media personality to the extent that you identify with his or her views on a variety of matters, this is plainly a different category of effect. It may stay with you long term, is based on admiration or identification, and has an effect on your outlook.

How can these different types of media effect be classified? In his book *Mass Communication Theory*, Dennis McQuail proposes various categories of media effect. His list, or 'typology', is constructed on various distinctions, which are framed here as questions:

• Is the effect long term or short term?
• Is the effect intentional or not?
• Is the effect at the level of the individual or the collective?
• Is the effect simple or complex?
• Is the effect based on information given?
• Is the effect based on emotional or instinctive factors, such as fear or sexual arousal?
• Is the effect linked to other significant social events, such as an election, war or revolution?

You may be able to add further distinctions to this list of questions. It is important to emphasise that describing a media effect as a particular type of effect only identifies it as a possibility; it does not necessarily mean that the effect actually exists.

▶◀   *See Activity 10, page 70*

The following sections look at two examples of theories of media processes, which act as models of both audiences and media effects.

The agenda setting model

The media often seem to have a 'searchlight effect'. A subject in the landscape is picked out, kept in the spotlight for a while and then the searchlight moves on, leaving the subject in the dark once more.

An influential example of an effects model is the agenda setting model proposed by McCombs and Shaw (1972). This is founded on the idea that the topics the media select for attention, and the attention and priority they give to the topics selected, has a matching effect upon what the audience perceives as important. McCombs and Shaw wrote:

❝ *Audiences not only learn about public issues and other matters through the media, they also learn how much importance to attach to an issue or topic from the emphasis the media place upon it. For example, in reflecting what candidates are saying during (an election) campaign, the mass media apparently determine the important issues.* ❞

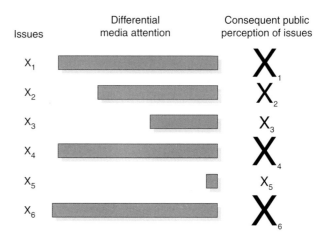

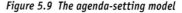

Figure 5.9 The agenda-setting model

This model is typical of much 'effects theory' research in three ways:

• It exaggerates the influence of the mass media to lead.
• It portrays sources in the media as having deliberate intentions to control issues and their debate in a manner that resembles conspiracy theory.
• It portrays the audience as unthinking and easily manipulated (a passive recipient of the process).

The uses and gratifications model

Sometimes it is difficult to relate models to your own experience of the media. What do all these models and theories have to do with your own experiences of, reactions to and pleasures from media texts? The uses and gratifications model may give you a persuasive answer.

One of the discoveries which has moved on effects research is the realisation that media audiences are active. There are various theories which reflect this, including the uses and gratifications model of audience behaviour, which emerged in academic research and discussion in the 1950s. In his book *Media Analysis Techniques*, Arthur Asa Berger gives the following list of what the media may offer to do and the possibilities which we, as audiences, may take from media products:

1 To be amused
2 To see authority figures exalted or deflated
3 To experience the beautiful
4 To have shared experiences with others
5 To satisfy curiosity and be informed
6 To identify with the deity and the divine plan
7 To find distraction and diversion
8 To experience empathy (sharing in the joys and sorrows of others)
9 To experience, in a guilt-free and controlled situation, extreme emotions such as love and hate, the horrible and the terrible, and similar phenomena
10 To find models to imitate
11 To gain an identity
12 To gain information about the world
13 To reinforce our belief in justice
14 To believe in romantic love
15 To believe in magic, the marvellous and the miraculous
16 To see others make mistakes
17 To see order imposed upon the world
18 To participate in history (vicariously)
19 To be purged of unpleasant emotions
20 To obtain outlets for our sexual drives in a guilt-free context
21 To explore taboo subjects with impunity and without risk
22 To experience the ugly
23 To affirm moral, spiritual and cultural values
24 To see villains in action.

If you carry out any analysis using uses and gratifications as a tool, try to assess how important each description of a use or a gratification is. Each one you describe will not be the same in importance for everyone. Find evidence that the use or gratification is possible, either by reference to something actually in the product (something in the story being told, for example), or reports from other members of the audience (preferably both).

Media ideology and audience decoding

Have you noticed how different people can have a completely different interpretation and response to something in the media? Have you noticed that if people have different values they tend to see things in the media differently?

How individuals and different groups interpret a media text is based on their own personal circumstances and the different groups they fall in with.

Sometimes those who discuss messages in the media talk and write as if ideology concerns only the power of media institutions and products, rather than people. As an audience, we are seen as sensitive beings who are hit over the head with a media text which will influence, hoodwink or even damage us. But we all have our own experience of the world and make sense of it.

When you receive or read a media text you can:

- go along with the messages and bias of the text as 'reasonable' (dominant)
- disagree outright with the point(s) of view it is slanted towards (oppositional)
- take a 'middle way' which goes along with the text so far, but modify it with some of your own personal experience (negotiated).

These categories of audience interpretation and response (dominant, oppositional and negotiated) were first put forward by Stuart Hall (1973). Hall argued that television media products are put together in ways which put the audience in a position to interpret a dominant response. For example, factual television presents 'experts' in such a way that the audience is encouraged to think of them as knowledgeable, of high status and reliable (academic experts are filmed with imposing shelves of books in the background). However, Hall suggests that products are open to many interpretations, including those which move away from or oppose the dominant response. Many people are not convinced that a bookshelf in the background of a shot means that the person being filmed has read those books, or works as a sign to change their status, and some will recognise the trick being played. Sometimes we go along with the text, but 'negotiate' a response by bringing in personal experience, such as recognising one of the books on the shelf.

Media research seems to be making progress towards the understanding that we are not 'empty vessels' waiting to be filled, or blotting paper to be imprinted by what we last took in. When we consume or use the media we engage in a dialogue in which we actively and imaginatively make sense of what we read, hear or see.

David Morley studied 29 groups of people and their reaction to a news programme called *Nationwide* (Morley, 1980). Morley says that he expected to find different groups within the programme audience with different kinds of response to the programme:

> ❛ The TV message is... a complex sign, in which a preferred meaning has been inscribed, but which retains the potential, if decoded in a manner different from the manner in which it has been encoded, of communicating a different meaning. ❜

Television programmes, like other media products, carry many different meanings. The producers of the programme will have structured and presented these meanings in a way that agrees with their own interpretations of the programme content. A person viewing the programme can react to this presentation, or 'structured polysemy', in different ways.

The data which Morley collected, in the form of recordings of group discussions, showed that different groups of people have different responses. According to Morley's analysis, the groups viewing the programmes reacted in ways which fell under the three headings of dominant, oppositional and negotiated:

- People who went along with the presentation and structure of the text and more or less agreed with the bias that results showed the 'dominant response'.
- Those who showed understanding of the message and its dominant bias but fundamentally disagreed with these showed the 'oppositional response'.
- Those who showed an intermediate position, in that they took the meaning broadly as it had been put across but modified or slightly reinterpreted it according to their own experience or knowledge, showed a 'negotiated response'.

Conclusion

Questions about media texts and the activities and power of the media hinge on their relationship with the audience. This overlaps with many issues which are dealt with elsewhere in this book, such as how to detect bias, who the media are accountable to, the right of reply and what limits, if any, should be put on the activities of the media. When politicians are asked about their problems, they often say that the media have exaggerated or even created the difficulties. There are dangers in simplistically 'blaming the media', not least because it often lets off the hook other institutions and people who may bear responsibility (Connell, 1984).

In this chapter you have looked at how the media industries research their audiences. You have thought about yourself as a member or representative of various audiences. You have looked at how those who study the media for academic purposes research audience as a topic, and explored some of the theories put forward as a result. You have also learnt that the audience is a very important aspect, perhaps the most important aspect, of any media product.

▶◀ *See Activities 11 and 12, page 71*

ACTIVITIES ▼

Activity 1

Consider the relationship between satellite television and its audience in terms of strengths, weaknesses, opportunities for future developments and negative possibilities ('threats'). Use the following questions as prompts to help your analysis and discussion.

1 How are the audiences for satellite television assured of receiving programmes which relate to them?
2 How far is it possible to predict the effects of satellite television produced in one area of the globe on other areas? You could begin, or even restrict yourself, to the effects of satellite programming produced in the Western bloc (mainly Europe and the US) on the rest of the world.

Activity 2

Draw and label a diagram of Lasswell's model. Give a concise explanation of the model, including some comments on its strengths and weaknesses.

Activity 3

1 Make a list of different types of people: young, old, working class, middle class, black, white, gay and lesbian people, Gameboy players, car mechanics... Think about all the people you know. Stamp collectors, insomniacs, teenage boys, teachers... Don't stop until you've covered at least a page.
2 Look down the list and tick off all the words which describe you.
3 Divide the list into at least five different categories, such as gender, hobbies, occupations, class and lifestyle. Now look at the list and consider which categories you fit into and which you don't.
4 You may have found that you share characteristics with other people. This makes you a member of an audience, which the producers and distributors of media products can target. Look again at the categories and words which include you. Which will stay with you all your life and which will change?

Activity 4

According to the media economist Dallas Smythe, media owners are like slave owners when they trade with advertisers selling audiences. What is your assessment of this model of the sale of audiences resembling slavery? In what ways do you find it true, and in what ways false?

Activity 5

Conduct your own research into how media audiences are researched and measured for commercial and other industrial purposes.

Write to the organisations which survey and measure media audiences and their responses, asking for information about their activities. There is advice on how to do this in the 'Useful addresses' section below. You should also get copies of magazines which give audience information, including *Broadcast* and *UK Press Gazette*, both published by EMAP.

Contact local media outlets, such as cinemas, local newspapers, local radio and cable TV, and ask for information on how they measure and respond to their audiences. You will have to decide how best to do this (by phone, survey, personal letter and so on).

Produce a poster on an aspect of audience measurement based on your findings. If you work with others, you could put this together in the form of a display.

Activity 6

Design a survey of your school or college in order to measure an aspect, or aspects, of its media consumption.

You should construct a quota sample of the student population, either in part or as a whole. Your school or college marketing representative may be interested in commissioning you to do such a survey, with a view to where and how to market the institution and/or its courses.

Activity 7

When you choose to read, watch or listen to a media product, you are behaving actively. When you copy a fashion or role model in a media product, it could be argued that you are passively taking in messages. In this activity you are asked to think about these two different views of audiences as active and passive.

Which end of the audience spectrum do you usually belong to? Are there situations in which you become more active or more passive? Describe ways in which you might be seen as a passive and/or active receiver of media products.

What about your views of other audience groups? Are there any audience groups or behaviours which you tend to see as passive? Are there any audience groups or behaviours which you see as active?

Make a list of examples or ways in which audiences receive media products passively, and another list which shows examples of audiences actively responding to them. Produce an explanation or discussion in the format of your choice, looking at how audiences can be seen differently.

Activity 8

This is a class activity.

- One half of the class should write a questionnaire which seeks to find evidence that the *Sun* audience is swayed and influenced by the newspaper's views (you might include examples of investigations of the effects of actual stories chosen from the paper).

- The other half of the class should write a questionnaire which looks for evidence that *Sun* readers interpret the paper in different ways and make different uses of it. You should also seek evidence that *Sun* readers are sceptical about the truth of stories, causing them to question the information value of news.

In each case, you should try out the questionnaires and then rewrite them to make them as 'objective' as possible, making sure none of your questions are ambiguous or leading.

Each 'side' should make presentations about the results of their questionnaires, before writing a report on the investigations and what they seem to show about the *Sun* audience.

Activity 9

Conduct your own piece of research into children's media consumption and write up your results.

For example, you might do something as simple as record interviews with children about their favourite media products, transcribe what they say, then write a report on what you make of what they are saying.

At the time of writing, there is a debate about the nature and effects of *Teletubbies*, a BBC children's programme. You might find it rewarding to watch this programme with some children in the target audience and talk to them about it afterwards.

Activity 10
Media effects

Organise the following made-up examples of possible media effects into different types or categories, using ideas selected from Dennis McQuail's description and the questions on page 66. For example, you could classify the effects in terms of their duration (short or long term), and their intentionality or otherwise.

1 After hearing a traffic report about an accident on the M25 near Junction 21, I avoid that stretch of the motorway on that day.
2 An advertising campaign for Cadbury's Flake is followed by a 5 per cent increase in sales.
3 The campaign for Flake leads the Advertising Standards Authority to tighten its regulations concerning the content of adverts.
4 News coverage of the Rosemary West trial increases public support for the death penalty.
5 Screenings of Leni Riefenstahl's film *The Triumph of the Will* in 1930s Germany boosts support for the Nazi Party among adult German males.
6 A public information campaign about Aids contributes to the decline in its growth rate in the British population.
7 Regular showings of police and detective series reinforce public acceptance of law and order.
8 Audiences of *Robin Hood: Prince of Thieves* have their view that peasants were oppressed because of the unpleasant personalities of some lords reinforced.
9 The widespread sale and rental of videos contributes to the closure of some cinemas.
10 The combined influence of TV and radio prevents families from making their own entertainment.
11 News coverage of politics results in voters seeing their choice as being between the Anti-Corruption Party and the Monster Raving Loony Party.
12 Rumours, reported in the news, of large increases in petrol prices result in panic buying.
13 Systematic representation of women in adverts as home-makers influences girls' ambitions and expectations about their future.

Activity 11

Devise your own model of the role of an audience in a mass communication process. Begin by dividing what you want to model into different parts, giving each part its own label. Then describe the relationships between these parts of the process. Finally draw a diagram or an illustration which represents your model.

If you are unsure what to model, you could try using one of the following ideas:

- choosing a newspaper to buy
- audience responses to advertising
- becoming a fan
- relationships between the participants in, and audience of, a magazine problem page
- the relationship between copycat behaviour and the media fad or craze connected with it
- a map of local newspapers and their audiences
- a diagram of media likes and dislikes among a group of people.

Activity 12

Analyse a media product of your choice in terms of its audience. Using at least some of the ideas in this chapter, and making sure you use at least two different methods, come to a description of the audience.

- Who is the product aimed at? This is the concept of target audience.
- What is the actual audience and how is it measured?
- What does the audience do with the product? This brings in the uses audiences make of the product, and the pleasures they take from, or find in it.
- What ideologies and bias does the text refer to? What different responses might different audience members take up?
- How does the audience 'read' or interpret the product? From this point of view the media product is a text, and the audience may interact with the text as if in a dialogue, or react against it.
- What is the relationship between the audience and the product? How is the audience positioned in the product? What spaces are there in the media product or text for the audience to occupy?

BIBLIOGRAPHY ▼

Anderson, D R, and Lorch, E P, 'Looking at Television', in Bryant, J, and Anderson, D R, *Children's Understanding of Television*, Academic Press, 1983

Ang, I, *Watching Dallas*, Methuen, 1986

Barker, M, and Petley, J, *Ill Effects*, Routledge, 1997

Berger, A A, *Media Analysis Techniques*, Sage, 1982

Branston, G, and Stafford, R, *The Media Student's Book*, Routledge, 1996

Buckingham, D, *Public Secrets, EastEnders and its Audience*, BFI Publishing, 1987

Connell, I, 'Fabulous Powers: Blaming the Media', in Masterman, L (ed.), *Television Mythologies*, Comedia, 1984

Eldridge, J, Kitzinger, J, and Williams, K, *The Mass Media and Power in Modern Britain*, Oxford University Press, 1997

Glasgow University Media Group, *Getting the Message: News, Truths and Power*, Routledge, 1993

Hall, S, *Encoding and Decoding the TV Message*, CCCS Mimeo, University of Edinburgh, 1973

Hovland, C I, Lumsdaine, A, and Sheffield, F, *Experiments in Mass Communication*, Wiley, 1949

Kent, R (ed.), *Measuring Media Audiences*, Routledge, 1994

Lasswell, H, 'The Structure and Function of Communication', in Bryson, L (ed.), *The Communication of Ideas*, Harper, 1948

Lewis, P, and Pearlman, C, *Media & Power: from Marconi to Murdoch: A Graphic Guide*, Camden Press, 1986

Marcuse, H, *One Dimensional Man*, RKP, 1964

Masterman, L (ed.), *Television Mythologies*, Comedia, 1984

McCombs, M, and Shaw, D, 'The Agenda Setting Function of the Mass Media', in *Public Opinion Quarterly 36: 176–87*, 1972 (see also McQuail and Windahl, 1981)

McDonald, C, and Monkman, M (eds), *The MRG Guide to Media Research*, Media Research Group, 1995. (Available at the time of writing by mail order: contact Nick Hiddleston, The Old Bakery, Wintersloe, Wiltshire FP5 1PP.)

McQuail, D, *Mass Communication Theory*, Sage, 1994

McQuail, D, and Windahl, S, *Communication Models*, Longman, 1981

Morley, D, *The Nationwide Audience*, BFI Publishing, 1980

Palmer, P, 'Favourite TV Programmes, Progress Report 2', University of Sydney, 1983

Philo, G, *Seeing and Believing*, Routledge, 1990

Salomon, G, and Leigh, T, 'Predispositions about Learning from Print and Television', in *Journal of Communication 34*, 1984

Smythe, D, *Dependency Road: Communications, Capitalism, Consciousness and Canada*, New Jersey, 1981

Watson, J, and Hill, A, *A Dictionary of Communication and Media Studies*, Arnold, 1997

USEFUL ADDRESSES

Advertising Association
Abford House
15 Wilton Road
London SW1V 1NJ
Tel: 0171 828 2771

ABC (Audit Bureau of Circulations)
Black Prince Yard
207–209 The High Street
Berkhamstead
Herts HP4 1AD
Tel: 01442 870800

BARB (Broadcasters' Audience Research Board)
Glenthorne House
Hammersmith Grove
Hammersmith
London W6 0ND

BARB does not answer enquiries from the public, however a pack about its work is available. Please apply to BARB for details.

Cinema Advertising Association
127 Wardour Street
London W1V 4AD
Tel: 0171 439 9531

ITVA (Independent Television Association)
200 Grays Inn Road
London WC1X 8HF
Tel: 0171 843 8000

JICREG (Joint Industry Committee for Regional Press Research)
Bloomsbury House
Bloomsbury Square
74–77 Great Russell Street
London WC1B 3DA
Tel: 0171 636 7014

The Market Research Society
15 Northburgh Street
London EC1V 0AH
Tel: 0171 490 4911

The Newspaper Society
(same address and telephone number as JICREG, above)

NRS Ltd.
Garden Studios
11–15 Betterton Street
London WC2H 9BP
Tel: 0171 379 0344

RAJAR (Radio Joint Audience Research Ltd)
Collier House
163–169 Brompton Road
London SW3 1PY

RAJAR will send information if you write to them enclosing two first-class stamps.

The *Guardian Media Guide* includes further contacts, sources of information and their addresses.

CHAPTER 6

Popular culture and television

Introduction

Popular culture is all around us. Whenever you read a magazine, enjoy a package holiday, watch a football match, listen to the radio, watch a TV programme or just talk about it to a friend, you are taking part in popular culture. This chapter aims to raise your awareness of popular culture, focusing in particular on television.

It looks at:

• the meaning of popular culture

• the relationship between popular culture, traditional folk culture and carnival

• television and popular culture – including the development of popular television in Britain and America, the role of television in the home, and the relationship between popular television and melodrama.

At the end of the chapter there is a detailed analysis of *The X-Files* television series as an example of popular culture.

What is popular culture?

One way to start thinking about a definition of popular culture is to look at what is meant by 'culture' and 'popular'.

▶◀ *See Activity 1, page 84*

Culture is a way of life. Your media studies class will have its own culture. Different ethnic groups, social classes and religious groups each have their own identifiable cultures. Activities which involve you consuming the mass media, such as those described in the introduction, are part of the wider culture of society. Buying and reading a magazine, for example, interacts with other activities outside the media, such as daily routine, going on a train journey and looking for information.

The 'popular' attracts large audiences. Hit singles, blockbuster films and tabloid newspapers are all popular. They are consumed by such large numbers of people that their audiences may be described as part of the majority. However, something does not have to have a majority following to be popular. Popularity can also refer to a growing audience. Popular products have an appeal which tends to spread; they include as many people as possible, and do not exclude. A 'cult' media product, for example,

Figure 6.1 A music festival and a cinema classic: the 'popular' attracts large audiences

may have a minority audience, but if it is a product of popular culture its appeal will not depend on excluding mass audiences.

▶◀ *See Activity 2, page 84*

Taken as a whole, popular culture encompasses not only mass media products such as print and broadcast media, film and multi-media, but also other activities such as shopping, holidays, fashion and home life. These activities and the consumption of mass media products usually take place in leisure time outside work.

Popular culture can be divided off from, and compared with, its 'opposite': high culture. High culture includes cultural pursuits which are not part of the way of life of the mass of people, such as opera, ballet, classical theatre, serious poetry and intellectual novels. These pursuits tend to be associated with the élite: people who are upper class, highbrow, educated and wealthy.

Popular culture is not exclusive or intentionally difficult. Unlike high culture, where difficulty is often cultivated and you may have to work at understanding a product before enjoying it, popular culture makes a virtue of being easy. For example, if you study the background to an opera or a ballet, it may well increase your enjoyment of the product. You do not need to study anything to enjoy a soap opera; you simply have to watch an episode, or even just dip in occasionally. Although guides have been written exploring the background to serials like *EastEnders* (such as Smith and Holland, 1987), these are very much optional extras. Like all popular cultural products, *EastEnders* is immediately accessible to the ordinary person.

▶◀ *See Activity 3, page 84*

The activities and products of popular culture follow patterns, or formulae, which offer pleasure to the emotions and the senses. *EastEnders* is a very inventive programme, but it follows the soap genre in its multiple plots and cliff-hangers. It is typical of British soap operas in the way it recreates everyday life as a spectacle and an object for discussion. The pleasures of *EastEnders* are similar to those of gossip. There are comments on the events of the plot and the personalities of the characters in the dialogue, and the audience is encouraged to talk about these outside the limits of the programme.

Popular culture, folk culture and carnival

Folk culture is the original popular culture: the culture of working-class folk, with roots going back before the industrial and the modern. Folk culture remains today in folk songs, traditional festivals and fairs, and the history of working-class communities. Folk culture is made 'by the people, for the people', in the shape of entertainment, pastimes and rituals.

Mass media popular culture is not produced 'by the people'. Instead, small groups of people working in the mass media industries make media products 'for the people' (O'Shaughnessey, 'Box Pop: Popular Television and Hegemony', in Goodwin and Whannel, 1990). However, mass media popular culture is in touch with culture made by the people. Some popular culture is still controlled and produced by the people who participate in it, for example holiday activities such as games

which people make for themselves. This form of popular culture goes back to folk culture, as the diagram below shows.

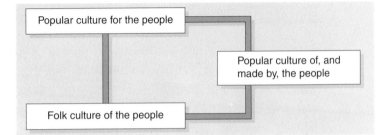

Figure 6.2 Culture of, by and for the people

Studies of the role of carnival and the 'carnivalesque' indicate that it has strong relationships with popular culture (Stallybrass and White, 1986). Carnivals were originally linked to religious holidays and festivals, taking place on dates with emotional and religious significance, and often marking difficult or celebratory times of the year. They involved, as they still do, feasting, dancing, games, competitions, processions, spectacle and public celebration, and often preceded or followed fasts, when people deprived themselves of food. As *Encyclopaedia Britannica* (1997) explains, carnivals, like other feasts and festivals, 'provide psychological, cathartic, and therapeutic outlets for persons during times of seasonal depression'. During carnival times everyday conventions are suspended, and people are allowed to break the rules. The Hindu Holi festival in February–March allows participants to make obscene gestures and shout obscenities in public. In Switzerland and Bavaria, participants in the Fasching carnivals wear masks, and the carnival has a reputation for sexual activity which at other times would be illicit and judged immoral.

An example of carnival alive and well in Britain today is the Notting Hill Carnival in London, which is the largest street festival in Europe. Carnival pleasures can also be found in traditional holiday resorts and seaside towns, such as Brighton, Blackpool, Clacton and Margate.

When you look at popular culture, you may be able to pick out elements of the carnivalesque: audience participation, the meeting of the professional and amateur performer, the turning upside-down of everyday restraint, and an abundance of colour, movement, rhythm and melody in a fairground atmosphere. The quiz show, for example, has many of these features (Nicholas, 1994).

▶◀ *See Activity 4, page 85*

Television and popular culture

In the 1950s television took over from cinema and radio as the leading medium of mass entertainment and the main broadcasting medium. Today, television remains dominant over cinema, radio and more recent alternatives. The number of channels available has continued to increase, and each new channel brings changes in what popular television can offer.

This section takes a brief look at television in Britain and America since the 1950s, and then explores the importance of the home in television culture.

Figure 6.3 Notting Hill Carnival

Television in Britain

In 1955 the opening of the ITV network delivering commercial television financed through advertising brought a more populist approach to television. Before then, BBC television had produced a balance of information, education, high culture and light entertainment, reflecting a philosophy of giving people what was 'good' for them. ITV put more emphasis on light entertainment. Many of its most popular programmes were imported or copied from the United States, for example the quiz shows *Double Your Money* and *Take Your Pick*.

The BBC fought hard to regain the large audience which justified its existence and its licence fee. It produced current affairs programmes such as the early evening news magazine *Tonight*, first broadcast in 1957, which had a more relaxed and informal tone than previous BBC news programmes. It also took a pioneering role in the development of science fiction as popular television programming.

The *Quatermass* series (1953, 1955 and 1958) and *A for Andromeda* (1961) combined the BBC's strengths in producing drama with a popular cultural genre, and spoke confidently to a wide audience. *The Quatermass Experiment*, produced back in 1953, told the story of the crash landing of a British/Australian space rocket in which the only surviving astronaut was contaminated by an alien organism. *A for Andromeda* focused on a future British society contacted by extraterrestrial intelligence. Both have intertextual links with *The X-Files*, popular today. Indeed, the narrative of *A for Andromeda* includes conflict between scientists and government bureaucracy, directly anticipating the concerns of *The X-Files* stories.

Television in America

Although the first American television broadcasts were slightly later than in Britain, the American television industry was ahead by the 1950s. British television broadcasts shut down during the Second World War years of 1939–45, while

Figure 6.4 ITV's 1950s quiz show Take Your Pick copied from USA

Figure 6.5 A family watching television in the 1940s

broadcasting continued in the United States. Commercial television dominated the US networks by the late 1940s (Boddy, 1995), and during the early 1950s there was an explosive growth in sales of TV sets. By the mid-1950s middle and low income households were the main audiences, influencing programming decisions. The American public has always had more channels to choose from than the British, with a strong tradition of local television stations.

American television began marketing its products overseas early. In the 1950s its main targets were the BBC and stations in Mexico and South America. In 1954 CBS Inc. boasted that it was the world's largest single advertising medium, with affiliated stations in Canada, Mexico and the Caribbean. By the end of the 1950s the US networks were the leading exporters of TV programmes to the rest of the world (Boddy, 1995). American television had established itself as the leading national producer in global television culture, a position which it has maintained to date.

▶◀   *See Activity 5, page 85*

Popular television and the home

'Television is a domestic medium.' Silverstone, 1994.

The place of television within the home is often taken for granted. However, in the early years of television, many countries associated it with public places. This was the case for some time in Italy, and remains so today in a number of developing countries.

When television took over from radio and cinema in Europe and America, it established a relationship with the home which transformed popular culture in these parts of the world. It made the greatest impact when taking the place of radio as the focal point for popular entertainment in most households. It also brought the pleasures of the moving image, previously only available at the cinema, inside the home.

▶◀   *See Activity 6, page 85*

Television interacts with the home in various ways. Programmes overlap with domestic activities and provide representations of homes and home life. Cookery and gardening programmes provide entertainment and information related to

domestic activities. Situation comedies and soap operas offer representations of domestic life.

One reason that popular culture and the mass media are thought to be important areas for study is that they provide evidence of the preoccupations and changes in society and domestic history. For example, British sitcoms of the 1960s were preoccupied with social class. In *Hancock*, *Steptoe and Son*, *The Likely Lads* and *The Liver Birds* much of the comedy revolved around the desire of some members of the working class to 'better themselves', while others resisted change. In the 1970s, *Butterflies* and *Agony* began to ask questions about the role of women in society. In the 1970s and 1980s, comedies such as *'Allo, 'Allo, Hi de Hi* and *Last of the Summer Wine* showed a nostalgia for a kind of British society which had passed into folk memory. The households portrayed may not have been typical or even 'normal', but they reflected experiences of change, topics of debate and shifts in domestic habits.

▶◀   *See Activity 7, page 85*

Figure 6.6 Terry and Bob from The Likely Lads

The time slots and patterns into which programmes are scheduled over the day reflect ideas about domestic routines. In Britain, the schedules which programmes follow seem to have traditionally fitted in with the needs of a stereotypical nuclear family with young children. In his essay 'A Suitable Schedule for the Family' (in Goodwin and Whannel, 1990), Paterson describes this pattern of scheduling:

> ❝ *In the early evening, domestic life is assumed to be devoted to meals and the audience is understood to be unable to concentrate for long periods. Television is in the control of the child audience with parents available intermittently until about 7.30 pm. From this time the mother is thought to control the television, which functions for the next 90 minutes as a focus of the family. After 9 pm, when the rules on content are less strict, children's viewing is seen as the responsibility of the parent.* ❞

As Paterson goes on to point out, only one-third of British households includes children. However, the traditional ideas about audience needs that he describes have a big influence on those who plan the schedules.

▶◀ *See Activity 8, page 85*

Popular television and melodrama

The original meaning of melodrama is 'drama with music'. Victorian melodramas were theatrical dramas which combined various elements in order to provide sensational popular entertainment. In a typical Victorian melodrama, a hero and heroine would suffer at the hands of a persecuting villain, with a sentimental ending in which virtue is rewarded and vice or evil punished. Visual effects were more important than dialogue, and often included special effects. Action would be mimed, with much emphasis upon stylised facial expressions and gestures. Here are some extracts from Victorian playbills (a kind of advertisement, or flyer) promoting melodramas.

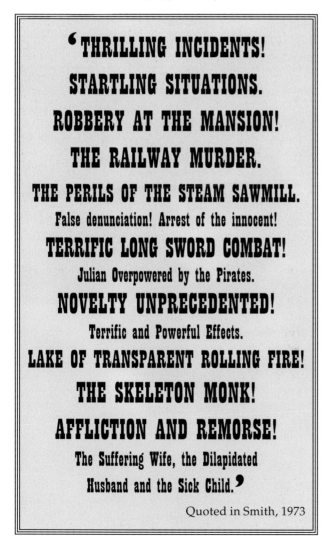

' THRILLING INCIDENTS!

STARTLING SITUATIONS.

ROBBERY AT THE MANSION!

THE RAILWAY MURDER.

THE PERILS OF THE STEAM SAWMILL.

False denunciation! Arrest of the innocent!

TERRIFIC LONG SWORD COMBAT!

Julian Overpowered by the Pirates.

NOVELTY UNPRECEDENTED!

Terrific and Powerful Effects.

LAKE OF TRANSPARENT ROLLING FIRE!

THE SKELETON MONK!

AFFLICTION AND REMORSE!

The Suffering Wife, the Dilapidated Husband and the Sick Child. '

Quoted in Smith, 1973

Nineteenth-century melodrama had a huge influence on the silent cinema of 1900–30. There is also much evidence supporting the argument that melodrama is a fertile source for, and a strong influence upon, twentieth-century audio-visual culture, including film and television.

The following features of many popular television programmes and films reflect the creative force of melodrama.

- The use of both tragic and comic effects. This is evident in comedies such as *One Foot in The Grave*, where comedy is often combined with tragic material about loneliness and death.
- The exaggeration of emotional content and manipulation of the audience's feelings. For example, in quiz and game shows the studio audience exhibits 'naked emotion' and an involvement in the show's drama which the viewing audience can share.
- The expression of feelings which people usually hide, such as anger, fear, lust and romantic attraction. The horror genre, for example, represents extreme feelings born of people's worst fears.
- The use of music to dramatise character and action. Genres such as thrillers, romances and horror all have characteristic music.
- The use of effects to excite the visual sense through the image (mise en scene) and the use of space, light and dark, colour, gesture and other dramatic movement. Melodramatic visual effects like these are widely used in television crime thrillers such as *Cracker* and *Prime Suspect*, especially during the enactment of crimes.
- The involvement of strong, central female characters. For example, television soap operas have female characters who are central to stories and initiate action.
- The involvement of 'simple' characters, tending towards the one-dimensional. Heroes and villains are either clearly differentiated, or revealed through the plot. In tragedy the hero is 'divided': for example Hamlet is unable to avenge his father's death without becoming a murderer himself. In melodrama the character is essentially 'whole': the hero is wholly heroic, the villain wholly villainous. The stock characters of a genre are also melodramatic in the way in which 'a single impulse... absorbs the whole personality' (Smith, 1973). For example, investigative documentaries and crime programmes such as *Crimewatch* set up melodramatic effects in the contrast between the heroic, truth-seeking journalist and the villainous criminals they expose or seek to find.
- The use of exaggeration. Melodrama presents extreme situations and over-the-top versions of the way people live. The sitcom *Absolutely Fabulous* shows this well. The character of Patsy is a recognisable but exaggerated figure in her crude lust for young, virile males and her prodigious appetite for alcohol, cigarettes and other drugs.

▶◀ *See Activity 9, page 86*

The X-Files as popular culture

This section gives a detailed analysis of *The X-Files* as an example of popular culture. It explores the programme's:

- context
- relationship with reality
- popularity
- imagery
- relationship with different genres
- relationship with folklore and melodrama
- characters
- messages.

It also includes an analysis of the series from a postmodernist perspective.

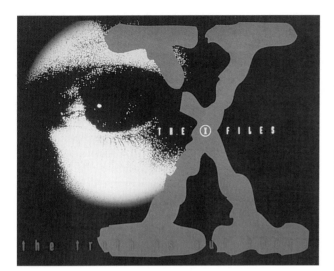

Figure 6.7

The context of *The X-Files*

The X-Files series was conceptualised and written by Chris Carter, a television writer. Carter submitted a first script to Fox, the US television studio, which accepted it on a pilot basis. The script was filmed as a pilot in a co-production between Carter and 20th Century Fox Television in 1992, and went out on Fox Broadcasting in the United States on 10 September 1993.

An important ingredient in the programme's commissioning as a series was its success with advertisers and TV critics. Although *The X-Files* was initially very low in the US Nielson audience measurements, it attracted sales in its advertising slots. The social class and lifestyle of the programme's viewing audience were important factors for advertisers. The audience included a high percentage of educated, urban-dwelling 18 to 34-year-olds, who were a target for many advertisers (Lovece, 1996). The early production context of *The X-Files* shows that the nature of the audience and its behaviour is a factor in success: it is not only the size of the audience that counts.

> ❛ *X-Philes were bright, usually well educated, white collar workers who were still young enough to spend any loose change in their pockets. They were in an age group which it was as difficult for advertisers to capture as it was for network programmers to understand. More importantly, those fans were **talking** about the show.* ❜
> Genge, 1995

Fox includes Fox Broadcasting, the national network of US television stations on which *The X-Files* was first shown, and 20th Century Fox Television, a production studio. Fox Television was bought by media mogul Richard Murdoch in 1985, and is now a subsidiary of the world-wide Newscorp media conglomerate.

The series has since been sold around the world, and in Spain it is the most popular television series ever. Chris Carter cites *The Avengers*, the British TV series of the 1960s, and *The Night Stalker*, the US series of the 1970s, as predecessors and influences.

The X-Files and reality

The sources of *The X-Files* pose a double-edged question: what is real and what is illusion? Paranoia often has some factual basis, and so it is with *The X-Files*. The series links with conspiracies, some of which are confirmed as fact, some of which reach out into illusion, and some of which fall into the grey areas in between, where conspiracy theory breeds.

The heart of doorstepping

X-FILES news from Royal Tunbridge Wells, Kent, where police were recently summoned by a worried householder who claimed to have found a pair of human lungs sitting on his doorstep.

As the *Tunbridge Wells Courier* suggests, the officers were less perturbed than the caller. Their note in the police log read: 'They are not breathing!' Kent police's answer to Agent Scully was dispatched and concluded that it was nothing more sinister than the heart of a small animal.

'We don't want to embarrass the man by revealing his identity,' said a police spokesman. 'He fancied himself as a student of biology as he was insistent that it was human lungs. But we think it was something the cat brought in.'

Tristan Davies, 'Parish Pump', *Daily Telegraph*, 8 March 1997

Figure 6.8 Intertextual link: The X-Files invades all areas of the media

The conspiracy which seems to have had a special influence on *The X-Files* is the Watergate affair (Lovece, 1996). On 17 June 1972 Washington police caught burglars in the headquarters of the Democrats, the US political party at the time in opposition to the Republican President Richard Nixon. Two reporters on the *Washington Post* investigated the cover-up of this break-in and its political links, guided by a mysterious informant nicknamed 'Deep Throat'. They revealed that the FBI investigation into the break-in was blocked by the President himself. The result of their work was a court case and, on 9 August 1974, President Nixon left the White House in disgrace.

The X-Files as a media product interacts with life and more virtual realities. A news story which involves conspiracy, extraterrestrial life, psychic phenomena or just a little weirdness will often contain an explicit reference to the series.

Why is *The X-Files* so popular?

In its early days, *The X-Files* had a below average audience in the United States for a programme of its type. However, audiences grew after the first series, with ratings approaching 20 million for a single broadcast.

The series is now popular around the world. This is reflected not only in the size of its audiences, but also in the amount of attention and discussion it attracts. Some of *The X-Files'* followers have turned the series into something of a cult: in the UK on BBC2 the programmes typically attract audiences of between 5 and 7 million.

The X-Files seems to appeal to people living in the 1990s for a number of reasons.

It ties in with the nineties obsession with New Age ideas and practices which challenge the rationality of science and Western common sense.

Figure 6.9 Three graphics from the Emmy award-winning title sequence of The X-Files

It is easy to enjoy. The characters include an attractive hero and heroine with an intriguing relationship. The stories are accessible to adults and teenagers, following the type of 'classical' linear narrative which viewers and readers expect. The stories unfold a mystery, which Mulder and Scully set about solving. The concept, or premise, on which they are based is clear to the viewer: 'The combination of a smart woman and a sensitive guy chasing giant parasites and little green men across the country' (Genge, 1995).

The endings of the stories are often open in the sense that mysteries remain partly unsolved and/or the full truth evades the detectives. However, there is always some degree of closure: Scully and Mulder defeat a threat, or find at least partial explanations.

The programmes exist on the border between a serial, in which episodes are part of a greater whole, and a series, in which each programme is a new story. *The X-Files* is like a soap in the way that endings are left open, in the constant relationship between Scully and Mulder, and in the recurring themes of the storylines.

The 'look' and texture of *The X-Files* are enjoyable on an immediate, sensory level. The series uses lighting, camerawork and what we see in the frame (the mise en scene) to give the viewer pleasure. The one-hour pilot episode was shot at a cost of $2 million, and the lighting and sound quality in the horror-inspired sections of the story were used to convey suspense and excite the viewer. Overall, the quality of *The X-Files* aspires to that of film, and the effects are often described as cinematic.

The imagery of *The X-Files*

The opening sequence of *The X-Files* in the early series shows its characteristic imagery, themes and stories. It includes:

- *The X-Files* logo
- film of a 'classic' flying saucer
- a pointing hand moving over a large blue-lit map, resembling a radar screen showing patterns of lines
- a sphere surrounded by white lines of electrostatic
- a distorted, screaming male face
- what appear to be two sprouting beans
- the title 'paranormal activity'
- a faint and ghostly white figure appearing on video film
- Mulder's FBI ID card with the title credit David Duchovny
- the title 'Government denies knowledge'

- Dana Scully's FBI ID card with the title credit Gillian Anderson
- a falling white silhouette of a human figure
- a blue hand with a single red bone
- film of Scully and Mulder in action
- stormy blue skies with clouds scudding on speeded-up film, accompanying the title 'The Truth is Out There'.

This is all conveyed in 40 seconds, and is set off by appropriately spooky title theme music.

What does this miscellaneous collection, or montage, of images make you think of? It includes images of the paranormal, science, suggestions of government cover-up, and the human being in physical evidence (body and signature). The images are thrown together like evidence from some kind of enquiry. They suggest questions rather than answers. For example, why do Scully and Mulder's signatures look as if they are in the same handwriting?

Modern recipes: No 19

X-Files rip-offs

1 pair investigators
1 conspiratorial cartel
1 gross aliens
1 shadowy military organisation
Half-dozen government agencies
Assorted psychopaths and serial killers

Take the government agencies and leave them in a warm, damp environment to spoil slowly. When they are thoroughly corrupted, add the pair of investigators.

Whichever you use, be sure to ask your local shop for agents with psychic or deductive abilities that make Cracker's Fitz look like Rodney Trotter.

Suspend the conspiratorial cartel above the mixture, allowing it to shed crumbs of baroque plotting into the bowl. Infiltrate with half the aliens. Layer the shadowy military organisation over the top, lasagne style, and pelt freely with the remaining extra-terrestrials.

Puree the result until thick, dark and murky, then seed with the assorted psychopaths and serial killers. Season with mysticism, paranoia, astrology and psychobabble. Taste. Wonder why it's nowhere near as good as the original.

Serve by torchlight in order that people will think it is a documentary.

David Bennun

Figure 6.10 The X-Files recipe is now much copied as these ironic comments from the Guardian point out

In and from popular culture, the *X-Files* draws upon attractions which parade the bizarre, exploiting human interest in the unusual, abnormal, magical and unexplained. It uses signs and images of nineties science and technology as a backdrop for contemporary stories of ghosts, monsters and alien visitors from outer space. In 'high culture' this type of material is associated with surrealism: dream-like images which represent the irrational and the workings of the unconscious mind. It is also associated with the Gothic tradition in English literature, as exemplified by Mary Shelley's novel *Frankenstein*. The Gothic literary tradition has been carried on in popular culture and the mass media through the horror genre.

The following key images crop up in the stories told in the first ten episodes of the first series of *The X-Files*:

- the corpse of a dwarf-like 'alien'
- a futuristic aircraft with spotlights
- the trophies collected by a serial killer
- sand smelted to glass (at 2500°F)
- a hairy, 'devil-like' creature
- the blurred image of a ghost
- a computer with a life and intelligence of its own
- an alien worm which lives in Arctic ice
- a face-like land formation on the surface of Mars
- a UFO, or flying saucer.

Images like these mix technology, folklore and the stuff of hysteria and dreams. The carnival procession of *The X-Files* seems to be dominated by the topics of death, other worlds, the paranormal and the spiritual. It evokes feelings of awe, fear and wonder, mixed with the representation of sides of human life which are not part of the normal or everyday.

The X-Files and genre

The X-Files draws upon the genres of:

- horror
- film noir
- science fiction
- the detective series.

It has several features typical of film noir, including the use of darkness and shadow to indicate moral ambiguity or evil, a strong 'whodunnit' or mystery element, and half-heroic detectives who face conspiracies to conceal the truth. It also includes science fiction in its subject matter, since it goes beyond conventional common science and common sense in its account of things such as alien abduction, human mutations and other paranormal phenomena. The influence of the detective series is evident in the fact that the two heroes are FBI investigators, and in the way that the storylines revolve around solving mysteries.

The series also draws on features from outside fiction, for example the style and iconography of documentary. As in many documentaries, written captions are used to establish places, buildings, dates and times.

The *X-Files* has been characterised as 'speculative fiction': fiction that speculates about what might be possible beyond the present established borders of fact. It is not alone, and can be grouped with other material which is speculative, challenges conventional science, contains material characterised by sources such as rumour and urban folklore, and includes subject matter from the paranormal and the unexplained.

The X-Files, folklore and melodrama

The X-Files is an example of a popular cultural product made for the people. However, its relationship with folklore shows links with areas of popular culture which are also 'of the people'.

The series links back to folk culture concerned with the unexplained and the paranormal, including mysteries, legends, mysticism and magic. However, it also connects with modern urban folklore. The story of a government conspiracy to conceal the crash landing of an alien spaceship is essentially a modern legend. The story that motorists have been kidnapped by aliens, examined and returned to earth is an example of an urban legend:

> ❝ Urban legends belong to the subclass of folk narratives, legends that – unlike fairy tales – are believed, or at least believable, and that – unlike myths – are set in the recent past and involve normal human beings rather than ancient gods or demi-gods. Legends are folk history, or rather quasi-history. As with any folk legends, urban legends gain credibility from specific details of time and place or from reference to source authorities. ❞
> Brunvand, 1983

Figure 6.11 A futuristic aircraft and Eugene Tooms from the first series of The X-Files

The aliens in *The X-Files* are the modern equivalent of 'the little people' in traditional folklore, who included leprechauns, trolls, fairies, elves and hobgoblins. One episode is even called 'Little Green Men'.

A clear example of the use of urban folklore in *The X-Files* is episode 2.02, 'The Host'. This story concerns the tracking down of a killer who lives in sewers or septic tanks. The killer turns out to be 'the flukeman': a mutant combining features of a human being and a liver fluke. The mutation is the result of atomic radiation from the Russian Chernobyl nuclear accident.

The X-Files variation on this legend stretches belief even further in the story of the mutation of a humanoid parasite which appears to pass through a life cycle between the human liver and the sewer. However, it links this mutation to a specific time, place and cause: the explosion of the Chernobyl nuclear reactor on 26 April 1986.

*Figure 6.12
'The Host'*

 ❛ *"The Host" draws upon urban legends of "dreadful contaminations", such as "the Kentucky fried rat" or "the spider in the hair-do". As Brunvald explains: "Americans, on the whole, are a clean people with a low tolerance for unhygienic conditions, especially in their food, persons, or homes. Yet, as much as they despise the company of germs and vermin, some of their folklore depicts the penetration of these creepy invaders to the very heart of their sterile sanctuaries."*

Dreadful contamination stories include the flushing of dangerous animals down the toilet, which is explicitly referred to in this episode when one of the sewer workers talks about people flushing away pets, such as alligators and snakes. In modern legend, these creatures breed in the sewers and end up attacking people: "One of the sillier folktales of the 1960s was that the New York sewers were becoming infested with alligators, presumably unwanted pets that had been flushed down the toilet." ❜

Minton, 1973

As well as linking with folklore, *The X-Files* draws on the tradition of melodrama. Mulder and Scully operate in a melodramatic world. The monsters and freakish phenomena they investigate are over-the-top: what could be more so than the hermaphrodite in 'The Host', which lives down the toilet and combines features of a human being, a worm and a liver fluke? The strange phenomena under investigation seem no more evil, however, than those mysterious figures in authority over Mulder and Scully's immediate superiors. Which are more villainous – the 'parasites and little green men' who prey on humanity, or the shadowy figures who conspire to manipulate government, democracy and withhold the truth?

The key characters

Scully and Mulder are played by actors who have attained star status. They are idealised heroes bound together in a relationship which combines features of the professional double act with a family relationship and a sexual chemistry which never becomes physical. Scully seems to mother Mulder as if he were a precocious child. They also seem attracted to each other, although whether this is brotherly/sisterly or based on sexual attraction remains unclear.

In the pilot episode of *The X-Files*, Scully was despatched by the FBI to watch and report on Mulder's activities. One way in which the series has developed is that the two characters have gradually become tied together by some bond of meaning, while remaining strikingly different. According to the show's creator, Chris Carter, they are opposites: 'One is sceptical (although things begin to change), the other is a true believer.'

The jargon term for this code of opposites in media studies is 'binary oppositions', and it belongs to semiotic analysis. Looking for opposites in the Mulder–Scully characterisation can be helpful in understanding the meaning of their characters and relationship in *The X-Files* text.

Mulder	Scully
male	female
passion	calmness
imagination	rationality
belief	scepticism
religion	science
child	parent

Mulder is religious in that as a child he experienced alien abduction, and is now a prophet and true believer in the 'little green men' (Braithwaite, 1996). Scully is a forensic scientist with a background in medicine, who conducts post-mortem examinations on the corpses returning from Mulder's investigations. Mulder is the adventurer (child) who identifies the new phenomena which swim into view. Scully is the authority (parent) of the pair, who questions and confirms what Mulder has found.

It is interesting that the oppositions between Mulder and Scully challenge and oppose stereotypical views of gender. Mulder, the male, confounds certain expectations in that he is child-like and intuitive; while Scully, the female, is the more rational and scientific of the pair.

Figure 6.13   Gillian Anderson and David Duchovny: Scully and Mulder from The X–Files

Messages of *The X-Files*

What are the underlying messages of *The X-Files* text? As an analysis of the characters reveals, it is concerned with the human desire to believe in something of a spiritual or religious nature beyond the physical and material. As Chris Carter explains:

> ❛ *There's some degree of hope in all of us that our faith can be tested, that we'll see something that shakes us and moves us and lets us believe there's something beyond the mortal coil, beyond the temporal and the mundane and the facts that we're going to live and die.* ❜

Carter's comments here seem to agree with psycho-analyst Carl Jung's analysis of flying saucers as a symptom of 'a religious vacuum at the heart of modern man', and as a sign that religious feelings had become fixed upon an external, extraterrestrial force. In *The X-Files* however, it seems as if the aliens, UFOs and other paranormal phenomena express not only post-modern images of heaven, but also the shades of hell.

▶◀   *See Activity 10, page 86*

Postscript on postmodernism

This section presents some starting points for understanding and using a postmodernist approach to analyse popular culture such as *The X-Files*. It is a postscript in the sense that it is an alternative view to some of the popular cultural analysis presented above. It is not essential, and if you do not find it helpful or useful, you can skip it.

The phase of modernism was characterised by a division between a mass culture which was easy and accessible, and a high culture which protected art and tradition and was difficult or even obscure. In contrast, postmodernism, which

has followed on from modernism during the late twentieth century, says that anything goes.

Frederic Jameson identifies features of postmodernism, or 'Pomo', in his essay 'Postmodernism or the Cultural Logic of Late Capitalism'. Here are some of them:

> ❛ *The effacement... of the older (essentially high modernist) frontier between high culture and so-called mass or commercial culture, and the emergence of new kinds of texts infused with the form, categories and contents of that very culture industry so passionately denounced by all the ideologues of the modern, from Leavis and the American New Criticism all the way to Adorno and the Frankfurt School. The postmoderns have been fascinated precisely by the whole "degraded" landscape of schlock and kitsch, of TV series and Reader's Digest culture, of advertising and motels, of the late show and the Hollywood B movie, of so-called paraliterature with its airport-bookstall paperback genres of the gothic and the romance, the popular biography, the whodunnit, the SF or fantasy novel: materials they no longer simply "quote" as a Joyce or a Mahler might have done, but centrally incorporate.* ❜

You may recognise some of the features of *The X-Files* here.

The X-Files are not 'original'; instead the series constitutes a well-made piece of postmodernist popular art. The episodes draw attention to the fact that they are reproducing and recycling the material of popular sources such as 'the Hollywood B movie, the gothic, the romance, the whodunnit and SF' (Science Fiction), and in this sense they parade the fact that their purpose is not to be 'original'. Postmodernist analysis draws attention to this 'hall of mirrors' effect, where a text refers more to other media texts than to things in the real world.

Only (re)Produce

The opposite of knowledge is not ignorance but deceit and fraud.

Baudrillard's notional scepticism is unconvincing. But his exaggerated views on media cyberpower highlight a condition that needs urgent emphasizing.

The last 25 years of the 20th century will go down in history as unique in one respect. These "postmodern" years are symptomatic of a total lack of originality. Our scanty resources of invention are all parasitically confined to **reproduction**. Everything apparently "new" - whether it be CDs, cyberspace Virtual Reality or even the DNA Genome Project and postmodern cosmology - is feeding on the originality of the past, on a data bank not simply of information but of **already experienced** reality.

Why have we come to this unprecedented technologically-streamlined **cannibalization**? Could it be that we are commanded by an unconscious, biologically determined will (a "selfish gene") to proceed with the absolute demolition of the past for a reason that we cannot comprehend? Are we "wiping the slate clean" for the coming of the artificially engineered human?

This is a paranoiac vision of reproduction, a sci-fi pessimistic advent of the **in**human.
We might do better to reconsider Marx's view of capitalist reproduction. The reality of capitalist production is that of a process which unfolds in time, one cycle of production succeeded by another: a question of **continuity** in short, which is a problem of social and economic **re**production.

For capitalist production to be continuous in time, it must not only reproduce itself completely but **expand** the fundamental conditions of its mode of production. The question arises: How can this continuity of production be maintained, when the value and global extent of this production seem to result from individual decisions by thousands of businessmen who **hide their intentions from each other**?

The players of the capitalist game must inevitably be "in deceit", and a sort of acceptable consensus of fraud must be basic to the continuous reproductive expansion of its mode of production.

And this is why everything "postmodern" so nakedly depends on and stems from reproduction. The game is about fabricating a sort of knowledge, which although it **looks** to be expanding and becoming accessible to a vast public on the Internet superhighways, is in fact becoming industrially controlled.

So, when Lyotard replaces the traditionally-trained knower with the "knower as consumer", he is not valorizing either the "new" knower or the novelties of knowledge, but is implicitly acknowledging the omnipotence of the free market economy.

The new-born consumer of knowledge enters with amnesia into an already established game of deceit. He, she, is a myth of postmodernity.

Now let's continue our walk on the wild side, in search of this mythical "knower as consumer" in his or her postmodern habitat, the **Cyberian streetscenes**...

Figure 6.14 *'Only reproduce': postmodernism draws attention to ways in which 'lack of originality' has been transformed from a negative to a positive*

Figure 6.15 *The knowledge and facts behind The X-Files are recorded in books, magazines and on the Internet. Analysis or 'trivial pursuit'?*

The X-Files, like most postmodernist texts and products, has a pick-and-mix effect. Postmodernism tells us that the late twentieth century has rejected the clear frontier between high culture and popular culture.

The X-Files series challenges and overrides distinctions between 'the popular' and 'high art'. It takes the anti-Utopia of novels such as George Orwell's *1984* and Aldous Huxley's *Brave New World* which have high cultural status, and demolishes the boundaries between this and popular culture. *The X-Files* may have elements of schlock and kitsch (i.e. the more 'cheesy' aspects of popular culture), but it also has an aspect of political satire. Scully and Mulder are like the heroes of anti-Utopian fiction: they struggle to find answers to explain the political landscape in which they find themselves, against a background of shadowy figures who use their power corruptly and conspire to withhold information from 'the people'.

The X-Files also invites the viewer to recognise the 'quotations' or 'allusions' which have been included in the mix. Scully and Mulder's characters are like a comment on the many double acts which precede them; Chris Carter has underlined their relationship to Emma Peel and Steed from the sixties TV series *The Avengers*. The cliff-hangers and unresolved endings of episodes and stories look back through soap opera to old cinema serials such as *Flash Gordon*. Printed guides to the series even give the fan help in the 'trivial pursuit' of identifying references.

'The Host' is a self-consciously postmodern piece in that it refers to the 1950s Hollywood B movie science fiction genre of 'dreadful contaminations' in the form of monstrous threats to humanity, and makes explicit the link with that genre's fear of Soviet Russian Communism. One of the legacies of the Soviet era is the consequences of the explosion of nuclear reactors at Chernobyl. The host monster is a mutation created from this radioactive pollution, so it is a kind of throwback, or inheritance, from the Cold War.

The X-Files mixes up melodramatic and realistic, fact and fiction, normal and incongruous. It blurs the frontier between hallucination and reality, so that watching it is similar to being in a dream:

> *It is a smart point about The X-Files that at the end of each episode the evidence of UFOs or some other strange phenomenon always disappears, or is stolen by the chief conspirator, the dreaded Cigarette-Smoking Man. Mulder and Scully have nothing to show. At the end of the dream we wake up to our mundane world where things are what they seem to be – most of the time.*
>
> Harrington, 1997

It is paradoxical that *The X-Files* series refers so much to other texts, yet at the same time creates a parallel world which becomes mixed up with the real world. The effect is that the distinction between reality and unreality becomes blurred. Scully and Mulder are not real people, but they have become part of the real world. Are Gillian Anderson and David Duchovny more real than Scully and Mulder, or is it the other way about? Conspiracies and cover-ups really happen. Should we follow *The X-Files* slogan: 'Trust No-one'?

ACTIVITIES ▼

Activity 1

Design a mini-survey to establish how 'ordinary people' define the term 'popular culture'.

Ask ten people what they understand by the term and record their answers.

On the basis of their answers, construct a mini-questionnaire to find out what is understood by the term 'popular culture'. Provide multiple choice answers, including a 'get-out' choice saying something like 'other'. For people who choose this get-out option, write an open question asking how their understanding of popular culture differs from the answers you have provided.

Try out your mini-questionnaire on a sample of people, and write a short report on what you find.

Activity 2

Using the most recent edition of the *Guinness Book of Records* you can find, collect examples of the most popular products of all time in different countries and different media.

Collate the results and present them on a wall poster to be displayed wherever you decide (and have permission).

Activity 3

Find a classical piece of music and its presentation/packaging, and a 'pop' piece of music and its presentation/packaging. Ideally, this should be music presented on television (e.g. *Top of the Pops* compared with a classical music concert), but you may go beyond this if you wish.

What signs of high culture do you find in the classical music and the way it is presented?

What signs of popular culture do you find in the popular music and the way it is presented?

Activity 4

Analyse *Blind Date* or any other suitable game show in terms of its carnivalesque elements. You may use the following features as prompts:

- abundance
- community – people getting on better and co-operating more than normal
- competition
- escape
- fun and enjoyment pushed to their full
- 'saturnalia' (i.e. the breaking or overturning of everyday restraint and moral rules)
- the use of rituals to bring people together and confirm the equal footing of participants
- wish fulfilment.

Activity 5

Watch and compare some examples of popular British and US television programmes from the 1950s. Then compare them with similar products of the 1990s.

What conclusions can you draw about the contrasts in popular culture?

Activity 6

Discuss the place of television in your home, organising the points which come up under headings. If you wish, you can use the following headings to distinguish between your points, adding any extra headings you think are necessary.

1 Television and the relationship between home and the world outside.
2 The place of television within the home.
3 The role of television in defining the home and its particular identity.

Activity 7

View at least one episode of the British sitcom *Till Death Us Do Part* and/or the American sitcom *Love Thy Neighbour*.

What social changes are registered? How do these impact upon the home and family life?

Activity 8

1 Using a weekly television guide, chart the schedules for evidence for and against the model of evening scheduling which Paterson describes in the quote on page 76.
2 Can you find any other watersheds (i.e. common times when programming changes, such as in the morning)?
3 Produce a diagram showing the influence of family audiences on programme planning and scheduling. You can do this by blowing up a schedule for one day's television, and labelling and annotating it with comments on scheduling decisions and watersheds.

Activity 9

Choose an episode from a melodramatic television genre such as a soap, and analyse how the programme shows and uses the features of melodrama.

Activity 10

Undertake your own analysis of a popular cultural media product.

It is suggested that you address the issue of how the product has changed over time.

If you choose to investigate *The X-Files*, for example, you could analyse early and more recent episodes of your own choice. If you can gain access to *The X-Files* sites on the Internet, you should be able to use these as a resource for your research.

BIBLIOGRAPHY ▼

Boddy, W, 'The Beginnings of American Television', in Smith, A (ed.), *Television: An International History*, Oxford University Press, 1995

Braithwaite, R, 'Truthspotting', in *20/20* magazine, Arts Council, Winter 1996

Brunvand, H J, *The Vanishing Hitchhiker: Urban Legends and their Meanings*, Picador, 1983

Carter, C, 'Trust No-One', in *Guardian*, 6 June 1996

Genge, N E, *The Unofficial X-Files Companion*, Macmillan, 1995

Goodwin, A, and Whannel, G (eds), *Understanding Television*, Routledge, 1990

Harrington, M, 'The Alien Half-Century', in *The Spectator*, 7 June 1997

Jameson, F, 'Postmodernism, or the Cultural Logic of Late Capitalism', in *New Left Review 146*, July–August 1984

Jameson, F, *Postmodernism or the Logic of Late Capitalism*, Verso, 1991

Lovece, F, *The X-Files Declassified*, Hodder & Stoughton, 1996

Minton, S A, *Giant Reptiles*, Scribner's, 1973

Nicholas, J, 'Quizzical Culture', in *Media Education Issue 23*, 1994

Silverstone, R, *Television and Everyday Life*, Routledge, 1994

Smith, A, *Television, An International History*, Oxford University Press, 1995

Smith, J L, 'Melodrama', The Critical Idiom, Methuen, 1973

Smith, J, and Holland, T, *EastEnders, The Inside Story*, BBC Books, 1987

Stallybrass, P, and White, A, *The Politics of Transgression*, Methuen, 1986

CHAPTER 7

News: sources and selection

Introduction

> ❝ *Students cannot claim to be media literate if they are incapable of reading a newspaper with an informed and critical eye.* ❞
> Masterman, 1980

The next two chapters should help you understand and think critically about:

- what news is
- how it is produced
- how it is processed and presented
- how it is interpreted by the audience.

To do this, you will need to become familiar with as many different news products as possible. You should read a variety of newspapers thoroughly, over a period of time, and watch different television news programmes. In both cases, you should get to know a range of styles and compare how different products treat the same day's news. This chapter focuses on:

- where news comes from
- how organisations influence the content of newspapers and news broadcasts
- how news is selected
- news values – the criteria which journalists use when deciding what is important.

News sources

As you study news, you should try to train yourself to ask where each story has come from. Reporters do not usually just go out and find stories, picking them up 'as if they were fallen apples' (Chibnall, 1981). This would be too haphazard for organisations which need to produce papers or programmes to very precise deadlines.

Some events which demand attention are unpredictable, such as murders and natural disasters, but editors can't sit around waiting for these to occur. Newspapers and news programmes have to be filled and presented. You can't have a 'no news' day.

To make sure they always have a range of news stories to draw on, news organisations set up contacts or sources of information (for instance, they may employ foreign correspondents); cover predictable events, such as court cases and football matches; and use information provided by other organisations seeking publicity.

Most news organisations have a news editor, who usually makes the day-to-day decisions about what to include in newspapers or broadcasts. The news editors and their teams are at the centre of a web of lines of communication, bringing information into the news organisation. This supply of information comes from a range of sources, as the following list shows.

1 Stories from **news agencies** such as the Press Association and Reuters. These are news-gathering organisations which employ journalists to find and write stories. The stories are then made available to any news organisation which pays an annual subscription.

2 Stories written by the organisation's **own staff**, often at the direction of the news editor.

3 **Press releases**. These are statements and information from organisations which seek publicity, written by press officers or publicity specialists. Press releases are sometimes used verbatim, although they are usually rewritten or summarised by the organisation's own staff.

4 **Emergency services**. Police, fire and ambulance services are contacted regularly during the day, to see if there are any incidents which are important enough to report on.

5 Letters and phone calls from **members of the public** often provide good leads for stories.

6 **Other media**. News desk staff scour other newspapers and broadcast news for stories which they can follow up and develop. Local news organisations sometimes take a national story and do a local angle on it. Occasionally, national organisations decide that a local story is important enough to be given national coverage. If the news department is big enough, someone may be assigned to reading specialist magazines such as the *Lancet* (for medical stories), or pressure group publications such as the feminist *Bad Attitude* for stories of general interest.

7 The magistrates' and crown **courts** are regularly monitored. Court cases provide the bulk of stories in the *News of the World*, for instance.

8 **Diary stories**. Journalists are invited to attend scheduled meetings, and go to meetings which are open to the public. Local newspapers cover council meetings as a matter of routine, for instance. Sometimes organisations invite prominent speakers to promote issues or to highlight a controversy. News editors decide which of these meetings reporters should cover.

9 Journalists have their own **contacts**. These are often people in subordinate positions in organisations, who are willing to give alternative views from those presented by official PR sources.

> ❛ In the book of Genesis, it is God who brings order out of chaos; in the modern world, television journalists have to make a stab at doing it. They subdue into harmony a mountain of telex printouts, miles of videotape and a pandemonium of ringing telephones. They organise into a coherent picture a riot of impressions, a chaos, a bedlam of attitudes and opinions that would otherwise send us scurrying to the hills in panic. And they have to construct this world at lightning speed, in a welter of instant judgments. ❜
>
> Colin Morris, Controller of BBC Northern Ireland, 1986 (quoted in Glasgow University Media Group, 1993)

Journalist John Pilger proposes the following survival kit for all journalists.

> ❛ Beware all news from official sources. As the great muckraker Claud Cockburn once said: "Never believe anything until it has been officially denied."
> Beware the pack and fashions in news. The stories crying out to be done are almost always passed over.
> Beware all background briefings, especially from politicians. Indeed try to avoid, where possible, all contact with politicians. That way you will find out more about them. Certainly never go to work for them. Campaign to abolish the lobby system.
> Beware celebrating technology until you find out who owns it. The Internet is brilliant, but its most fervent bedfellows are the American government and a cluster of multi-national companies whose message posting is outstripping all others. Finally, take pride in the knowledge that the media barons can't stand the sight of us journalists. ❜

Sources and power

Many news sources tend to reflect the distribution of power in society. There is more likelihood of a well-organised publicity department having its message heard than an organisation with poor public relations procedures.

However, the best stories sometimes come from maverick individuals or small organisations which wish to challenge the status quo. Popular newspapers in particular like to see themselves as the champion of the 'little person' against impersonal systems and bureaucracy.

It is important to ask where information has come from and whether there is a hidden agenda behind it. Sometimes the sources of information are concealed; sometimes they are inferred. Journalists may be given summaries with interpretations which they can reproduce without challenge, rather than detailed information which is too complex to absorb. For example, a government press release accompanying a detailed report may claim a 'great success' in the improvement of SATs results in English and maths, producing figures to prove it. However, a journalist with time to read the whole report might find out that the tests have been made easier since the previous year. The problem then is that the story is not quite so appealing, and it might be easier to give the public the 'good news'. 'Never let the truth get in the way of a good story' is a common contention in news rooms.

In his book *Seeing and Believing* (1990), Greg Philo illustrates how authoritative sources tend to influence a story. He quotes as an example the BBC television news coverage of the 1984–5 miners' strike. At the start of each day the Coal Board issued information on the number of miners returning to work, using the phrase 'drift back' with its suggestion of inevitability. The headline in one news bulletin was: 'More than 1200 miners have returned to work, the largest number to end their strike on any day since November.' Not until the very end of the story was it revealed that these were Coal Board estimates, and that the figures were disputed by the unions. Moreover, because the story was established in the headline, information which did not accord with it was omitted. Figures from three areas were presented in a graphic, but South Wales, where there was no return to work, was missed out.

The relationship between sources and the media

Once a news organisation has established its sources of information, custom and habit mean that the news it covers tends to be concerned with certain types of events and topics. In addition, the events being reported are often interpreted by the source.

In his study of crime reporting (in Cohen and Young, 1981), Steve Chibnall analyses how this can happen.

As he explains, crime reporting is in the hands of a small number of specialist reporters working for national organisations. These journalists rely on one major institutional source for their information: the police ('a cautious and secretive organisation', according to Chibnall). Although the police have information officers who disseminate information to the media, crime reporters rely on personal contacts with individual CID officers, as the official sources are cautious.

Figure 7.1 A police appeal at a press conference – the police and journalists have established a reciprocal working relationship

The relationships that journalists build up with CID officers are reciprocal. The police provide information, and reporters uncover evidence which a police officer would find difficult to obtain. The media can also offer help by broadcasting or printing appeals to the public. Sometimes this involves deception; for example there may be a public declaration that robbers have stolen £1 million when in fact they have stolen much less, in the hope that this might make the thieves fall out. The media can also give promotional aid to the police by portraying police activities favourably.

Ostracism

Relationships like these have obvious consequences for the way crime is portrayed by the media. A crime reporter will always be aware that portraying the police in a bad light can lead to being cut off from the source of information. This is known as 'ostracism'.

Ostracism also occurs in other areas of journalism. The following article shows how bad publicity, in this case criticism of Newcastle United football club, led to a local paper being ostracised. The club demanded the sacking of a reporter which it felt was not portraying the team positively enough. The editor of the *Newcastle Journal* refused to comply, and the paper's press facilities were withdrawn. This made it difficult for the journalists to do their job: they no longer had access to the technology they needed to communicate with their office, and could not interview players or the team manager. This is a particular blow for a local paper, which usually carries daily reports on its local football team.

Newcastle United and *The Journal*

By **Bill Bradshaw**, *editor*

NEWCASTLE United withdrew press facilities from *The Journal* last night when a hand-delivered letter – written by Sir John Hall – arrived at our offices.

That disappoints me as it must disappoint our readers.

The board decided, after a recommendation from manager Kevin Keegan, to impose a 'blanket ban' on this newspaper.

Kevin Keegan does not like the reporting style of executive sports editor Tim Taylor. He was prompted into recommending a ban to the directors after Taylor questioned the varying accounts of Andy Cole's exclusion from the England squad.

This upset assistant manager Terry McDermott who was asked about Cole's fitness to play for England at a press conference at Aston Villa last weekend. McDermott said he knew nothing about it.

Later it emerged that Kevin Keegan had asked England manager Terry Venables, the day before the Villa game, not to consider Cole.

The Journal was only one of several newspapers to highlight the inconsistencies between Newcastle United's version of events and that of England manager Terry Venables.

It is to be regretted if Kevin Keegan and Terry McDermott were offended by the sort of language we felt at that time to be appropriate.

Kevin Keegan, in a telephone call to me, suggested we were not behaving like a local paper. If by that he is suggesting that we are not sycophants, he is absolutely right. And I refuse to apologise for it.

I applaud Keegan, a magnificent player, supreme soccer ambassador and inspirational manager, for all his achievements for Newcastle United and Tyneside.

I also applaud Sir John for providing the kind of backing and vision so obviously lacking in days gone by. These are exciting times for ALL to share.

But, while it is our right and duty to criticise when necessary, I would not dream of telling Keegan which players he should hire and fire.

So, with respect, he can't expect to pick my team.

Meanwhile it is business as usual. This newspaper will be reporting on Newcastle as fully as ever.

The Journal is proud of its association with Newcastle United through both the glory and gloomy days. We want it to continue and our door is open to Sir John, and his directors, and Kevin Keegan.

We hope they are big enough to reopen theirs.

Newcastle Journal,
7 October 1994

Figure 7.2 The Journal's response to being ostracised by its local team

Economic influence

Economic weapons can also be used against a newspaper. In another example from football, a club chairman who was peeved at readers' letters criticising him and the club's management, threatened to withdraw his car sales advertising from the local paper unless it suppressed the letters. The paper's editor refused to change his policy and the paper lost, temporarily, a considerable amount of advertising revenue.

'Feeding' the media

When you are studying news, it is important to be aware of the interdependence of sources and the media. In politics, sources often 'feed' the media: parties give journalists information which portrays their cause positively. According to Marcus Linton, writing in the *Guardian* in 1997: 'Newspapers do not like admitting they are fed stories by political parties.'

Linton gives as an example the *Daily Mail* printing 'virtually verbatim' a press release from Conservative Central Office in 1979 under the headline 'Labour's Dirty Dozen'. The story was about Labour's predictive 'lies', most of which, according to Linton, came true. He says that this left the *Daily Mail* with 'egg on its face', but presumably the Conservative party had achieved its goal with the story.

Linton goes on to say that more sophisticated methods are used when Central Office gives research material to journalists which they can present as their own work. He refers to an 'insider source' who 'recalls with pride how he stored anti-Labour stories in his safe for two years before the election [1992] and drip-fed them to friendly journalists, who presented them as their own work in the final seven days of the election campaign.'

A key part of the strategy is to create stories targeted at particular newspapers. So the *Sun* was fed stories that a Labour government 'would let in tens of thousands of immigrants', and that applications for building conversions would have to be approved by gay and lesbian groups.

Linton goes on:

> ❛ Both parties and papers have an interest in denying cooperation, but it is an effective division of labour. The party provides the research, the journalists present it as their own. The politicians can't be blamed, the journalists can't be questioned. In the run-up to the last [1992] election it also proved to be an effective destruction of Labour. It caused, or at least coincided with, a sharp swing to the right among Sun readers. ❜

The lobby system

Another form of sourcing used in politics is the lobby system, where journalists are given unattributable information from the government. Bernard Ingham, Chief Press Secretary during Margaret Thatcher's premiership, describes this well in his autobiography *Kill the Messenger*. His job was to give selected journalists information about government policy, portraying the government in a favourable way. As Ingham puts it: 'Number 10 Press Office is entitled to make judgements about what best serves the Prime Minister and his or her office.' He did not believe that he should help 'those who are either trying to take the mickey out of Number 10 or just being gratuitously awkward'.

What is particularly interesting in Ingham's account is how the issuing or repression of information was affected by his own personal feelings. He apparently ostracised journalists he did not like. Ingham recalls one occasion when BBC reporter Martin Dowle treated him to lunch at Beotys, one of Sir Bernard's two favourite London restaurants. But things started to go wrong when Dowle used information from their informal chat to suggest in a news programme that Margaret Thatcher had privately criticised two of her ministers. Ingham considered he had been misreported, and angrily told Dowle so. But he goes on to say in his book: 'Nor did he... ever have a personal briefing from me subsequently... Those who seek to impugn my integrity have to pay a price, and the more inconvenient the price for them the better.'

Ingham took a similar line with Sunday newspapers when he felt that they had misrepresented him over Mrs Thatcher's relationship with the Queen, 'and the Sunday lobby went on short rations for a few weeks'.

Ingham also took a dislike to BBC reporter Brian Redhead. He believed that the BBC was not so much either left or right wing as 'anti-government. It feels as if it has to challenge authority of whatever political colour.' Seeing Redhead as a prime example of this attitude, Ingham objected in particular to Redhead calling him 'a conspiracy'. Once again Sir Bernard turned to ostracism: 'From then on I was [a conspiracy]. His failure to apologise meant that he never got another interview with Mrs Thatcher as Prime Minister.'

Relationships between Ingham and journalists were often difficult. The press variously depicted him as 'Mrs Thatcher's personal Rottweiler', 'an omnipotent ogre ruling over us all with a malignant eye' and 'the Iago of Downing Street'. Three newspapers, the *Guardian*, the *Independent* and the *Scotsman*, actually withdrew from the lobby system in protest at his behaviour.

Ingham in turn thought that some journalists believed that 'the government is inevitably, irrevocably and chronically up to no good', and that they would 'never go for the simple explanation when an elaborate theory can be constructed. After all it reads better.' He accused them of a 'refusal to check any fact lest a paragraph is lost to truth'.

Figure 7.3 Bernard Ingham – Margaret Thatcher's 'personal Rottweiler'

Stifled sources

Ostracism in this case is a denial of information to certain parts of the media. A similar tactic, which is more difficult to detect, involves stifled sources: issuing information in such a way that it gets the minimum attention.

For example, if government is obliged to issue information which will produce bad publicity, it can choose the timing of the release to coincide either with a low level of activity in news rooms (Friday at 4 p.m. is a good time), or when a big story will grab the main headlines.

By Francis Wheen ....

By hallowed tradition, December 24th is the day on which government departments quietly announce any bad tidings to which they do not want to draw attention, safe in the knowledge that MPs and journalists will be busy wrapping up their presents or getting sloshed on disgusting mulled wine. And so it was that Barbara Mills, the Director of Public Prosecutions, revealed on Christmas Eve that none of the officials criticised by Sir Richard Scott for their antics in the arms-to-Iraq scandal would be prosecuted.

Had this statement come at any other time, there would have been a tremendous fuss. The Scott Report concludes, with ample evidence, that some civil servants were guilty of 'impropriety' which amounted to 'an impeding of the course of justice'. But now we learn (or, rather, we don't learn, since Mills's press release went largely unreported) that interfering with the course of justice is no longer an offence.

● ● ● ● ● ● ● ● ● ● ● ● ● ● ● ● ● ● ●

Guardian,
8 January 1997

Figure 7.4 Hiding bad news

Subverting sources

Although sources are sometimes reported unthinkingly or uncritically, especially if journalists are working against the clock, it is also possible for the writer to subvert the source. The feature in Figure 7.5, taken from *Today* newspaper, is an example of this. The government of the day held a public relations event to launch National Bike Week as part of a healthy living campaign. A photo opportunity was organised for the media, who were invited to take pictures of two ministers riding a tandem in Trafalgar Square. However, reporter Adrian Lee did not tell the story the way the government had intended.

The paper emphasised the point of the story by printing the publicity shot of the bike alongside a picture of Mrs Bottomley getting into her car.

The leak

Leaks involve the release of information which is embargoed, not allowed to be printed until a certain time, or not meant to be made public.

For example, in autumn 1997 the editor of the *Mirror* was sent a copy of the Budget by a man with a grudge against the government. All Budget information is supposed to be kept secret until the Chancellor of the Exchequer makes the Budget speech in Parliament. It was the biggest Budget leak in history, and should have been one of the biggest ever scoops. But editor Piers Morgan, fearing legal problems if he used the material, sent it back to the government and led on the fact that the secrets had been leaked: 'Budget Secrets Leaked to Mirror'.

Figure 7.5

Ginny, Ginny, give us your answer do

We're half crazy, and all because of YOU..

Still in the saddle: Virginia Bottomley tries out the tandem with Stephen Dorrell as she promotes healthy living yesterday

Figure 7.6 Max Clifford

Healthy cycling call – then off in a car

by ADRIAN LEE

VIRGINIA Bottomley came close to doing us all a favour yesterday – by getting on her bike.

It was too good to be true, though. For after a quick pedal around London's Trafalgar Square, she was soon back behind her desk at the Health Department putting a spoke in the wheel of the NHS.

Mrs Bottomley tried her best to look sweet upon the seat of a bicycle made for two as she climbed on a tandem with Heritage Secretary Stephen Dorrell.

The pair were launching National Bike Week – supposedly to promote the benefits of cycling to health and the environment. But soon after the cameras stopped clicking, Ginny apparently decided that people can have too much of good clean air.

Back to reality: Mrs Bottomley about to climb into her car for the long trip to Westminster

FUMES

She ducked into her comfortable gas-guzzling ministerial Rover Sterling to head for her next appointment.

And before you could say asthma, she was off in a cloud of exhaust fumes pumped out by the Rover's powerful 2.7 litre engine.

Aides said she needed the motor to get to a pressing ministers' meeting on time.

There was clearly no alternative like, say, a bike. After all, the meeting was in Westminster, which is several yards away from Trafalgar Square...

Today, 10 May 1995

The maverick

There are a few individuals, known as 'mavericks', who make a living from selling stories, especially scandalous ones, to the news media.

Max Clifford is an example of a maverick news source. He maintains that he has taken the place of the type of investigative journalist which much of the press cannot seem to afford. He is a public relations expert who understands the kind of stories papers want and knows how to negotiate deals for his clients. One of his major stories was Antonia de Sancha's affair with Cabinet Minister David Mellor, which contributed to Mellor's resignation.

Clifford does long-term PR work for major clients such as Muhammed Ali, represents companies such as the car manufacturer Seat, represents infamous mistresses, and performs 'the work I can't talk about for celebrities caught or about to be caught with their pants down'.

The hoax

The news media must always beware of being hoaxed. Hardly a day passes when a tabloid news desk is not offered a fake story. Some are from people who are innocently misinformed; others are malicious; and some are from people seeking cash or fame.

Even vastly experienced journalists can be deceived. In 1996 Stuart Higgins, the editor of the *Sun*, was given an 80-second videotape purporting to show, from a distance, Princess Diana 'cavorting with her lover' Captain James Hewitt at her Highgrove home. Higgins did his best to authenticate the material. He brought in experts who knew the couple well to view the tape. He contacted Hewitt himself, who agreed that the pictures were accurate and that he had probably been spied on. So the *Sun* devoted five pages to the 'Di Spy Video Scandal' story. But someone contacted Max Clifford (the maverick described above), and told him that the video was an elaborate hoax, staged with look-alikes. Clifford in turn sold an exclusive to the *Sun*'s rival the *Mirror*, who proclaimed: 'We expose Diana and Hewitt sex video as a cruel hoax'.

▶◀ *See Activities 1, 2 and 3, pages 93 and 94*

News selection

> ❝ *In relation to the press, news values may vary considerably from title to title and they can only be discovered through close scrutiny of the newspapers themselves. In this area, it is particularly important that the notion of "news values" should not be used in a formulaic way, or as an instant and universally applicable check list.* ❞
> Masterman, 1980

The media selects and edits from the stories offered by its variety of sources. In other words it mediates, emphasising some events and repressing others.

When so much information is available, what criteria do journalists use to select and prioritise stories? What is and isn't newsworthy?

Journalists have notions of newsworthiness which seem to have been gathered from experience and tradition rather than through any formal and accepted training. The author has heard all of the following definitions over the years from different editors and news editors.

> ❝ *"News is anything which makes you sad, mad or glad."*
> *"News is anything that you hope will never happen to you, or that you wish would happen to you."*
> *"Nobody is interested in education."*
> *"Politics is boring."*
> *"It's whatever interests the general reader."*
> *"Its news if it's light, trite and shite."*
> *"Sex, money, health and crime – that's what people are interested in."* ❞

Close to a deadline with a 'hole' in a page, news selection can even be reduced to: 'Can anyone send me a 10 centimetre story?'

According to Larry Lamb, the first editor of the *Sun* under Rupert Murdoch:

> ❝ *The basic interests of the human race are not in politics, philosophy or economics, but in things like food and money, sex and crime, football and television.* ❞

Views such as these are often just hunches, or a sort of journalistic folklore. However, news organisations do carry out research to discover what their readers like and dislike about the content and style of papers or broadcasts. Ultimately news products need to satisfy their consumers, so the attitudes of readers are taken very seriously.

Market research can sometimes leave editors with dilemmas, especially if they are aiming for a family audience. What one group particularly dislikes may be valued by another. Unless a news product is being aimed at a very narrow, specialised market, it has to try to be many things to many people: a compendium of minority interests. The oldest challenge in journalism is how to appeal to new, young readers without alienating established, older readers.

Figure 7.7 Newspapers have to try to appeal to readers from all walks of life

News values

Academics have tried to categorise news values, or 'newsworthiness': what makes a good story. One of the most influential studies was by Galtung and Ruge (1973), who described the following general news values:

- the time a story takes to happen – the shorter the time, the more likely it is to be selected
- how big an event is
- how easily understood the event is
- how close the event is to the cultural background of the readers
- stories from alien cultures are valued if they affect the readers' culture
- predictability in the sense that the media expect something to happen and then 'make' it happen
- how rare an event is
- running story – covering a story for a few days, keeping it going by adding new details or looking at it from new angles
- balance – choosing a story because it is a contrast to others.

They also identified four characteristics which are of particular importance to western media:

- reference to elite nations
- reference to elite persons
- reference to individuals – stories which are easy to personalise
- bad news.

In turn, Louise Clara identified the following ten points which determine what makes news.

1 Immediacy (news which is new to the communication media).
2 Nearness (involving people and places that readers know).
3 Consequence (news which affects readers, for example, rises in taxes).
4 Prominent people (people who are important to many of the readers).
5 Suspense (information about things which have to be resolved, for example a murder trial).
6 Oddity (man bites dog type of story).
7 Conflict (so that the reader can take sides).
8 Human interest (stories which involve the readers emotionally).
9 Magnitude (stories which shock because of the enormity of the events).
10 Progress or lack of it (advances in medicine, travel, education etc.).

It is important to treat such lists with caution. Galtung and Ruge produced their findings after studying the foreign news sections of Norwegian newspapers. There will be variations from country to country (Louise Clara's list is based on the USA), and between different types of newspaper (for example, local and national). There may even be different values in different departments within the same news organisation.

▶◀ *See Activities 4 and 5, pages 94 and 95*

Selecting crime news

In his study of the selection of crime news by the press, Bob Roshier looked at what journalists select and why. He analysed the percentage of news space devoted to crime news in a wide range of newspapers, looking at the types of crimes reported, the stage at which they were reported, the sentences given out, and the kind of information given about offenders. He then compared the findings with the official criminal statistics.

He followed this quantitative study with a qualitative study which looked at readers' attitudes to questions such as:

- Is there too much crime reporting?
- Do newspapers make crime appear attractive?
- Do newspapers make heroes out of criminals?

Roshier's findings showed that:

- crime news is not prominent in any national daily papers, accounting for only a small proportion of all news
- the relative frequency of crimes reported bears no relation to the actual crime figures
- newspapers give a distorted impression by concentrating on solved crimes and tending to over-report more serious punishments, so that the public has an exaggerated impression of the chances of being caught and the severity of punishment
- very little information is given about offenders
- there is an over-reporting of older and higher social class offenders
- the press does not exaggerate the extent of youthful crime, nor does it purvey a lower class stereotype of offenders
- the press does not glorify crime or make it seem profitable and attractive.

Roshier argues that these last two conclusions in particular run counter to popular opinion.

Roshier also analysed the types of crime that the press select for coverage, and found that:

- the offence was more likely to be reported if it was serious (for example a murder or a big robbery)
- the offence was more likely to be reported if there was some element of humour or irony in it, such as a thief stealing a detective's car or a man just released from jail finding his first job in a bank
- sentiment or drama, whether relating to the victim or offender, add to a story's appeal. For example, 'Boy steals Arthur's budgies – 25 years' work ruined!'
- the involvement of a famous or high-status person adds to a story's appeal (for example an Olympic champion on a drugs charge).

Roshier also found that readers are able to reinterpret the information they receive, and that they do not necessarily take media presentations of real events to be representative of real life.

▶◀ *See Activity 6, page 95*

ACTIVITIES ▼

Activity 1

Read all the news stories in a single newspaper and list the identifiable sources for each story.

- Look for attributed quotes (for example 'German boss, Berti Vogts, insisted "England can be happy. Klinsmann will not play." ').
- Look for press release sources. These are sometimes difficult to spot, but if there is a phrase such as 'it was revealed' followed by a reference to an organisation like 'The Hospital and Consultants Association', this suggests the information was from a press release.
- Look for mentions of reports and meetings (for example 'after a two-and-a-half hour meeting of the local party's executive...').

- Look for clues which are mentioned late in a story (for example 'Contacted by the Telegraph when her name appeared on a list of bankrupts...').
- Look for references to courts (for example 'outlined today at Winchester crown court').

Choose a few stories and comment on the quality and relevance of the sources. Could other sources have provided a different angle on the stories?

Activity 2

Do the same kind of analysis on broadcast news.

Activity 3

You have information from the following sources which are all seeking publicity for one reason or another. Discuss which other sources you would consult for each story and why.

- Greenpeace has told you that it is staging a protest about a redundant oil rig which its owner, BP, is planning to sink in British territorial waters.
- A local residents' association has complained to you about some New Age travellers who are camping on a common near their houses.
- A political party in opposition is claiming that a leaked document shows that the government is planning to require all public schools to accept 10 per cent of their pupils from poor inner-city areas.
- The news desk has received an anonymous letter complaining that there are secret spy cameras installed in all local council offices.
- You have been offered information and pictures about the manager of the local football club accepting bribes to lose games. The pictures were taken in a motorway café and look authentic. You have been told that there is also a tape recording of a conversation relevant to the circumstances. Your informant says he comes from a company called TABSON which is based in London. It specialises in revealing scandals to the media.

Activity 4

Divide your group into four or five different news organisations, each with a target market identified by age, gender, geography, interests and size.

Each group should be given, or should design for itself, a brief like this:

You are the news team for a local radio station in the Midlands. Your audience is made up mainly of people in the 18–25 age group, with a high proportion of females. Twenty per cent of the students at your local university claim to listen to the station, especially in the evenings. Your station manager wants to keep this audience, but wants to try to add more under-18s if possible. A recent piece of market research has shown that most of your listeners think there is too much bad news on the station.

As a group, organise an editorial meeting and consider the following news items. Each group must select its top three stories and give reasons for their choice.

1 A famous pop star has suggested that the taking of Ecstasy is not harmful and that the drug should be legalised.
2 The government has announced a snap general election.
3 A holiday plane has crashed into the Indian Ocean killing over 200 passengers. There may be some Britons among the dead.
4 A nine-year-old girl has gone missing in the Midlands. Police have organised a search for her. Her parents are distressed and the police are very concerned about her safety.

5 Police in London have uncovered a major credit card fraud.
6 The Home Secretary has been having an extra-marital affair with a Soho stripper.
7 Twenty people in the Hebrides are reported to be suffering from serious food poisoning.
8 Protesters against a nuclear waste disposal site have been arrested by the Cumbrian police.
9 Scientists have discovered a new cure for the common cold.
10 A new report claims that pregnant women are putting their unborn children's health at risk when they eat brown bread.
11 Twenty people in the north of Norfolk have reported seeing a spacecraft in the night sky. One man claims to have spoken to an alien and has pictures to prove it!

Activity 5

Compare the news values of different newspapers and/or broadcasts. Make a list of every news item selected by each paper or programme you are studying, and note their prominence in terms of placement or amount of coverage. Do this over a period of time (at least a week) and then draw conclusions about what each paper or programme considers important and what each neglects. If you have access to old papers or programmes, you could carry out a historical comparison.

Local newspapers usually store back issues and you may be able to obtain photocopies of them. Local libraries also have back copies of local papers and may have them on microfilm. Most national newspapers have their own libraries, but the public is not usually allowed in and telephone calls are not always welcome, especially at busy times (late morning onwards).

The British Library Newspaper Library has stored all UK newspapers since 1986 on microfilm. A double-page photocopy costs about £1.50, and a postal service operates at a small charge. For more information, contact The British Library Newspaper Library, Colindale Avenue, London NW9 5HE. Tel: 0171 412 7356.

Some reference libraries may have newsreaders' typescripts from the 'BBC Home Service Nine O'Clock News, 1935–45'.

It is very difficult to locate old TV news programmes, though the British Film Institute (BFI) has a National Film and Television Archive with TV news from 1985 onwards. Access to this is limited, but possible to arrange, and there is no copying service. Contact BFI, 21 Stephen Street, London W1P 2LN.
Tel: 0171 255 1444.

Activity 6

Analyse the crime reporting of a local news organisation. Collect information under the headings:
- type of crime
- solved or unsolved
- information about offenders
- information about punishment.
Collect this information over a period of time, and then compare the portrayal of crime with published crime statistics for your area. These can usually be found in the Chief Constable's annual report, which will be in your local library. What conclusions can you draw about how accurately crime is portrayed by the media?

BIBLIOGRAPHY ▼

Bagnall, N, *Newspaper Language*, Focal Press, 1993

Chibnall, S, 'The Production of Knowledge by Crime Reporters', in Cohen, S, and Young, J, *The Manufacture of News*, Constable, 1981

Clara, L, *Creating the Mature Reader,* The Commercial Appeal, 1972

Cohen, S, and Young, J, *The Manufacture of News*, Constable, 1981

Fowler, R, *Language in the News*, Routledge, 1991

Galtung, J, and Ruge, M, (1973), quoted in Cohen, S, and Young, J, *The Manufacture of News*, Constable, 1981

Glasgow University Media Group, *Bad News* and *More Bad News*, Routledge, 1976 and 1980

Glasgow University Media Group, *Getting the Message*, Routledge, 1993

Goodwin, A, and Whannel, G (eds), *Understanding Television*, Routledge, 1990

Hartley, J, *Understanding News*, Routledge, 1990

Ingham, B, *Kill the Messenger*, Fontana, 1991

Linton, M, 'It's still up to you my *Sun*', in *Guardian*, 6 January 1997

Masterman, L, *Teaching about Television*, Macmillan, 1980

Philo, G, *Seeing and Believing*, Routledge, 1990

Roshier, B, 'The Selection of Crime News by the Press', in Cohen, S, and Young, J, *The Manufacture of News*, Constable, 1981

CHAPTER 8

News: presentation and effects

Introduction

The last chapter looked at where news comes from and how it is selected. In this chapter you will explore:

- how news is interpreted by the people who work in news departments
- how news is presented on television, in print and on radio

- whether news can be, or should be, impartial
- the extent to which the public is influenced by the messages it receives through mass media news.

How do media professionals interpret the news?

As you found out in the last chapter, news is partly determined by the organisations which feed information to the media. However, as you will find out now, the character of news is also partly determined by the professionals who process it.

When professionals present news, they have an assumed audience in mind. To communicate with this audience, they have to tell stories using frames of reference which are familiar; they have to relate events to other events which the audience knows about. This involves bringing unusual or unexpected events into contexts, or 'maps of meaning', shared by a particular culture. To do this, media professionals continually make assumptions about what society is and how it works. One crucial assumption is that society works by consensus: that we all share particular values and concerns. This is sometimes called a 'central value system' (Hall *et al.* in Cohen and Young, 1981).

As a result of presenting news within familiar contexts:

- references are continually renewed, and existing beliefs and values are reinforced
- media professionals not only select and define what is significant as news, but also tell the audience how to interpret events through their implied attitudes to the people and groups involved.

For example, consider the use of the word 'mainland' by London-based media professionals when addressing the issue of Irish nationalism and Northern Ireland. Spokespeople for Sinn Fein, the Irish republican movement, challenge the use of the word because it implies that the island of Ireland is somehow less important than the island of England, Wales and Scotland. They emphasise that there are actually two adjacent islands, not a mainland and an offshoot which by implication is inferior. It is most unlikely that the media professionals would deliberately use the word 'mainland' to imply superiority; it is more a question of this being their accepted terminology and cultural map.

Mode of address

Hall and others argue that each news organisation develops its own mode of address, and that the language used by a newspaper or programme is a version of the language spoken by its main target audience.

In this way, the statements and viewpoints of organisations which determine the news (as described in chapter 7) are translated into a public idiom with which the audience is comfortable. Staid and unexciting officialese is turned into newspaper rhetoric (i.e. persuasive language) and made accessible to large numbers of readers, viewers or listeners.

The *Sun*, for instance, tends to report Trade Union affairs in terms of conflict, using clichés with which it assumes readers are familiar. So in a report in the *Sun* on 9 September 1996 on the negotiations between Tony Blair and the TUC over a minimum wage, we find the following statements:

- 'Blair and TUC in 76p *Wage War'*
- 'The TUC *were at war* with Labour leader Tony Blair last night over 76p.'
- 'But Mr Blair insists that is too high and wants it *slashed* by 76p.'
- 'Wednesday's vote... will *smash a hole through* Labour's wages policy.'
- 'He has already *warned* union leaders they will be *left in the cold* if they don't *toe the line.'*
- 'Mr Blair is also *on collision course* with the unions over plans *to crack down* on public sector strikes.'
- 'It will be a *test of his strength* if he can *steamroller* his party's union paymasters.'

I have added the emphasis to show the familiar images and references which make it difficult for readers to think about the problem in a non-confrontational way. This reinforces the idea that trade unionism equals conflict, and that the unions are dangerous.

Creating themes

News organisations can also create an interest in issues of their own choosing. Thus a particular publication or programme can determine that, for instance, stories about

Brussels bureaucracy are a topical issue, and devote staff, time and space to making it a theme. As other news organisations will then follow up this newly defined area of interest and try to find other angles on it, it may well seem to the public that there is in fact a real problem because they read so much about it.

Mark Fishman shows how this process works in his essay 'Crime Waves as Ideology' (in Cohen and Young, 1981). He argues that 'crime waves' are a construct of the mass media, who determine an issue of interest and then 'make it happen'. He looked at the media coverage of a 'surge in violence' against old people in New York in November and December of 1976. The story was that old people were being mugged, murdered and raped, and that the criminals were black or Hispanic youths with long juvenile records. The youths lived in ghetto neighbourhoods next to enclaves of elderly and fairly affluent whites. According to Fishman, the story developed because one editor, working for a television news programme called WAVE, was looking for a theme or issue on a slack news day. He scanned the stories listed on the computer, and grouped them together as follows:

- a story about the mugging of an elderly couple in the Queens district of New York
- a meeting of a senior citizens' crime prevention group in the same district
- a feature on an organisation called the Senior Citizens Robbery Unit.

None of these three stories merited much attention by itself, but grouped together they became a theme: crimes against the elderly by dangerous minority groups. And, as Fishman says, a crime theme is a potential crime wave. Every crime that could be seen as an example of the theme was seen and reported as such, and incidents which had previously gone unnoticed became more important because of the 'crime wave' against the elderly. As other news programmes and newspapers noticed the theme, they began to reinforce it by picking up more stories. Between 1 October and 1 November 1976, stories in the New York media about crimes against the elderly increased sixfold.

Fishman then looked at the crime figures produced by the New York Police Department and found that there was no unusual surge of crimes against the elderly during that period; in fact, there was a slight decrease in robberies, purse snatchings and homicides. Nevertheless in May 1977 a Harris Poll in New York found that 60 per cent of respondents thought that crimes against the elderly were increasing.

Fishman argues that this process of finding news to fit a theme applies to other areas of life, as well as crime. As an example he gives the huge 'bureaucratic apparatus... set up... to feed the media with fresh instances of the Watergate theme. Once [President] Nixon was deposed, this apparatus was dismantled, and so was the Watergate "news wave".'

News themes like this can lead to 'moral panic'. Roy Greenslade, writing in the *Media Guardian*, describes how many newspapers never miss an opportunity to highlight a 'supposed decline of Britain from those misty, happy, crime-free days of yore... Newspaper columnists endlessly decry the falling standards in schools, the lack of innocence of youth, the decline of manners, the lost authority of the police, the absence of churchgoing. Television and movies are blamed for encouraging young people to grow into violent, sexually promiscuous lager louts.'

According to Greenslade, once the disease has been identified, a cause has to be named. This will depend on the demonology of the individual writer or publication, but one common culprit is 'liberalism', especially liberalism of the 1960s.

▶◀ *See Activity 1, page 106*

News presentation

This section focuses on the way news is presented:

- on television
- in print
- on radio.

It explores the different codes and conventions used, and looks at the variations found in different types of news products.

News on television

When studying the presentation of television news, the method of analysing presentation outlined in John Hartley's *Understanding News* can be a useful starting point.

First consider the visual structures:

1 The newsreader who frames, links and rounds off each programme.
2 The correspondents who set the context and explain things.
3 Film reports.

Then look at these four modes of presentation:

1 The talking head.
2 Graphics.
3 Nomination, or naming the participants in the news and establishing their status with captions or verbal introductions.

Figure 8.1 Different styles of presenting television news – Trevor MacDonald of I Kirsty Young adopting the informal approach of Channel 5

4 Actuality (film, or occasionally live transmission). In turn, this can be divided into:
  • film with voice-over
  • 'stake out' (where the reporter talks directly to camera)
  • 'vox pop' (where the interviewee is seen full frame).

Look for the different types of talk you are presented with. Hartley identifies what he calls 'institutional voices' and 'accessed voices'.
  • Newsreaders and reporters are institutional voices.
  • Accessed voices are granted access to the audience via the implicitly more powerful institution. Accessed voices are usually pictured talking to an unseen reporter, so that they are separated from the institutional figure. Other accessed voices are not even seen or heard directly, working through press releases and being delivered as institutional voices.

Making this distinction helps you to understand how certain voices carry more authority than others. There is a hierarchy of information-givers, with the anchor-person who sits in a studio behind an impressive desk in charge. The impression given is that he or she controls the stories, allowing reporters and correspondents to contribute. They are to be trusted because they are professionals, but they do not seem as powerful as the anchor-person. The accessed voices, introduced by reporters and answering their questions, are by implication the least important. Occasionally an accessed voice tries to subvert these conventions during a live interview by challenging the questions they are asked, but this is rare. Most of them 'know their place'.

Question styles

What are the different types of question interviewees on TV news programmes are asked? What effect do these have?
  Hartley describes the following three forms of question.
  1 'How does it feel?' This type of question leads to personal-ising the story and neglecting more abstract issues.
  2 'Isn't it...?' A question designed to let the interviewee make a statement, tacitly giving approval to the accessed voice.
  3 'But surely...?' A question designed to challenge the interviewee, tacitly showing disapproval of the accessed voice.

You may want to use these definitions of question styles, or you may prefer to devise your own.

Presenting a confrontational view

Critical viewing of television news presentation should lead you to consider whether a confrontational view of the world is being implied. Is there a 'them' and 'us' interpretation of news, with 'us' being the nation, the public, the viewer, the newsreader, and the news organisation, and 'them' being foreign powers, strikers, weather, fate, bureaucracy and so on?
  The labelling of interviewees, either overtly or by suggestion, can contribute to this. Different groups of people may be defined as troublemakers, extremists, perverts, deviants, dissidents and so on, influencing the way news is presented.

How can TV news improve?

According to Stephen Marshall, director of the Canadian Channel Zero, television news has to change radically in order to appeal to a younger audience which is used, for instance, to the amount of information available on the Internet. He argues that 'anchor-driven' news, which has led the way for 30 years, will have to change. Channel Zero news programmes use the screen as a palette containing lots of different types of information. The presenter is given a small corner of the screen, while the rest is used for text and visuals, such as maps and film.
  Marshall argues that today's audiences can cope with several images at once. He also believes that if people are interested in particular stories, they tend to record news programmes and study them more closely later on.

Figure 8.2 Bloomberg TV broadcast news combining a live anchor, a dynamic information panel and market and weather tickers

This approach could be one way to prevent television news becoming mere 'infotainment', as veteran American news anchor-man Walter Cronkite fears (Snow, 1997). According to Cronkite, the main problem facing TV news is that it is an 'inadequate substitute for a good newspaper'. Although television is a powerful way of presenting people and events in moving pictures, it 'fails in outlining and explaining the more complicated issues of the day. For those who either cannot or will not read, television lifts the floor of knowledge and understanding of the world around them. But for the others, through its limited exploration of difficult issues, it lowers the ceiling of knowledge.'
  Cronkite argues that the volume of television news is very small, and that half an hour's TV news is equivalent to only two-thirds of a standard newspaper page. As a result, news is compressed, distorted and oversimplified. As Cronkite says: 'With inadequate time to present a coherent report the correspondent seeks to craft a final summary sentence that might make some sense out of the preceding gibberish. This is hard to do without coming to a single point of view – and a one-line editorial is born.'

▶◀ *See Activity 2, page 107*

A different style of TV news

In his book *Reading the Popular*, John Fiske argues that if news is to be more meaningful to its audience, it should be produced as entertainment rather than information. Informative media programmes attempt to be objective, aim to present 'the truth', and see themselves as educational and important. Entertaining programmes, on the other hand, see themselves as subjective, fictional, escapist and trivial.

Fiske believes that TV news should judge its effectiveness solely in terms of its popularity:

'We should demand of our television news that it make the events of the world popular, that it subject them to popular taste and attempt to make them part of the popular consciousness of society.'

Fiske argues that to achieve this, television news should be relevant to people's everyday lives. Although people may watch news about national and international issues because they feel that they ought to, they do not talk about the issues involved and absorb them into their lives.

The attitudes to news expressed by an interviewee in David Morley's *Family Television* seems to illustrate this well:

'I don't want to know about the Chancellor somebody in Germany and all that. When I've seen it I don't want to watch it again... It bores me. What's going on in the world? I don't understand it all so I don't like to listen to that. I watch – like those little kids – that gets to me, I want to know about it. Or if there's actually some crime in Wandsworth [local] like rapes and all the rest of it. I want to read up on that, if they've been caught and locked away. As for like the pound's gone up and the pound's gone down, I don't want to know about all that 'cos I don't understand it.'

Fiske argues that the more open and interrogatory television is, the more it will be talked about and incorporated into the microculture. Soap operas do this well, being full of open-ended stories which pose questions about characters' feelings, possible courses of action, and judgements about behaviour. TV sport is also open, full of contradictions which invite engagement, disagreement and therefore popular productivity. Fiske explains this comparison in more detail:

'Rather than trying to be important and responsible, TV news should be more like sport and soaps, striving after entertainment and trying to stimulate its audiences into taking up its information and using it in their everyday lives. It should aim to be talked about, which means it must discard its role of the privileged information giver, with its clear distinction between the one who knows (the author) and those who do not (the audience), for that gives it the place and tone of the author-god and discourages popular productivity... Instead of promoting a final truth then, it should provoke discussion (like soap opera) or disagreement (like sportscasting).'

Journalistic conventions and professional practices would need to change to allow this different style of news production. Objectivity would be replaced by the practice of presenting multiple perspectives and avoiding clear hierarchies. There would no longer be a need to disguise the selection and editing processes. According to Fiske, journalists 'should open them up to reveal news as a production, not as transparent reportage'.

Instead of aiming to present the 'true facts', popular news would emphasise contradictions, with narratives left open and unresolved so that news could be not 'these things happened today', but 'we are in the middle of these events'. Popular news should not aim to preach or teach, but to encourage viewers to make their own interpretations. As Fiske says:

> ❦ *Far from wishing to improve its objectivity, its depth or its authority, I would wish to increase its openness, its contradictions, the multiplicity of its voices and points of view.* ❦

▶◀ *See Activities 3 and 4, page 107*

News in print

When studying news in print, you should be aware of:
- conventions which journalists tend to use
- presentational techniques, which vary according to the type of audience a publication is aimed at.

Thus the use of headlines to label stories is universal; but jokey, monosyllabic headlines such as 'CROSS CHRIS QUITS' are characteristic of tabloids such as the *Sun*, from which this was taken. Similarly all newspapers use photographs to illustrate stories, but only some will use pictures of near-naked women in 'sexy' poses.

The following sections explore some of the conventions which are widely used in newspapers.

Brevity

Journalists are trained to keep their writing brief and to the point: their motto is 'kiss (Keep It Short and Simple) and tell'. Sentences in news stories are seldom longer than 35 words, and in tabloid newspapers and many local papers they are even shorter. Long subordinate clauses are avoided.

The reason for this and many other conventions is that newspaper readers have a short concentration span. Newspapers are designed to be read quickly and discarded, not pored over like a textbook.

In turn, paragraphs are kept short because newspapers are printed in columns with small type. Long paragraphs would be too daunting for the reader, especially a reader in a hurry. Lead paragraphs in news stories almost always tell the essence of the story as succinctly as possible. Again, this is to help readers identify quickly whether or not the story interests them. Headlines perform the same function.

Structure

Journalists are trained to think of five Ws when presenting a story:
- Who?
- What?
- Why?
- When?
- Where?

Often, all five Ws are given in the lead paragraph of a story. For example:

> ❝ *A young woman teacher from Cheshire was jailed yesterday for sending filthy notes to an 11-year-old boy in her class.* ❞

This has two whos (teacher and pupil), a what (teacher jailed), a why (for sending filthy notes), a when (yesterday) and a where (Cheshire).

The 5W formula can, of course, be used throughout a story. For example:

- the reader might want to know a little more about **who** was concerned, or about other people such as the boy's parents
- more information about **what** happened could be supplied (e.g. details about the content of the notes)
- the **where** could be more precise (e.g. the name of the school where the incident happened)
- the audience might want to know **when** the teacher will be released
- most interesting of all would be to find out **why** such bizarre behaviour occurred.

The *who* is important as stories are 'hung on people': journalists avoid abstractions and concentrate on people. This tendency becomes more marked the more popular the paper. Thus a story in the *Mirror* about an anti-European movement in Britain begins: 'Tories loyal to Michael Howard are spearheading grassroots demands for a nationwide vote on Britain's role in Europe.'

The *when* is important because news has to have a sense of urgency: the more recent the story the better. A 'today' is good; a 'yesterday' is acceptable; a 'last week' means the story is probably dead.

Popular papers tend to heighten the emotional appeal of stories by adding adjectives and adverbs. In the teacher story mentioned above, we find 'perverted Angela...' whose notes were 'disgusting and evil' and whose husband shouted 'angrily' and 'sobbed uncontrollably'. There are often strong value judgements implied in journalism of this sort.

Quotations

Journalists are encouraged to 'add life' to their writing by using quotations, and this is how accessed voices (see page 99) are introduced into newspaper stories.

Quotations are usually turned into standard English, and are hardly ever strictly verbatim. For example:

- fillers (such as 'erm', 'sort of', 'like' and other sounds, words or phrases which fill gaps in spoken English) are usually missed out
- swear words are indicated by asterisks
- grammatical mistakes are corrected.

Conversational words are included to give authenticity where appropriate, but the convention is to tidy things up and formalise them.

The following extract from a story about '*Eastenders* Romeo Howard Antony' printed in the *Mirror* is typical of tabloid style.

> Only his dad's beatings stopped him getting into serious trouble.
>
> He revealed: "A lot of my friends' parents were villains doing time.
>
> "When I was about 11 or 12 my mates encouraged me to nick a bike. The best thing that ever happened to me was getting caught.
>
> "I was riding home after stealing it when I was stopped by the police.
>
> "The father of the kid who owned the bike was sitting in the police car. I heard him saying he wouldn't press charges.
>
> "He said he realised I probably took it because I didn't have a bike of my own.
>
> "When the police told my father what had happened, he gave me the biggest thrashing of my life."
>
> *Mirror*, 4 January 1997

Figure 8.3 A typical tabloid news style

Attribution

It is a journalistic convention for opinions to be attributed (for it to be made clear whose opinions are being given). For example:

> ❝ *Between £200 million and £1 billion would be saved if the decision on building a nuclear waste depository at Sellafield were deferred for ten years, according to an independent report by the science policy research unit at Sussex University.* ❞
> *Observer*, 1997

This convention is particularly important when reporting on court cases, when newspapers are not allowed to present opinions.

As a thinking newspaper reader, you need to be alert to *unattributed* opinions which appear to carry authority or seem to be expressing a 'common sense' reaction. Words and phrases such as 'the shock findings', 'the so-called', 'astonishing' and 'staggering' are used to interpret facts for the reader.

 *See Activity 5, page 107*

Headlines

Headlines are used to attract attention to a story or give it a label. They are in larger type than the story they accompany, and may also be in a different type style.

Individual newspapers have their own headline styles, but in general:

- popular newspapers opt for much bigger headlines in proportion to the size of the page than the quality press
- headlines in the popular press are usually more startling and sensational. For example on the day that the *Sun*'s 'CROSS CHRIS QUITS' headline appeared, the *Guardian* had 'No-show Evans works his Radio 1 ticket amicably' alongside a typically quiet but informative 'Bank governor calls for rate rise'

- journalists working on popular newspapers tend to have more fun with their headlines, for example 'PADDY PANTSDOWN' (*Sun*), 'FREDDY STARR ATE MY HAMSTER' (*Sun*), later parodied in 'FREDDY STARR ATE MY LUNCHBOX' (*Star*)
- popular newspapers have a preference for monosyllabic headlines such as 'MISS FILTH' (*Mirror*) and 'CROC BITES OFF HAND THAT FED IT' (*Mail*). This may be because they can be printed in very large fonts
- there is a trend in the popular press towards using nicknames, alliteration, assonance, puns and invented words, for example 'GAZZA'S SHEZZA HAZZA BRAND NEW BRAZZA' (*Sun*) and 'BALDIE ARNIE'S ERAZOR-SHARP HAIRCUT' (*Sun*).

▶◀ *See Activities 6 and 7, page 108*

Still pictures

All modern newspapers make use of pictures to illustrate stories and give them authenticity. As Roland Barthes says in *Mythologies*, 'pictures are more imperative than writing, they impose meaning at one stroke, without analysing or diluting it.' Sometimes a picture is a story in itself, perhaps needing just a single caption to add essential information (see Figure 8.4).

In his essay 'The Determination of News Photographs' (in Cohen and Young, 1981), Stuart Hall argues that news photographs appear as 'the facts', speaking for themselves and representing the 'having-been-there'. However, he goes on to point out that although pictures seem to guarantee objectivity, the selection of a picture is a highly ideological procedure.

According to Hall, every press photograph has two levels of meaning. One is the 'news value level', where the picture plus text are selected according to professional criteria of what constitutes news. So on this level, the picture in Figure 8.5 was chosen because of its topicality, as the government had just

Held by hooks through his flesh, a Hindu devotee hangs from a pole during a religious procession in India's southern city of Madras. Hundreds endure similar hardships each year, believing they will win favour with the god Murugan and have their wishes fulfilled

Figure 8.4

announced a replacement for the royal yacht *Britannia* at a cost to the taxpayer of £60 million.

The second level of meaning is an ideological one. This is governed by the newspaper's policy, political orientation, presentational values, tradition and self-image. On this second level, the picture of *Britannia* depends for its ideological meaning on the 'token force' of just four people waving to the yacht, a meaning which is emphasised by the headline and caption. This interpretation fits with the *Guardian*'s tendency towards iconoclasm and its lack of reverence for the power and symbolism of the monarchy.

As this suggests, you should be able to determine something about a newspaper's ideology simply by studying its choice of pictures and captions over a number of weeks.

▶◀ *See Activity 8, page 110*

Symbol of a nation's pride?

A token force of well-wishers waves from the shore as the royal yacht Britannia sails out of Portsmouth harbour on the seven-month overseas tour that will be her last before the vessel is decommissioned

Figure 8.5

Newspaper picture desks have modified pictures for many years, for example brightening the sky, taking out intrusive objects, and adding a football to a picture of a striker's shot. However, the advent of computers has made this doctoring process much easier and more effective. Today we can have manipulated images of Paul Gascoigne 'kissing' Princess Diana at her wedding, of Pamela Anderson apparently embracing the Archbishop of Canterbury, of John Prescott's bottle of beer being digitally disappeared and replaced with a bottle of champagne to show that he is a 'champagne socialist'. Such practice can be dangerous, and not all newspapers will use this type of trick editing. The National Union of Journalists is campaigning (1997) to have a mandatory symbol on all photos that have been manipulated.

Figure 8.6 Photographs can be manipulated to produce striking effects, but there are calls for regulation to prevent harmful trick editing

Radio news

Radio news is similar to TV news in the way that it gives emphasis to particular stories. A newspaper can indicate the importance which editorial staff attach to a story by its positioning, the amount of space it is allocated and the size of a headline. However, broadcast news can only use positioning and time to do the same job. It would be possible for a newsreader to mimic the size of headlines in a paper by increasing the volume of his or her voice, but this is not done in practice. A newspaper's audience has more choice in terms of which stories to read and in what order. TV and radio audiences must wait to find out what story comes next.

The following section explores some of the presentational variables found in radio news.

Context

The introduction of a radio news programme gives the listener some idea of the style of presentation to follow. Radio 4 headlines read between the chimes of Big Ben give the impression that the transmission comes from the centre of political power in the UK and carries authority, suggesting that the listener is in for some serious newscasting. On the other hand, a short, snappy introduction with a station jingle on a predominantly music station suggests that news will be pacey, brief and easy to follow, without analysis and gravity.

Voices

Accessed voices in radio news are sometimes quoted, but are more effective when recorded and played as part of a script. The aim is to produce credibility and to 'bring the story alive'.

The institutional voices (newsreaders and reporters) are chosen to appeal to the radio station's target audience. As with TV news, the aim of having institutional voices is to give news objectivity and authority, an illusion of 'this is the truth'.

The more upmarket the news programme, the more likely it is to favour readers and reporters who use 'received pronunciation' or 'BBC English', which is really the accent of middle-class people from the south of England. The style of delivery in such programmes tends to be calmly authoritative. In the early days of radio, newsreaders were not only expected to have impeccably 'proper' accents, but were also expected to dress formally while reading the news.

Middle market news programmes, on Radio 5 for instance, tend to include some 'provincial' regional accents, as long as they are not too strong. The delivery is often more relaxed and conversational.

News on programmes aimed at young people tends to be read by younger announcers with a more animated delivery. Newsreaders on this kind of programme tend to be trained to read 'as if they are talking to a friend'.

Figure 8.7 Reading the news on radio

Background noise

Reporters presenting 'live' reports, which are usually pre-recorded and edited, will use different styles of background noise to add atmosphere. The reporter may also add some descriptive words if the sounds alone are not descriptive enough.

▶◀ *See Activity 9, page 110*

Impartiality

> 6 *There is no fundamentally non-ideological, apolitical, non-partisan news gathering and reporting system.* 9
> Gerbner, 1964

The issues of bias, partiality and fairness are central to all discussions of news.

There are some levels of information-giving which must be impartial: some information can never be biased. For example, you might have a biased report of a football match, but you would not expect a biased result. Beyond basic facts and evidence, however, news soon becomes storytelling characterised by selection and interpretation.

The BBC is obliged by its Royal Charter to 'refrain from... expressing the opinion of the Corporation on current affairs or matters of public policy'. However, the press, without such restraint, is able to express opinions freely. Newspapers have to appeal to their readers, who may well *want* biased opinion. People tend to buy newspapers which reflect and reinforce their own opinions rather than those which challenge their views.

Complaints about bias

Complaints about bias on television news come from a variety of sources. After analysing TV news over a period of time, the Glasgow University Media Group found that it systematically favours socially dominant groups, tends to favour the right of the political spectrum, and tends to support management rather than workers in industrial disputes.

In some cases this bias is expressed through selection; for example choosing to highlight trade union stories only if they involve strikes. Union behaviour tends to be portrayed as irrational and unmotivated, and reporters' language tends to be biased against workers. Strikes are portrayed as the 'workers' strikes', suggesting that the workers have caused them. Terms such as 'demand', 'threaten' and 'reject' are used to describe workers' actions, whereas softer words such as 'offer' and 'promise' are used to describe management actions. The Glasgow University Media Group also argues that interviewers are more likely to adopt hostile attitudes when interviewing workers, and that even the choice of locations for interviews can be biased. Workers tend to be interviewed in streets and managers in offices, with implied contrasts of disorder and order. The Group claims that this bias is not an organised conspiracy against a certain class of people, but that it is the result of unconscious professional practices and the class background of television journalists and producers.

Detection of bias does not just come from the left of the political spectrum. The BBC has long been criticised for being too left-wing by some newspapers and Conservative politicians. During the Falklands Conflict of 1982 it was criticised for lacking patriotism and sometimes giving the impression of being pro-Argentinian. The director general of the BBC was summoned to the House of Commons, along with the chairman, to face the media committee of the Conservative party, where he was accused of being a traitor.

He vigorously denied this charge and refused to change BBC policy, maintaining that: 'We have no sense of guilt or failure.' Senior Conservative politician Sally Oppenheimer's view (quoted in Cokrell, Hennessy and Walker, 1984) was different:

> 6 *I know how strongly many people feel that the case for our country is not being put with sufficient vigour on certain – I do not say all – BBC programmes. The chairman of the BBC has assured us, and has said in vigorous terms, that the BBC is not neutral on this point, and I hope his words will be heeded by the many who have responsibilities for standing up for our task force, our boys, our people and the cause of democracy.* 9

In 1986 Norman Tebbit, the chairman of the Conservative Party, produced a critical analysis of BBC news coverage of the bombing of Libya by American forces (supported by Prime Minister Margaret Thatcher). He criticised the BBC for not being enthusiastic enough about America's actions. He wanted more emotive words used to describe terrorist killings; he thought 'murdered' would be more appropriate than 'killed', for instance. It was clear to Tebbit who the villains and heroes were in this story, and he objected to the BBC's detached style of reporting.

In his book *Seeing and Believing*, Greg Philo quotes the following passage which gives an idea of Tebbit's concerns:

> 6 *The BBC then chose a particularly damaging phrase to describe America's response, "in Washington the mood is one of jubilation", which is then sandwiched between phrases such as "children are casualties" and "causing deaths and injuries to men, women and children as they slept in their homes", suggested extreme callousness.*
> *It also devoted far more of the opening paragraph than ITN did to words and phrases designed to arouse anti-American emotion:*
> *"across the world there is great concern", "deaths and injuries to men, women and children as they slept in their homes", "Colonel Gaddafi's own family was hit", "in intensive care with serious injuries".*
> *The point is not whether these statements should be made but whether they should be given such prominence in the first, "audience conditioning" part of the report.* 9
> Conservative Central Office, 1986

Philo expresses concern that this Conservative critique is based on the notion that news should support particular interests. He sees this as a threat to the BBC's belief in fairness, balance and the expression of basic human values.

Can news be too impartial?

Veteran war reporter Martin Bell did not see the BBC in this light when he threatened to resign in January 1997. He was concerned about the organisation's introduction of 'rolling news' – non-stop news programmes. According to Bell, this meant journalists standing on rooftops doing a series of 'live shots' one after the other, reciting words fed into an earpiece by a producer in London instead of finding out what was happening. 'That is not

Figure 8.8 Martin Bell reporting from the Gulf War in 1991

journalism, that is puppetry', he said. He called for an end to 'bystander's journalism' based on the old tradition of detached, cool and neutral reporting. 'I do not believe we should stand neutrally between good and evil, right and wrong, aggressor and victim. My answer is what I call the journalism of attachment, journalism which cares as well as knows.'

The influence of the news

> 6 From the shelves-ful of research into the effects of the mass media, in particular of television, few firm and generally agreed conclusions can be drawn. This does not mean that there are no effects, only that this kind of effects analysis is in its infancy. 9
> Hoggart, 1995

To what extent is the public influenced by the messages it receives through mass media news? If we accept Hoggart's view, this is an area ripe for exploration, and there is much work that today's students can do. However, although it is fairly straightforward to analyse news output, to move on to making assumptions about the audience's understanding of that output poses many problems.

Researching effects

Research into the 1985–6 miners' strike concluded that television news did not set the agenda for the viewing public (Cumberbatch, 1986). For instance, their content analysis showed that the topic of 'talks and negotiations' was most widely covered by TV news, whereas pit closures came top of the public's list of important topics. However, their report has been criticised for oversimplified categories of topics and for 'removing words from the context in which they are

understood' (Philo, 1990). There were differences between the categories measured by the researchers and what the news actually meant, both to those who produced it and those who watched it. The problem here, as with much research, is that statistical summaries disguise shades of meaning. You may count the number of times a word or phrase is used in a news programme, but you cannot measure what it conveys or how it is understood.

Some research has seemed to indicate that television and radio news has limited influence on its audience:

> 6 People seem to be failing to grasp much of what it has been assumed is getting across... My colleagues and I found, in work supported by the IBA, that knowledgeable, well motivated grammar school sixth formers retained little more than 60% of the detailed news information they were tested on minutes after viewing. 9
> Colin Berry, 1986

However, the type of information the audience was tested on in this research has been questioned. It may be true that people cannot remember details such as times, dates and place names, but if they had been tested on their understanding of themes, would the results have been different? Philo argues that his own research indicates that they would. He believes that 'we might be better off employing methodology which illustrates the explanatory frameworks of the news and how audiences relate to these, rather than simply noting the percentage of information which is forgotten'. Philo also suggests that how much the audience remembers might depend on how interested it is in the news items.

You could carry out your own investigation to see whose viewpoint your findings agree with.

Does social group affect understanding?

Some research has focused on whether there is a relationship between viewers' social group and their understanding of what they see in the news. In *The Nationwide Audience*, David Morley analysed audience responses to the news and current affairs programme *Nationwide*. He wanted to know whether differences in class and social experience made people interpret a programme differently. To do this, he needed to analyse not only the programme, but also the uses which people made of it. Morley believed that people's ability to make meaning out of what they experience is influenced by the kinds of questions they ask and do not ask. He was interested in how far the intended meanings of the programme coincided with the meanings and definitions the audience were familiar with. The degree of fit between the two determines how easily a programme is accepted or rejected by the viewer. He suggested three categories of interpretation or 'decoding': dominant, negotiated and oppositional (for more on this, see chapter 4).

This concept is important whenever you analyse news products or think about your own response to them. Try to become more aware of the levels of acceptance and rejection of messages, and determine what it is about the cultural and social background of the receiver of the messages that determines these levels.

Reception studies

As Masterman says in his book *Teaching the Media*: 'Teachers and students alike will need to widen their examination of media texts to include analysis of the sense which is made of them by their audiences.'

This interest in how people interpret media messages in the context of their everyday lives is called 'reception studies'. This was the focus of research carried out by Jensen, who recorded in-depth individual and small group interviews both before and after programme transmissions. After analysing 600 single-spaced pages of transcript, he concluded that:

- people do make different sense of the same programme
- their interpretations are socially patterned – they are not just individual differences
- the social interpretations do not differ in the traditional categories of social class, but in terms of subcultures
- meaning is not final and stable, but is an ongoing process: 'this is what I understand it to mean at present, but I'm still thinking about it'.

This suggests that TV news is polysemic – that is, it offers an array of possible readings.

▶◀   *See Activity 10, page 110*

ACTIVITIES ▼

Activity 1

How far do the news media emphasise a supposed decline of standards and values, especially among the young? As a group, collect examples of stories about young people from news broadcasts and newspapers. You could assign one programme or paper to each person in the group, trying to cover a range of news styles and genres.

Once you have collected the material, classify it under the following topics:

- standards in schools
- youth social behaviour (e.g. in public places, manners, attitudes to older people)
- youth crime
- sexual promiscuity among the young
- young people and drugs.

Consider the *amount of coverage* of these issues relative to total news output, and make comparisons within and between news forms and genres (e.g. television news and newspaper news, local radio and national radio, news aimed at very different audiences such as *Channel 4 News* and the *News of the World*).

Discuss any evidence of *presentational bias* towards a particular editorial interpretation of the events. In particular, consider emotive language, the use of captions to interpret images and the treatment of accessed voices.

After research and discussion, write an essay based on the statement:

'Contemporary news media misrepresent young people, portraying them as problems and therefore encouraging confrontational attitudes and a sense of social decline. Having created a sense of unease, the media then 'identify' the causes of the problem, which are often political (loony left/repressive right) or social (soft treatment of criminals/poverty).'

How far do you agree with this analysis? In your answer refer to specific examples covering both broadcast and print news.

Activity 2

Discuss Walter Cronkite's assertion that television news is an inadequate substitute for a good newspaper. Write about the relative strengths and weaknesses of print news and televised news.

Activity 3

Write two stories for a television news programme based on real or imaginary events. One should be a happy story, and the other a tragic one. Your two stories should last exactly 90 seconds when you read them. Now, without practice, have somebody video your news 'broadcast'. View your recording and determine what you need to do to make your presentation more 'professional'. Consider whether you were able to look at the camera while reading your news, whether you filled your time slot precisely, whether you varied your tone of delivery between the stories, whether your speech was clear and audible, and whether the 'set' was appropriate. Now practise for another timed recording, and try to implement any improvements.

Activity 4

'Far from wishing to improve its objectivity, its depth or its authority, I would wish to increase its openness, its contradictions, the multiplicity of its voices and points of view.' Fiske, 1989.

Record a television news programme. Discuss in your group how you would modify the presentation of that news to achieve the style suggested by Fiske in the quotation.

Produce a storyboard which shows in detail the way one story would be presented on screen using your alternative style.

Activity 5

Make a collection of unattributed opinions from news stories, either broadcast or in print. Try using the technique to subvert other stories; for example, 'The so-called Prime Minister, in an emotional outburst in the Commons today, made the staggering claim that his party was the party of low taxation!!!'

Activity 6

Read the following story taken from a *Viz* annual.

What presentational characteristics (language, layout, cultural references) of popular tabloid newspapers are parodied here? Look in particular at:

- typographical style
- the way people are described
- the emphasis on money
- the language used to hint that something improper has been going on
- the liberal use of quotations.

ELTON AND THE GENERAL PURPOSE BUILDER

World Exclusive

A man who has been seen working at the home of millionaire pop star Elton John is a self employed general purpose builder, we can exclusively reveal.

Steve Fairbrother, a stocky 32-year-old, runs his business from a small yard in Guildford, Surrey, not far from Elton's £2.5 million mansion.

YELLOW PAGES

Elton, 44, met Steve after reading an ad in the Yellow Pages. In it Steve described himself as 'Prompt, friendly and reliable'. 'No job too big or too small', the ad continued. It also boasted 'Free Estimates'.

THOMSON LOCAL

Steve has been a regular visitor to the pop millionaire's lavish £6 million luxury home, often seen coming and going in his £4,500 red Escort van – believed to have been paid for using the profits from his building work, some of which has come from Elton.

BONES

The singer, 46, who often wears hats, makes no bones about his relationship with the handy man. 'It's true, I've employed him to do some plastering, to build a fireplace and tile the bathroom. He's a reliable tradesman, and his prices are competitive,' he confided to friends recently. And people close to the billionaire singer say that Elton is 'delighted' with the work that has been done.

In the past few months Fairbrother is believed to have:

- **PLUMBED** in a sink in Elton's lavish £80,000 utility room.
- **REPOINTED** a chimney stack above the south facing gable of the star's £12 million farmhouse.
- **BUILT** a small retaining wall around flowerbeds outside the star's lavish £40,000 kitchen window.

SCOTTY

Neighbours living close to the multi-billionaire's £14 million hideaway describe Fairbrother as 'quiet'. 'He regularly comes and goes bringing plaster, lengths of wood and tools. Sometimes he has a ladder on the top of his van,' one neighbour told us.

UHURU

When we rang Tewson's Builders Supplies of Guildford, a spokesman confirmed that Fairbrother had an account with them, and revealed that he had collected several lengths of dressed timber from them only last week.

'He ordered them on Monday, and said he wanted them on Wednesday,' we were told. Unfortunately the spokesman could not confirm that this wood was for Elton's mansion. 'I don't know what it is for,' he told us.

WIFE

When we rang Fairbrother's home – a small flat which he shares with his wife – he wasn't in. His wife Shirley, a pretty 24-year-old, offered to take a message. 'My husband's out on a job at the moment,' she said. 'But if you give me your number I can

Elton - paid Steve for home improvements

get him to ring you back when he comes in. Probably after six,' she added.

DIVORCE

Elton, whose short-lived marriage to Brazilian beauty Renata Blauel ended in divorce, has admitted to friends that he is concerned about hair loss on the top of his head.

The Pan Handle,
Viz annual, 1994

Activity 7

The following two articles – 'Health staff face widespread attacks surveys reveal' and 'ANGELS IN PERIL' – are two very different treatments of the same source material.

- Compare the two stories in terms of their presentational values.
- What was the source of the story?
- What techniques has the *Sun* used to make the basic story more appealing to its readers?
- How far do you think that the *Sun*'s approach has trivialised and distorted the story? Or has it made the story more relevant and meaningful to its audience?

Health staff face widespread attacks surveys reveal

By Nicholas Timmins
Health and Social Services
Correspondent

EVERY YEAR one in 200 health service staff is likely to suffer an assault requiring hospital treatment or admission, and one in 10 is likely to suffer a minor injury, a survey by the Health and Safety Commission shows.

Staff in accident and emergency departments are known to face a high risk of assault. But Pat Woodcock, chairman of the health services advisory committee, said yesterday that attacks, verbal abuse and threats with weapons are more widespread throughout hospitals than is generally thought.

He told a conference on hospital security in London that the survey of 600 staff in five health authorities had shown that in the previous twelve months one in four of those working in mental illness facilities had suffered minor injuries requiring first aid. The figure was one in five in geriatric hospitals and mental handicap units.

Almost five per cent, or one in twenty, of all staff had been threatened with a weapon and more than one in six had been threatened verbally. Of those suffering major injuries – broken bones, being knocked unconscious, deep puncture wounds or cuts requiring stitches – one tenth were admitted to hospital and more than a third had more than three months off work.

'As expected, accident and emergency departments showed high rates of all assault categories from serious injury to verbal abuse. But the returns also showed that experience of violence is widely, if more thinly, spread in other departments,' Mr Woodcock told the conference, organised by the National Association of Health Authorities.

Nurses, including students, and ambulance staff appeared at the highest risk, but doctors and catering and domestic staff also reported attacks and threats.

The commission's figures coincide with a survey of 110 health authorities by the national association which show that a third have seen an increase in violent attacks in the past two to three years. In one case the rise was 47 per cent.

Staff at risk included community nurses visiting patients in their own homes, who had suffered physical intimidation, violence and sexual harassment. The conference was told that in Liverpool health visitors and community nurses had to organise their work so they do not go out alone.

Douglas Hogg, the Home Office minister who chairs a ministerial group on crime prevention, told the conference that the Government will shortly produce a booklet for wide distribution advising women on how to avoid violent attacks. Efforts would be made to ensure that nurses and others at high risk receive copies.

Health authorities are starting to take many more measures to combat violence and to try and stem losses through theft and vandalism, Philip Hunt, director of the national association, said. These included teaching self defence, issuing personal alarms, increasing floodlighting in hospital grounds and installing closed circuit television.

'The dilemma we face is how to improve our security without diverting massive resources from patient care and without creating a fortress-like environment in our hospitals,' he said.

Independent, 14 November 1986

ANGELS IN PERIL

Shock report from the violent front line of our hospitals

Attacks drive
nurses away

One in ten medical workers is attacked badly enough to need treatment every year, according to a shock new official report.

The Government's health and safety executive says victims – many of them teenagers and half the size of their attackers – are threatened with knives, broken bottles and chairs.

Accident and emergency departments are the main targets and student nurses and ambulance men suffer most.

The Royal College of Nursing now holds self-defence classes for its members.

A spokesman said: 'We are extremely alarmed by this report. We knew attacks on nurses were increasing, but not so drastically.'

Violence has now joined low pay, stress and unsocial hours as a reason why 27,000 British nurses –a tenth of the total – leave nursing for good every year

Attacks are not confined to London. All over the country health chiefs are taking emergency action.
■ **BURLY** male nursing auxiliaries have been drafted in as 'minders' to protect nurses in North Warwickshire.
■ **EMERGENCY** panic buttons have been installed at South Birmingham.
■ **PERSONAL ALARMS** have been issued to staff at Wolverhampton.
■ **A BOOKLET,** Violence, Crime and You, is issued to nurses in North Staffordshire.
■ **CLOSED CIRCUIT TV** identifies troublemakers at Sandwell, Staffs.

Dr Vera Dallos, consultant at the Emergency department of Whipps Cross Hospital, East London, says:

We've had one nurse who had her jaw broken and another staff member was stabbed.'

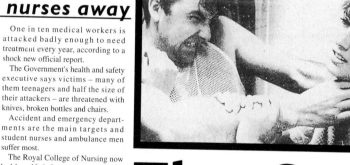

The Sun
sees real Casualty

By Fiona Webster

It was just another week on the night shift in casualty. One nurse was thrown to the ground and kicked by a gang.

Another ducked the swing of a blood soaked drunk. A third had to flee the murderous clutches of a drug addict.

These were not plots in TV's Casualty – they were for real. Caring for the sick can be very bad for your health.

Small wonder that staff nurse Cherry Bowden cannot wait until next month, when she leaves.

For Cherry, a nurse for six years, is one of the front line fighters facing increasing violence in our hospitals.

Angry, argumentative, aggressive patients arrive at casualty wards drunk, drugged and downright dangerous.

And they are putting angels like Cherry through hell.

SCRAPES

Cherry, 25, talking of her week in charge of the accident and emergency ward at London's St Bartholomew's Hospital, mentions the scrapes she has missed rather than the scrapes she has healed.

'The gang fight that turned on me was the worst moment this week,' she says. 'There was a huge bust up in Islington and they brought in the wounded victims.

'I was patching up one bloke with stab wounds and left the room to get some bandages.

'My back was turned for only a minute, but I happened to glance through the glass and saw two of the rival gang had him up against the wall, punching him.

'I tried to pull them off and the next thing I knew I was on the floor, underneath all three being kicked and shoved.

'One of the doctors tried to pull them off and it ended up one massive struggle until, thankfully, security finally arrived.'

It was no isolated incident that week – or any week.

Cherry works with three other nurses, two of them students. Sometimes they see 50 patients a night and half of them may be abusive or violent.

Policemen are as common as stethoscopes on the ward, and there is a hotline link to nearby Snow Hill Police Station for emergencies.

BLUSH

When the pubs turn out, Arthur, a middle-aged drunk, rolls in with a head injury, his clothes smeared with blood, booze and vomit, and lunges at a student nurse.

She manages to dodge the flailing fist. Two others come to her rescue.

It takes all three ten minutes to persuade the man to lie on the trolley. Even then his arms are thrashing and his language would make a merchant seaman blush.

Jamie, a 24-year-old drug addict is brought in suffering from an overdose, cursing every nurse who comes near him. They calm him down a little but they know that in a few hours he'll be fighting mad for a fix.

Nurse Sue Hoerchener has seen it all before.

'One of them tried to strangle me a few weeks ago,' says Sue, 32.

'She was a 20-year-old addict, a regular here, known to be violent, who'd hit nurses before.

'I gave her a bed pan and the next thing I knew she was trying to strangle me.

'I tried to pull her hands away but she just squeezed harder and I couldn't breathe!

'Fortunately, I managed to signal security for help, and one of them came and pulled her off me.'

Sun, 26 November 1986

Activity 8

In discussion with others, analyse the picture above from the point of view of its news value and its ideological meanings. It was taken during a Republic of Ireland v England soccer match which had to be abandoned because of disruptions.

Activity 9

Research and write a 90-second story for local radio based on an event at a local indoor sports venue. Record the story with, then without, background noise. Which version is more effective and why?

Activity 10

Tape or video-record a controversial running news story (one that goes on for a few days) and play the recordings back to a group of four or five people. Ask them to discuss the story and the way it was portrayed by the programme. Let the discussion flow for about an hour, prompting it where necessary with open questions, but staying neutral yourself. Don't let one individual dominate the discussion, as this stops the others from saying what they really think. Record the discussion and see if you can identify examples of preferred, oppositional and negotiated readings. You can take this research further by conducting an in-depth interview with just one of the group to see if his or her opinions change under different circumstances and with more time for reflection.

BIBLIOGRAPHY ▼

Bagnall, N, *Newspaper Language*, Focal Press, 1993

Barthes, R, *Mythologies*, Vintage, 1993

Brown, C, *Learning from Television News*, IBA/NELP, 1986

Cohen, S, and Young, J, *The Manufacture of News*, Constable, 1981

Cockerell, M, Hennessy, P, and Walker, D, *Sources Close to the Prime Minister*, Macmillan, 1984

Cumberbatch, G, *Television and the Miners' Strike*, Broadcasting Research Unit, 1986

Fiske, J, *Reading the Popular*, Routledge, 1989

Fowler, R, *Language in the News*, Routledge, 1991

Gerbner, G, 'Ideological Perspectives and Political Tendencies in News Reporting', in *Journalism Quarterly 41*, 1964

Glasgow University Media Group, *Bad News* and *More Bad News*, Routledge, 1976 and 1980

Goodwin, A, and Whannel, G (eds), *Understanding Television*, Routledge, 1990

Greenslade, R, 'Cut the moral hysteria', in *Media Guardian*, 23 October 1996

Hartley, J, *Understanding News*, Routledge, 1990

Hoggart, R, *The Way We Live Now*, Chatto and Windus, 1995

Jensen, K, *Making Sense of the News*, Aarhus University Press, 1986

Masterman, L, *Teaching about Television*, Macmillan, 1980

Masterman, L, *Teaching the Media*, Routledge, 1985

Morley, D, *Family Television*, Routledge, 1986

Morley, D, *The Nationwide Audience*, BFI Publishing, 1980

Philo, G, *Seeing and Believing*, Routledge, 1990

Snow, J, 'More bad news', in *Guardian*, 27 January 1997

CHAPTER 9

Film fiction: narrative structures and strategies

9

Introduction

This chapter shows you how to analyse the way in which films tell their stories. Film analysis is such a broad topic that it cannot possibly be covered in a single chapter. Rather than attempting to look at every aspect of understanding a film – from commercial influences and the input of professionals to genre characteristics – in this chapter you will focus on storytelling. This involves analysing:

- the stories themselves
- themes
- the use of mystery, suspense and contrast
- cinematic techniques
- the way time is manipulated
- narrators
- settings
- characters
- underlying structure.

The chapter ends with an analysis of *Don't Look Now*, directed by Nicolas Roeg.

Analysing stories

A good place to begin an analysis of a fictional film is by summarising the story. If there is more than one story you will need to show how they interrelate, but do this as succinctly as possible. It can be helpful to use a chart, as Figure 9.1 shows.

You will have to devise different kinds of charts for different films. This process should help you to see each film as a constructed scheme. You can then start asking questions about why stories have been arranged in a particular way, and 'what would happen if...?' For example, what would happen in the *Psycho* story if you started with Norman murdering his mother?

▶◀ *See Activities 1 and 2, page 121*

Looking at themes

Once you have analysed the story, you could think about the film's themes. Although most of the enjoyment in watching a film comes from following or predicting the story, reflective enjoyment can also come from thinking about and discussing the underlying messages or ideas. Some themes may have been intended by the film-maker; others may be discerned by you, the spectator.

For example, director Tim Burton (in Salisbury, 1995) describes some of the intended themes in his film *Edward Scissorhands*:

> ❦ *The idea came from a drawing I did a long time ago... It came subconsciously and was linked to a character who wants to touch but can't, who was both creative and destructive... The manifestation of the image... probably came to the surface when I was a teenager, because it is a very teenage thing. It had to do with relationships. I just felt I couldn't communicate. It was a feeling that your image and how people perceive you are at odds with what's inside you.* ❦

Figure 9.1 Chart showing the narrative structure of Psycho

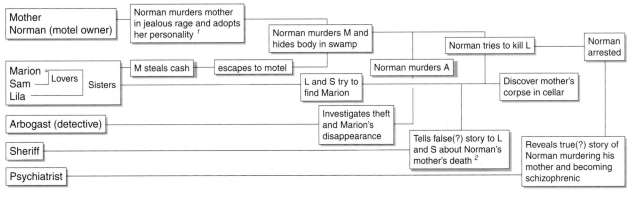

Notes: 1. *This story is revealed only in flashback so as to keep audience in suspense.*
2. *Example of a story within a story - 'embedded narrative'*

Burton goes on to say that the film was also about categorisation; about being taught from an early age to conform. As he explains: 'I remember sitting there as a child, looking at the teacher saying some other kid is stupid, and really he's not stupid, he's much more intelligent than a lot of the others and has a lot more spirit, it's just that he's not conforming to the teacher's image.'

Other people saw themes which Burton did not intend, but which are still there. At the end of the film, when the mob confronts the monster (Edward), critics have drawn parallels with the story of Frankenstein. Others have seen the film as a Beauty and Beast fable. Burton recognises that this is a theme, but says: 'It wasn't something I dwelled on very much. It wasn't the overriding impulse to do the film.'

Analysing mystery, suspense and contrast

Most narratives depend on there being some kind of conflict or disruption, followed by a need for the conflict to be resolved. Effective storytelling involves the use of techniques which keep the reader guessing about the resolution. We are all aware of this, which accounts for the way we do not want to 'spoil the film' by revealing the ending to others who intend seeing it.

Each significant event in a film raises many possibilities of what might happen next, and the audience is in a constant state of anticipation. At the start of *Psycho*, for example, we want to know whether Marion will meet up with her lover, whether she will be found out and caught for stealing money and, when she

Figure 9.2 The 'monsters' from Edward Scissorhands and Frankenstein are both treated as outsiders

You will probably begin by suggesting themes as hypotheses. You can then test these by analysing the details of the film and discussing possible themes as a group.

In the case of *Psycho*, for instance, what does the film say about the nature of schizophrenia? Does it tell us anything about possessiveness? How does it reflect on chance and fate, or crime and punishment? What does it say about sex and cruelty?

You may find that certain questions recur. You could consider questions such as the following with reference to different films:
- What is love, and how is it connected to emotions such as jealousy, obsession, hatred, protectiveness and loyalty?
- What is the nature of evil? How far is it innate and how far is it learned? What is the effect of social environment?
- Who should make and enforce laws, and in what way?
- How do people behave in the struggle for power in relationships?
- How does society adapt and change in the face of calamity?
- Is revenge ever justifiable?
- In what ways, and why, do we fear the unknown?

decides to return it, whether she will be punished in some way. All these unresolved questions suddenly become irrelevant when she is stabbed to death in the shower. The suspense has been interrupted by a shock and we now have a new, more intense puzzle: who has done the murder and why? In this way, the film's suspense is heightened.

But storytelling is also about different levels of intensity, and there is a need for contrast in the story's flow. Film-makers tend to introduce emotional peaks and troughs in the narrative, where dramatic events are followed by moments of comparative calm. However, this is not always the case. Some films, such as *The Fugitive*, try to sustain and intensify the emotional excitement throughout.

Try studying a film's peaks and troughs of excitement by compiling a chart of your own emotional reactions to its events.

▶◀ *See Activity 3, page 121*

The use of cinematic techniques

Telling stories in film is different from telling stories in other forms of media. Film has its own techniques which you need to be aware of and be able to comment on in your analysis. Here are some of the main techniques:

Choice of shot

When analysing a fictional film, you should be aware of the film-maker's choice of shot. This involves considering the following points.

1 Whose point of view is being shown – do you see things from a particular character's viewpoint, or as a detached observer? This can determine how easily the audience identifies with a particular character.

2 The distance of particular shots – from what distance does the camera show things? The choices made can influence the mood and atmosphere of the film. If grand settings are important to the story, as they are in many Westerns, then long shots are important to show landscapes. A film shot mainly in close-ups will give you the feeling that you are getting to know the characters intimately, and can be very claustrophobic. Close-ups can also conceal (e.g. keeping a murderer's identity secret by just showing his or her feet), or reveal (e.g. by focusing on a significant feature of a person's face).

3 The mix of different types of shot or the length of time a particular shot is shown can also be significant. Conventional Hollywood dialogue style involves lots of head and shoulder shots with frequent cutting from speaker to speaker. Often we see each speaker from 'over the shoulder' of the other, giving the unusual experience of seeing something from someone's point of view and at the same time being physically separated from it. Some film-makers prefer to show a couple together without cutting from one to the other. This is presumably because it is more 'realistic', although there is no general agreement that this is the case. A good example of this can be seen in *Secrets and Lies*, in the long scene in the café where the mother 'discovers' her daughter.

4 Different sorts of focus can be used. The camera-person can keep everything in the frame in focus (deep focus, used especially effectively in *Citizen Kane*, for example) or can focus on the foreground, middle ground or background (shallow focus). There is also a choice between soft focus, usually associated with romantic moods, and hard focus, which makes things appear real and authentic.

5 The angle of a shot can be changed. Eye-level shots are the most commonly used. A high-angle shot (looking down on someone) usually makes the subject look vulnerable or unimportant. A low-angle shot (looking up) suggests power.

6 The camera can be moved on tracks, taking it closer to the subject or moving it away, or it can be mounted on a crane and lowered or raised. It can also be strapped to the operator or be hand-held. There is much debate over the effect of these techniques. Some people feel that they enhance realism, while others feel that they detract from the subject and draw the audience's attention to the film-making process instead.

Figure 9.4 By holding both the mother and daughter in shot for a whole scene in Secrets and Lies, Mike Leigh actually intensified the impact of the emotion felt by both characters because the audience had to confront it in the most 'real' way

Figure 9.3 The use of long-distance and close-up shots explores different aspects of character in Citizen Kane

Figure 9.5 This low-angle shot looking up at Clint Eastwood reinforces the power of the character. The shadow hiding his face also creates a sense of darkness in the character that emphasises that he is a figure to be feared

Lighting

There are many choices available to the film-maker in terms of lighting. In Hollywood films, and much current television work, the normal practice is to light scenes thoroughly. This minimises shadows and produces a 'natural' effect, presenting no barriers to the viewer. However, some argue that far from being natural, such lighting is unrealistic.

Using limited lighting can emphasise the contrast between light and shade, and is sometimes used to provide a moody or sinister atmosphere. It can also allow the camera-person to produce some dramatic highlighting effects, such as emphasising a killer's or victim's eyes.

Figure 9.6 Sombre lighting helps to create a classic film noir atmosphere in Farewell My Lovely

Framing

What limitations does the frame of a picture impose? How is the image within a frame composed?

For example, you could consider whether landscapes and location shooting are more effective in wide-screen formats such as Cinemascope and Panavision, or whether the traditional 4:3 ratio of the cinema and television screen is better for intimate conversations.

The film-maker can choose to follow the subject and keep it in frame ('closed form'), or can let the subject move out of the frame and re-enter ('open form'). Open form means that the audience is more aware of the area outside the frame.

The relative size of subjects within the frame may also be significant. A small human figure dominated by a vast landscape could well be meant to emphasise the power of nature and the insignificance of human endeavour. On the other hand, a face which dominates the frame because it is filmed in extreme close-up can be used to heighten emotional impact.

Other framing techniques which may be used include:
* masking part of the frame to change its shape
* splitting the screen to show two or more images at once
* double exposure, which mixes two separate images.

Figure 9.7 The framing of this early shot from Psycho, and in particular the use of the mirror, dramatically highlights the unease of the character and intensifies the sinister atmosphere of the film

Sound

At a simple level, you should be able to comment on how well a film's soundtrack communicates. Bad dubbing of dialogue can be disconcerting, as can poor recording of speech.

Beyond this, you should consider how significant music and sound effects are in terms of creating mood and atmosphere, or even conveying meaning. For instance, the irony of the brass band in *Brassed Off* playing 'Land of Hope and Glory' as their open-topped bus passes the Houses of Parliament is unmistakable; the government having just closed their home town colliery.

Montage

Montage refers to the way different bits of film are joined together. It involves the skill of editing.

As viewers of films, we have become so used to the Hollywood style of editing that it seems natural to us. Notice how often a sequence begins with an 'establishing shot', which tells us where we are (and sometimes more). As James Monaco explains in his book *How to Read a Film*:

> ❛ *Hitchcock was a master of the establishing shot. The opening pan and track of Rear Window, for example, tells us where we are, why we are there, whom we are with, what is going on now, what has happened to get us there, who the other characters of the story are, and even suggests possible ways the story might develop – all effortlessly and quickly and without a spoken word!* ❜

We have also become used to the Hollywood-style editing of dialogue, which involves mixing a master shot with shots from each character's point of view. This makes it seem natural, although in real life we could not possibly listen to a conversation in this way.

Another technique of montage is the jump cut, which is used to compress time. The editor cuts from, say, someone entering a room, to a shot of another character, back to a shot of the first character having crossed the room. This eliminates the action of the character crossing the room.

You should also be aware of the rhythm of editing in techniques such as using progressively shorter alternations of shots as a chase scene comes to its climax.

▶◀ *See Activities 4 and 5, page 121*

Manipulation of time

Events by their nature happen chronologically, but storytellers can change the order of events to make a story more compelling. The film-maker can use a range of techniques to manipulate time:

- Flashforwards can be used to tease the reader about what action is to come. Flashbacks are often used to supply missing information.
- Simultaneous action can be shown by cutting back and forth between separate shots.
- Action can be condensed as a kind of summary of events. For instance, the break-up of a marriage that takes years can be summarised by short clips of significant incidents, with the actors 'ageing' with each successive shot. There is a particularly good example of this in *Citizen Kane*.
- Time can be 'stretched' using slow motion or freeze frame.

You should try to be aware of these techniques, but assessing their effects will depend on individual films. Generally speaking, the fewer time manipulation techniques are used, the less the audience will be aware of the narrator and the more 'natural' the film will seem.

The effect of the narrator

A story's effect is always influenced by the person who is telling it.

In film, there is often an all-seeing but anonymous narrator that the audience is not consciously aware of. A narrator like this, who you might think of as the scriptwriter or director, is outside the story looking in, can show events from different perspectives, and can penetrate into a character's mind.

Alternatively, the narrator can be within the story itself. Narrators within plots are found in many film noirs, especially those based on the novels of Raymond Chandler. Notable among these are *Farewell My Lovely*, in which the narrator is the world-weary detective Marlowe (portrayed by Robert Mitchum in the 1975 version of the tale), and *Double Indemnity*, scripted by Chandler but based on James M Cain's hard-boiled classic, in which the narrator is dying insurance salesman Walter Neff (Fred MacMurray) who has been caught out by his own greed and his lust for femme fatale par excellence Phyllis Dietrichson (Barbara Stanwyck). Narrators like these are less knowledgeable and powerful than the omniscient narrator, but their stories can be more emotional and personal.

Unreliable narrators can be found in films as varied as *Little Big Man* and *Sunset Boulevard*. In the former, Dustin Hoffman plays a compulsive liar who may or may not have been present at some of the great moments in American history. In the latter, the narrator is looking back on events from beyond the grave: the opening shows William Holden's character dead in a swimming pool.

A narrator's story may be coloured by the distance in time between the event and the telling, becoming more nostalgic and reflective with distance, and more urgent and immediate with proximity.

The effect of settings

In order to analyse the effect of setting on a film's plot, you need to consider its geographical or physical location, and its social setting.

Geographical location

When looking at a film's geographical setting, you should ask questions such as:

- Is the film urban? If it is, what type of city is the film's backdrop? Is it a specific place? Compare the use of Los Angeles in *Heat* or *Swingers* with the representation of Las Vegas in *Leaving Las Vegas* or *Casino*; or compare the London of *The Long Good Friday* with the Sheffield of *The Full Monty*.
- Is the place real? Gotham in the *Batman* movies is a famous example of a city which does not exist. Tim Burton explains how it was designed: 'For Gotham City we looked at pictures of New York. *Blade Runner* had come out and any time there's a movie like that, that's such a trend setter, you're in danger. We had said early on that any city we were going to do was going to get the inevitable *Blade Runner* comparison... We decided to darken everything

and build vertically and cram things together and then just go further with it in a more cartoon way. It has an operatic quality to it and an almost timeless quality... Every time I do anything I start with the character. Batman's character likes the dark and wants to remain in the shadows, so it's a city at night without many day scenes.' (Salisbury, 1995)

- Do specific buildings play a key part? These might be haunted houses or hotels (as in *The Haunting* and *The Shining*), decaying mansions (as in *Rebecca* and *Mandingo*), apartments (as in *Someone to Watch Over Me* and *The Apartment*), or famous landmarks (as in *Sleepless in Seattle* and *King Kong*). The decaying attic in a gothic castle in *Edward Scissorhands* was designed by the director to show not only

isolation, but also a reaction to the pastel-coloured boxes of the suburban houses, which are 'like being inside a shoe box'.

- If the setting is not urban, what use is made of natural landscape? Is the non-urban represented as a threat (as in *Anaconda* and *The Evil Dead*)? As wilderness (as in *Mad Max* and *Waterworld*)? As community (as in *To Kill a Mocking Bird* and *Mississippi Burning*)? As the indicator or backdrop for romance (as in *The English Patient* and *Map of the Human Heart*)? Or as space to be conquered (as in many Westerns, and *1492: Conquest of Paradise*)?

◀◀ *See Activity 6, page 121*

Figure 9.8 How do the cartoon character of the set for Gotham City in Batman and the looming presence of the Bates Motel in Psycho influence the atmosphere of the two films?

Social setting

As well as looking at a film's geographical location, you can examine its social milieu and how this is portrayed.

Good examples of films which explore different social settings include:

- the adaptations of the novels of Jane Austen, which portray a certain English upper-class lifestyle at the beginning of the nineteenth century
- the films of American director Spike Lee, such as *Do The Right Thing* and *Clockers*, which portray the multicultural underclasses
- British films such as *Kes* and *The Full Monty*, which explore working-class lifestyle, along with Mike Leigh's *Secrets and Lies* and *Naked*
- unusual American takes on the subject of class, such as Whit Stilman's subtle comedy of manners *Metropolitan*, Scorsese's visually dazzling *Age of Innocence*, and the amusing *Clueless*, which was inspired by Jane Austen's novel *Emma*.

Social milieu can also be explored through the portrayal of social groups, with narratives influenced by characters' jobs and the world of work. The characters of cops, teachers, lawyers, soldiers, secret agents and even criminals bring with them a setting which affects the outcomes of the stories their films tell.

You should also recognise that settings are temporal: films can chronicle stories which unfold over days, months, years or even centuries. A famous example of the latter is the moment in Stanley Kubrick's science fiction masterpiece *2001: A Space Odyssey* when he audaciously cuts from a bone sent hurtling into the air by an ape at the dawn of man, to a spaceship orbiting thousands of years later.

Analysing characters

There are two key aspects to bear in mind when analysing the characters in a film:

- the actors playing the parts
- the characters themselves.

An actor's influence

Each actor brings with him or her a history with which the audience may be familiar.

Different stars come from different backgrounds: when we watch Mel Gibson in *Braveheart*, for example, we cannot overlook the fact that the same actor appeared in the *Mad Max* films, as *Hamlet* and, of course, as a loose cannon cop in the *Lethal Weapon* series. Mel Gibson is undeniably leading-man material with a slightly manic edge.

Tim Burton had the opportunity to have Tom Cruise in the leading part in *Edward Scissorhands*, which would have made commercial sense. Instead he chose Johnny Depp. Burton liked his eyes, which is important in a character who doesn't say much, and he also thought that the actor had a lot of the character in him: 'I felt very lucky to have Johnny because he brought to it a lot of themes that are nearer his life, which, when I started talking to him, I liked very much.'

▶◀ *See Activities 7 and 8, pages 121 and 122*

A character's role

Having considered the actors chosen for particular parts, you should analyse the characters themselves.

What function does each character perform? For example, is he or she:

- a hero or villain?
- an initiator of events or a victim of events?
- a helper/assistant or an opponent?
- a rebel or a conformer?
- a law-breaker or a law-enforcer?
- a bringer of comic relief?

Figure 9.9 The same story but set in different centuries and social milieaux – Emma and Clueless

Figure 9.10 Clint Eastwood is the mysterious stranger who comes to town in Pale Rider – a classic character in Westerns

Certain roles are associated with particular genres, such as the mysterious stranger in a Western, the femme fatale in film noir, or the bent copper in crime films.

Other questions to think about include:

- How does the character develop?
- How is the character defined in relation to other people?
- Is the character a major or minor player in the narrative?
- What motivates the character – why does he or she act in a particular way?
- Is the character complex or uncomplicated?

Analysing underlying structure

Critics have devoted much time and thought to trying to discover underlying structures in stories. Some theorists have argued that all stories are governed by a set of unwritten rules and have tried to specify these, although no single format has gained general acceptance.

Vladimir Propp studied Russian fairy tales and identified 31 functions such as 'the villain attempts to deceive his victim in order to take possession of him or his belongings', and 7 types of character (hero, villain, donor, dispatcher, false hero, helper, princess and her father). Many critics have found it illuminating to try to apply these categories to film and television analysis.

Gustav Freytag, a German playwright, saw plays as having a pattern of exposition describing a state of affairs, a rise of tension through various complications to a climax, followed by a resolution of crises and a new state of affairs.

The Classic Five Part Narrative and *Unforgiven*

Critic Robert McKee finds what he calls the Classic Five Part Narrative Theory useful in his analysis of films. The five parts are:

- inciting incident
- progressive complications
- crisis
- climax
- resolution.

The following sections show how this theory can be applied to *Unforgiven*.

Inciting incident

A prostitute in the town of Big Whiskey is mutilated by a cowboy customer. The town's sheriff, Little Bill (Gene Hackman), deals out light punishment to the cowboy and his companion. The prostitutes are appalled at this lack of justice and club together to offer a reward to anyone who kills the two men.

Complications

A short-sighted bounty hunter calling himself the Schofield Kid tries to recruit William Munny (Clint Eastwood) to help him carry out the revenge killing. Munny has been reformed by his deceased wife. He was once a drunkard and a ruthless killer, but he now tries to run a pig farm and look after his two children.

Munny is tempted by the reward and follows the Schofield Kid, persuading his friend Ned Logan to help him.

Meanwhile English Bob comes to Big Whiskey to carry out the revenge killings but is prevented by Little Bill who beats him up savagely, revealing a disturbingly sadistic streak which sits uneasily with the other side of his character – the self-reliant citizen who is building his own house with a porch where he can sit in the evenings and watch the sunset.

Munny receives similarly sadistic treatment when he arrives in Big Whiskey and it takes him three days to recover from his injuries, inflicted by Little Bill. He is nursed by the prostitute who had been mutilated.

Munny, Logan and the Schofield Kid try to carry out the assassinations. Logan freezes and decides to return home and take no further part in the venture. The Kid is too short sighted to do much, so it is left to Munny to kill one of the men.

The Kid later kills the second cowboy and he and Munny escape to await the payment of their reward.

Crisis

Logan is captured and taken to Big Whiskey, where he is beaten and tortured to death by Little Bill. His body is displayed in the main street with a warning that this is what happens to assassins.

Climax

Munny now decides that he must avenge his partner's death. He has been troubled all along by his conscience, but now he returns to being the kind of man he was before his wife reformed him. He goes to the town and confronts Little Bill in a bar-room shoot out. His former shooting skills seem to have returned, and he kills five men while remaining unscathed.

Resolution

By becoming ruthless and wicked again, Munny has been able to gain revenge for the way the prostitute was treated and has 'cleaned up' the town by ridding it of a sadistic sheriff whose dying words are: 'I don't deserve to die like this... I was building a house.' The ending brings a catharsis, but also leaves us feeling uneasy because the hero on the white horse has had to

use violence to combat violence, and rides into the blackness with the threat: 'Bury Ned and don't cut up no whores, or else...'

Or perhaps the resolution is what follows briefly when credits tell us that Munny became just an 'ordinary feller' again, and looked after his kids and ran a respectable business on the west coast of America.

Figure 9.11 Unforgiven – a classic five part narrative

DON'T LOOK NOW

The 1973 psychological thriller/horror film *Don't Look Now*, directed by the respected British film-maker Nicolas Roeg and starring Donald Sutherland and Julie Christie, is a well-documented film text which can be used to illustrate some of the points made in this chapter.

Taken from a short story by Daphne du Maurier – whose other film adaptations include Alfred Hitchcock's *Jamaica Inn*, *Rebecca* and *The Birds* – *Don't Look Now* tells the haunting and deeply affecting tale of a couple who lose their young daughter in a drowning accident and go to Venice to attempt to come to terms with their grief. Once there the husband begins to have visions of his dead daughter, and his wife is told by two weird sisters (played by Hilary Mason and Clelia Matania) that the husband's life is in danger. It all ends terribly in one of the cinema's most shocking moments.

This synopsis does not do justice to the profound effect of the film, as, of course, no synopsis could.

A story is simply a structure upon which a film-maker hangs the thematic and intellectual concerns of the movie.

In *Don't Look Now*, director Roeg, his screenwriters Allan Scott and Chris Bryant, his actors, his editor Graeme Clifford, his director of photography Anthony Richmond and his composer Pino D'Onaggio, have all worked together to create a film which has the power to remain with you long after you have first seen it; which sustains repeated viewings and which never fully gives up its secrets.

It is a film which explores beautifully the effects of location upon individuals. Out of season Venice is a major character in the film and is shot with an eye for the locale's decaying grandeur. It delicately presents totally believable and fully rounded characters and their relationship to us.

Figure 9.12 Donald Sutherland and Julie Christie in Don't Look Now

Don't Look Now challenges its audience to think about issues such as the nature of time (in its editing, the film is a piece of technical virtuosity), love, loss (this is a film which deals with bereavement, one of the hardest emotions to bear) and the supernatural (dealt with here in a way which makes many other discussions of the subject appear rather trite).

As novelist Leslie Dick observes in his essay 'Desperation and Desire' in the January 1997 edition of *Sight and Sound* (which also gave away a free copy of the film's screenplay):

> ❛ *The film is about… loss, about the ways a marriage might survive such a terrible blow, or not, and about the compelling power of the wish to have the lost child again, to make contact, to hold her in your arms once more. It's about desperation, and the crazed persistence, against all reason of desire.* ❜

Which, of course, might suggest that for a viewer reared on post-1980s horror films, for whom the genre is linked with *Halloween*, Wes Craven, low-budget slasher thrills and grisly special effects, *Don't Look Now* might be a rather pretentious and unrewarding struggle.

Nothing is further from the truth. *Don't Look Now* shows exactly what a much maligned genre is capable of achieving and, in terms of its depth of character and feeling, goes to show how hollow the visceral thrills of some recent examples of the horror genre really are.

In its use of non-linear editing, *Don't Look Now* provides you with a model of how stories can be, but seldom are, told. The film's use of D' Onnagio's memorable score is masterly, with music central to the point of the film, not simply tacked on to enhance atmosphere. Sutherland and Christie's performances are brave and uncompromising; the film is explicit without pandering to voyeuristic lowest common denominators. By respecting the intelligence of the audience, Roeg produced a film which is, in turn, always respected by its viewers.

Don't Look Now is indeed a film classic, and one which will help you understand the power and possibility of the medium.

Admirers of the film might also want to analyse further works by director Roeg. These include the David Bowie science fiction film *The Man Who Fell to Earth*; Art Garfunkel's starring vehicle *Bad Timing*; the under-rated *Eureka*, which stars Rutger Hauer and Gene Hackman; and the menacing children's film *The Witches*.

The film is available for purchase on video, and Mark Sanderson has written an invaluable book about it in the BFI Modern Classics series.

ACTIVITIES ▼

Activity 1

Write a synopsis of a film you have seen recently. This should be about 300 words long.

Activity 2

Produce charts to show the story development of two different films, each of which has more than one storyline.

Activity 3

Construct diagrams to show the emotional contrasts in a film of your choice.

Activity 4

Describe some of the cinematic techniques used in a short extract from a film you have found especially enjoyable.

Activity 5

Compare the editing patterns and techniques used in two chase sequences from different films.

Activity 6

Describe (in words, pictures or both) two settings which you would use to depict one of the following:

- isolation
- urban decay
- the power of nature
- a city of the future
- teenage revelry
- romance
- pomp and circumstance
- gladiatorial conflict
- drugs.

Activity 7

Imagine you are producing a film of the Little Red Riding Hood story. How would you cast the main parts if it was to be done in the style of:

1 a fairy tale for a very young audience
2 a contemporary horror story
3 a spoof horror for a 20-something audience.

Explain your choice of actors in each case.

Activity 8

Choose a star, and write an article about how his or her performances have contributed to at least three different films. You should consider:

- the roles played
- the contribution to the role made by screenwriter and director
- the star's public persona
- the star's performance itself.

BIBLIOGRAPHY ▼

Dick, L, 'Desperation and Desire', in *Sight and Sound*, BFI, January 1997

Ellis, J, *Visible Fictions*, Routledge, 1982

Freytag, G, *Technique of the Drama: An Exposition of Dramatic Composition and Art*, Benjamin Blom, 1968

Kozloff, S, 'Narrative Theory and Television', in Allen, R (ed.), *Channels of Discourse Reassembled*, Routledge, 1992

Kuhn, A, and Radston, S, *Women's Companion to International Film*, Virago, 1990

Monaco, J, *How to Read a Film*, Oxford University Press, 1991

McKee, R, Lecture series on story structure in film, Annual

Propp, V , *The Morphology of Folk Tales*, University of Texas Press, 1970

Salisbury, M (ed.), *Burton on Burton*, Faber & Faber, 1995

Sanderson, M, *Don't Look Now*, BFI Modern Classics, BFI Publishing, 1996

Wall, I, *Reading Movies*, Film Education, 1990

CHAPTER 10

Film and TV documentary

Introduction

Documentary is a way of presenting factual material which spans film television, radio, theatre and the press. This chapter concentrates on film and TV documentary, looking at:
- what we mean by documentary
- typical forms and conventions of documentary
- different types of documentary
- the analysis of documentary (focusing on an analysis of *The World at War*, a TV series, and *Night Mail*, a classic cinema documentary)
- what happens when documentary and fictional techniques are mixed.

What do we mean by documentary?

The difference between classic documentary and fiction is that documentary presents actual incidents and statements which can be tested against reality. For example, characters presented in a documentary are from real life, and what they look like and say can be compared with the reality they represent. Fictional characters have a different purpose, and are not seen as lacking if they fail to measure up to the details of real people.

Documentary has changed and developed throughout the history of TV and film. In television, it overlaps with categories such as current affairs and news. It is also part of the area known as 'true stories', and rubs shoulders with the 'based on a true story' type of drama (or 'faction').

In the history of film, the documentary offers an alternative to the fictional world, created characters and clear narrative shape of the classic feature film:

> ❝ *The documentary film differs from Hollywood narrative film... It is primarily a rhetorical form which both offers the audience information and attempts to put forward an argument, to persuade the audience to think in a certain way, to do something, to accept the argument. It achieves this by presenting the truth of its argument as self evident, unified and non-contradictory. Most often an authoritative voice-over is used to frame and contain the images which are seen as unmediated recordings of the "real world".* ❞
> Cook, 1985

Many definitions of documentary concentrate on the purpose of documentary, rather than its characteristics of form:

> ❝ *Methods of recording... so as to appeal either to reason or emotion, for the purpose of stimulating the desire for, and the widening of, human knowledge and understanding.* ❞
> Rotha, 1952

> ❝ *The documentary is distinguished from the factual film by its sociopolitical purpose. Great art can be an instrument for social influence and change... the documentary film does have this purpose.* ❞
> Barsam, 1974

These definitions emphasise the point that, unlike much fiction, documentaries are rarely intended purely for entertainment. They usually contain messages of educational, social and/or political importance.

However, some commentators would disagree with these definitions. The difficulty seems to lie in agreeing the relationship between documentary and reality, or 'truth'. The four points below summarise the main views, or 'positions', on this relationship (see Goodwin, 1986).

1. Documentary is fiction. Documentaries give only one version of 'the facts' of any situation. They have characters, just as the rest of fiction. They tell dramatic stories and distort time in order to have the same build-up as more obvious fiction. Thus, documentaries give you no less a distorted picture of 'reality' than fictional stories.

2. Documentary gives facts. When documentaries fall short of reality, the distortion is a failure caused by human fallibility or the limits within which they are working. No documentary can give reality as it is, but it can strive to stay as close to the truth as possible.

3. Documentary is a mixture of fact and fiction. The aims of a documentary are to entertain and engage as well as to inform. Facts are essential ingredients, but so also are interesting characters and stories, dramatic complications and climaxes. Therefore, documentaries must always use elements and techniques from fiction in order to make the documentary dramatic.

4. Documentaries, regardless of their factual truth or use of fictional techniques, are made to convey messages about the 'realities' they portray. These messages colour, bias and

control the portrayal. In this sense, documentaries give political and ideological messages in what is shown, and how it is shown.

This chapter will give you opportunities to explore these ideas for yourself.

Figure 10.1 *Fiction films such as* In the Name of the Father *(top) draw on documentary realism, in this case the story of Paul Hill of the Guildford 4, seen here having been freed from prison, and question the distinctions between documentary truth and fiction*

Forms and conventions of documentary

Documentary is a way of speaking about the world. It cannot be tied down to specifics of character and storyline in the same way as a genre can. However, it is typified by certain forms and conventions:

> ❝ *the conventions of documentary* **are** *just that – conventions. Many of these – "natural" lighting, indistinct sound, jerky camera movements – may be motivated by the conditions of recording, but they remain conventions. The "documentary look" needs to be carefully examined, so that its constructed nature is established... When we perceive a low level of light in a scene in a film or television [programme], it is read as "natural" or maybe "bad" lighting. In documentary this gives the impression of being more "real" than a scene lit with high levels of lighting. Yet this "natural" light is read in this way not because of its relation to the world, but because it differs from the higher lighting levels we have learned from television drama or Hollywood cinema.* ❞
>
> Goodwin, 1986

These forms and conventions change, just as those of the classic fiction narrative change. The following sections summarise some of the traditional forms and conventions of documentary, which are typical of the straight 'factual' documentary.

Actuality

The term 'actuality' is used to describe recordings of actual events as they happen. In true actuality footage, the camera is present at events which would have taken place whether the camera was there or not. The so-called home movie is usually a form of actuality.

The action in early actuality footage was often staged (as it often is in the home movie). In the early cinema, the term actuality was used to describe any factual film, such as the work of French film-makers the Lumière Brothers. A short piece of film shot in 1895, *Workers Leaving the Lumière Factory*, which begins with the factory gates opening, is often called the first documentary.

At the beginning of this century most films were actualities. In the 1920s the term 'documentary' took over from 'actuality', which is now used to refer to one ingredient of documentary.

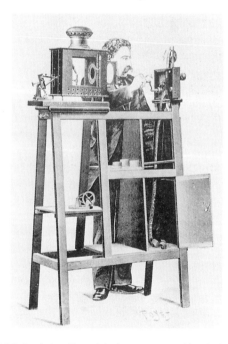

Figure 10.2 *Louis Lumière with the camera used by the Lumière Brothers to make* Workers Leaving The Lumière Factory *in 1895*

'Fly on the wall' filming

In fiction films, what is seen on the screen is scripted. In documentaries, the camera records people going about their real lives, usually without a script. The real events themselves – such as war, famine, or more personal crises – may be dramatic in themselves, and the camera is present to record them as they take place.

In some documentaries the camera is placed with people, or in places, for long periods of time. The final product is then edited down to a much shorter piece of film. There are thus two aspects of this selection process. During the production stages there are the choices of when to bring the camera into full operation and film.

During the post production stages there are choices of what to edit into, or out of, the final product from what was actually filmed.

> ❝ *"Fly on the wall" could be seen as a genre of documentary. However, it seems to have broadened out to become simply a documentary technique. In documentaries based wholly on the fly on the wall technique, the people observed seem to forget they are being filmed. New camera technology also means that cameras can be concealed so that people are totally unaware they are being filmed. In both cases, fly on the wall techniques raise issues of privacy and consent. Fly on the wall documentaries have been described as "designed to invade privacy".* ❞
> Denton, 1983

Figure 10.3 A scene from Frederick Wiseman's fly on the wall documentary Hospital

The use of film originally shot for other purposes

In documentaries, film images are selected for their use in illustrating and evidencing an argument. These images may include film shot for other purposes then kept in film libraries, archives, museums and other collections. This is often known as 'library film'. Images may be borrowed and reused from any source: documentaries will even 'quote' from and use fiction film to illustrate a documentary point.

Voice-over

Traditionally this is the voice of an actor, who plays an invisible controlling role in 'telling the story' rather than participating in it. Voice-over is not necessarily restricted to one voice; for example it can also include participants, or eyewitnesses, in the narrative.

In documentaries, the voice-over often has the role of uncovering or solving a mystery. In the drama documentary *Death of a Princess*, which explores the execution of a Saudi Princess in 1977, the voice-over has a particularly interesting 'film noir' effect, as well as a documentary tone. The mystery is not solved by the investigation; in fact it can be argued that it makes the story more complex and mysterious. Similarly, voice-over is often used in the detective fiction film noir genre to record the thoughts of the hero, or to recount the story in flashback.

Written text

The term documentary implies that what is presented has a link to written documents. A central characteristic of traditional documentary is the authority given to writing and a reliance on the written word as a touchstone of fact.

Many documentaries use writing in the form of subtitles, references to time and place, and the appearance of written documents in the frame. These written documents may include newspaper headlines, magazines, quotations from books, legal documents and government proceedings.

Graphics

Documentaries often use graphic illustrations as well as written text. Computer graphics are now common, and may be used alongside maps, artists' drawings, cartoons, still photographs and other visual aids. Some documentaries also use statistics shown in the form of graphs, tables and charts.

Visible recording and disruption

In documentaries the camera is simply 'there'. It does not control, and may seem, metaphorically speaking, to be surprised by the action. In this sense, shots seem only partially premeditated, and have the quality of a witness.

In line with this, many documentaries incorporate footage which might, in a fiction film, appear to be accidents, mistakes or poor-quality filming (see the extract from Goodwin, page 124). For example, it is now common for documentaries to include what happens if someone tries to stop filming by placing a hand over the lens. In some documentaries an awareness of the camera's presence and other technical paraphernalia may be used to increase realism. If the camera shook or wobbled in a fiction film, this would be seen as poor camerawork. In documentaries, a wobble or a blurred effect when a camera pans too quickly can be seen as a guarantee of the reality of the recording.

Techniques such as grainy film and the hand-held camera are sometimes referred to as 'cinema verité'.

The use of interviews

Documentaries are based on painstaking research, and this is most apparent in the use of interviews. The results shown are highly edited, and the interviewer and questions asked are not always included.

The presentation of interviewees has its own forms and conventions, which overlap with other types of film such as news. For example, the background often establishes information about the interviewee (shelves of books convey expert status, and so on).

The use of the 'talking head'

A shot of someone talking directly to the camera is often called a 'talking head' in film and TV jargon. The talking head is associated with authority and presentation of facts. It is a form used across a wide variety of factual film and television, including news, current affairs and documentary.

Figure 10.4 John Romer talking to the camera in his Channel 4 documentary Byzantium

The use of the 'expert'

The expert is often a key character in establishing truths and facts in documentaries. The status and authority of experts are usually established by the situation in which they are shown and through titles explaining who they are, their position and qualifications.

Vox pop

In film and television, consultation with the ordinary person in the street is referred to as 'vox pop'. This phrase comes from the Latin 'Vox Populi': the voice of the people. Typically, the scene behind the person being interviewed will establish his or her status as the man or woman in the street.

The use of eyewitnesses and participants

People 'who were there' are often used to establish facts, truth and reality. Eyewitnesses and participants may speak directly, or an actor may be used to speak their words. If a real person's identity needs to be withheld, this is used to justify the use of an actor. In some cases actors are used because the real people are dead, for example in a historical documentary.

The use of music

Music is normally used to open and close documentary programmes and films, and the type of music chosen will reflect the tone of the documentary. Traditional, serious documentaries tend to open with sober, dramatic music.

Within programmes, music may signal mood and encourage the audience to take up a particular attitude. Music tends to be used as a 'commentary' to accompany events, rather than to indicate central characters (as is often the case in fiction films). Sometimes the music itself is part of the social reality being presented, for example when popular songs from different times and places are used in historical documentaries.

Reconstruction

Reconstruction is the performance of constructed action and events for the benefit of the camera, to represent 'real' action and events which have taken place. Although the use of reconstruction and actors, whether amateur or professional, is now the subject of some debate and controversy, it is an old ingredient of documentary. There are two types of reconstruction:
- simulation with the 'real participants'
- reconstruction using actors.

I wore a tunic, a dirty khaki tunic,
And you wore your civvy clothes . . .

Figure 10.5 Oh What a Lovely War: a theatrical production which mixes the forms and conventions of documentary with the use of actors and drama

Simulation

While film was still an expensive commodity, equipment was bulky and film crews a crowd, it was common practice for documentary film-makers to observe situations and then ask the participants to repeat them for the camera:

> *In 1955, documentary films looked much as they had looked for the previous twenty years... People were rehearsed in their everyday activities so that they could perform them convincingly in front of a crowd of technicians with their forbidding mass of equipment, cables and lights.*
> Vaughan, 1974

This convention was called 'simulation', and in many circumstances its use has continued as a documentary tradition. As a BBC internal document of 1972, 'Principles and Practice in Documentary Programmes', explains:

> *The need for some element of simulation... is clearly a matter of some delicacy, and is frequently a cause of misunderstanding. For example, it is virtually impossible to convey an accurate impression of a board meeting or discussion by filming it as it happens... The director, cameraman and sound man will find it impossible to follow a rapid and spontaneous interchange... Therefore the producer must to some extent prepare such a discussion.*

Simulation – hidden to varying degrees – has undoubtedly continued as a documentary technique. However, it has come under increasing criticism due to the possibility of more direct and naturalistic observation, the drama documentary debates (see page 132) and arguments about documentary truth.

▶◀ *See Activity 1, page 133*

Reconstruction using actors

Documentaries which are not dramatised in the full sense may still use segments of reconstruction with actors. The practical reasons for this are usually made clear, with a spoken or written label announcing that the following piece of film is a reconstruction.

What types of documentary are there?

Documentary is a broad area within which there are a number of genres with their own distinctive character types, storylines, key signs and so on.

Different types of documentary include:

- investigative
- consumer interest
- educational
- artistic/cultural
- scientific
- historical
- wildlife
- travel
- ethnographic documentary about cultures, peoples, customs
- documentary based on a place or institution
- personality-based documentary about a person or group of people
- the 'soap opera'
- propagandistic
- political
- campaigning
- social issue.

Many of these types of documentary overlap. For example, *The Nightcleaners* (by the Berwick Street Collective, 1975) is a documentary about the struggle of women office cleaners to get a union. This combines three types of documentary – propagandistic, political and campaigning – and has other elements which the list above does not cover.

▶◀ *See Activity 2, page 134*

Figure 10.6 The Nightcleaners

C A S E ▼ S T U D Y

ANALYSIS OF A TELEVISION DOCUMENTARY: *THE WORLD AT WAR*

The World at War is a documentary series of 26 episodes made by Thames Television in association with the Imperial War Museum. It covers the period from the ascendance of the Nazis to power in the 1930s, to the dropping of nuclear bombs by the USA on Hiroshima and Nagasaki in 1945. It has been shown a number of times on television, and was released on video in 1982 (it has recently been re-released on four video tapes).

The World at War was first broadcast on British television in 1973–4. At that time, Thames Television was part of the ITV network, providing TV broadcasting to the London area (it is now an independent television production company, not an ITV franchisee). The programme was also sold and distributed to television networks abroad.

ACTUALITY AND OTHER INGREDIENTS

The World at War presents the history of the Second World War from the point of view of the time that it was made, but uses documents and film footage from the time that it describes. Historians describe this way of looking at the past with a new eye as 'revisionist': telling history from a new perspective.

The World at War consists mainly of a narrative edited from 'actuality' interspersed with testimony from various talking heads involved in events at the time. The actuality film comes from diverse sources, including film crews working for the governments and military forces of the time, newsreel film and propaganda. It is crucial to realise that in most cases the way the actuality film was shot and used originally was very different from the way it is used in *The World at War*.

The actuality film is in black and white, whereas the talking heads interviewed are in colour. Dubbed sound effects were added to the actuality, replacing the previous soundtracks which would have used the images for different purposes and comment.

Other ingredients include radio broadcasts, stills, written text in the form of newspaper headlines and stories, graphics in the form of maps, and animation in the form of arrows moving over the maps. The result is a montage of different documentary ingredients.

The main voice-over is spoken by Laurence Olivier, a famous actor with a commanding voice which unifies the narrative. The voice-over also includes the voices of people who were involved commenting on events. The use of music 'orchestrates' what is going on and sets moods. The music combines dramatic music resembling that of the fiction thriller genre with patriotic and popular music, war songs and national anthems.

EPISODE 2: 'DISTANT WAR'

The first episode of the series deals with the build-up to the war in Germany. Episode 2, 'Distant War', deals with the period from September 1939 to May 1940. It opens with actuality film of the invasion of Poland by Nazi German forces, accompanied by sinister music.

The narrative of the episode deals with the following main events:

- the Nazi invasion of Poland
- reference back to the treaty of Versailles ceding parts of East Germany to Poland
- in Britain, the evacuation of one and a half million children from London and other urban bombing targets
- the call-up of civilians into the armed forces
- in Britain, the imposition of the blackout to remove light from any source which might be visible to bombing planes
- the invasion of Finland by the Russians
- the mining of Norwegian waters by British and other Allied forces
- the invasion of Norway by Nazi Germany
- the landing of British troops in Norway and their defeat by the Nazis
- following the British defeat in Norway, the humiliation of Prime Minister Chamberlain and his replacement by Churchill.

Figure 10.7 'Actuality' footage from The World at War documentary series

The World at War has the unity of the traditional documentary. It is obviously based on extensive research, and masses together a great range of documentary evidence from different sources. It puts these together into a narrative which has great authority and apparent integrity.

In some ways, the episode 'Distant War' maintains a seeming objectivity and balance:

- Although it deals with events very much from the British point of view, the previous episode had concentrated on the build-up to the war by looking much more closely at Germany.
- The way in which the episode presents Britain is not all positive. There is criticism of Britain for its unpreparedness. The British campaign to resist Nazi domination of Scandinavia is presented as something of a fiasco.
- The ways in which Germany and Soviet Russia are portrayed are equally negative. They both share blame for the occupation of Poland, which they divided up between them. In Scandinavia, the Soviets invaded Finland; the Nazis invaded Norway.

However, there are also a number of ways in which the episode is loaded towards messages with a 'patriotic' bias:

- Music establishes a 'preferred' attitude towards the participants and the events. Similar kinds of sinister music are used when the German and Russian invasions are shown (the 'villains' in this episode). In contrast, the music associated with Britain is of a more 'popular' kind, and includes patriotic songs.
- The British failure to halt the Nazi invasion of Norway looks forward to other defeats. In contrast, the 'action' around the Battle of the River Plate, and the scuttling of the German battleship, the *Graf Spee*, is used to tell a story of British naval dominance and courage. This establishes a storyline of British victory which precedes the failure in Norway, and looks forward to other British victories in the story which all the episodes will tell.
- The story told is influenced by the versions of history based on personalities. The personalities who dominate this episode's narrative are the two British politicians, Chamberlain and Churchill. Prime Minister Chamberlain had tried to appease and make peace with Hitler at Munich. The episode concludes with the replacement of Chamberlain by Winston Churchill, the war leader. There is a bias towards the role of leaders and the important personalities, who are named and identified. In contrast, the 'ordinary' people and the working classes tend to be represented by anonymous 'types'.

EPISODE 15: 'HOME FIRES'

This episode deals with the war from the point of view of the British 'at home' from 1940–44: civilians, the working population and British domestic politics.

The narrative includes the following:

- the bombing of British cities, looking particularly at Coventry and London
- the response of Government and local authorities to the devastation
- the evacuation of women and children
- the censorship of news and the use of propaganda in newsreels

- the detention of foreign 'aliens' in internment camps
- the role of Parliament and important politicians such as Bevin and Beaverbrook
- the build-up of 'the war effort' and production of arms
- the call-up of women to the forces and to work on the land and in factories
- relations with Soviet Russia, support for its eastern front with Germany, and pressure to open up the 'second front'
- the domestic economy: rationing, the encouragement of home-grown food ('Dig for Victory'), and the black market in food and luxuries
- culture and the mass media: the BBC, radio, entertainment, music and art
- strikes by miners complaining about pay and conditions
- the arrival of the first Nazi rocket bombs: the V1s.

Activity 3 gives you an opportunity to investigate and analyse this episode further.

▶◀ *See Activity 3, page 134*

Figure 10.8 Vera Lynn from 'home' keeps up the morale of troops

CONCLUSION

In conclusion, *The World at War* is an achievement in television documentary. One measure of this is the fact that it is still widely available 25 years after it was first shown, and has recently been reissued on video. The episodes of *The World at War* show evidence of objectivity, but overall the series gives a version of events biased towards dominant British views of history. To take just one example, the attraction of members of the British ruling classes towards Nazism and their sympathy with the rise of Hitler in the 1930s is largely omitted from the first episode on the origins of the war.

You should look at at least one episode from *The World at War*, and come to your own conclusions about it.

CASE ▼ STUDY

ANALYSIS OF A CINEMA DOCUMENTARY: *NIGHT MAIL*

Night Mail is one of a number of films associated with the work of the British film-maker John Grierson, who led a group including Basil Wright, Stuart Legg, Paul Rotha and Arthur Elton. Their work is sometimes referred to as the British Documentary Movement, and received the backing of state organisations such as the Crown Film Unit. Grierson's first film was *Drifters* (1929). Other films associated with the movement include *Song of Ceylon* (1934), and *Housing Problems* (1935), which was made with the backing of the gas industry.

Night Mail is a documentary account of the London to Scotland Postal Special train. The film was first released in 1936 as a two-reel cine film 'short', although it can now be seen on video. It was made by the Post Office Film Unit under the direction of Basil Wright and Harry Watt, working with John Grierson as producer. The music was written by the British composer Benjamin Britten, and the poet W H Auden wrote a poem, 'Night Mail', used in the commentary in the final part of the film. The following extract is taken from the first part of the poem:

> This is the Night Mail crossing the Border,
> Bringing the cheque and the postal order,
> Letters for the rich, letters for the poor,
> The shop at the corner, the girl next door.
> Pulling up Beattock, a steady climb:
> The gradient's against her but she's on time.
> Past cotton grass and moorland boulder,
> Shovelling white steam over her shoulder,
> Snorting noisily, she passes
> Silent miles of wind-bent grasses,
> Birds turn their heads as she approaches,
> Stare from bushes at her blank faced coaches.
> Sheep dogs cannot turn her course;
> They slumber on with paws across.
> In the farm she passes no-one wakes,
> But a jug in a bedroom gently shakes.

AN INNOVATIVE APPROACH

The film has many of the features of a traditional documentary in the use of voice-over, statistics given in the commentary and the use of music. However, the film was seen as innovative, experimental and 'avant-garde' at the time, and it still possesses a freshness and the capacity to surprise the viewer.

The technology and expense of film in the 1930s meant that scenes had to be carefully constructed. It is clear that the workers for the LMS railway and the travelling Post Office were aware of the film crew, and indeed 'performed' for them and the cinema audience. Much of the soundtrack has been edited onto the action from sound tape during post-production. None of the participants in the film is named.

CHARACTERS

The train performs a character-like role in the narrative. The heroic portrayal of its climb up a gradient is now a cliché in films about trains, but it is typical of the Futurist optimism in technology which was a feature of British culture of the 1930s.

Apart from the train, the primary character role is the Worker, a role which is noticeably male dominated. There may be some Soviet influence in the way that the working people are elevated to hero status. Memorably, there are low-angle shots of men at work, such as the shot up through the signal levers of the signalman. *Night Mail* belongs to a type of documentary portraying 'the dignity of labour', which dramatises and acknowledges workers and their institutions. Arguably, the representation of the working class in the film is positive.

Figure 10.9 The representation of workers in Night Mail is positive

UNITIES

The film constructs various 'unities' on which the narrative turns. The unity of time is the train journey. The unity of place is the railway line, the train which runs upon it and the surrounding landscape. The camera appears to view the train with an 'all-seeing' eye. There are aerial shots of it snaking along the lines. There are shots from the train lines and the line-side. There are shots inside stations, signal boxes and the train itself. There are shots from individual points of view, including shots on and from the footplate of the steam engine, and from the viewpoint of the engine driver. These shots are dramatic and are edited together to give a sense of movement and action. There is some suspense, for example in

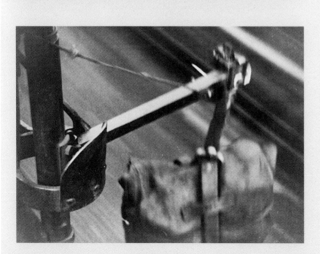

Figure 10.10 The train and its journey is a central 'character' in the narrative of Night Mail

the sequence where postbags are swung out from the train and are caught in the net of the line-side mechanical grab.

The portrayal of state, industry and workers in *Night Mail* is of a unity, or a pattern. It is notable that there is no conflict in the narrative between these institutions and the people, or between classes. *Night Mail* is quite typical of films of the so-called British Documentary Movement of the 1930s, and of Grierson-influenced documentaries in particular. It shows the interdependence of workers, industry and society through the activities of the railway and the Post Office. The filming of the sorting of the mail and the emphasis on the names of the places across the country which the mail links carry messages of social and national unity. Grierson's world view and political beliefs were that co-operation and duty were positive, and that individualism and the personal were negative. His positive vision of society, which is conveyed in *Night Mail*, was that society consisted of a pattern of interdependent relations:

'Sleeping or waking, we are concerned each day in an interdependency... This is the fact of modern society.' Quoted in Hardy, 1966.

Grierson believed that documentary film could serve the modern industrial democratic state as a means of public education and persuasion.

CONCLUSION

This analysis of *Night Mail* reveals the politics of the film's messages. These politics go beyond the obvious state politics of party political debate into the politics of how people live and the principles on which society goes about its business in everyday life. The term commonly used in media studies for this kind of far-reaching politics is 'ideology':

'Ideology is a term which refers to the coherent set of beliefs and values which dominate in a culture, and which is particularly held by those who have power. Ideology is concerned with social and power relationships, and with the means by which these are made apparent. The media communicate ideology to their audiences. This ideology can be found in the material by looking for covert messages.' Burton, 1990.

The ideologies of documentary films such as *Night Mail* are relevant to the messages and portrayal of issues in British documentary since the 1930s. Documentaries often seek to establish a 'middle ground' of common agreement between the interests of individuals, groups and the state. The term used for this ideology of the middle ground is 'consensus'.

Night Mail draws its audience into a consensus of common values: the value of work, teamwork, a national identity reflected in language, landscape and industry. A common link between many of the political and social documentaries of today and those of the 1930s is this attempt to construct a unity of mutual understanding through 'middle ground' consensus politics.

▶◀ *See Activity 4, page 134*

Drama documentaries

So far in this chapter, documentary has been distinguished from fictional drama in two main ways.

- Fictional drama uses actors, whereas documentary uses 'real people' who carry on with their lives whether the camera is there or not.
- Fictional drama comes from the imagination and experience of its writer (or writers), and may only reflect what goes on in the writer's head. Documentary bears a direct relation to people and events in the world, and the truth of its portrayals may be measured against the documented facts.

There is, however, a grey area between what is drama and what is documentary. Not everyone would agree with the clear distinctions given above. When the forms and conventions of drama and documentary are mixed together, it draws attention to the grey area between the two.

Some films and programmes have features of documentary, but also use the resources of fiction, such as scripts and actors. These mixtures of drama and documentary borrow the realism of factual programmes and often have a similar purpose to 'straight documentary'. They may:

- have messages and propagandise
- campaign to right injustice or uncover cover-ups
- seek to engage with the 'real world' in order to right wrongs, awaken public opinion and re-educate.

Productions which mix drama and documentary in this way are known as 'drama documentary', 'documentary drama', 'drama-doc', 'docu-drama', 'faction' and 'true stories' (Paget, 1990).

Documentary and drama have been mixed in the theatre, as well as in film and television. A famous theatrical documentary drama is *Oh What a Lovely War* (Theatre Workshop, 1965), which includes screening of actuality stills, quotes from documentary sources, and the use of popular contemporary music and songs (see Figure 10.5 on page 126).

Productions which mix drama and documentary have been seen to provoke a number of debates (Goodwin, 1986).

▶◀ *See Activity 5, page 134*

Mixing fact and fiction

One of the features of drama documentary hybrids is that they can be controversial. Part of the reaction that they stir up is often involved with their 'mixing of fact and fiction'.

A famous example of this is Peter Watkins' 1965 film, *The War Game*. This dramatises what would happen during and after a nuclear attack upon Britain, highlighting the inadequacies of civil defence plans. The film was censored by the BBC and withheld from broadcasting until 1985. Much of the justification for this ban was based on the argument that its documentary form would confuse and frighten the audience.

The furore *The War Game* caused peeled away the thin veneer of impartiality and consensus which concealed a bias towards the established views of BBC management. There is a very useful account of this affair in *Nukespeak, The Media and The Bomb* (Aubrey, 1982).

Terms and definitions

Another area of debate centres on terms and definitions. In 1980 John Caughie wrote an article in *Screen* magazine entitled 'Progressive Television and Documentary Drama', in which he makes a distinction between two ways of combining drama and documentary. This distinction seems to be based in the first instance on the sources of the two forms. Caughie uses the terms:

- 'drama documentary', or 'dramatised documentary', to refer to work which originates from journalists and current affairs departments, and thus uses techniques such as scripting, staging and actors
- 'documentary drama' to refer to work by drama producers and writers which takes on the 'documentary look'; in other words, drama which borrows the codes and conventions of factual television to add a further dimension of realism.

Caughie points out that dramatisation has been an ingredient in documentary throughout its history, beginning with early pioneers of dramatised actuality such as Melies, and carrying on through the revolutionary cinema of early Soviet Russia:

> ❛ *Dramatic reconstructions of actuality have a history in cinema as old as cinema itself, beginning with Melies' reconstructions of coronations and assassinations, and continuing with Soviet cinema's celebrations of the revolution.* ❜
> Caughie, 1980

Caughie goes on to identify the way in which documentary dramas use a 'documentary look'. This is not simply the way

Figure 10.11 The War Game from 1965 (opposite) and Hillsborough from 1996 – both documentaries 'fictionalised' events based on documented facts

they 'look like' documentaries, but also the way they put together the social world in which they take place:

> ❝ By the "documentary look" I mean the system of looks which constitutes the social space of the fiction, a social space which is more than simply a background, but which in a sense constitutes what the documentary drama wishes to be about, the "document" which is to be dramatised. ❞

Cathy Come Home is a documentary drama directed by Ken Loach. It tells the story of children being taken away from a homeless couple by the social services. It is a television film with the 'documentary look'. Caughie describes the way in which *Cathy Come Home* puts together a 'social environment' of social forces and bureaucrats which cause the distress of the homeless family at the centre of the drama. This realistic picture of oppression by landlords, bureaucrats and social workers is thus part of 'the documentary look' in *Cathy Come Home*.

Analysing the overlap between documentary and drama

It is useful to study the overlap between drama and documentary. Analysing and discussing the drama-documentary mix increases awareness that the distinction between fact and fiction is not as clear as some people think. The processes of selection and construction which underlie both factually and fictionally oriented media products mean that they have much in common.

Documentary dramas and drama documentaries will continue to be made, and will probably continue to be controversial. If you wish to do so, you should be able to find more contemporary examples appearing on television on which to undertake your own work and analysis.

▶◀   *See Activities 6 and 7, page 135*

ACTIVITIES

Activity 1

View any documentary made before 1955 and see where and how you can identify the use of simulation in the performance of activities for the camera.

For example, you or your teacher could try to get access to a copy of Robert Flaherty's 1934 documentary, *Man of Aran*. This is particularly interesting in terms of the reconstruction and simulation of activities. As Ivor Montagu explained in 1983:

'Man of Aran – made by the studio I was working in – is centred around the killing of a shark to get fuel for oil lamps. No-one had killed a shark for about eighty years in Aran. Flaherty had to show them how to do it, and Aran had electric light!'

Activity 2

Documentary genres

Look at the list of different types of documentary given on page 127. Find as many examples as you can of these types of documentary (a copy of a TV listings magazine will probably help).

Can you find, or think of, any types of documentary which are not listed?

Activity 3

Home fires

Watch episode 15 from the series *The World at War* and write an analysis of the episode and/or an excerpt from it. The prompts and questions below are guidelines. You may decide to address them all, or to concentrate upon one or more in particular. You are advised to include a response to question 5 in any analysis.

1 What personalities, or 'characters' are there in this episode, and what parts do they play in the narrative?
2 What is the role of the main voice-over, spoken by Laurence Olivier? How does it unify and bring together the subject matter? In what ways does it limit controversy or other possible points of view?
3 Look at how the representations in the film are selected and put together. How are the social classes portrayed? How are gender differences represented, and men and women portrayed? (You may concentrate on the excerpt dealing with female call-up, if you wish.)
4 Consider the coverage in the episode of popular culture and the media. Carry out some research of your own into British culture and media of the period, and compare your findings with the picture given.
5 Consider the dominant politics and ideology of this episode. In particular, you should consider the portrayal of the 'British people' and the representation of a 'British character' in the face of the adversities of war and Nazi bombing.

Activity 4

The work of the British Documentary Movement

Watch *Night Mail* and another example of the work of the British Documentary Movement, such as *Song of Ceylon* or *Housing Problems*.

Write a comparison indicating what they have in common in terms of technique and content. Include a response indicating how far you find evidence of the ideologies of social cohesion and consensus, as outlined in the *Night Mail* case study on page 130.

Activity 5

Obtain a copy of the script for *Oh What a Lovely War*. How would you make this as a television drama documentary?

Storyboard a scene from the play as a TV documentary (e.g. look at the opening of Act Two).

Activity 6

Identify a suitable dramatised documentary, or drama documentary, for analysis as a case study. You are recommended to consult your syllabus, and if necessary your exam board, for ideas. NEAB gives particular guidance.

You may wish to investigate a contemporary example, or something from the history of the form (see Goodwin, 1986, for ideas). The following prompts are guidelines.

1 Research the context in which the drama documentary or dramatised documentary was made. Find out about the production company, director, writers, researchers and so on.
2 Research the 'true story' on which the documentary was based. Make note of any selections, omissions and treatment given.
3 When viewing the film or programme, log and make notes on the forms and conventions from documentary and drama which are used. What types of drama conventions are used? Do they draw upon any particular genres?
4 Identify the elements which give the film a 'documentary look'.
5 Can you categorise the character roles? Are there heroes? villains? any stock characters?
6 What impact does the use of actors have upon the characterisation of the people involved?
7 Can you separate the 'fictional' from the 'factual'?
8 What dominant messages/politics/ideology shape the film?
9 Are there any alternative ways of interpreting the film which oppose the dominant message?
10 Investigate the response to the film. Forms which mix drama and documentary normally arouse criticism and debate for doing so. What debates are aroused in this case?

Activity 7

Documentary and drama documentary can be an interesting form for practical work. The following activity should help you to learn about the selection and construction that takes place when presenting factual programming.

Find a suitable story reported in the press and gather as much information as you can. Then work through the following tasks.

1 Make a list of all the character roles.
2 Write down all the questions which an investigative reporter might want to ask to get at 'the truth'.
3 Working as a group, assign character roles and rehearse your own versions of the story individually or in pairs, writing role play cards if necessary. One or two will have to play the reporter role needed to 'run' the programme.
4 Now decide the format you would like the programme to follow, and set about planning and production.

A short cut, if you do not want to produce a documentary, is to produce a discussion programme about the 'truth' behind the news, in which each character is cross-questioned by the reporter. From this you can move on to a more informal debate among the characters involved, until the programme runs out of time.

BIBLIOGRAPHY ▼

Aubrey, C (ed.), *Nukespeak, The Media and The Bomb*, Comedia, 1982

Auden, W H, *Collected Shorter Poems*, Faber & Faber, 1966

Barsam, R M, *Nonfiction Film, A Critical History*, Allen & Unwin, 1974

BBC, 'Principles and Practice in Documentary Programmes', BBC (internal document), 1972

Burton, G , *More than Meets the Eye*, Arnold, 1990

Caughie, J, 'Progressive Television and Documentary Drama', in Goodwin, A, *Teaching TV Drama Documentary,* BFI Publishing, 1986

Cook, P (ed.), *The Cinema Book*, BFI Publishing, 1985

Denton, R, article in *Listener*, 13 January 1983

Goodwin, A, *Teaching TV Drama Documentary*, BFI Publishing, 1986

Hardy, F (ed.), *Grierson on Documentary*, Faber & Faber, 1966

Montagu, I, quoted in 'The Grierson Influence', in *Undercut,* Number 9, 1983

Paget, D, *True Stories? Documentary Drama on Radio, Screen and Stage*, Manchester University Press, 1990

Post Office, *Night Mail*, Central Office of Information, 1936

Rotha, P, *Documentary Film*, Hastings House, 1952

Thames Television, *The World at War*, Thames/Futurevision, 1982

Theatre Workshop, *Oh What a Lovely War*, Methuen, 1965

Watson, J, and Hill, A, *A Dictionary of Communication and Media Studies*, Arnold, 1997

The video of the Post Office *Night Mail* documentary is available from DD Video, North Harrow, Middlesex HA2 7SA.

CHAPTER 11

Radio

11

Introduction

With the expansion of television since the 1960s, the role of radio in people's lives has changed. This chapter focuses on radio today. It looks at:

- what makes radio unique
- how technological change has affected recording, sound sources and receiving equipment
- the structure of the radio industry, including BBC radio, commercial stations and independent companies

- issues of public service and accountability
- the radio audience, including how programmes are targeted at different groups of people and how audience research is conducted
- scheduling programmes
- programme genres
- radio production techniques
- how to analyse a radio programme.

Radio: a unique medium

The most important thing about radio – and what differentiates it from all other media – is the fact that it communicates entirely in sound. This has both advantages and disadvantages.

There used to be an official at the BBC with the wonderful title 'Controller of the Spoken Word'. He (and it was always a 'he' in those days) no longer exists, but 'the spoken word' and, for that matter, 'the sung word', are still what radio is all about.

Although it has been around for less than a century, radio imitates the oldest form of communication: voices and sounds. As such, its foundations are much older than printing, or even writing itself.

Radio today

Every aspect of the media has been affected by technological change, and radio production is no exception. The quality of sound has improved greatly with the use of digital recording and higher frequencies, both of which give much better sound definition. Important changes have also been made to the receiving equipment – the radios themselves – which have profoundly altered the way we listen and, in turn, what we listen to.

How has recording changed?

Almost everything involved in radio has become much smaller in recent years. For example, instead of huge outside broadcast vans with long aerials, today's radio cars look like ordinary cars or taxis with the recording gear tucked away in a corner. The exception to this rule is the control desk in a studio. This is noticeably bigger; crammed with a breathtaking range of controls (many of them rarely used) that can do a host of things to the sounds they receive from the microphones.

Figure 11.1 A modern recording studio

In the 1940s most broadcasting went out 'live', and once it had been broadcast it would be lost for ever. When a recording was made it was done on huge wax discs or great reels of steel tape that were extremely difficult to edit.

Today all shows are recorded: even when they are going out live, a copy is made and kept for the records. Recordings are made on tiny DATS (digital audio tapes), compact discs or, increasingly, directly into computers called digital audio workstations. Here the recorded sound goes straight on to hard disc and it is always possible to try something, change your mind and retrace your steps if you don't like it.

Just 20 years ago, tape was still edited with a sharp razor-blade. Now workstations like SADiE (Studio Audio Disc Editor) turn the sound into pictures. A wavy line on the monitor screen

137

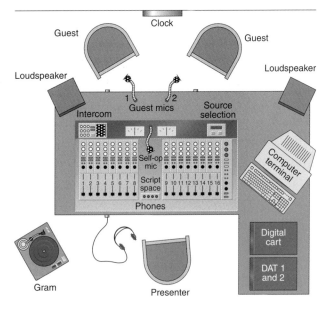

A typical layout for the 16 self-operated channels would be as follows:

1 Spare	9 Guest mic 1
2 News booth	10 Guest mic 2
3 Cart	11 CD 1 (Remote jukebox)
4 Computer hard disk 1	12 CD 2 (Remote jukebox)
5 Computer hard disk 2	13 Outside source 1
6 Telephone 1	14 Outside source 2
7 Telephone 2	15 DAT 1
8 Presenter's mic	16 DAT 2

Figure 11.2 A radio studio control desk

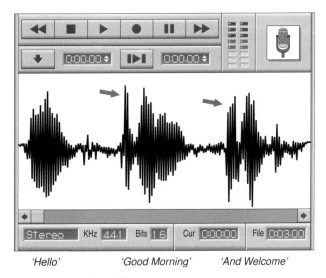

'Hello'   'Good Morning'   'And Welcome'

Figure 11.3 Digital editing

rises up like a great wave for the loudest sections and remains flat when there is no sound at all. The sound editor uses a cursor to locate exactly where to cut, or where two sounds should start to overlap. It's much more accurate, much quicker – and a lot less dangerous than the old razor-blades for absent-minded editors.

Sound sources

Modern radio is not studio-bound. What you hear may have come via:

- a satellite link – favoured by reporters working abroad
- cable

- the telephone system – reporters usually screw a higher quality microphone into the mouthpiece to send material in this way
- an OB (outside broadcast) van – a travelling studio used for major outside broadcasts. OB vans have a complex control panel and numerous microphones, which are rigged in a nearby town hall or church
- a radio car – often used for interviews. The interviewee can sit in the back with an interviewer, and be beamed straight into a programme via a tall telescopic aerial on the car's roof
- a reporter on foot with a 'backpack' – used to transmit to a nearby studio, from where material can be retransmitted all over the country
- a tiny machine such as a Sony Walkman Professional – used if the recording does not need to be transmitted live. As long as the reporter uses a high-tech microphone, this will record as clearly as if you were in a studio.

Figure 11.4 A small outside broadcast van

Figure 11.5 Interview being conducted in a radio car

Studios themselves vary enormously, from the smallest 'self-op' (self-operating) studio, where speakers work the equipment themselves, to the largest drama studio with built-in doors, kitchens, sets of wooden, metal and stone stairs, a huge variety of different acoustics, and a control desk that can do amazing things to the human voice.

Pre-recorded sound can come from:

- wax, vinyl or CD discs (these can be either commercial discs or archive recordings)
- quarter-inch wide reels of tape
- multi-tracked tape
- cassettes
- DATS
- 'carts' (cartridges in which the tape is spooled so that it runs continuously). These are used for sound effects and advertisements.

Receiving equipment

The quality of sound being broadcast is sharper, clearer and covers a wider vocal range than in the days before VHF (Very High Frequency). However, most people – listening in cars as traffic rushes by, or maybe pushing a vacuum cleaner with a baby bawling in the background – are not really aware of this. They may be conscious that most programmes are now in stereo, but often stereo speakers are placed too close together to give the proper effect. The exception, and it is a very important exception, is when you listen on a personal stereo. Headphones are ideal for stereo sound.

In fact, for the majority of people, the most important technological change is not in the quality of sound or the way programmes are made or broadcast, but in the way we receive them. Radios are much smaller and more mobile today, so we can now listen in circumstances that would have been impossible in the past. Modern radio is intimate. Gone are the days when the whole family sat round a big wooden box in the corner, eating jam sandwiches, drinking Horlicks and listening to *Dick Burton Special Agent*, *Riders of the Range* and *Journey into Space*.

Figure 11.6 A family listening to the radio in the 1930s

This transformation of listening habits came about as a result of the introduction of the transistor in the 1960s. There had been radios of a sort in cars for years, but from then on the much higher quality reception and cheaper cost meant that car radios became almost universal. Portable radios too became the norm. You didn't have to go to where the radio lived; you took it with you.

Today, radio broadcasters have become friends who can go everywhere with us. TV performers remain caged in a box in the corner, while radio people, from disc jockeys to the actors in *The Archers*, seem friendly and down-to-earth. In a word, they provide companionship.

There's a wonderful expression used in radio – 'zoo format'. This refers to a discussion programme in which a group of people talk among themselves, not unlike a group of friends in a pub (*Loose Ends* on BBC Radio 4 is a good example). This sort of show creates the feeling that you're there with the participants: you're not sitting back watching them talk, as is the case with a TV chat show. If a discussion takes place on a phone-in programme, you can even ring up and play a part. In effect radio plays are another sort of 'zoo format', except that in some there is a narrator who talks directly to the listener.

Figure 11.7 Recording Start the Week with Melvyn Bragg on BBC Radio 4 – an example of a 'zoo format' conversational radio show with guests around a table

Trainee radio producers are taught to think of themselves as broadcasting to a single listener, because most of us listen on our own. Radio is about personal, one-to-one communication. Its presenters, newsreaders and DJs go to bed with you at night and wake you in the morning. The whole cast of a radio play can be with you in the bath or even on the loo, you can carry a football match with you in your car and, since the introduction of the personal stereo in 1980, DJs can chat to you as you jog round on your morning exercise.

In short, you watch TV, but radio talks to you. Smaller radio sets have increased its intimacy, but did not create it. There has always been something about people speaking to us that draws us into the conversation in a way which no other medium can. In one of the most famous radio plays of all, *Under Milk Wood* by Dylan Thomas, first broadcast in 1954, the narrator (played by Richard Burton) talks directly to the listeners and takes them into his confidence:

> ❛ Only you can hear the houses sleeping in the streets in the slow deep salt and silent black, bandaged night. Only you can see, in the blinded bedrooms, the coms. and petticoats over the chairs, the jugs and basins, the glasses of teeth...❜

Listen With Mother, a programme for small children, went even further, trying to give its little listeners the illusion of a two-way dialogue. It used to begin:

'Are you sitting comfortably?' (pause for response)

Of course it was an illusion. Even if the targeted toddler had been screaming back, 'No, I'm not sitting comfortably', the cosy voice would still reply:

'Then I'll begin...'

The radio industry

As radios have been getting smaller, the radio industry has been getting bigger.

Changes in government policy over the last 30 years have resulted in major developments in the radio industry. The BBC's monopoly of sound broadcasting has come to an end, and there is now a proliferation of local and national commercial stations. Today, radio is the fastest-growing advertising medium in Britain.

BBC radio

Until 1974, your only official choice of radio listening came from four BBC radio stations: Radios 1, 2, 3 and 4. Since then another BBC station – Radio 5 (now Radio 5 Live) – has been added.

Each of these radio stations aims to meet the listening preferences of a different audience:

- Radio 1 was introduced in the 1960s when pirate radio stations (which broadcast from ships offshore) were suppressed. It aimed to replace them by offering the same sort of pop music format. Many of the early DJs on Radio 1 were recruited from the pirate stations.
- Radio 2 puts out mainly pop and light music programmes, catering for an older audience than Radio 1. Terry Wogan actually makes a joke of this older listenership and the BBC Public Relations department provides car stickers for 'TOGS' (Terry's Old Geezers). Radio 2 also has more speech programmes than Radio 1, including comedy like The News Huddlines and some drama serials (often radio versions of television successes).
- Radio 3 inherited the role of the old 'Third Programme'. Its main focus is broadcasting classical music, but for many years it also put out a wide range of more demanding specialist speech programmes, including features, poetry programmes and over 100 plays a year. Sometimes it could appear a little ridiculous: *Private Eye* once wanted to parody a typical day on Radio 3, but dropped the idea when that week's output included a feature called 'The Place of the Potato in English Folklore', which was far more absurd than anything Peter Cook, Willie Rushton and Co. could make up. Today, although Radio 3 still broadcasts a few plays and other speech programmes, it is essentially a classical music station, consciously competing with Classic FM.
- Radio 4 still has a unique role in British broadcasting, with its wide range of speech-based output including current affairs programmes, in-depth news, quizzes, many plays and serials, comedies and readings. And, of course, the only radio soap: *The Archers*.

- Radio 5 began as a gallant attempt to recapture a younger audience for radio. In the daytime it broadcast sport, but in the evenings concentrated on readings, features and drama for children, and on vaguely defined 'youth' programmes. Although the audience share was making steady progress (in percentage terms it was building more quickly than any of the other stations), in 1994 the BBC got cold feet and replaced it with Radio 5 Live. This is a much safer mix of sport and popularly presented news, indistinguishable from some commercial radio stations. Significantly, it shifted from programmes that were unique to radio to programmes that could generally be done better by commercial TV. Who wants to listen to a football match when they can watch the same game on Sky? Radio 5 Live is a good example of a radio station targeted at people who would rather be watching television, but who are doing things that prohibit them from doing so.

Figure 11.8 Ron Jones commentating for Radio 5 Live

This brings up the whole question of whether the BBC, and BBC radio in particular, has a public duty to make certain sorts of programme which are not available elsewhere, even though they may not be as popular as sport and news.

Despite the success of commercial radio, in the foreseeable future the BBC will remain the largest and most varied supplier of radio programmes. It still has an almost complete monopoly of radio drama, for instance. At the time of writing (1997), its only real competitor in this area is IRD (Independent Radio Drama), which broadcasts short, imaginative dramas on the London News Station every weekday.

Commercial radio

As already explained, if you wanted to listen to radio before 1974 you had to listen to the BBC, unless you were one of those dedicated pop fans who tuned in to:

- pirate radio, broadcast from ships offshore
- Radio Luxembourg, broadcast in English from the tiny country of Luxembourg.

Both of these paid for themselves by putting out advertisements.

Licensed commercial radio began in 1974, nearly 20 years after commercial television. At first the commercial stations were only allowed to serve local areas, but since 1993 Britain has had national stations such as Classic FM, Virgin Radio and Talk Radio.

Generally, new commercial stations gain their audience from the BBC rather than from other commercial stations. In 1997 the BBC only attracted about 50 per cent of all radio listening. Indeed Liz Forgan, the ex-Head of BBC Radio, estimated that this share would drop to 30 per cent by 2005 – which may be one of the reasons why she's the ex-Head.

The growth of commercial radio has resulted in a much more complex system of radio broadcasting regulation, along with a more professional analysis of who listens to what and when.

Figure 11.9 One of London's ' local' commercial radio stations

Types of radio station available

Today you have the choice of tuning in to more different types of radio station than ever before, including:

- BBC network radio. As described above, the BBC has expanded to match the competition from commercial radio, and now offers five channels.
- BBC local radio. For many years, BBC local radio stations competed directly with local commercial stations, offering pop music. Now there has been a change of policy, and BBC local radio is speech-based. As such it is more conscious of its duty to serve the public and to offer a real alternative to the commercial local stations. However, the result has been some loss in audience.
- National commercial radio. Stations such as Classic FM or Virgin Radio tend to specialise in particular areas of broadcasting, rather than competing across the board with the BBC. National Talk Radio is a speech-based station, but offers a far more limited (and cheaper!) range of programmes than the BBC speech-based Radio 4 and Radio 5 Live.
- Local commercial radio stations. These rely mainly on pop music, although many specialise in a particular type of pop (for example the so-called 'Gold' stations, which concentrate on hits from the past).
- Community radio stations. Small-scale, non-profit-making stations with a limited licence. They are dedicated to serving the needs of a local community, a single town or country area.

Public service and public accountability

Despite the efforts of the Director General, John Birt, to turn it into a business, the BBC is still the only real 'public service' station. Critics would say that as such it can be pretty patronising; giving the listeners what it thinks is good for them, rather than what they want. This is one reason why the BBC is nicknamed 'Aunty' (because 'Aunty knows what's good for you'). Even though you want a ray-gun for Christmas, Aunty will give you a Children's Encyclopaedia.

However, commercial radio also has to be aware of its duty to the public, in particular in the way it handles advertising. The Radio Authority has been set up to keep an eye, or an ear, on the output of commercial radio, and especially on its advertisements. Its Code of Advertising Practice disallows any advertisements that could be confused with an ordinary programme, advertisements by political parties, those which attack other products unfairly, those which play on fear, and those which contain sounds that could be a hazard to drivers.

You can't advertise cigarettes, guns, pornography, the occult or betting shops. Advertising isn't allowed during a religious service, a royal ceremony, or a schools programme of under 30 minutes. If you want to advertise alcohol, medicines or contraceptives, or if you want to use children in your advertisement, you have to send your copy (the text of the advertisement) to the Authority. It then decides whether to allow the advertisement to be used.

▶◀ *See Activity 1, page 146*

Independent companies

At one time, all BBC radio programmes were made 'in-house' by BBC staff producers. But since the early nineties BBC Radio has followed in the footsteps of BBC Television by buying programmes made by independent companies. These are usually well-established companies that have been making advertisements for commercial stations or producing the huge variety of talking books now available. The original Radio 5 was particularly open to offers from such 'independents', which was one reason why it had such a refreshingly different sound.

At the moment about 10 per cent of BBC radio programmes, other than news, are made by independents (1997). However, this percentage is likely to increase in line with what happened at BBC Television, where over 25 per cent of non-news output is now made by independents.

It is difficult to assess the effect of so much independent production on the traditional BBC. On the one hand any large organisation tends to get in a bit of a rut, and independent productions have sometimes brought a new sound to the airwaves. On the other hand many people see them as undermining the BBC's commitment to public service. They are not so tightly bound by contractual agreements as the BBC, their studios are not always as well-equipped, and there is always the temptation to cut corners to increase profits. Unfortunately this new reliance on independent producers has led the BBC to get rid of several of its superb drama studios, resulting in a marked reduction in the quality of radio drama. These included a marvellous studio in Bristol, on which it had recently spent £900,000.

Producer choice

Even BBC producers themselves are no longer limited to using BBC facilities. Since 1993, in line with television practice, BBC radio producers have to include a payment in their budgets for using BBC facilities such as studios and editing channels, which have a notional cost attached to them. If they find they can get these facilities more cheaply outside the BBC, they are free to use non-BBC studios and editing. This system, which can mean that for cost reasons complicated dramas are made in rather inadequate studios, goes under the name of 'producer choice'.

The audience

Speech on radio has to be both appropriate to, and comprehensible by, its audience. This means that it has to be in the right style for the person you want to talk to, in words they will understand.

In order to achieve this, radio stations need to have a clear idea of who their audience is. Many stations, especially those which carry advertisements, spend a lot of time and money trying to identify their 'targeted listener'.

The targeted listener

In Britain today there are a lot of radio stations and a lot of radio channels (although not yet as many as in the USA, where the average listener can pick up over 50). Each of these radio stations has to have a fair idea of who it wants to broadcast to. A Radio 1 listener doesn't want the same thing as a Radio 4 listener, for example. A Radio 2 listener is usually a good deal older than a Radio 1 listener. A Radio 5 Live listener is usually interested in news and/or sport. A BBC World Service listener probably has English as a second language. A local radio listener in Wigan doesn't want to hear about events in Watford, while the listener in Watford doesn't care about the weather in Wigan. Radio 3 and Classic FM listeners are mainly interested in classical music, so the spoken bits between the records have to be suited to the sort of people who like classical music.

BBC and commercial local radio stations used to target similar audiences. However, the BBC made a deliberate change in policy in order to target a different audience from its rivals, and today BBC local radio tends to be speech-based, while commercial radio tends to be music-based (usually pop music).

Finally, even pop music stations can differ from each other in style by catering for fans of different sorts of pop. Advertisements too can be tailored to appeal to the sort of people who listen to a particular sort of music.

▶◀ *See Activity 2, page 146*

Radio Joint Advertising Research (RAJAR)

Radio stations, and especially the companies which advertise on them, want to know a lot more than just the general character of listeners. That is where Radio Joint Advertising Research (RAJAR) comes in.

For years the BBC and independent companies each had their own audience research organisations (the BBC one always showed the BBC on top; the commercial one always showed the commercial stations on top). So in 1992 a joint BBC/commercial system was set up: RAJAR.

RAJAR gives figures for:
- weekly reach – the number of people who listen to a station for at least five minutes each week
- audience share – the total listening time devoted to a particular station (the number of listeners multiplied by the number of hours they have tuned in).

Because RAJAR breaks down its figures by sex, age range and social grouping, it helps advertisers and broadcasters to select types of broadcasting suitable to the audience.

RAJAR also breaks up the day into 30-minute chunks, on the grounds that different people listen at different times of day and that the same listeners' tastes vary from morning to evening.

RAJAR is without doubt the most comprehensive radio audience research system in the world. But even it has problems. In the mid-1990s modifications to its sampling technique produced major disparities between the old and new figures, which rather undermined its credibility.

The problem with audience research lies in getting a big enough sample; asking enough people to get a representative selection and therefore a trustworthy answer. You can ask 1000 people, and maybe only 20 or 30 will have listened to their local radio that day. Three Counties Radio for instance, a BBC local radio station, was rather proud of the success of its minority ethnic programmes for people of West Indian background, until suddenly the listening figures dropped drastically. It turned out this was because one family had moved out of the area.

Virgin Radio has decided to supplement RAJAR by offering its own research system to advertisers. This analyses when particular advertisements were broadcast and the size of audience that heard them.

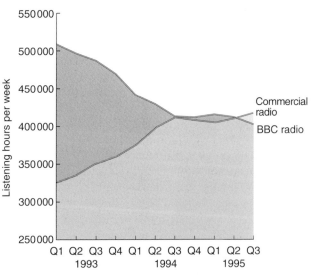

Figure 11.10 RAJAR analyses have highlighted the recent decline of audience figures for BBC radio as commercial radio has grown

Is there anyone out there?

Despite the proliferation of new stations, the overall audience for radio is not what it used to be. In 1974, when commercial radio began, 92 per cent of adults listened to the radio at least once a week. By 1995 the figure was 87 per cent. Listening hours have also declined. In 1977 the average listener took in 22.9 hours of radio a week; by 1995 the figure was 20.00 hours.

In fairness, it should be pointed out that these figures have remained pretty constant since 1988, despite the introduction of satellite television and CD players in cars.

As you might imagine, younger listeners tend to prefer music while older listeners prefer speech radio. Commercial radio has always been strong in the under-44 age group, while the BBC leads the way with the over-55s.

Listener loyalty

Radio listeners seem very loyal. Research carried out by RAJAR indicates that about one-third of all listeners tune in to just one station, and half listen to fewer than three. This is despite the fact that some 20 stations are available in London.

This loyalty has its down side. When the BBC realised its Radio 1 audience was getting a bit middle-aged, it decided to make changes. Familiar voices like Dave Lee Travis and Simon Bates went, and the channel stopped being based on chart-based broadcasting. There was more live music, more comedy and more documentaries. All good innovative stuff. They lost five million listeners.

But times are changing. New technology could again shift the pattern of listening and undermine audiences' loyalties. As more and more of us get sets with digital displays so that we don't have to remember where to find particular stations, it will become much easier to sample different programming. We could start zapping round our radio channels as quickly as we do round TV channels with our hand-held controls.

Scheduling

RAJAR's analysis of audience size throughout the day is shown in the form of graphs, with the points at which the audience is largest standing out like mountain peaks above the general level. At the moment, radio 'peaks' at breakfast time and then declines steadily throughout the day. Radio advertisers are aware that lots of mums listen in the morning before they go shopping. Around 4.30 p.m., when the children arrive home from school, television becomes more dominant than radio.

More detailed audience research has revealed that we tend to want to hear different things at different times of day: one sort of programme when we're getting breakfast, another when driving to work, another if we're at home in the daytime, something different in the evening if there's nothing much on TV, and something else again if we're lying in bed late at night with the light off. The people responsible for scheduling radio programmes have to bear this in mind.

In 1997 BBC Radio brought in a system where the day and the week is split up between different commissioning editors, who are supposed to be aware of the type of audience likely to be listening during their time-slot and commission programmes accordingly. This means that different editors commission programmes for the morning, afternoon and evening, with others again working on programmes for the weekends.

◀ *See Activity 3, page 147*

Choice of programmes

Once they know the audience they are catering for, schedulers have to decide what type of programme they want to put out, at what time. This mix of programmes is often called a 'menu'.

Not all radio is about voices. Radio 3 and Classic FM broadcast orchestral music; natural history programmes include the songs of whales, the chirrups of crickets, the growls of tigers and the calls of birds; sport gives us the roar of the crowd and clunk of bat on ball. However, the vast majority of programmes scheduled are dominated by the human voice, either singing or speaking.

The voices on radio are picked up by a microphone. From the microphone they can come straight to the listener live, or they can be recorded, messed around with in various ways by skilled technicians and expensive machinery, and then broadcast. This simple concept allows for many different kinds of programming, each with its own character.

Speech-based programmes

Even discounting news (which is dealt with in chapters 7 and 8), there is a bewildering variety of spoken programmes on the radio. Speech-based shows can be either live or recorded, and can take the form of:

- phone-ins – good cheap radio that involves the listener
- discussions – group of people sit round a table and, hopefully, disagree
- outside broadcasts which involve taking a mobile studio on location – such as sports coverage, or a panel of gardening experts in a village hall answering questions from local people
- strip programmes – shows lasting several hours, made up of pop music interrupted by live chat interviews and phone-ins (the stock-in-trade of local radio)
- dramatised features – real events such as famous trials recreated by actors
- actuality features – field recordings of real people living real lives, recorded with background sounds on a small tape recorder and then edited down to get rid of the boring bits and give the programme a structure
- investigative features – usually a mixture of studio-based comment and recorded inserts
- talks – the simplest radio of all, with one person sitting at a microphone telling the listeners his or her ideas on a topic
- readings – one person sitting at a microphone and reading a book out loud. Books are usually cut by about three-quarters, even for a fortnight's worth of fifteen-minute readings
- quizzes – audience shows with the 'teams' sitting on a platform trying to be clever
- light entertainment – audience shows with the actors standing on a platform trying to be funny. Nowadays a high proportion of these are made in a studio like ordinary dramas

Figure 11.11 Recording the Goon Show

- documentaries – an extended examination of something of public importance
- poetry – in the past recorded in the studio, but now more often performed before an audience, either by the poet or by actors
- drama – a group of actors pretending they aren't reading scripts in a radio studio, perform plays either specially written for radio or adapted from stage plays or books.

Music programmes

While it is true that the main element on radio is the human voice, it is also true that on the majority of stations that voice is usually singing. As with speech programmes, there is a wide variety of music programmes:

- live concerts – concerts involving a whole orchestra, like the Proms (Promenade Concerts), are the most expensive things broadcast on radio, which is why you only find them on the BBC
- session programmes – pop, jazz or folk programmes featuring a live band and usually discs made by the band
- music documentaries – now virtually the only documentaries regularly appearing on Radio 1 and Radio 3
- chart programmes – programmes based on the Top Twenty, Top Forty and so on, with minimal interruption by the presenter or DJ
- presenter-led programmes – the most popular format on Radio 2. In these programmes the personality of the presenter, such as Jimmy Young or Terry Wogan, is at least as important as the music they are playing. Some presenters even talk over records

- personal choice programmes – the most famous of these is still *Desert Island Discs* which, because it actually contains a lot more talk than music, is broadcast on Radio 4.

▶️ *See Activity 4, page 147*

Figure 11.12 Pete Tong at work for Radio 1

Making an impact on the radio

It is estimated that 90 per cent of people listening to the radio are doing something else at the same time. Indeed many people choose to listen to the radio rather than watch TV or videos *because* they are doing something else; perhaps preparing breakfast, or doing the housework. The old

Afternoon Theatre used to be nicknamed 'plays to hoover by'!

If you are producing *The Archers*, it is drummed into you that clarity of sound is more important than clever background effects. It is more than likely that a lot of the audience will be listening to the show with all sorts of other noises going on in the background. Apparently the soap is particularly popular with tractor drivers.

Radio is fleeting

Listeners have to catch the spoken word on the wing: they have to understand what is being said as it is being said. In the early days of the old BBC Third Programme, at least one academic who was used to publishing learned papers sent in the script for a commissioned talk with footnotes! Radio is not like that: you haven't got time to look something up if you don't understand it. Sometimes, if you are talking about a technical subject, you may feel you have to use a *recondite* word. But, with care, you can usually find a way to explain this *little-known* or *obscure* word within the general text of what you are saying.

The simplest way to do this is to give the explanation in sort of parentheses (in verbal brackets, as it were). Sentences should be constructed in a way that makes them easy to understand at a single hearing. They should be short, straightforward and direct, not cluttered with adjectives and adverbs.

The 'grammar' and sounds of spoken language

Spoken language has its own grammar that is not always the same as that of written language. On the page, spoken language can look incorrect, even though the style is often quite intentional.

Sentences without verbs. Terse statements. Everywhere nowadays. Even in the carefully crafted speeches of the President of the USA. They give an impression of urgency and economy. At least that's the idea...

Spoken language also has its own rhythms and forms. Indeed, if language is too carefully grammatical it can sound stilted and artificial. On the other hand, if it is too smoothly written and flows too easily and comfortably into the ear, there's a real danger it will flow straight out the other side.

Speech also has tools that are not available when using the written word. Radio speech uses pauses, timing, pace, volume, pitch and inflection to create variety and to make clear what is being said.

Pauses

The most important tool which professional broadcasters use to recapture our attention is the pause. Just as you are aware when your clock stops, so an actor, presenter or newsreader will highlight a word by *pointing* it. This means putting a brief pause before it, occasionally after it, and sometimes both before and after. These tiny sudden silences wake the ear up, making us pay attention.

In fact you don't even have to pause at a significant point.

Picture the poor newsreader who has to do a bulletin at six o'clock in the morning. She is dragged half-awake to the lonely, cold microphone by a BBC commissionaire. She sits in her pyjamas with a bacon sandwich in one hand and a mug of black coffee in the other, blinking at the typewritten sheet in front of her. The green light goes on, signifying that she is 'on air'. Without having had a chance to look at it, she 'sight reads' the news. She has no idea what she is saying, so she just sticks in pauses where she feels like it. But to the early morning listener it makes perfect sense. Because it is broken up, it sounds natural. If you don't believe it, get up early one morning to listen to the six o'clock bulletin and see where the pauses come!

One final point. We think much more quickly than we can speak. The pause we hear in our head as we read something seems much longer than it really is; much longer than the pause the listener hears. If you are speaking a script, remember to leave a long enough silence for it to register. In radio drama actors are sometimes told to count a certain number of beats to make sure their pauses are long enough for the effect intended. Samuel Beckett once had a 30-second pause in a radio play. It would have been extremely effective, had the BBC Control Room not panicked and assumed there was a technical fault.

Pace and timing

Pace is quite simply the speed at which you speak. One way to create variety, and therefore interest, is to vary the pace within a speech so that it doesn't just rumble over the ear.

Timing – the exact amount of pause left before saying something – is often said to be the key to great comedy. Good timing enables you to catch the audience's attention and keep them in suspense, so that you surprise them into a laugh. On the other hand, if you want to create an atmosphere of danger and horrors, the usual trick is to speak quickly but to have long pauses.

Try saying the following quickly without the pauses, and then with the pauses:

> ❛ *Suddenly she heard footsteps behind her.* [pause] *They were getting nearer.* [pause] *She began to run, quicker and quicker,* [pause] *she was panting with the effort, running as for her life,* [pause] *but the footsteps, without seemingly to hurry* [pause] *were gaining on her, getting closer.* [pause] *Again, she ran and ran and ran,* [pause] *until she could run no more.* [pause] *Exhausted, she collapsed against a wall.* [pause] *The footsteps were now right behind her.* [pause] *Gritting her teeth, she turned to face her pursuer.* [pause] *And there was no-one there.* ❜

Volume and pitch

Volume is quite simply loudness. This is not a very useful tool on radio, as it can make the microphone distort what is being said.

Pitch varies depending on whether speech is in a high voice or a low voice. When we are calling out, we tend to use high notes because we seem to know instinctively that they travel further than low notes.

Inflection/intonation

Inflection, or intonation, is a mixture of everything applied to individual words. Take the simple word 'well'. Depending on the way it is spoken, it can convey quite a number of different

meanings. Try saying:
- 'Well?',
- 'Well!'
- [pause] 'Well I...'
- 'Well,' [pause] 'I...'.

Quite often a broadcaster will use these tools simply to make sure the listener is listening and not just hearing, rather than for dramatic or comic effect.

▶◀ *See Activities 5, 6 and 7, page 147*

Analysing a radio programme

When analysing a radio programme, you may find it helpful to work through the following steps:

1 Look at the format. At the simplest level, is the show live and spontaneous? Is it recorded with lots of different elements carefully edited together? Or is it a mixture of the two? Does it include listener participation by telephone or letter?

Does it rely on one presenter or does it have a 'zoo format'?

2 Is it purely for entertainment, or is it also intended to inform?

3 What is its style? Is it chatty and friendly? Deliberately confrontational? Specialist? Of general interest? Mad? Fast-moving or evenly paced?

4 What is its target audience? What age? Is it for both sexes or just for women or for men? What will you expect the audience to be doing while they are listening to it?

5 If it is on a commercial station, how do the advertisements relate to the general style of the programme?

6 How does it stop you switching off or switching to another programme?

7 Taking all these elements together, try to decide what the producers set out to do with the programme. Why did the station choose to put out this particular programme?

8 Did the station achieve what you think was its purpose in broadcasting the programme?

ACTIVITIES ▼

Activity 1

Discuss what you feel is the difference between 'public service' and pure entertainment programmes. As a group, go through radio listings in the *Radio Times* and decide which programmes you would consider 'public service'. Would you listen to them yourselves?

Activity 2

Here is the script of a radio advertisement for a large chain of record stores in the north of England. It is targeted at a particular audience in a particular place. (**MVO** simply means 'Male Voice Over'.)

THE HARRISON AGENCY

Client: Andy's Records

Area: Grimsby

Title: Razamatazz

Length: 40"

MVO: It's a razamatazz tazz tazz and all that jazz is a gazz eee baby who said, Jazz. I mean solely solely soul rock 'n' roll blues and peeeezazzz... that's peezazz like a pizza (that's Italian food wid'da cheeese n'things y'know) with the sleepy sounds you put out like the zzzzzzeds and adding them on to the best range of music you've ever heard from Andy's Records... the record store to beat them all... where you're never alone with a pink satin elephant night-dress holder, which is this week's competition to see how many famous names from the Andy's range you can spot, if only to tell you that Massif Centrale is a large French meatloaf and just wait until the day breaks before covering your knees up... so who said there's lots going on at Andy's Records at 31 Victoria Street, Grimsby. 'Cos they've got all the rock 'n' roll in the world to be goin' on with. But don't listen to me, just listen to Andy's... 'cos they know what you're talking about.

MVO: Andy's Records. 31 Victoria Street, Grimsby. We know what you're talking about.

What audience do you think this advertisement is aimed at? What kind of image is Andy's Records trying to project? On what sort of radio station would you expect to find this advertisement?

Activity 3

Carry out your own survey among your group and family to find out where and when people listen to the radio (if they do), and what programmes they listen to. Draw a graph to show listening patterns throughout the day.

Compare your results with those of professional research organisations such as RAJAR (Radio Joint Audience Research Ltd, Collier House, 163-169 Brompton Road, London SW3 1PY). Many of RAJAR's research findings are printed in *Broadcast*, a weekly magazine for the broadcasting industries.

Activity 4

Research different stations and try to work out what their programming policy is. What sort of target audience are they aiming for?

Activity 5

Take a short article from a broadsheet newspaper and turn it into a piece that could be spoken on the radio for a general audience. You will probably need to shorten and simplify the sentences, get rid of quite a few long words, and maybe cut down the number of adjectives and adverbs. Where a technical expression is essential for the meaning of the article make sure you explain it, preferably more than once in case your audience misses it the first time.

Activity 6

Write a five-minute talk for radio on a subject that interests you and you know a lot about. The talk is for people who do not know anything about your subject. Remember to keep your sentences uncomplicated and reasonably short, and to repeat any really important information to make sure the listeners grasp it (without making it too obvious!).

After you have given your talk, see how much people learned. Did they grasp the main facts? Were you able to communicate your enthusiasm? Five minutes is about 900 words.

Activity 7

As a group, plan a radio soap opera to rival *The Archers*. To do this you will need to work out the following:

- Format. Where is it set? A town? A street? A school? Somewhere else? What sort of town, street, school or other location? Where is it? What sort of people are involved? What are the issues and situations that concern them?

- Characters. Invent about 15 characters, allowing for different ages and interests. Make sure that they are connected in some way – through work, family relationships, friendship or hostility. Make sure you know what they do for a living and what they earn, and make sure there is plenty of variety of types.
- Storylines. The best storylines are the ones that grow out of the characters themselves. Work out a variety of storylines that will each last at least four weeks. Each should be about one page.
- Episodes. Plan six episodes, each covering several storylines. Remember all the storylines don't have to start at the same time, but once a storyline has started it should be referred to in each episode, even if it isn't the main theme, or the audience will lose touch with it. Several of the storylines can be left in the air at the end of the sixth episode, as long as you know how they will be resolved. If you want to be really clever you can devise references so that even if someone misses an episode they can still follow the story! Each episode should be about a page of notes.

Remember: your soap is for radio, not for TV!

BIBLIOGRAPHY ▼

Briggs, A, *The History of Broadcasting in the United Kingdom*, vols. 1–4, Oxford University Press, 1961–79

Drakakis, J (ed.), *British Radio Drama*, Cambridge University Press, 1981

Extending Choice: The BBC's Role in the New Broadcasting Age, BBC, 1992

The Future of the BBC: A Consultation Document (Cm2098), HMSO, 1992

Horstmann, R, *Writing for Radio*, A & C Black, 1991

Lewis, P M, *The Invisible Medium: Public, Commercial and Community Radio*, Macmillan, 1989

The Radio Authority Pocket Book, Radio Authority, 1993

Thomas, D, *Under Milk Wood*, Everyman, 1979

Took, B, *Laughter in the Air: An Informal History of Radio Comedy*, Robson Books, 1982

CHAPTER 12

Pop music

Introduction

This chapter outlines a range of approaches to the study of popular music as part of a media studies course. It begins by showing how pop music relates to the central concepts of media studies, before going on to look at:

- record labels
- recording artists
- recordings themselves
- pop videos.

The activities at the end of the chapter give ideas on how you can carry out practical projects on pop music as part of your media studies.

Why study pop music?

> *The "death" of rock in the 1980s is sometimes described in terms of its fragmentation. There are now just scattered "taste markets", and the central rock institutions of the seventies – the music press and certain TV and radio shows – can no longer put together a general audience. This is not simply a matter of statistics. The important point is that there is no single pop taste, no particular rock fragment seems any weightier, any truer than any other.*
> Simon Frith, 1988

As this passage suggests, the world of pop music is not as simple as many people assume. In fact, the study of pop music can make a major contribution to your understanding of many of the key concepts of media studies, including:

- genre – the marketing of genres can be illustrated by a detailed analysis of, say, reggae or heavy metal
- representation – the impact of representation can be explained by looking at how popular figures such as Madonna, the artist formerly known as Prince, Michael Jackson or the Spice Girls are portrayed in the music press, on album covers or in videos
- audience – audience analysis and research can be carried out with pop music as a focus
- industry – a detailed study of how record labels operate can form the basis for an interesting case study on the structure and organisation of a media industry.

Looking at pop music over time can also be a good way to study the history of a media industry and how the media have affected social attitudes, trends and fashion. Pop music recordings on vinyl, tape or CD are durable and deletion of recordings by major artists is rare, although original pressings may become unobtainable. Therefore, at any given time, recordings from a range of historical periods are available. A visit to Our Price, HMV, Virgin or any independent record dealer can be a visit to Aladdin's cave if you wish to gather media representations of the sounds, looks and attitudes of the past. This means that pop music can be used like documentary film evidence, raising the same debates about the reliability of such material and the way in which it is controlled, edited, selected and disseminated.

The study of pop music can also develop your appreciation of the art of journalism. For example, you could study the codes and conventions which dominate journalist's writing about music, then attempt to write reviews or articles in the style of *NME* or *Select*. You could produce your own pop music fanzine as a practical project; design your own CD covers or promotional packages; or, if you happen to play in a local band or produce your own recordings at home, use your own music as part of your studies.

▶◀ *See Activity 1, page 159*

If you are interested in learning about the technical aspects of video production, then 'experimental' pop videos can be both exciting and challenging to produce. Recording audio programmes about pop music which feature, for example, a profile of an artist or the history of an act, can be useful if you wish to develop your skills as a radio presenter. Designing concert programmes or flyers for local concerts can forge a link between yourself, your course and the local community.

One word of warning: opinions run deep when it comes to popular music. Battles have been fought over it (as the film *Quadrophenia* shows); generations have defined themselves by their taste in music; and modern 'youth culture' and rebellion are inextricably linked to the sounds and styles of the pop music produced during a given period. Therefore any attempt to discuss pop music is likely to provoke fierce, sometimes confrontational debate.

If you wish to study pop music 'seriously', which is what this chapter will help you to do, then you might find it necessary to arm yourself with more than your passion for music. You will also need a willingness to listen to the musical preferences of others, and a thick skin to prevent your love of certain artists or genres being dented by the merciless assaults of other students who don't share your musical taste.

▶◀ *See Activity 2, page 159*

The record label

> *Being able to sell in the international marketplace is something that only the large majors can do. They can press, distribute and sell all around the world through subsidiary companies and licensees. It is this ability that makes them giants of the business and enables them to dominate the markets of the world. Independent companies are simply not large enough to sell in the international marketplace.*
> Blanchard, Greenleaf and Sefton-Green, 1989

Any study of a pop music product should start with the record label, just as the study of a film or television programme should begin with the studio or channel.

Record labels act as signifiers to the consumer. They indicate whether recording artists have the support of a major label such as EMI or Warner Brothers, or whether they are in the hands of a small, independent company such as Factory, Cherry Red, 4AD, Creation or Fax. This, in turn, can say a great deal about a recording artist's style of music.

Major labels

In 1997 approximately 70 per cent of recordings sold worldwide were produced, manufactured and marketed by five major companies: Sony Music Entertainment, EMI Music, PolyGram, Warner Music International, and BMG music group.

These companies are all owned by large, transnational companies:

- Sony is owned by the Sony Corporation of Japan. Its interests include telecommunications, domestic and visual products, Columbia Pictures, Hollywood.
- EMI is owned by Thorn EMI of the UK. Its interests include lighting, domestic appliances, retail outlets and computer software.
- Warner is owned by Time Warner, the largest entertainment company in America.
- PolyGram is owned by the Philips Corporation of Holland. Its interests include lighting, domestic appliances, retail outlets and technological systems.
- BMG is owned by the Bertelsmann group of Germany, a large media conglomerate whose interests include newspapers and cable TV networks.

In addition, a further 12 to 15 per cent share of the world's pop music market is owned by two other leisure and entertainment groups: Music Corporation of America, and the Virgin Music Group of the UK.

In most instances, an artist on a major label is promoted and represented with little reference to the record label itself. The label's name often only appears as a logo on the artist's recording, or as a small part of the promotional material. In the same way, it is unusual in the 1990s for a feature film to be publicised as 'From the studio which brought you...' (although the director, actors and sometimes producer and scriptwriters are often used).

Instead, artists on major labels are usually marketed according to:

- the genre of the music they produce
- their 'unique' image which the label wishes to promote.

Figure 12.1 Record label logos

Independent labels

Some independent labels, on the other hand, actively encourage the comparison of acts on their label by employing the same team to produce the graphics and cover artwork for different artists' recordings. They may also use the same engineers or producers to work on recordings, which can have a major impact on the overall effect of a recording on the consumer. The impact of a major record label on an artist is harder to define, and is much harder to research.

Although most record labels 'sign up' a range of pop music artists with differing influences, it is sometimes possible to see links in the sound, style and 'overall feel' of an independent label's artists.

▶◀   *See Case Study, page 154*

The recording artist

> *For women musicians, though, there's a problem. Rock is a man's world, and women musicians are still treated as something unnatural, as needing some sort of gloss.*
> Simon Frith, 1988

As with other media industries, certain codes and conventions have been established in order to enable recording artists to be easily marketed to their target audience. Just as genre movies directed by very different directors share similarities, so do the images of artists performing music of similar styles or genres:

- a look at promotional photographs or interviews with Blur, Oasis, Gene, Kula Shaker, Lightning Seeds and the Manic Street Preachers will soon establish that they are male British guitar bands that share a love of traditional (and some might argue great) song writing
- The Prodigy, Orbital, Underground and The Orb are all defined by their uniquely British take on dance music
- Pearl Jam, Soundgarden and Pavement are male American guitar bands made popular by the Nirvana phenomenon
- R Kelly is an R and B performer
- Gabrielle and Whitney Houston are female balladeers
- Take That were, and Boyzone are, pretty boy teen pop bands. The Spice Girls are a far more interesting female equivalent.

Codes and conventions used to present artists

The bands and artists mentioned above are all very different, but the conventions dominating their representation remain, even today, rather conservative. These include the use of:

- sex appeal
- the rebel image
- the lads' image
- the loser
- street culture
- pretty boys and girls.

Figure 12.2 Studying images can help you identify pop genres, such as the three contrasting genres of British pop music represented by Oasis, The Spice Girls, and The Prodigy

The representation of men

Sex appeal is a key factor in the representation of both men and women. However, as with most advertising (record sleeves, like film posters and book jackets, should be seen as advertising products), men are usually represented with more variety than women:

- rebellious males are signified by their clothing (leather jackets, torn jeans etc.)
- lads are linked by the backdrop of the pictures, their poses and attitude (e.g. The Smiths' *The Queen Is Dead* contains a classic lads' image which has been much imitated)
- losers are shabby, unshaven, rough but 'tragically' noble (e.g. Tom Waits)
- representatives of 'the street' are hard, dangerous, aggressive, angry and (probably) black (e.g. Public Enemy)
- 'pretty' boys are non-threatening boys next door, charming and handsome (e.g. Boyzone, Take That).

▶◀   *See Activity 3, page 159*

Figure 12.3 Alternative images of male bands: the moody lads of The Smiths and the boys next door of Take That

A quick scan of the shelves in a record shop reveals the extent to which male recording artists appear to dominate the industry and define the genres which exist within styles of pop music.

The subject of masculinity within pop music has been hilariously ridiculed in Rob Reiner's 1989 spoof 'rockumentary' *This Is Spinal Tap*, a film which, along with Martin Scorsese's *The Last Waltz*, can be used as an invaluable aid to the study of pop music. Both, in their very different ways, give a unique insight into the backstage world of rock music.

The representation of women

Women popular music artists are often 'sold' on record sleeves or in promotional material with less variety and according to the artist's perceived sex appeal. This manifests itself in the usual stereotypical ways: lots of exposed flesh, 'fetishistic' clothing (by colour, texture and design), unnatural poses, an emphasis on make-up and hair, a propensity for looking glamorous, and so on.

Even respected women artists such as Kate Bush, Alanis Morisette, Joni Mitchell and Diana Ross have found themselves represented with undue emphasis on their sexuality. Recent notable exceptions to this rule might be said to include Skunk Anansie, Elastica and Tori Amos.

The 1980s saw a significant shift of emphasis from traditional stereotypes, with the new popularity of all-girl bands like Bananarama and the representation of women with 'attitude' on record sleeves. Other conventions which are now commonly used to represent women in pop music include:

- 'the mature chanteuse' (e.g. Celine Dion, Mariah Carey, Annie Lennox)
- 'the solo folkie' (e.g. Suzanne Vega, Tracy Chapman)
- 'the torch singer' (e.g. Nico, Marianne Faithful)
- 'the bubble gum' pop star (e.g. Shampoo, Kenickie, early Cyndi Lauper).

Figure 12.4 Women in pop music include the 'bubble gum' star like Cyndi Lauper and the 'mature chanteuse' like Annie Lennox

Madonna's career has consciously taken in almost all of these conventions: from the bubble gum image of *True Blue*, through the sex appeal of *Erotica*, to the mature chanteuse of *Bedtime Stories* and *Evita*.

Incidentally, the American Country and Western genre provides a number of interesting examples of a more 'positive' representation of women in pop. Sheryl 'Leaving Las Vegas' Crow has been presented with a cross-over appeal, while the tragic cases of Patsy Cline and Loretta Lynn have both been charted in Hollywood biopics (*Sweet Dreams* starring Jessica Lange, and *Coal Miner's Daughter* with Sissy Spacek). Both films are worth watching to get further insight into these performers' lives. The cable TV station CMT will give you opportunities to look closely at the video and lyrical concerns of this ever-popular, but much maligned, musical genre.

Figure 12.5 Sissy Spacek as Loretta Lynn in Coal Miner's Daughter (left) and Jessica Lange as Patsy Cline in Sweet Dreams

Dress codes

It is also possible to identify recording artists by their use of the dress codes which exist within the genres of pop music:

- a heavy metal act may be defined by long hair and certain types of guitars (Flying Vs used to be a sure-fire sign of the genre, for example The Scorpions and Michael Schenker)
- sunglasses are signifiers of aloof pop celebrity
- a reggae act may be represented through the use of Rastafarian colours (green, red and yellow) and 'dreads'
- a rock 'n' roll artist may still adhere to a classic 1950s look
- techno performers often appear dressed in the latest fashionable 'rave' wear
- Goth bands (such as Sisters of Mercy and The Cure) wear black.

Even something as simple as trouser style can tell you a great deal about a performer's target audience. Think for a moment about the difference between tight leather and flares.

Codes and conventions over time

If you look at pop music of the 1960s and that of today, you will find that although there is a great deal of difference in the sound of music being produced, the codes and conventions surrounding the representation of recording artists remain relatively unchanged. A detailed analysis of the 'changing face' of The Beatles might reveal that all of the aforementioned codes and conventions were used (or perhaps established) on their record sleeves.

Another artist whose career is marked by a constant 're-invention' of his public face is the singer David Bowie, who, to this day, attempts to surprise and sometimes unsettle his fans and critics by attempts to redefine his image (and the sound of his music). There can be little doubt that the Bowie of *Diamond Dogs* or *Ziggy Stardust* is different to the Bowie of *Heroes* and the recent *Earthling* sessions.

Figure 12.6 The reinvention of David Bowie

CASE ▼ STUDY

4AD

> ❛ *It was his [Ivo Watts-Russell] intention to encourage bands that the leading labels passed up because they were too eccentric, too intelligent and too much of a risk. He succeeded in nurturing some of the most acclaimed alternative rock acts of the past decade.* ❜
> Emma Forrest, 1993

THE 4AD IDENTITY

Although fans may want to disagree, it is undeniable that while on the 4AD record label bands as musically diverse as the Cocteau Twins, Lush, Pixies, Red House Painters and The Wolfgang Press all shared a certain type of image.
The label cultivated this image through its innovative and ground-breaking sleeve designs. It might also be suggested that, since leaving the label, both the Cocteau Twins and Red House Painters have taken the label's 'look' with them, in order to keep their fan base. Even the record's catalogue

Figure 12.7 4AD covers for albums by the Pixies and The Breeders

number (which always includes the letters 'AD' in the case of 4AD) acts as a signifier to the consumer of the record label.

The fact that 4AD has released a compilation record featuring many of its artists (*Lonely is an Eyesore* – CAD 703), sells T-shirts and poster packs bearing the label's logo and designs, and has encouraged many of its artists to work together on a marvellous trilogy of records under the name This Mortal Coil further suggests that the label sees itself as a signifier and representative of its artists.

4AD's approach to marketing its artists ensures that the label has a strong identity, and that fans of one band on the label may be persuaded that other bands on the same label might be worth 'checking out'. 4AD markets itself as a club worth joining.

THE IMPORTANCE OF DESIGN

When surveying the racks in a local record store, a fan of one 4AD act would probably have little difficulty in realising that an album belonged to the 4AD label if the sleeve was designed by Vaughan Oliver/23 Envelope/V23, the company responsible for the label's artwork. They might, therefore, buy the product on spec.

A close look at the sleeve design of records released on 4AD further reinforces the label's method of maintaining and establishing an identity:

- the Venus fly-trap on the cover of Heidi Berry's eponymous LP (CAD 3009) is photographed in a similar way to the fossil which is mounted on the front of the Cocteau Twins' ground-breaking 'Aikea–Guinea' single (AD 501)
- the sepia hues dominating the Pixies' releases 'Here Comes Your Man' (AD 909) and *Monkey Gone to Heaven* (BAD 904) are also reflected in the Red House Painters' *Down Colorful Hill* (CAD 2014)
- there is a strong similarity between the graphics and layout of releases by Swallow, Richenel and Xymox.

The 23 Envelope sleeve designs are also linked in that there has been an obvious decision made to not represent the artists on the record sleeve (Frank Black and The Wolfgang Press are notable exceptions). Instead, haunting, luridly photographed and obliquely laid-out images dominate the album covers. These are images, like those of Dave McKean who designed the imaginative *Sandman* comic-book covers, which suggest mystery, the exotic, the erotic and sometimes the wilfully 'strange'.

ALBUM TITLES

The titles of the albums, like the names of the bands, share semantic similarities: links with nature, the Romantic poets, words associated with time and memory. For example, 4AD titles include:

- *The Moon and the Sun* (Heidi Berry – BAD 3010)
- *Lullabies* (Cocteau Twins – BAD 213)
- *Within the Realm of a Dying Sun* (Dead Can Dance – CAD 705)
- *Filigree and Shadow* (This Mortal Coil – DAD 609).

STYLE OF MUSIC

The anonymity of the performers and the atmosphere of the sleeve designs also reflect, to a certain extent, similarities in

Figure 12.8 Heidi Berry and Cocteau Twins

Figure 12.9 Pixies and Red House Painters

the music produced by many of the label's artists. It would be churlish to say that all bands on 4AD 'sound the same' (this is a lazy approach often taken by music journalists, for whom the label will always be linked with the Cocteau Twins, its most successful signing). However, a quick listen to a selection of the label's releases reveals that the 'strangeness' alluded to earlier can definitely be found somewhere on 4AD recordings, whether the artist is the ambient composer Michael Brook, the mournful Red House Painters, or the liltingly harmonious Voix Bulgares.

It is certain that the bands on 4AD have been signed because the label's gatekeepers – its A and R team, its producers and its chairpeople (especially Ivo Watts-Russell) – have similar 'good' taste. Watts-Russell confirmed this himself in an article by John Paveley in *Indie Cator* magazine:

> ❝ *I make most of my decisions on an absurd emotional level as I can truly say that I have never got to grips with what will work commercially. I think that if I have that intense feeling about something, then we should release it. It must be said that I totally indulge my fantasy for releasing music that I think is dead good.* ❞

▶◀ *See Activity 4, page 160*

As this case study shows, a record label like 4AD can act as a strong signifier of its artists. However, this is only possible while the label remains small enough to do so (4AD has approximately 40 artists). In most cases it is the recording artist, not the label and what it represents, who is 'sold' on a recording.

The recording

As with most media products, the recording of a popular music product must be considered as a collaborative project. As we have already seen, the impact of a record label on a recording should not be underestimated. Nor, of course, should the work of the studio engineers and producers who work on it.

Therefore, before actually listening to a recording, you should consider the record label, the people involved in the recording in addition to the artist, and how the recording is packaged (its title, cover artwork, any printed lyrics and so on).

Production factors

Some artists align themselves with producers they feel they work with particularly well; for example:

- The Beatles with George Martin
- The Smiths with Stephen Street

- The Blue Nile with Calum Malcolm
- Joy Division with Martin Hannant
- U2, Talking Heads and James with Brian Eno
- Talk Talk with Tim Friese-Green.

All have worked together on the production of memorable albums. Other producers stamp their personality on recordings by a wide range of recording artists. Producer Trevor Horn, for example, has given recordings by artists as diverse as Yes, ABC, Frankie Goes To Hollywood, Propaganda and Rod Stewart a certain epic and, at times, innovative 'production sound'.

In some cases, artists produce their own recordings, in order to retain greater control over the finished product. The artist formerly known as Prince, Edwyn Collins and the Cocteau Twins have all chosen to do this.

It is even possible to argue that where a record is recorded may influence its 'feel'. To this day artists still queue up to record at Abbey Road studios in London, Oasis being one of the latest to seek out the studios' ambience.

Record titles

The name given to a recording can provide a useful 'way into' the product, which can then be approached in the light of its title. In literary studies this is a commonly used approach. For example, poems such as 'The Waste Land' and 'Paradise Lost' are often analysed by showing the link between content and title.

Cover artwork

As with books, comics and films, there is usually a strong link between a recording's title and the images used on the cover to sell the product. Much of the genius of cover design work goes unnoticed, partly because so much gets lost. Books and films are often reprinted or re-released with changed artwork to reflect the attitudes of the day. A study of how 'classic' novels are marketed or how old movies get repackaged for a new generation of film-goers can show a great deal about social change and the media's effect upon, and reflection of, public perception.

However, it is rare for a pop music recording to be significantly repackaged, giving you an opportunity to focus upon the original artwork designs.

Album covers certainly merit study. The images we are able to scrutinise as we listen to our favourite recordings are imprinted on most of us:

- Pink Floyd's 1974 *Dark Side of the Moon* is forever linked to the Hipgnosis designed black and white prism on the cover
- Prefab Sprout's Steve McQueen motorbike captures the band's insouciant charm and, most importantly, an image cleverly associated with the actor and his film *The Great Escape*
- The Smiths and sixties icons are permanently linked on the brilliant covers designed by Caryn Gough for their singles 'This Charming Man', 'Hand in Glove' and 'Heaven Knows'
- Peter Saville's ground-breaking work on New Order's single 'Blue Monday' imaginatively heralded in the 'techno/dance' era
- it is hard to imagine 1970s prog-rock giants Yes without Roger Dean.

▶◀ See Activity 5, page 160

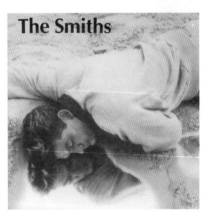

Figure 12.10 All memorable covers: Pink Floyd's Dark Side of the Moon, Caryn Gough's designs for 'Hand in Glove' and 'This Charming Man' by The Smiths, and New Order's 'Blue Monday'

The lyrics

The packaging of a recording often includes lyrics for the consumer's attention.

A close analysis of a recording's lyrics will give some indication of its target audience. Although it is foolish to generalise, love songs still dominate pop music recordings, with artists as diverse as Babybird, Pet Shop Boys, The Divine Comedy, The Beautiful South, Edwyn Collins and Massive Attack achieving success in 1996 and 1997 with pop songs apparently about the traumas of heterosexual relationships ('Candy Girl', 'Before', 'The Frog Princess', 'Don't Marry Her...', 'A Girl Like You', and 'Protection'). The song in tribute to a particular girlfriend is almost a sub-genre of popular music: just think of all the pop songs which have girls' first names for their titles.

Obviously, like any poets, lyricists are not exclusively limited to writing about love. Pop music has always thrown up artists who wish to use the medium to tackle more challenging concerns; for example:

- the protest songs of Bob Marley, Bob Dylan and The Sex Pistols
- the heart-felt street portraits of Mark Eitzel, Tom Waits and Tindersticks
- the druggy ramblings of Jim Morrison and Syd Barratt
- the humour of Lloyd Cole, Microdisney, Momus and Blur
- the anger of the Manic Street Preachers and Public Enemy
- the wilful obscurity of Kate Bush, Talk Talk, Talking Heads and David Sylvian.

All go to show how diverse and inspirational pop music can be.

Music without dialogue

Obviously not all pop music has lyrics, and the dance music explosion of the late 1980s has meant that music supported by sampled dialogue or entirely without the contribution of a vocalist has grown in popularity. Often artists rely on 'guest vocalists' when there is a need for a more prominent vocal line (Noel Gallagher, Beth Orton, John Lydon and Tracy Thorn have all consolidated their status by guesting in this way).

Material by The Orb, Future Sound of London, Leftfield and the Chemical Brothers has taken pop music in a very different direction to the guitar-dominated 'song' approach which characterised the industry throughout the 1960s and 1970s. It is possible to argue that the work of these artists is playing a major part in defining the sort of music we will be buying in the next century.

The composer

When looking at a recording's packaging, it is important to note which of the artists on the recording is cited as the composer of the songs.

Some artists credit the lyrics to one member of the group (often the singer) and the music to another. The Smiths' Morrissey and Marr follow this pattern. Often two of the band members are named as responsible for song-writing duties, although they may not actually write songs together. This was the case with The Beatles' Lennon and McCartney, who rarely wrote songs together but whose names were linked for contractual reasons. Some artists credit composition to the entire group (as with Blur on *Parklife*). Others will list the individuals responsible. Solo artists such as Madonna and Michael Jackson often have songs composed for them by professional song-writers. It is also common for artists who are 'created' and have a very high media profile (such as The Spice Girls) to co-write material with their producers.

Analysing the recording itself

Having gathered as much information as you can from a recording's packaging, you can then go on to make a subjective analysis of the recording itself. This might be in the form of:

- an objective review
- a critical essay
- a series of notes
- a piece presented in audio or audio-visual format (e.g. a feature for radio, or a segment of a pop music TV show).

The pop video

> *Video killed the radio star.*
> The Buggles

Probably the most significant development in terms of the promotion of popular music in the 1980s was the arrival of the pop video. Traditionally, pop music had been promoted on the radio, through concerts, and through 'live' appearances on television programmes (either those aimed at fans of pop music, such as *Top of the Pops*, or those with a magazine-type format which allowed performances by artists keen to 'plug' their latest release).

Since the 1980s, videos have been cheaply and quickly slotted into a wide variety of TV shows. They regularly feature on programmes ranging from the ever-popular Saturday morning children's show and breakfast TV, to late-night 'alternative' shows and music-specific programmes like ITV's *The Chart Show*.

Not only does the video provide a major source of 'visibility' for pop music artists and their record labels (the proliferation of video-based TV stations like MTV is evidence of this), but the pop music video industry, like the advertising industry, also provides an invaluable training ground for directors and other technicians who seek employment in the world of film or television.

The limitations of the pop video

It is possible to argue, however, that during its infancy the pop music video has not matched the pop music recording in terms of 'greatness'. The following are often cited as exceptions:

- Peter Gabriel's 'Sledgehammer'
- Michael Jackson's 'Thriller' and 'Bad', directed by major Hollywood film directors John Landis and Martin Scorsese
- Pulp's 'Do You Remember the First Time?'
- Brian Eno's ground-breaking 'Thursday Afternoon'
- The Prodigy's 'Firestarter'.

You will probably have your own favourites, but overall there is little doubt that the pop video medium is limited by its 'literalness'. Ultimately, a pop video is usually produced to visually represent the recording. In some cases, a video may simply be an opportunity for a record company to promote a song which is being featured in a new movie by using an edited series of 'highlights' from the film interspersed with fairly routine footage of the artist (Seal's 'Kiss from a Rose', the love theme from *Batman Forever*, and Bryan Adams' long running 'Every Thing I Do...' from *Robin Hood: Prince of Thieves* are good examples).

Technology has meant that it is now possible for fans to purchase pop music recordings in the form of a video or CDi and play them at home through home entertainment systems rivalling the CD or tape player in terms of quality. This has also led to increasingly 'image conscious' recordings.

Figure 12.11 A truly great pop music video amidst the mediocrity? 'Firestarter' by The Prodigy

Analysing a pop video

When analysing a pop music video, you might find it helpful to ask the following questions:
- does it feature the recording artist, actors or both?
- does it feature a narrative or story with a traditional beginning, middle and ending?
- does it contain 'live' footage of the artist in concert?
- does it reinforce the representation of the artist found on album covers or in promotional photographs?
- does it make any sense with the sound turned down?
- is it possible to detect similarities between this video and others produced for the same artist or by the same director (if known)?

Answering these questions will not, in itself, provide all the information you require to analyse a pop video. However, collectively your answers should help you to comment upon the effectiveness of certain videos.

▶◀ *See Activity 6, page 160*

The Internet as an alternative

Recently, the championing of the Internet by certain acts (often dance music artists like Future Sound of London) and the increasing and controversial use of web sites for promotional purposes look set to usurp the video from its place at the centre of pop music promotional activities. Over the next few years it is likely that this form of communication will become a prime source of study for media students and teachers.

Approaching pop music

> ❝ Aren't you glad to live in the kind of times that make people produce music like this? ❞
> Charles Shaar Murray, in a review of
> Joy Division's 'Closer', 1980

This chapter has introduced you to some approaches to studying pop music. However, these are not meant to be prescriptive.

The key thing to remember when studying pop music is that it is essential to maintain your awareness of what is happening in the pop world. Music papers like *NME* and *Melody Maker* regularly provide readers with the latest news and reviews, as do the glossy magazines *Vox*, *Select*, *Q*, *Uncut*, *Mix Mag* and so on. The Cable TV station MTV provides opportunities to watch hundreds of pop videos on a daily basis, while terrestrial TV shows like *Top of the Pops*, *The Chart Show* and *Later with Jools Holland* enable you to study live performances, the charts and top 10 videos. Radio is an invaluable source of information about pop music artists, latest releases and trends (Radio 1 and many of the independent stations excel). A regular scouring of the *Radio Times* or the pages of listings magazines to find out what is being broadcast will also enhance your studies.

It is also worth attending live concerts and noting the sort of merchandise available; paying close attention to the marketing of recording artists in advertisements for new releases; and taking an active interest in the way the news media present pop music.

Most importantly, though, you should keep listening to pop records with an open mind. Remember that it is your enjoyment of music which will best support your studies.

The following activities may help you to see ways of including pop music in your media studies. All of these activities assume that you have prepared by reading this chapter and taking part in the usual range of pre-production activities outlined elsewhere in the book. These are all complex pieces of work, requiring time and thought if they are to be used effectively in your media course.

ACTIVITIES ▼

Activity 1

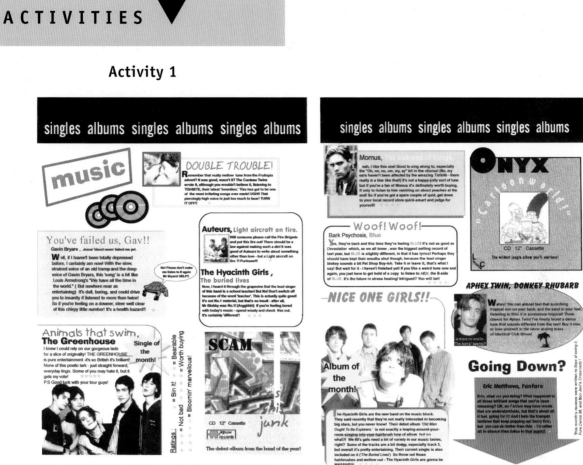

Listen to a range of pop music recordings and attempt to produce your own singles and albums review page for a magazine like *Smash Hits* or *Vox*, or for the pages of the *NME*. Alternatively, you could produce a radio programme in the style of *Juke Box Jury*.

Activity 2

Imagine you are to appear on Radio 4's *Desert Island Discs* programme or its equivalent. Make a list of the eight records you would 'take with you' and explain why these records are important to you. You might like to do this with reference to either your favourite songs or your favourite LP. This could form the basis for a presentation to the rest of your class.

Activity 3

Imagine that you have been asked to market a new all-boy pop band. Think of ways in which this band might be 'sold' to its target audience of (mostly) young women. You might design a logo, T-shirts, pencil cases and so on. Present your ideas to the rest of your group and evaluate the results.

Activity 4

Analyse the two album covers from the 4AD label. In what ways do you think that the label establishes its own identity on these sleeves? Make notes and discuss.

Activity 5

Design a CD cover for a real or imaginary pop artist which either attempts to represent the artist using some of the conventions outlined in this chapter or presents the artist in a new way.

Activity 6

Storyboard the opening sequence for a pop video based upon your favourite song or the music produced by a local band. Pay close attention to the way you use images to support your interpretation of the recording artist's image and the song you have chosen.

BIBLIOGRAPHY ▼

Blake, A, *The Music Business*, Batsford, 1992

Blanchard, T, Greenleaf, S, and Sefton-Green, J, *The Music Business*, Hodder & Stoughton, 1989

Forrest, E, 'Into a different dimension', in *Sunday Times*, 25 July 1993

Frith, S, *Music for Pleasure*, Polity, 1988

Goodwin, A, *Dancing in the Distraction Factory: Music, Television and Popular Culture*, Routledge, 1993

Lloyd, F (ed.), *Deconstructing Madonna*, Batsford, 1993

Paveley, J, 'Label of Love', in *Indie Cator*, 19 April 1993

Shaar Murray, C, Review of 'Closer' by Joy Division, in *NME*, 19 July 1980

CHAPTER 13

Sport in the media

Introduction

This chapter shows you how to investigate sport across different media. It provides key information to help you explore issues, gives advice on analysing the way sport is portrayed in broadcast media and the press, and suggests practical activities to help you use your knowledge and insight.

The chapter is divided into the following main sections:

- sport on television, including the relationship between sport and TV and a brief history of televised sport

- sport on the radio, including an investigation of commentary techniques and how different types of radio station present sport

- sports coverage in newspapers, looking at how it differs in popular tabloids, 'quality' broadsheets and local papers.

Guidance is included on how to analyse sports coverage in each medium, highlighting conventions and approaches you should consider. At the end of the chapter there is an investigation of women and sport, which looks at how the media represent sportswomen and speculates on how this might change in the future.

Sport on television

Sport and television have always had a close relationship. Sport provides TV with excitement, entertainment, intimacy and a 'safe' spectacle: television provides sport with money and publicity. Whether in the process television has made or ruined sport is a question for debate. Certainly changes in sport have been dictated by television. For example:

- snooker has become more popular, both as a game to watch and as a 'respectable' game to play, since it was transmitted in colour on television

- Premiership soccer matches have been re-scheduled from the traditional Saturday afternoon timing to Sundays and Mondays, so that BSkyB can show them 'live' without affecting gates at other matches

- the rescheduling of matches has altered football supporters' social habits, and pubs with big screens have become substitute venues for mini-crowds of supporters

- in tennis, television has led to the introduction of the tiebreak to prevent matches lasting too long

- in cricket TV has led to the introduction of 'pyjama cricket' – limited overs matches played on Sundays with teams wearing brightly coloured gear

- Rugby League in Britain is now being played in the summer rather than the winter, again because Sky television has bought the rights for televising games.

In return, sport is demanding more and more from television. Television has been responsive, recouping its costs through advertising revenue or subscription or license fees.

The history of televised sport

Although the first televised sport in Britain dates back to 1937, it did not become popular and significant until the 1950s. The Coronation of Elizabeth II in 1953 resulted in a huge increase in TV ownership. It also happened to be the year of sporting dramas such as the 'Stan Matthews FA Cup Final', England winning the Ashes for the first time in 20 years and Hungary beating England 6-3 at Wembley (revealing that we were no longer superior to foreign football teams, as we had smugly imagined).

Televised sport was characterised by a remarkable congruence of interests. Sports bodies were able to publicise their sport more; players were better rewarded; sports followers had more access to high-quality events; sponsors gained more attention for their products and services; and broadcasters were able to fill air-time cheaply (compared to drama and news).

The increasing power of television as a means of bringing sports to a massive audience was emphasised in 1962, with the first transatlantic live broadcast via the satellite Telstar. In 1966, when the BBC transmitted the Soccer World Cup live to a world-wide audience, it also introduced the instant replay. What the naked eye missed television caught, replayed, slowed down, froze and showed again and again. England's third goal against Germany in the World Cup Final (where there was endless argument about whether the ball had crossed the goal-line or not) was gift-wrapped for television. Since then television has given its audience views which a spectator at an event could never have.

Figure 13.1 That goal! England take a 3-2 lead in the 1966 World Cup Final against West Germany

Figure 13.2 Dickie Davies Of ITV's World of Sport

During the 1960s the notion of a sports family audience developed. The BBC led the way initially with *Sportsview*, a Wednesday evening magazine programme which concentrated on human interest stories. *Grandstand*, another sports magazine programme, dominated Saturday afternoons, and football highlights were shown on Saturday evenings.

Sport on commercial stations

At first commercial stations were fragmented and regionalised, and could not compete with the BBC's established expertise and strong links with sporting body officials through the 'old-boy' network. The only real challenge from commercial television came with its coverage of wrestling on a Saturday afternoon, which attracted five million viewers compared to BBC's four million for *Grandstand*.

In 1967 ITV established a central sports unit to acquire transmission rights for the network. The unit aimed to build up a strong team of producers and presenters and to improve technical equipment.

After franchise reallocation in 1968, LWT (London Weekend Television) assumed initiative for sport. It introduced *World of Sport* to compete with *Grandstand*, employing Richard Davies as anchor-man. He changed his name to Dickie, was asked to grow sideburns and a moustache, and soon became a personality presenter.

Constrained by its need for advertising breaks, ITV arranged its magazine into five sections:
• 'On the Ball'
• racing
• 'International Sports Special'
• professional wrestling
• a results sequence.

Problems sometimes arose from the need to balance commercial demands with the unpredictability of sport. Cricket's Gillette Cup Final of 1968 was scheduled to finish at 6.45 p.m. but overran. ITV had to go off the air three overs from the end, causing much outrage. The MCC, cricket's controlling body, cancelled its option for a second year.

Duplication and alternation

The 1970s saw a growth in the coverage of major sports. Since the 1954 Television Bill there had been a voluntary agreement to share coverage of certain events. However, this sometimes led to sport appearing simultaneously on all three channels, which annoyed many viewers.

In 1974 there was an attempt to establish the principle of complementary transmissions (alternation) of World Cup matches. The BBC opposed this, arguing amongst other things that audiences simply preferred BBC coverage. The following year the BBC offered an alternation deal on the European Cup which was eventually accepted. However, in 1976 there was no alternation agreement on coverage of the Montreal Olympics, so ITV decided not to cover the games.

In 1977 alternation and duplication were the main sporting issues for the Annan Report, which recommended:

> *The broadcasting authorities should not jointly televise the same event with the same pictures but should agree to share their coverage of such events. They should also reduce other instances where they cover the same event at the same time to the barest minimum, and, after holding discussions on this matter, should make a public announcement of the agreement reached.*

The BBC was reluctant to let ITV gain by negotiation what it was failing to win by competition, and conflict continued. However, the 1970s saw companies such as LWT and Thames adopt a more aggressive attitude, while the BBC's economic power declined because of governments holding down the licence fees. Meanwhile, ITV's main source of revenue – advertising – kept pace with inflation.

In the 1980s, ITV obtained exclusive contracts to broadcast British athletics (1985), the Football League (1988) and the Rugby World Cup (1991). It developed the attitude that if it could not get exclusive rights it would ignore the event: it did not cover the 1992 Olympic Games from Barcelona, for instance. The break-up of the old sharing agreements affected football in particular, as the authorities could now sell the game to the highest bidder and attract increased revenue for the game.

The start of satellite

Further significant changes occurred in the late 1980s with the start of satellite systems.

By 1990 the BBC was beginning to lose ground. It kept exclusive coverage of Wimbledon but had to pay £9 million over three years, almost twice the cost of the previous five years.

Satellite television won major boxing matches such as Bruno v. Tyson (Britain's first pay-per-view programme) and cricket's Benson & Hedges trophy.

In 1992 BSkyB was formed in a merger between the satellite companies BSB and Sky. The new company bought exclusive rights to cricket's World Cup, but not to test matches as the cricket authorities thought that their sponsors would prefer BBC's bigger audiences. In the same year BSkyB outbid ITV for live Premiership football, while the BBC had to be content with edited highlights.

At the Annual General Meeting of News Corporation in 1996, Rupert Murdoch declared that he would use sport as a 'battering ram' to draw a wider market for his pay television services. He maintained that sport 'absolutely overpowers' film and everything else in drawing viewers to television.

The advent of pay-per-view football in Britain in the late nineties has wide repercussions. It only takes 100,000 viewers to pay £10 each to watch a Premiership match and the teams pocket £1 million in 90 minutes. What counts is not people attending stadia, but people tuning into television. In fact people attending stadia become a bit of a nuisance, with clubs having to spend money on safety measures, catering, policing, transport and so on. In the future, the only value of supporters attending matches might be to provide a 'crowd atmosphere' for the television presentation.

▶◀ See Activity 1, page 172

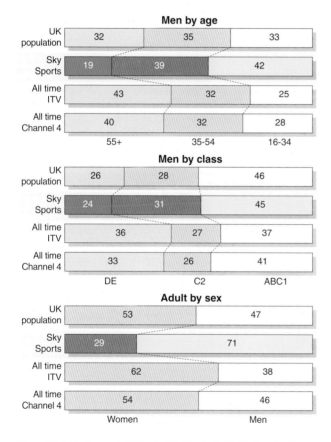

Figure 13.3 Audience statistics for Sky Sports in the first week of April 1996

Money in TV sport

Because of TV, some sports have become of particular interest to advertisers. Both kit and stadia advertise commercial products to huge audiences. Even the names of the competitions establish brand names. In 1989 in America, Macintosh advertised a new computer during the screening of the Super Bowl and the next day clocked up sales of $3.5 million. As early as 1976 sponsorship of sporting events in Britain had reached £16 million, with events such as cricket's Benson & Hedges trophy.

Murdoch's sporting empire

United States

FOX TV

- **American Football**
  £1 billion for four years' coverage of NFL National conference
- **Baseball**
  Rights to World Series (alternate seasons) - estimated at £370 million
- **Ice Hockey**
  £96 million for five years of NHL

Germany

VOX 49.9% owned by Murdoch

- **American Football**
  £45,000 for World League
- **Football**
  Murdoch has stake of 'up to 49%' in broadcasting firm owned by tycoon Leo Kirch. Kirch paid £1.4 billion for non-US rights to 2002/2006 World Cups, raising possibility of UK terrestrial channels being frozen out of World Cup football.

Latin America

GLOBO

- **Football**
  Bidding for rights to Spanish football league

United Kingdom

BSkyB 40% owned by Rupert Murdoch

- **Football**
  £674 million four-year deal
- **Rugby Union**
  £87.5 million deal with English RFU has caused split among home unions
- **Golf**
  £6 million deal including Ryder Cup, highlights of Open Championship
- **Rugby League**
  £87 million deal for exclusive coverage
- **Boxing**
  Deal reportedly worth £60 million with Frank Warren and Don King includes four Tyson fights
- **Cricket**
  £58 million deal for Benson & Hedges Cup until 1999, home one-day internationals, county championship and Sunday League; coverage of England overseas tours.
- **Racing**
  Evening racing

- **Tennis**
  US Open, ATP Championship series
- **American Football World League**
- **Basketball**
  British and NBA leagues

Asia

STAR TV 63.6% owned by Murdoch

- **Football**
  Chinese football: £16 million for 10 years, World Cup
- **Badminton**
  £11 million for 10 years of all competition
- **Basketball**
  Japanese World Series
- **Cricket**
  Asian Cup, World Masters, World Cup, rights to tests in West Indies and Pakistan
- **Motor cycling**
  500cc Grand Prix
- **Motor racing**
  Formula 1 grand prix
- **Rugby Union**
  Five Nations tournament
- **Table tennis**
  World championships
- **Tennis**
  Grand Slam tournaments, Davis Cup
- **Hockey**
  Indian broadcasting rights

Australia

CHANNEL SEVEN 15% owned by Murdoch

- **Olympics**
  £45 million for Atlanta and Sydney 2000
  £67.5 for exclusive rights to summer/winter Olympic games between 2002-2008
- **Australian Rules Football**
  £32 million for seven years of AFL
- **Rugby Union**
  £7 million for five years of Super 12 Regional rugby, home Tests
  Tri-nation tournament between Australia, South Africa and New Zealand
  1999 World Cup
- **Golf**
  Australian Open/Masters
- **Tennis**
  Australian Open, Davis Cup

Figure 13.4 Murdoch's sporting empire in 1997

Analysing live sport on television

This section looks at the different elements you need to consider when analysing live sport on television:

- planning and the unpredictable
- reporting and entertaining
- maximum action in minimum space
- manipulation of time
- assessing what's missing
- production techniques
- the 'crossing the line' rule
- personalisation
- commentary
- TV screens at events
- the use of 'experts'
- narrative continuity
- frames of reference
- the use of 'stars'
- immediacy and suspense.

Planning and the unpredictable

A live sports programme depends on some predictable things which can be scheduled and planned for, but is also at the mercy of the unpredictable.

In live football, for instance, it is predictable that there will be a contest between two teams involving players named before the match starts. The officials will be known. The size of the pitch and the length of time the match lasts are predetermined (although referees do add time to compensate for things like time lost through injuries to players). Producers will be able to plan around these predictable things. For example, they can arrange background research on participating players, time commercial breaks and place cameras.

However, other things are unpredictable: the scoring of goals, the ebb and flow of the game, refereeing decisions and injuries. The images of a football match are governed by actuality; the cameras have to follow the game as it develops, and there is no way of predicting when key moments such as goals, fouls and crucial refereeing decisions will occur. Occasionally there are more serious problems, such as a game being abandoned because of a freak snowstorm or a floodlight failure.

When analysing a live sporting event on TV, you need to consider how effectively the producers use the predictable, and how well they respond to the unpredictable.

Reporting and entertaining

How far is there tension between the journalistic part of reporting sport – showing events as they happen – and the need to guarantee entertainment? In other words, how is the portrayal of the world as it is mixed with the need to highlight action, focus on stars and tell stories?

A crucial question to consider is how far the images presented to the audience are dictated by the events themselves, and how far they are interpreted by the production team.

Maximum action in minimum space

If the space in which an event takes place does not fit the screen well, then more work has to be done in order to make it fit. For example, the challenge of televising boxing or darts

is very different from that of televising golf.

Try to determine what techniques are used to overcome problems of space, for example the use of cameras on cranes, or the use of hand-held cameras.

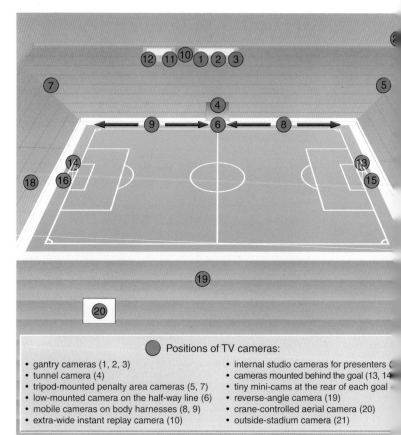

Positions of TV cameras:

- gantry cameras (1, 2, 3)
- tunnel camera (4)
- tripod-mounted penalty area cameras (5, 7)
- low-mounted camera on the half-way line (6)
- mobile cameras on body harnesses (8, 9)
- extra-wide instant replay camera (10)
- internal studio cameras for presenters (
- cameras mounted behind the goal (13, 14
- tiny mini-cams at the rear of each goal
- reverse-angle camera (19)
- crane-controlled aerial camera (20)
- outside-stadium camera (21)

Figure 13.5 Typical placement of BSkyB cameras at a football stadium

Manipulating time

Programme-makers manipulate time by using techniques such as split screen, stop action, slow motion and instant replay. During lulls in live action, the producer may decide to interrupt the action to examine and relive key moments using slow motion techniques. The same incident in any event, but especially in team games, can be shown from different angles in order to prolong the drama or analyse how the incident occurred.

What's missing?

What is missed out? Sometimes speculation on what is not shown but could have been helps you to understand the version and interpretation of events which is being offered. Is there a tendency, for instance, to ignore losers, neglect foreign competitors, or fail to mention team players who are not 'stars'?

Variations in production techniques

How are different production techniques used for different sports? For instance, how much use is made of the prime position camera? Does it predominate, as in ice skating, or are there lots of cuts to other camera shots, as in cricket and Rugby Union? How much use is made of roving cameras, as in horse-racing?

Deciding how much cutting to close-ups to use is important. Too much cutting can be disconcerting; too little and an event can seem boring. Cutting is also linked to the balance between realism and entertaining by personalising (that is focusing on individual athletes). Motor-racing commentator Raymond Baxter asked for two cameras at each vantage point, so that there was always the choice of long shot or close-up.

The miniaturisation of cameras has given producers a much wider choice of shot. The viewer can now be shown unusual shots such as a pocket's eye view of a snooker ball being pocketed, a cricket stump's view of a bowler dismissing a batsman, or a driver's eye view of a Grand Prix race. How far does the use of these cameras add to the realism of presentations, and how far does it contribute to entertainment value? You might consider how some camera positions, such as inside a racing driver's car, allow the audience to sense the excitement of the sport.

Crossing the line

In *The Grammar of Television Production* (Barrie and Rockliffe, 1960), Desmond Davis defines the 'crossing the line' rule:

> ❝ The rule is draw an imaginary line down the centre of the football field from goal to goal, down the cricket pitch from wicket to wicket, down the tennis court at right angles to the net, and keep all your cameras the same side of this line. It does not matter how close they get to this line as long as they don't actually cross it, but the moment they do actually cross it you will be in trouble and the audience will lose all sense of direction. ❞

However, like all conventions this can be defied. Australian Kerry Packer caused huge upheavals in the way cricket was played, as well as in the way it was presented. For the benefit of his Channel Nine television station, he introduced night-time cricket played under floodlights with a white ball and black sight-screens. Players had to wear brightly coloured uniforms instead of the traditional all-white gear. Packer's television style meant a faster cutting pace, different angles, superimposed captions and replays between deliveries. He also broke the 180 degree rule ('crossing the line'), so that the viewer could see from behind the bowler's arm whichever end of the ground the bowler was bowling from. Confusion was minimised by the use of captions to indicate when an unconventional shot was being used.

Personalisation

You should also look at the degree to which sport is personalised by television zooming in on individuals. This technique is particularly widely used in snooker and darts, where the indoor locations permit good quality lighting and the immobility of the participants makes it easier to frame them. Use of close-ups helps viewers to identify with particular sportspeople, who become like characters in a play (especially if intense or crucial moments are highlighted in this way).

Commentary

Commentators are in a privileged position, as they can see both the live event and the television pictures. They:

- act as an interpreter of visual images – 'A great shot by Ian Wright; must be a candidate for goal of the season'
- act as a complement to the images by identifying people and providing background information
- provide biographical information – 'He's been out with an Achilles tendon injury for a month'
- offer professional insight – 'Looks like he's taken out a number 9 iron, which will help him put backspin on the ball'.

Figure 13.6 The commentary box at Nottingham Forest's City Ground

Commentators have much power and can direct the viewer to interpret events in particular ways. However, the viewer can always reject a commentator's readings of events and make what is called an 'oppositional' reading, for example by detecting bias or questioning judgements.

As early as 1952 the BBC produced a guide for its television commentators. It included this advice:

- the need to watch the monitor
- not to be afraid of silence
- let the picture do the talking
- associate competitors with localities
- build up partisanship without being partisan
- single out star individuals to watch
- use a personalised form of address ('you'). Commentators should say, 'many of you may remember', rather than 'viewers will remember'.

By using a conversational tone, questions, imperatives and invitations, the presenter becomes a genial sports fan with a slightly greater knowledge, able to explain things with a privileged awareness of the delights to come. As BBC sports presenter Des Lynam said during Euro 96:

> ❝ There it is, England are out, but they played with pride tonight, and if you're going to have a drink at the end of the evening, perhaps you should do it with pride and not aggression tonight. It's been a good night for English football; we've all enjoyed it, I certainly hope you have. Bit disappointing but there it is. I'll see you Saturday. ❞

Des Lynam has told us how we should feel, how we should behave, and where we should be on Saturday.

One problem facing sports presenters is having to address a very mixed audience. There will be experts who resent having obvious things explained; but there will also be people who know little about sport and may want to learn. There will be others who have only a casual interest and may be more interested in the human angle, seeing the participants as people. As one experienced football commentator put it:

> 6 *The smallest group is the real soccer fan. Then comes the sports fan who is not particularly interested in soccer but will watch anything in the sporting line. The largest group of viewers is composed of people who are not sports fans but who are watching for entertainment. The commentator must see that the third and largest group gets its entertainment without upsetting any of the other two groups... almost an impossible task.* 9
> Kenneth Wolstenholme, 1958

"SPORTS PERSONALITY OF THE YEAR? IT'S A CONTRADICTION IN TERMS!"

Figure 13.7

Television screens at events

Television techniques have changed the audience's expectations of events themselves. Stadia are introducing television as a way of enhancing the experience of attending a sporting event. At better equipped grounds, spectators can now see instant replays of important action on screens. In some sports, TV replays are also used to help officials make decisions.

Experts

Experts can be called on to preview an event, comment on its flow and analyse it when it is finished. They are usually ex-professionals who are presented as being knowledgeable about tactics and skill levels.

Figure 13.8 Current and ex-players acting as expert rugby commentators for the Five Nations coverage on Sky Sports

The experts are often interviewed or chaired by a television journalist who prompts and directs. Their chats mimic the type of analysis that takes place among spectators at an actual event. There is a tendency to focus on personalities and to determine the story of the contest (usually before it starts). Favourite themes are how British competitors and teams compare with foreign rivals, favourites versus outsiders, flair versus discipline, and contrasting personalities. Some of these themes may be continued in brief analyses during or at the end of the event, although some have to be discarded or modified in the light of what actually happens.

Narrative continuity

Edited versions of live sport give television more scope to construct events as stories and entertainment. Where possible, edited programmes try to retain a narrative continuity, so that the 'story' does not seem disjointed.

For example, this is done in football by cutting on goal kicks, so that the actual flow of the game is replicated. In cricket, where it is more difficult, a narrator and/or superimposed captions are used. This helps to preserve narrative continuity, but makes it more difficult to maintain realist transparency (the illusion that you are watching the real event as it happens).

Frames of reference

Viewers are given ways of looking at a particular event, sometimes called 'frames of reference'. This means that they are guided towards making interpretations.

Certain values are established in sports journalism, such as men are more important than women, track events are more important than field events, and British sportspeople are more important than foreign. These values can affect the way an event is portrayed.

The emphasis on British success can sometimes make it difficult to establish an angle on an event. This happened in the 1988 Winter Olympics in Calgary, when there seemed no hope of British success. In the absence of a medal hope, the media found an anti-hero in Eddie the Eagle Edwards, expected to finish last in the ski jump. He was small, vulnerable and myopic, and his lack of skill served to heighten the danger of the event. These characteristics, together with his genial have-a-go attitude, provided a story for the media. In turn, they made him a minor celebrity.

Stars

People working in television sport determine 'stars' and then single them out for special attention. They are often featured in pre-event publicity and listings, introduced in title sequences, emphasised during events, and commented on in after-event summaries. Stars also appear as experts and are then turned into celebrities, sometimes with their own TV programmes or slots.

Immediacy and suspense

All sports coverage emphasises action and immediacy, especially in title sequences: 'all the action as it happens'. This is sometimes highlighted visually by sitting presenters in newsroom-style sets with workers in the background.

Uncertainty is also exploited as a major part of sport's appeal, with broadcasters trying to emphasise suspense, tension and mystery. To keep viewers in suspense, the score is never given before football highlights are shown. To heighten the drama, presenters and commentators have a fondness for theatrical metaphor, referring to a football ground as a 'stage', where great 'dramas' will unfold.

◀◀ *See Activities 2, 3 and 4, pages 172 and 173*

Sport on radio

The developing stories, sense of drama and suspense which make sport attractive as television entertainment are also conveyed effectively by radio. In fact because the equipment needed for radio broadcasting is cheaper and more portable than that needed for television, sport on the radio has greater flexibility. For example, radio is better placed than television to cover the climax of a football season involving several simultaneous games.

In many ways, the presentation of sport on the radio is similar to sport on television. In both cases it involves:
- an effort to maintain continuity in edited (post-event) highlights
- the use of experts to relay information and make judgements
- 'frames of reference' telling the audience how to judge and value certain happenings
- emphasis on immediacy
- highlighting of suspense.

Commentary techniques

Radio commentary techniques vary from sport to sport, ranging from the rapid delivery of a horse-racing commentary to the whispered tension of a snooker commentary. Cricket needs lots of background information and anecdotes to keep the commentary going (remarkably, even when there is no play because of bad weather). With tennis, on the other hand, the problem is to keep up with sudden frenetic bursts of activity despite using verbose terminology such as 'a cross-court forehand volley played deep to the baseline' to describe action which happens in a second.

Perhaps the main difference between television and radio is radio's use of language to create images in the listener's mind. This depends largely on the skills of the commentator and

what is happening. The best commentators are able to make the listeners feel that they are not just hearing a version of an event, but that they are actually experiencing the event. Wilby and Conroy explain this in *The Radio Handbook*:

> ❛ This is illustrated by the BBC's celebrated history of test cricket coverage with commentators offering arguably little less than an epic poem of five days' duration. People do not have to like cricket to appreciate the coverage. They just need to enjoy life. ❜

The development of commentary conventions

Radio coverage of live sport preceded television coverage by a decade, and established many conventions of commentary which later influenced television.

The first BBC outside broadcast was in 1926, when Captain H B T Wakelam commentated on a rugby match and aimed to use 'ordinary conversational language and to make natural spontaneous remarks'. He was the first to establish the convention of the commentator talking as if addressing a single listener. He soon included a 'number two' in the commentary box, helping the illusion of naturalness for which broadcasters were striving.

From the start there was a dual need to provide realism by describing a scene accurately, and to provide entertainment by creating suspense, highlighting action and shaping material into some kind of story.

John Arlott, the cricket commentator, described his job as a radio commentator in terms of the need to be a television camera, a news reporter, a poet to capture the atmosphere and a painter to capture the impressions:

> ❛ I regard the commentator as the equivalent of the artist – the occasion is his canvas, the action his colours and the tongue his brushes. ❜

Figure 13.9 John Arlott: reporter, poet and painter?

Conventions became more structured during the 1930s and 1940s under the influence of Seymour Joly de Lotboniere, head of BBC outside broadcasting from 1935. He encouraged the analysis of commentators' performances and established these conventions:

- keep it simple
- keep up the suspense
- explain and interpret
- let sounds speak for themselves
- sound spontaneous
- vary the pace
- give the score
- don't make jokes unless they are brilliant.

Local radio

Sports coverage is an important aspect of local radio stations because it helps to reinforce the identity of the station's area. As Wilby and Conroy put it: 'Listeners are able to relate to a local radio output through sharing an orientation to and a familiarity with the area it covers. Sport in particular offers a focal point for this relationship.'

Like local newspapers, local radio stations differ from national radio stations in that they are able, or even obliged, to be biased. They are expected to cover sporting events from a local perspective.

Analysing live sport on radio

This section looks at the different elements you need to consider when analysing live sport on radio:

- background noise
- commentary
- modes of address.

Background noise

Try to describe the background noise and its importance to the overall presentation of the event. How do noises differ from sport to sport? The crescendo of a large crowd at a football match is obviously very different from the tense silence followed by cheering or cries of anguish at a missed putt during a golf commentary, but do they each convey important messages to the listener?

Commentary

Consider the qualities of commentators' voices in terms of pitch, volume, cadence and emotion. How effectively do their voice qualities suit the event being described?

Do local radio stations prefer their commentators to have accents from their own region? Are there any accents which would be either inappropriate or desirable for particular sports?

Modes of address

When you are studying broadcast commentary and introductions from a studio anchor-person, it can be illuminating to consider the use of 'we' and 'us'. This is sometimes called analysing modes of address.

Look out for the following four modes of address:

1 'We' as the presenter and the production team – 'We'll have the other results as they come in.'

2 'We' as the donor when linked with 'you' – 'We've got a very busy programme for you this afternoon.'
3 'We' as viewer – 'We're about to see what happened next.'
4 'We' as a sharer of experience – 'We're in for a real treat this afternoon.'

Each mode suggests a different relationship between the presenter and the listener. This intimacy allows, for instance, references to domestic routines, drawing the listener into the programme and establishing a cosy rapport: 'If you've just come in from work, so pleased you could join us for what promises to be an exciting evening's sport.'

▶◀   *See Activity 5, page 173*

See Activity 5, page 173

Newspaper sports coverage

Newspaper coverage aims to complement sport on television rather than compete with it. As a result, there is less reporting of events and more emphasis on background stories, personality interviews and analysis of events.

Sports coverage in newspapers is regarded as a specialist activity which is featured in signposted sections of publications and dealt with by separate departments. In popular tabloid papers the convention is for sport to occupy the back page, which functions as a sports front page with a big headline and prominent picture accompanying a lead story. This is because many sports fans read the sports section first, and the back page needs to perform the same role as a front page.

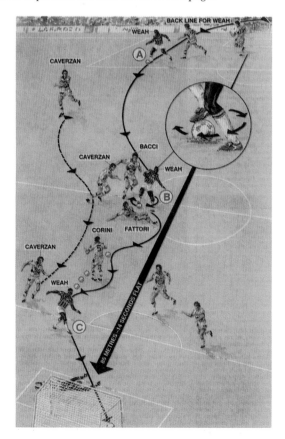

Figure 13.10 Graphic illustrating a great goal by George Weah for AC Milan in September 1996

Newspapers have followed Sky television's style of football presentation by including statistical charts analysing individual matches. There is also a tendency to make greater use of action pictures and graphics, as in Figure 13.10.

Sports reporting in newspapers has two main strengths: there is plenty of space to fill, and readers can take in information at their own pace. This enables newspapers to present large amounts of statistical information about a single popular sport, such as football, or about a variety of minority sports.

If you are studying the coverage of sport in newspapers, it is useful to think in terms of three categories of newspaper:

- popular tabloids
- 'quality' broadsheets
- local papers.

All have different functions to perform.

Broadsheets and tabloids

You can compare sports coverage in quality broadsheets and popular tabloids by conducting content research.

Count the number of column centimetres devoted to each sport, and express the figures as a percentage of the whole paper. You will probably find that the broadsheets offer more coverage of minority sports. For example, on 16 September 1996 *The Times* covered all of the following (some just statistically): sailing, mountaineering, basketball, golf, bowls, tennis, badminton, snooker, hockey, powerboat racing, horse-racing, athletics, water polo, cricket, rugby union, equestrianism, rugby league and association football.

Popular tabloids tend to cover only the most popular spectator sports, addressing the readers as if they are spectators rather than participants. For example, on 9 November 1996 the *Sun* devoted a huge amount of space to football and racing; gave some coverage of rugby union, cricket and boxing; and included nothing on minority interest sports.

The problem facing all sports editors is to decide how far to cater for the majority of their readers and how far they should see their paper as a compendium of minority interests. For instance, the racing page is one of the least read pages in a newspaper, but it may be the only reason why some people buy it. Certainly one of the reasons for the huge circulation increases of the *Sun* when it was taken over by Rupert Murdoch was its highly successful racing tipster.

Local papers

Local papers need to be partisan and report events involving local teams and individuals from a local perspective. They are concerned with the minutiae of local details that would be of no interest to a national audience, and have reporters whose main or even sole job is to report on the fortunes of local teams. If local teams feature in events of national importance, it is common practice for national journalists to tap the local specialists for background information.

The following extract shows just how trivial local sports reporting can be, and just how desperate local sportswriters can become, when they have to provide a daily diet of information for a local team's fans.

▶◀ *See Activity 6, page 173*

Andy Melville expects to toe the line as Sunderland challenge for a Coca Cola Cup tie at Watford tonight.

The Welsh international has played through the pain barrier in the last two matches and immediately after the defeat at Derby on Saturday was given no chance of facing the Second Division promotion hopefuls.

But his toe injury has improved and he is in no mood to give up his ever-present tag.

'My big toe was absolutely killing me after the game on Saturday,' said Melville. 'I've been given pain killers but apart from rest there is not much else I can do. It's my right foot and it's the worst possible place for kicking the ball.'

Sunderland Echo, 17 September 1996

Figure 13.11 Local sporting trivia

Analysing sports coverage in newspapers

If you are comparing different types of newspaper or individual titles, there are certain conventions which you should investigate.

Personalisation

Look at the degree of personalisation used, especially in the lead paragraphs. Compare these six statements, for instance:

- 'Barry Fry reckons being a football manager is the loneliest job in the world'
- 'Rory Underwood began this season as England's most capped player'
- 'Mike Tyson better get ready for war tonight'
- 'Students of English county cricket, its meteorology and horticulture, could possibly have made a field trip to Grace Road yesterday'
- 'In a two acre field on Roonith Hill, near Killadoon in County Mayo the words "Up Mayo" have been mown into the grass'
- 'The symmetry was wholly unwelcome when the season's final classic went the way of the first'.

The first three are taken from popular tabloids; the last three from 'quality' broadsheets. This is not to say that broadsheets do not personalise, but they do not seem to do so as consistently as popular tabloid newspapers.

Another indication of personalisation is the frequency of direct quotations, which in effect allow a personality to address the reader directly.

Look at whether or not a newspaper promotes individualism at the expense of collectivism by, for instance, selecting a 'man of the match' and giving players marks out of ten.

Language style

Look at the language styles of different newspapers, comparing the complexity of sentence structure, the choice of vocabulary and the use of metaphors.

In his house style guidelines for the *Daily Mirror*, writer Keith Waterhouse lays down guidelines for writing in a popular tabloid style. These include:

- Use specific words not general ones
  ('red and blue' rather than 'brightly coloured').
- Use concrete words not abstract ones
  ('rain and fog' rather than 'bad weather').
- Use plain words not college-educated ones
  ('began' rather than 'commenced').
- Use positive words rather than negative ones
  ('he was poor' rather than 'he was not rich')
- Use short sentences, but not all of the same length.
- Avoid elaborate constructions.

Levels of formality also differ between newspapers, with the more popular tabloids most likely to use colloquial language such as nicknames, especially in headlines. For example, 'COLLY FACES KOP PROBE' is a reference to Stan Collymore's problems at Liverpool, where part of the ground is nicknamed 'The Kop'.

Popular papers also seem more likely to use the term 'boss' when referring to managers and coaches. Does this tell you something about the paper's assumptions about its readers?

Look at the kinds of comparisons used in sports reports and try to categorise them to see if there are different underlying values. How far is sport compared to war, with terms like 'battle' and 'give them a rocket'? How far is it seen in non-aggressive terms? The following two quotations are taken from *The Times*: 'The Wales players walked away from the ground in single file, heads bowed, avoiding eye contact, like chastened schoolchildren' and 'They followed the ball, kicking it wantonly, until finally, the match became a dense broth of boredom'. How might the style be changed if for a tabloid newspaper?

Deciding an angle

Look at the angles that particular papers choose for stories. Journalists and editors can determine what each story is about. For instance, when Evander Holyfield took the world heavyweight boxing championship from Mike Tyson there were several readings of the story: nice man beats evil monster, sportsman beats cheat, 'old man' beats younger man, underdog beats favourite, and even Christian beats Muslim.

Choice of photographs

Looking at a newspaper's choice of photographs over a period of time can illustrate its attitudes to sport. Do photographs tend to emphasise conflict and aggression, or do they emphasise the aesthetic appeal of sport? How often are they humorous?

Other topics to consider are how far sports stories hinge on personal dramas, and how far sportspeople are seen as commodities, described in terms of their transfer value or as an envied rich class because of their earning power.

▶◀ *See Activity 7, page 174*

Figure 13.12 A newspaper's choice of photographs tells you much about its attitudes to sport

Women and sport

You may find it interesting to study the ways in which the media represent sportswomen. This is a rapidly developing area which is being increasingly researched.

Media and audience attitudes

In their content analysis study of American media, Mary Jo Kane and Susan Greendorfer found that:

- there is under-representation in the amount of media coverage women's sports are given
- media coverage trivialises and marginalises women by, for instance, focusing on physical attractiveness rather than athletic prowess
- women were often given an adolescent status (e.g. by referring to them as 'girls')
- the media suggested that women are plagued by character defects such as emotional dependency, anxiety, depression and sexual identity crises
- women were often the objects of jokes in the media
- women were treated as sexual objects
- women's sports fit into the 'unusual' category of news values
- women athletes who are attractive stand a much better chance of receiving media attention.

Kane and Greendorfer argue that this state of affairs can be changed by media organisations, and that sport can become an important area for empowering women:

> ❛ The media are active agents in the construction of meanings that come to be identified with specific images and themes. By the same token, they also have the ability, power and means to produce counter-stereotypical images. We would take seriously the notion that ideological bias, once recognised and acknowledged, is subject to modification... sport represents a potential site for empowering and liberating women. ❜

Some argue that sport, more than any other social institution, perpetuates the notion of male superiority and female inferiority: that in Western culture males are usually seen as active, aggressive, and spontaneous, whereas females are weak, passive and responsive (and therefore inferior).

Figure 13.13 Can sport 'empower' women?

How far do the media reinforce this attitude by the ways in which they represent women in sport? Consider this from Jill Turner writing on women's rugby in the *Guardian*:

> ❛ Yes rugby union chicks are hardy lasses. But contrary to popular belief, rugby playing women do not look like Brian Moore with long hair. In fact many of the women's squad at Richmond RFC are pretty and petite, some even with pretty pink gum shields. ❜

The problem does not only lie with media producers, however. Kane and Snyder (1989) found the following audience attitudes:

- women's sport is seen as inferior and less exciting
- people do not like the unknown
- some sports are seen as inappropriate for women
- women who play as well as men are seen as aberrant
- women who play differently from men are seen as inferior.

Women and sport in the future

The situation may be changing. The proportion of females competing in the Olympic Games has grown, and by the year 2000 there is expected to be an equal division of male and female competitors. When the modern Olympics began a century ago, women were banned from competing at all.

There was also a huge increase in the number of women who watched the Atlanta Olympics in 1996. This was partly due to the efforts of NBC, which insisted on female-friendly sports like gymnastics and swimming being scheduled in prime time slots at the expense of more macho sports such as boxing. The result was a 40 per cent increase in women viewers. In ancient Greece women were put to death if they were caught watching the original Olympics.

There is no doubt that sport will change over the years, partly because of the influence of the media. Perhaps it will also change because of the influence of women. In her essay 'Reawakening to the Co-essence Model of Sport', Pamela Sue Highlen suggests the following scenario for the future:

- Commercialisation, wealth, status and competitiveness no longer rule.
- Sport is seen as a performing art, along with music, theatre and dance.
- Athletes value co-operation, compromise, teamwork.
- Out are force, conflict, aggression and a win-lose mentality, and in are creativity, beauty and grace.
- More women and people of different ethnic backgrounds are reporting sport. They are allowed to develop their own voices.
- Sports broadcasters emphasise skill, courage, dedication, brilliance, co-operation, unselfish play and honorable performance.
- The sports sections of newspapers have been dropped, and sport is now in an expanded entertainment and arts section.
- Technology allows viewers a variety of perspectives to watch so that viewers choose which of several camera shots they can follow. They may watch several different shots simultaneously or shift to a full screen coverage of one perspective. There will

be a choice of watching with or without commentaries or tuning in to different styles of commentary.

• No longer does the television cover just professional and élite athletes. Amateurs are included and they tell their own stories. Audiences watch recreational and local sports because they see sport as a vehicle for understanding others and self-expression.

• Audiences see sport as athletes striving to bring the best out of themselves and their competitors. Spectators no longer focus on the importance of outcome and they express less violence and aggression at sporting events. In the Olympics, teams and individuals compete without national identification, thus enhancing the appreciation of sport as a performing art.

▶◀   *See Activity 8, page 174*

ACTIVITIES ▼

Activity 1

Design charts to compare the current coverage of sport on two TV channels during one week. Try to show:

• the percentage of time devoted to sport as a whole
• the range of sports covered
• the size of audiences (you can find this information in *Broadcast* magazine).

Give reasons for any contrasts which become apparent and put your findings into a historical context. For example, you might consider how one channel has come to have exclusive coverage of a particular event, or how a channel's remit obliges it to cater for minority interests.

Present your findings to the group.

Activity 2

Analyse live action football on television

Record a transmission of a live football match and then:

• make a chart to show the positioning of the cameras, working these out from the pictures you are shown
• make a chart to show the proportion of time allocated to each camera in a ten-minute sequence (preferably one containing a major incident, such as a goal or a missed penalty)
• work out which cameras are only used in replay sequences
• try to work out a cutting pattern for the sequence and comment on how the events of the match and the cutting pattern interrelate
• identify how slow and stop motion are used.

Consider what other choices have been made. For example, what interventions occur when a goal is scored? It is likely that the producer will select a close-up of the goal-scorer celebrating. What is the difference in meaning if the producer cuts to:

1 A helicopter shot of the ground and the surrounding streets, perhaps zooming to the distant horizon?
2 A close-up of the beaten goalkeeper?
3 Shots of the reactions of different sets of supporters?
4 Someone asleep in the club restaurant?

There are many other possibilities. The producer could choose not to show any close-ups at all but could stay with the main camera throughout, as in the early days of television. Would this be more realistic in the sense that it mimics the view of a spectator? On the other hand, a match could be presented in a continuous series of close shots without any general perspective.

If experts are used, what themes or topics do they focus on in the preview? Favourite themes are how foreign players are influencing the British game, favourites versus outsiders (especially in cup matches), flair teams versus disciplined teams, two contrasting personalities (the hard man and the sensitive, creative player) and players playing against their former teams. How far do the experts' stories or themes actually appear relevant during the game? How far have they changed by the end and the post-match analysis?

Activity 3

Analyse the title sequences of two different sports events. The titles will tell you what the programme-makers believe they are doing and who they believe they are doing it for. Consider the following questions:

- What action shots are included and why?
- How far do they feature 'star' competitors who will be recognised by the general public as well as knowledgeable sports fans?
- What sorts of action are shown?
- What is the pace of the montage of extracts? Is it slow and leisurely or fast and exciting?
- What sort of music, if any, is being played? What mood is it intended to produce?
- Is there a voice-over? If so, what messages are given and in what tone?
- Are there any logos or sponsorship messages? If there are, why are they there?

Based on your findings, take part in a discussion or write an essay on the topic:

How far do you think it is true that the titles provide the audience with instructions about how to read the programme?

Activity 4

Record a televised sporting event. Turn down the sound when you replay it and record your own commentary over a short extract, trying to follow the conventions of commentaries.

Repeat the exercise, but this time use an alternative style of commentary (e.g. by someone who does not understand the rules of the game). This exercise works well if you actually are unfamiliar with the sport.

Activity 5

Record a television commentary *and* a radio commentary of the same sports event. Write transcripts of a one-minute extract from each of the commentaries which features a key moment in the game.

Analyse the commentaries for:

- background information
- description of action
- statement of opinion or interpretation of events.

Write about the similarities and differences between the two commentaries.

Activity 6

Organise 'The Melville's Big Toe competition'. Each member of the group should try to write the most trivial sports gossip or news item which might just be published by a local newspaper short of news.

Activity 7

In an article in the *Observer*, Roy Greenslade made the following comment on some sports reporting:

'Too many tabloid match reports bear the hallmark of having been written by fans with laptops.

Drawing on a familiar lexicon of hand-me-down phrases, they stunt the reader's imagination rather than enlarge it. They indulge in a banal prose style that infects every paper, making writers interchangeable. They take up a theme and hammer it to death.'

To illustrate his point, Greenslade quotes this extract from a soccer report in the *Daily Express*:

'Tino Asprilla came up trumps last night... Keegan had thought long and hard over whether to throw his controversial Columbian striker into the tie... But Asprilla, whose future had been shrouded in doubt, provided the perfect response... He came up with two vital strikes in front of a packed house... That was Asprilla's emphatic answer to being left out... The controversial South American, whose future has been clouded in doubt... had been his customary jack-in-the-box self as Newcastle huffed and puffed to try to blow down Ferencvaros' 10 men back division.'

Re-write the passage, getting rid of what Greenslade sees as:

- ten clichés
- a repeated adjective
- a repeated phrase
- an 'inane' link between a nursery toy and a nursery rhyme.

Activity 8

Devise a contents list for a TV magazine programme which fulfils some of the criteria set out by Pamela Sue Highlen on page 171. You might like to base this on a diary of real events which you find in a Sunday newspaper. Produce a storyboard for the programme's introduction (about 30 to 60 seconds). Present your ideas to your group, explaining your decisions for what you have included and excluded.

BIBLIOGRAPHY ▼

Barnett, S, *Games and Sets: the Changing Face of Sport on Television*, BFI Publishing, 1990

Davies, D, *The Grammar of Television Production*, Barrie & Rockliffe, 1960

Cashmore, E, *...And There Was Television*, Routledge, 1994

Creedon, P J (ed.), *Women, Media and Sport: Challenging Gender Values*, SAGE, 1994

Greenslade, R, 'A Game of Two Clichés', in *Observer*, 3 November 1996

Highlen, P S, 'Reawakening to the Co-essence Model of Sport', in Kane, M J, and Greendorfer, S, *Women Media and Sport*, SAGE, 1994

Kane, M J, and Greendorfer, S, *Women Media and Sport*, SAGE, 1994

Kane, M J, and Snyder, 'Sport Typing – the Social Containment of Women in Sport', in *Arena Review* 13 (2), quoted in Kane, M J, and Greendorfer, S, *Women Media and Sport*, SAGE, 1994

Martin-Jenkins, C, *Ball by Ball – The Story of Cricket Broadcasting*, Grafton Books, 1990

Turner, J, 'Mud Sweat and Tears', in *Guardian*, 11 October 1996

Waterhouse, K, *Waterhouse on Newspaper Style*, Viking, 1989

Whannel, G, *Fields of Vision*, Routledge, 1992

Wilby, P, and Conroy, A, *The Radio Handbook*, Routledge, 1994

Wolstenholme, K, *Sports Special*, in Sportsmen's Book Club, 1958

CHAPTER 14

Advertising

Introduction

This chapter investigates advertising, focusing in particular on its relationship with the media. It includes:

- a profile of an adman and his analysis of an advert
- case studies of two high-profile campaigns
- an investigation of the role of media planners

- an exploration of the ideological significance of advertising and how recurrent themes are portrayed
- an explanation of how advertising and commercial media depend on one another, and how media commodities are promoted.

The advertising industry

Advertising is part of our culture, affecting the way we think and how we make sense of our lives. In this section you will explore the world of advertising from the industry's perspective.

Meet the adman

Trevor Beattie was the man behind the Wonderbra adverts. It was he who persuaded Playtex to go for posters on London Underground rather than confining its lingerie ads to women's magazines. It was he who came up with cheeky slogans to accompany the pictures of a model wearing the bra: 'Mind the Gap' (very appropriate for the Underground), 'Pull Yourself Together', 'Santa's Little Helper' and 'Hello Boys'.

Beattie is one of the most successful creative directors in the advertising industry. He is unconventional and opinionated, and he loves adverts. 'Advertising is the only thing I've ever wanted to do in my life', he says.

His unconventional approach to car advertising led to a particularly successful campaign for the Nissan Micra. There were none of the usual pictures of the car in dramatic locations, just a cartoon bubble with wheels, but the campaign caught people's attention because it was different. It fulfilled Beattie's main criterion for successful advertising: 'Get noticed'.

Figure 14.1 Beattie's cheeky slogan

One of Beattie's claims to fame is that he managed to get a copy of his 'Toys Aren't Us' poster in the bar of the Rovers Return in *Coronation Street*, in *Drop the Dead Donkey* and on a billboard in *Brookside* all in the same week.

Figure 14.2 The Nissan Micra getting noticed

In a feature in the *Guardian* by Paul Kemp Robertson, Beattie criticised people who work in advertising for being out of touch with ordinary people. For instance, he reckoned that no one in the industry would know about his successful poster placements because advertising people don't watch the TV programmes mentioned. 'They go and see film noir in Soho,' says Beattie. He also dislikes people who 'produce ads for admen'; who seem to be aiming to satisfy an awards jury rather than appealing to 'Mr and Mrs Average'. As he explains:

> ❛ *If you spend six million pounds on a car campaign and no one can even remember the name of the car, you should have given that money to cancer research, because that's a proper cause. There are loads of ads around that don't tell people about the product – or even what the product is. I don't think that's cool, I think it's crap. What's the point of being obtuse?* ❜

He is proud of his working-class origins and determined not to become a 'middle-class git'. Even when earning ten times the national average wage, he lived in a flat in Hackney and travelled to work by bus. 'I'm a normal bloke. I'm very passionate about that', he claims.

Analysing advertisements

This brief profile raises several issues which you can investigate further when analysing adverts:
- the relationship between the creators of advertising and the audience
- how, although advertising can be entertaining, it is primarily about generating business
- how advertising is just one form of marketing, and things like product placement are also important
- the need to persuade people and attract their attention.

In the article in Figure 14.3 Trevor Beattie analyses just one advertisement, relating it to his views on political correctness, party politics (this was written just after the general election of 1997), food and eating habits, and merchandising which purports to offer 'choice'.

▶◀ *See Activity 1, page 186*

Have you tried to buy a pint of milk in a supermarket recently? That's a Pint Of Cow's Milk. Not skimmed, not semi-skimmed, not calcium enriched. Not goat's milk, not sheep's milk, not breakfast milk. (Breakfast milk? Since when did breakfasts have udders?) Not homogenised, not UHT, not long-life ambient stable, not half-fat, not lo-fat, not no fat. Not a five litre plastic churn, not one of those slightly too tall two-pint tubey things with the revolutionary unresealable resealable snap up tops. Just milk. Very tricky innit?

Same with bread. White sliced bread in particular. Ask for white sliced bread in a sandwich bar in Soho and you might as well have asked for the Observer's Book of Necrophilia in the children's section of your local library.

It's the nanny state again, this time draped in the cloak of Choice. White bread? Kills you stone dead. Try this dark grey stale stuff instead, sir. Sure it's full of bits of old toe-nail and it tastes like stair carpet, but its very, very good for you. Really, and why's that then? Fibre, sir. It's a great fibre provider. Oh you mean it'll make me pooh? Everything makes you pooh. If I ate this newspaper it'd make me pooh.

I'm sorry but I just can't be doing with all this do-gooding. I don't want Good-For-Me. I want Bad. And I'm willing to pay top dollar for it. This is 1997. Prescott's in the House. I've waited two long decades to be governed by someone who eats bacon butties and doesn't rhyme class with arse.

Is fried bacon between white sliced bread really too much to ask for? I've lived through a Labour landslide. I believe I can fry.

So too, thank Hovis, does the wonderful Susan Oliver. Susan Oliver is a revelation. Susan Oliver is the star of the new Hovis Thick-Cut White Bread commercial. And Susan Oliver must be the only single, white, female, non-vegetarian, white bread-eating teenager in Britain. (What is it with this creeping vegetarianism in our young? Vegetables aren't food. Vegetables are what food eats.)

This commercial breaks every single rule in the foodie pc handbook. The bacon is fried. The bread is white. The sauce is brown. The sandwich... is a doorstep. Loyd Grossman must be turning in his gravy. Stuff the poncey little brats on Junior Master Chef. This is Junior Bacon Butty Builder.

And the best bit of all is that our Susie doesn't even bother to cut the bugger in two. She simply dives in, face first. All this to the haunting sound of Dvorak's New Hovis Symphony and a voice-over that sounds like everyone's mum. I love it. White bread's coming home. And it took the most famous name in brown bread to do it, an irony as delicate as the product itself.

I can't help thinking that this would have made a great Labour Party election broadcast. Think of the parallels... That was then, this is now. Beer and sandwiches at Number 10. It's as good for you today as it's always been. Don't say Brown, say Gordon.

All it needed was our Tony's voice drifting over the Grimethorpe Colliery brass band. 'And so I say to you... return to your constituencies and prepare your butties for government. White sliced bread is on the rise. New Hovis. No danger... eat white sliced. And I promise you, despite rumours to the contrary, you won't end up brown bread.'

Trevor Beattie, *Media Guardian*, 19 May 1997

Figure 14.3

CASE ▼ STUDY

AN ADVERTISING CAMPAIGN – MURPHY'S STOUT

This case study is an example of a company trying to increase the sales of a product at the expense of one of its competitors. In other words, the company is trying to increase its share of an existing market.

THE PROBLEM

Most campaigns are designed to solve a particular marketing problem. In the case of Murphy's, the problem was to try to challenge the huge market share of its main competitor, Guinness. Both Guinness and Murphy's are black beers (or stouts), which are heavier and darker than lager or bitter. For years Guinness had dominated the stout market in the UK, with 80 per cent of sales. Murphy's, owned by Heineken Worldwide and licensed to Whitbread, aimed to challenge this market domination.

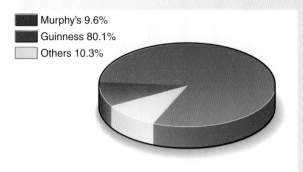

■ Murphy's 9.6%
■ Guinness 80.1%
□ Others 10.3%

Figure 14.4 The market share of stouts in 1993

THE MARKETING STRATEGY

The advertising agency Bartle Bogle Hegarty (BBH) decided to identify Guinness's weaknesses in order to see whether Murphy's strengths could be used to exploit them. This was a difficult proposition. Guinness had a very strong hold on sales and was backed by a successful advertising campaign featuring film star Rutger Hauer (the company spent £9 million on advertising in 1994).

Guinness had an image as a 'graduation' beer. Drinkers aspired to it. It represented individuality and discernment.

However, BBH's market research concentrated on whether there were any weaknesses in the Guinness product and image. This research seemed to suggest that the product's acquired taste which they had been fuelling could also be a latent disadvantage. The advertising campaign implied that Guinness was an acquired taste for the discerning drinker; but put another way this could mean that it was difficult to drink. As one of Murphy's selling points was that it was easy to drink and palatable, this was seen as an opportunity for attack.

The research also suggested that although many found the Guinness image of mystery and individualism attractive, some found it élitist and too intellectual. Of those who were aware of Guinness advertising, 18 per cent thought it 'pretentious'.

Another potential weakness in the Guinness image related to the perception of stout as a warm, friendly, relaxed sort of drink, associated with the atmosphere of a rural Irish community pub. In trying to appear sophisticated, Guinness had ignored its Irish connections and allowed Irish stout values to be neglected. This was seen as an opportunity for Murphy's to exploit.

BRAND VISION

The advertisers set about developing an image for Murphy's which emphasised its differences from Guinness. The image they wanted to create was of easygoing, friendly, relaxed, down-to-earth sociability, in contrast to Guinness's aloof, distant pretentiousness. The contrast between harsh and smooth tastes would also be highlighted, as would Murphy's Irishness. Murphy's would become the 'easy-drinking easygoing stout'.

TARGET AUDIENCE

Regular Guinness drinkers were not targeted, as their habits were regarded as fixed (if you have already acquired the taste for a more bitter pint there is little benefit in trading down). Occasional Guinness drinkers who might be inhibited by the taste were a secondary target. However, the main target group was 'stout wannabes' – people who wanted to aspire to stout drinking but were put off by the taste of Guinness or its intimidating imagery.

THE CREATIVE SOLUTION

The media team decided that TV advertising was the best way to convey 'the emotions of our brand positioning'. They found out the favourite programmes of their target audience and bought air time during those. They also looked for programmes which reinforced the Irish message, such as the film *The Commitments* and rugby matches involving Ireland. They spread their advertising throughout the year, although their limited budget meant that there were gaps. The press adverts were designed to be as different from Guinness press adverts as possible. Whereas Guinness had gone for small-space black and white adverts, Murphy's went for full colour double-page spreads.

Eugene inherited his Uncle Clancy's estate, but like the Murphy's he wasn't bitter.

Figure 14.5

Murphy's TV adverts were a series of mini-stories based on a central character who embodied the easygoing Irish personality that the advertisers wanted to suggest was the drink's main characteristic. The unnamed character is someone with whom the audience can identify. He narrates the stories in the first person, talking either as a voice-over or direct to camera as if confiding in the audience. Whatever misfortunes lie in his way he negotiates them calmly and with good humour.

In the 'Wedding Day' ad he appears to have missed out on marrying a beautiful girl. However, we then see the in-laws in a claustrophobic scrum around the actual bridegroom, and realise that the central character has been spared an ordeal. His bachelor status is intact and there are several bridesmaids to choose from should he wish.

In 'Novice' the main character loses a 'fool's' bet on a horse race: 'I took O'Brian's advice on the seventh horse in the accumulator, and it came in – seventh.' However, he takes the loss calmly and with good humour, before showing his independence by winning on his own choice in the St Barnabus Steeplechase, which is a 'race' of novice priests to the local church.

EFFECTIVENESS OF THE ADVERTISING

The Murphy's campaign began in August 1993 and by the end of the advertising period in December 1995 the volume of sales increased by 191,672 barrels. Murphy's increased share of the total stout market was worth £16.9 million in revenue. Of course there may have been other factors in this increase, such as pricing policy, competitors' advertising, special brand promotions in pubs and so on, so the advertisers had to apply some sophisticated statistical methods to demonstrate that the advertising campaign was largely responsible for the increase.

They also checked advertising awareness and found that the Murphy's adverts had been seen by the vast majority of beer drinkers. Over 60 per cent of those claiming to have seen any Murphy's advert could repeat the endline word-for-word without prompting. People's perceptions of Murphy's 'personality' were what the advertisers had aimed for: compared to Guinness it was seen as more sociable, friendly, down-to-earth and relaxed.

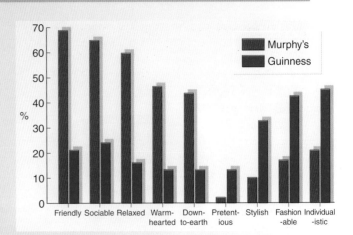

Figure 14.7 Murphy's personality conveyed via the advertising versus Guinness

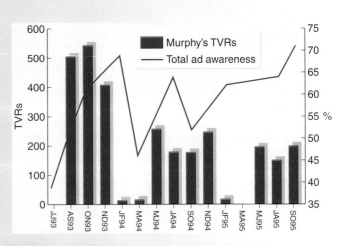

Figure 14.8 Total advertising awareness (spontaneous and prompted) among beer drinkers

▶◀ *For explanation of TVRs, see page 180*

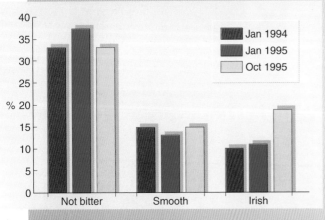

Figure 14.6 Spontaneous advertising communication showing % of people who had seen a Murphy's advert and understood its messages without prompting

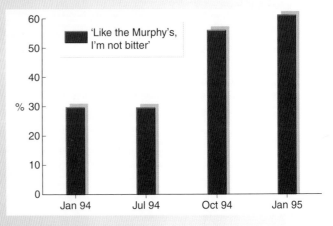

Figure 14.9 Awareness of Murphy's slogan among those who have seen Murphy's adverts

CASE ▼ STUDY

AN ADVERTISING CAMPAIGN – 'IT'S GOOD TO TALK'

BT's advertising campaign is an example of using adverts to increase a total market by changing people's attitudes (in this case, persuading them to use the phone more).

THE PROBLEM

BT was faced with a dilemma. It was obliged by OFTEL, the regulatory body for the telecommunications industry, to reduce its charges. Privatisation of the industry had led to the introduction of competition, which inevitably reduced BT's market share.

THE MARKETING STRATEGY

It responded to this problem by trying to increase the size of the market ('grow the market' in marketing jargon).

This meant trying to change the underlying attitudes which restricted people's telephone use. BT used three main strategies.

1 It tried to encourage heavy phone users (mainly women) to make more calls. Beattie, played by Maureen Lipman, was meant to be a role model who made the type of phone call BT wanted women to make more often, such as enquiries to shops and 'consolation calls'. The campaign was memorable and entertaining. However, instead of becoming a role model Beattie became a negative image of the wasteful woman chatting aimlessly on the phone, and the campaign was ended.

2 BT then introduced the 'Get Through to Someone' campaign. This still suggested the kinds of phone calls people could make, but tried to give a more sensitive portrayal of 'positive phone behaviour'. It was successful in prompting more phone calls, but BT also wanted to convey the message that people can get more out of their lives and relationships by communicating. It wanted to change the way that our culture values phone communication.

3 In 1994, advertising agency Abbott Mead Vickers BBDO devised the 'It's Good to Talk' campaign. This developed from research findings which showed that women think that just 'chatting' on the phone gives them pleasure, but men see the phone as a functional instrument for giving rational messages. Their conversations tend to be short and sharp. More worrying from BT's point of view was the finding that men tended to act as gatekeepers

in their homes, restricting the use of the phone. Their attitude was epitomised by remarks such as: 'She spends her time just wittering away about absolutely nothing. I just can't understand it, and I tell her to get off the phone 'cos it's just money down the drain you know.'

The advertisers tried to counteract this phone culture by promoting the value of female-style phone conversations, by weakening the power of the male gatekeeper and by getting men to think again about their own behaviour. They also had to try to counteract the perception of phone calls being expensive. Research showed that people overestimated the cost of a call by about 400 per cent.

It's good to talk

Figure 14.10 *BT's 'It's Good to Talk' campaign challenged an entire home culture*

THE CREATIVE SOLUTION

The messages of the 'It's Good to Talk' campaign had to be skilfully delivered because they were trying to change deeply ingrained habits. Bob Hoskins was selected to star in the adverts because he was seen by most people to be 'one-of-us', rather than a BT stooge. Women find him endearing. Men see him as 'hard' because of his film and TV roles, making it easier for them to accept his criticisms of their behaviour. He was made even more acceptable by being portrayed as an invisible conscience figure.

The laydown chart below shows how the campaign covered all but a period from February to April, when a different BT campaign about a change in national coding took place. The outdoor poster campaign was used to convey the idea that phone calls are inexpensive.

Figure 14.11 *Media laydown chart*

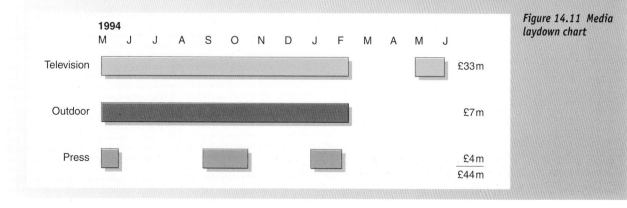

EFFECTIVENESS OF THE ADVERTISING

The advertising agency reported a 1.75 per cent increase in sales. This meant increased revenue of £297· million and represented a return of 6:1 on investment. Its market research appeared to show significant changes in attitudes (see the figures below).

BT's eventual goal is to change perceptions of using the telephone from a cost that should be kept down, to an investment in the quality of life: 'Yes it's good to talk, and I do admit that when I've seen Bob on the telly it makes me think how I'm actually a bit bad at it... and I ought to make more of an effort.'

▶◀ *See Activities 2 and 3, pages 186 and 187*

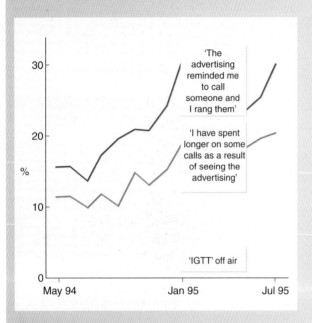

Figure 14.12 Percentage claiming to use telephone more

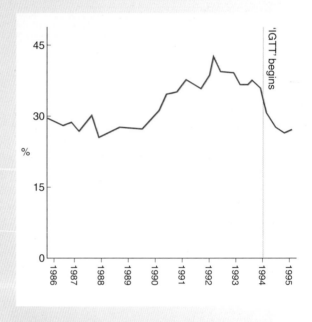

Figure 14.13 Percentage of people agreeing that 'BT call charges are high'

Media planning

The aim of advertising is to reach a target group effectively without spending too much money. The task of communicating advertising messages is usually the responsibility of media planners.

An advertising agency's media planning department is responsible for making sure that adverts are seen by the right people, in the right context, at the right time, and at an acceptable cost.

In the context of media planning, 'media' refers to the different ways in which advertising can be put before target groups, including poster sites and bus sides as well as TV, radio and newspapers. As the number of media grows, consumers have more choice about how they view, read and listen to media products. As a result they are becoming more selective, and therefore more difficult to reach from an advertiser's point of view.

Media planners work closely with the creative department to identify communication objectives. This means considering:

- which media to use – whether to buy space (e.g. in papers or posters) or air time (on the radio or television)
- what periods of time to advertise
- what combination of media to use
- what competitors are doing
- in which locations to advertise
- what the overall cost will be.

Comparing the effectiveness of advertising methods

Media planners must be able to work out the effectiveness of different advertising methods: how much exposure the target audience has to advertising messages delivered through different media. This exposure is measured either as 'Impacts' or 'Opportunities to See' (OTS).

Television viewing is measured in TVRs (television rating points). For example, if there are five million teenagers in a particular TV area and one million of them see an advert, that means that one-fifth, or 20 per cent, of the total possible teenage audience saw it. This is expressed as the advert having 20TVRs.

OTS can be different in quality. The fact that one million teenagers have had the opportunity to see an advertisement does not mean that they have all watched it. They could have been gazing into their partners' eyes at the time. Media planners need to take into account the amount of attention paid to different media. Compare the way you watch adverts in a cinema to the way you read them when flicking through a magazine. People are more likely to read adverts in a newspaper which they pay for than in a free sheet, although free sheets may have a wider circulation. A poster site next to traffic lights might attract people's attention for longer than one beside a road with free-flowing traffic.

Media planners produce cost-rank lists which compare the cost effectiveness of different media products, as in the example below.

Title	Readership	Space cost	Cost per thousand
Spicy	3,560,000	£14,000	£3.93
Fluffy	2,400,000	£11,300	£4.70
Tops Off	1,880,000	£10,000	£5.31
Hard Lads	450,000	£5,000	£11.11

The following factors are also important considerations in media planning.

Advertising spread

Timing is important for many reasons:

- The time of day can determine how receptive an audience is to a message (cornflakes ads on breakfast TV, Horlicks half-way through News at Ten).
- Certain times of the week may be significant: retailers may want to reach their target audience towards the end of the week, when most shopping is done.
- Sales of many items are closely linked to seasonal factors such as Christmas shopping or the weather.

Planners have to decide how to place advertising in terms of time. For example, when launching a new product it could be best to advertise heavily to begin with, so that retailers are encouraged to stock the product. However, recent research has suggested that more thinly spread advertising covering a longer period of time is more effective for some brands.

Positioning

Media planners also have to consider which is the most effective place for their message. For example, they need to decide whether:

- it should be first or last in a commercial break
- it would be effective to repeat a condensed version of an advert
- an advert should appear on a left-hand or right-hand page of a magazine.

Research has suggested the following tactics for press advertising:

- use colour
- use a large proportion of the page
- place next to editorial rather than another advertisement
- place on a back cover or an inside cover
- place early in a publication.

For television, findings suggest that commercials work best if they are:

- long
- appear during short commercial breaks
- appear early in a break, or last in a break in programmes which grip the attention of their audience.

Cost

Media planners have to balance:

- the length of a campaign
- its frequency

- the amount of coverage
- the cost.

Before deciding the size or length of an advert, planners need to take into account all of these factors.

Location

It is possible to vary a campaign by geographical area. Sometimes a company may want to target a small area of the country to test a campaign before a national launch. Often companies will use an ITV area and/or a regional newspaper for this purpose.

▶◀ See Activities 4 and 5, page 187

Advertising and ideology

There is a growing body of academic research about the ways in which advertising can shape people's social behaviour. Generally there seems to be agreement that advertising which relies on imagery is inevitably laden with cultural values, and that these values are conservative in terms of wanting to leave things as they are and resisting change.

Some people believe that advertising tends to reinforce the dominant ideology. Advertising, they argue, is not just about managing consumer demand, but about managing social consciousness.

People who produce adverts are often scornful of such suggestions. They say that they make adverts so that someone can sell something, and that selling things is what keeps a capitalist society going. Richard Phillips, creator of the Beattie adverts for BT, expressed typical scepticism in reacting to *The Hidden Persuaders*, a book on advertising by Vance Packhard:

> ❛ *The Hidden Persuaders perfectly summed up what people thought advertising was about. It suggested an image of shadowy Svengalis, fiendish manipulators who knew precisely how to bend the public to their will.*
> *Ah, but if only it were true. If only we did have some special insight into the sub-conscious; if only the subtle, hidden meanings that so-called experts are forever finding in advertising were actually there. In my experience, the truth is very different. The most vital ingredient for the concoction of any successful piece of advertising is a large slice of luck.* ❜
> Lipman and Phillips, 1989

And according to Michael Schudson (1993):

> ❛ *Advertising is much less powerful than advertising and critics of advertising claim, and advertising agencies are stabbing in the dark much more than they are practising precision micro-surgery on the public consciousness.* ❜

When studying advertising, it is probably wise to begin with some scepticism of your own about the claims of cultural studies theorists. Certainly you should be aware that the main function of advertising is commercial, and that the symbolism detected by people who analyse adverts may not have been intended by those who produced them. However, you should also be aware that observers and students of the role of advertising may have a better overview than an individual working in the industry.

For example, someone working on a campaign to sell the Renault Clio will be concerned with finding an actress who is young, attractive, sophisticated, a little elusive, a touch coquettish and so on. In contrast, a cultural theorist will be interested in what the actress represents in terms of current values and the status and identity of women (how advertising reacts and contributes to the changing role of women in society is a key cultural question).

In his book *Advertising: The Uneasy Persuasion*, Michael Schudson challenges many assumptions about the power of advertising in both commercial and ideological terms. He argues that when advertising works it does not work in the way most people imagine – by leading consumers to change their minds or to think a certain way about a product.

Instead, he believes that advertising works in these indirect ways:

- A sales force is more likely to work enthusiastically to sell a well advertised product.
- Retailers are more likely to be persuaded to stock a well advertised product. This means that widely advertised brands become the most widely available; consumers pick up what they find on the shelves whether ads influenced them or not; and the retailers are thus 'confirmed' in their conviction that advertised products sell well. In this case, availability equals sales.

It is difficult to assess the power of advertising because consumers are normally influenced by many different factors when making a decision to buy something. These include:

- their own experience of using the product
- the experience of friends and relatives who use the product: 'People take into account not only their own experience when they decide to buy something, but the experience of the people they know best, the people they trust most, and the people whose high opinion means most to them.' (Schudson, 1993)
- the opinions of family and friends (people want to buy things which their family and friends will approve of)
- information in the media besides advertising (e.g. reviews of books, concerts)
- consumer programmes and education
- other advertising (in terms of competing messages and the general 'clutter' of advertising messages)
- scepticism about advertising in general, on the part of the consumer or the salesperson
- price (either because people can't afford a product, or because they believe it can't be any good if it is cheap).

People who do not have these other sources of information at their disposal will be more likely to believe advertising messages. This includes people in Third World countries, children, the very old, and people with restricted mobility.

▶◀ *See Activity 6, page 188*

Representation in advertising

You can study representation in advertising in many different contexts. Here we focus on how men and cars are represented, so that you can see the type of approach to take and the kinds of questions to ask. However, you could choose to look at any number of categories of people and subjects in a similar way, including women, families, teenagers, homes, nature, science and technology.

The role of men in society

In his study of advertising and ideology in *Promotional Culture*, Andrew Wernick looks at the changing role of men in society and how this inter-relates with advertising (in particular the type of advertising which relies on imagery to reinforce its messages).

Wernick identifies the following main changes in men's social role:

- becoming more involved in actually buying things
- having more products targeted at them (e.g. personal care products and leisure goods)
- no longer being seen as the exclusive breadwinners
- no longer being automatically predominant in public life
- more often being seen as the prey rather than the hunter in sexual relations
- homosexuality becoming more acceptable as a lifestyle.

Faced with these changes, advertisers have had to rethink what masculinity means. In the 1950s men in advertisements tended to be portrayed in terms of their family roles: husband, dad and family provider. In car adverts, for instance, the man was usually depicted driving the car, with a 'pretty' wife by his side and two 'lovely' children in the back seat. Alternatively, in adverts aimed at women, men were seen as exotic strangers.

However, the 1960s saw the start of a trend away from mentioning family status, and since the 1980s the image of the young, single, affluent male has become more prevalent. This may have been a response to the Thatcherite ideals which encouraged ostentatious consumption, combined with a growth in the number of middle-class men going on to higher education.

During the 1990s there seems to be a preference for ambiguous images which consumers can relate to from different points of view.

The advert for Honda CR-V in Figure 14.14 typifies this ambiguity. Many things are undetermined by the image: the ownership of the vehicle, the social status of the two people, their relationship, their whereabouts. Readers can place themselves in the advertisement from a variety of positions, according to their own roles and living arrangements.

When men are shown with others, the most common grouping is the heterosexual couple, followed by a peer group of three or more men. The male-male twosome is rare, but no longer taboo. The family, however, is largely absent. Peer groups are different from family groups in that they are drawn from a single generation and have no fixed roles for their members. This allows the consumer to identify with different members of the group at will.

Figure 14.14 Ambiguous images

Figure 14.15 Have images of passive, weak men become more common?

Figure 14.16 The male as 'prey'!

Wernick describes how the depiction of male sexuality has changed from the traditional image of man as hunter and active partner, gazing at Woman. Such images still exist, but alongside them are other images of passive, weak and hunted man. As Wernick says:

> ❝ *The iconic conventions of promotion are becoming flexible enough to allow men and women to be positioned at either end of the objectified/objectifying sexual continuum.* ❞

The movement towards greater gender equality since the late 1960s has meant that advertising images of men identified with activity and power and women as passive, expressive and dependent have become less common. More often today, images show men and women occupying equivalent, if not identical, places in the world.

▶◀   *See Activity 7, page 188*

Cars as cultural signs

Cars are not just a means of transport; they are a cultural sign of their owners' social standing. Look out for the number of times people, especially young men, are defined by the cars they drive.

Like clothes, cars say something about their owners and go in and out of fashion. Car manufacturers take advantage of this by changing the appearance and styling of cars to encourage people to want something more 'up to date'.

Cars can be seen as a symbol of modern technological success and progress, giving people both private and occupational mobility. However, in some places the profusion of private and company cars is clogging up the transport system, and cars are destroying the very mobility which made them attractive.

In *Promotional Culture*, Andrew Wernick argues that there are three sorts of car image:

- the muscle car – associated with macho technology and styling, car racing, bullet shapes, feelings of rushing towards orgasm, the future and death
- the luxury car – associated with refinement and status
- the family car – associated with respectability, security and safety.

Figure 14.17 Nicole and Papa

According to Wernick, this third category is changing more quickly than the other two. As 'car ownership by youth and women has increased, the mass car has continued to reflect the prevailing family form, though in a way that is correspondingly more unisex, age-neutral and varied in size and composition.'

For example, the Renault Clio adverts were designed to attract mainly young, female drivers who could identify with the Nicole character in the series of stories. But men and older buyers can also relate to the advertising through the figure of Papa and other characters in the stories.

You can examine the current symbolic meanings of cars and trace the development of their meanings by looking at advertising from past decades. Look out for these types of symbol:

- the car as a person ('she handles really well'; lights designed to look like eyes) or a beast (names like Mustang and Colt)
- the car as a missile or aeroplane (e.g. SAAB adverts)
- the car as a sexual extension of a man (e.g. red Ford Capris)
- the car as a protector (womb-like)
- the car as sophisticated technology
- the car as a means of escape from urban environments
- the car as a means of developing more intimate relations with the opposite sex
- the car as a wrap-around experience (quadraphonic speakers, tape decks etc.).

Some images may well combine two or more of these themes.

> ❝ *Cars are second homes, places of intimacy, where people snog, make love, fall out, the family status symbol and the bit of home you take on holiday.* ❞
> Desmond Christy, 1997

▶◀   *See Activity 8, page 188*

Advertising and the media

Advertising influences almost every aspect of the media. The content of commercially produced publications and broadcast programmes, whether news or entertainment, is inextricably bound up with advertising.

Advertising, newspapers and magazines

Some newspapers now employ full-time writers of commercial copy or advertorials (information which is designed to sell something but which looks like a news feature).

All newspapers receive press releases about events that have been designed to draw attention to a product or service, or to give good publicity to an organisation. The pressure group Greenpeace is particularly good at creating 'stories' which draw attention to its campaigning activities. It attracted considerable national publicity, for instance, by getting scores of its members to dress up as penguins (birds not biscuits) outside the McVities biscuit factory in order to draw attention to the company's policy of using fish oil from millions of tonnes of sand eels in its biscuits. As a result of the publicity United Biscuits, owners of McVities, phased out the practice. Newspaper editors know that they are being exploited by such practices, but many accept that this is the price they pay for a 'good story'.

There is often a close link between advertising and the content of newspaper and magazine articles. In the case of specialist magazines, where the content is written to appeal to a group of people interested in a particular hobby or pursuit, a niche audience is created for advertisers. The same effect can be seen in magazines and supplements produced by the quality broadsheets, which have sections on travel to attract holiday advertising, food to attract adverts for restaurants, houses to attract property ads and so on. Thus advertising determines the construction and shape of the product. Sunday colour supplements were introduced to attract advertising revenue, not to give the reader more value for money.

As this shows, how advertisers choose to spend their money can determine the types of publication available. As advertisers will always be more interested in appealing to affluent groups in society, so these groups will inevitably have more printed products to choose from.

Advertising and television

The anger of the pop music industry when *Top of the Pops* was moved from a Thursday to a Friday shows how promotion and television are interconnected. When the programme was rescheduled, record companies feared a large drop in audience size because the show would be up against *Coronation Street*.

Figure 14.18 Top of the Pops: an excellent marketing opportunity, with young celebrities as presenters adding to the programme's particular youth appeal

According to a senior record company executive: 'Everything you see on *Top of the Pops* is supplied by the record companies – the artists, the backdrop, the lighting.' The companies were prepared to spend money transporting artists and equipment, sometimes across the Atlantic for a single show, because *TOTP* is the biggest marketing opportunity available in the UK for records and artists. In 1996 one company estimated that it had spent half a million pounds in one year supporting *TOTP*.

Television chat shows can be used for the promotion of books, films, theatre shows and so on, with writers, musicians and actors plugging their work.

Sponsorship of events is another way for products to be advertised on television (even on the BBC), with views of company logos on sports equipment and references to events such as the Cornhill Test and the Carling Premiership. Sponsorship like this can lead to huge financial rewards for the sportspeople who participate, with a wide media coverage. In turn, this can result in the media focusing on these individuals because of their fame, so distorting their presentation of events.

Advertising also affects the style of programmes on television. Adverts during an entertaining programme set out to entertain themselves, sometimes even consciously copying the programme's style or content. Thus we find:

- mini-soaps such as the Gold Blend adverts
- playlets with 'slice-of-life' situations such as the OXO ads
- comedy sketches such as Vic Reeves' Direct Line ad
- animations aping children's cartoons
- news-style vox pops where 'ordinary members of the public' express their satisfaction with a product.

The positioning of adverts in and around programmes can change the audience's viewing experience. Advertisements soon become part of the show.

The promotion of media commodities

Media products are commodities in themselves which are 'advertised' or promoted in different ways:

- They can be trailed before publication, broadcast or display with a package of extracts or highlights. For instance, commercially hired videos usually begin with trailers of other films available on the same label.
- They can be sold as serials in which each episode ends with suspense, so that people become addicted to finding out what happens next (as with soap operas and serialised stories in the press).
- They can be part of a series which does not have a continuous thread to attract attention but has continuity of characters and format; a theme with variations.
- A sequel or sequels can be made as a follow-up to a successful product. For example, the easily copiable formula of the film Rocky was repeated until the audience grew tired of it. These sequels are sometimes based on a genre, such as the 1970s disaster movies.
- Fan clubs can emerge as a continuation of the promotional effect, as happened with Star Trek after its serialisation.

Figure 14.19 Famous names help to sell a film

Famous names can also be a powerful tool for promoting media products. For example, people may have paid to watch the film *Evita* because:

- Madonna and Antonio Banderas were in it
- the music was composed by Andrew Lloyd Webber
- the title of the film was also the title of a successful stage production
- the musical was based on a famous historical figure, Eva (Evita) Peron.

A great deal of commercial effort goes into establishing the name of a new 'star', keeping it in the public's mind once it is known, and determining when to ditch it if it becomes a liability. Once a name has been established it can earn substantial rewards, becoming associated in the public's eye with material success and perhaps lavish lifestyle. The media may well feed the public with stories about the star, increasing the value of the name. In effect the star's name becomes a tradable commodity, which in some cases is even copyrighted.

A media product can also act as a promotional vehicle for the same product in a different form. Thus a successful novel such as *The Bridges of Madison County* becomes a selling point for the film based on it. The film then acts as a publicity vehicle for the novel.

ACTIVITIES

Activity 1

Make notes on the cultural references in Trevor Beattie's piece on the Hovis advertisement (see page 176) under the headings of what references would **not** be understood by:

- a visitor to the UK with no knowledge of our politics
- a reincarnated school dinner cook who died in 1947
- someone who has never watched television
- someone who has never seen or heard an advertisement on television
- someone who is unfamiliar with non-standard English.

Write a short character study of Beattie based on what you can learn about him from this article.

Study an advertisement to which you have a strong response. Relate its messages to your own perceptions and feelings, showing how it reinforces, confirms or challenges your ideas and attitudes.

Activity 2

Apparently boys in our culture tend to think 'reading is for wimps', because mothers and female teachers tend to be the main story readers for young children.

If you had to try to change this perception, what type of television advertising campaign would you devise? Your main target audience should be young fathers and, indirectly, young boys.

In small groups, discuss the casting, storylines and images you would use to bring about a cultural change. Produce rough storyboards for two thirty-second adverts using the same message and main character in two different situations/stories. Assuming you had a generous budget, in which TV programmes would you buy advertising time and why?

Activity 3

You have to try to increase the market share of a brand of crisps.

Your main target audience is children, but as 80 per cent of crisps are bought by adults (mostly for children) you will have to appeal to them as well. Market researchers have told you that 'irresistibility' is the characteristic that crisp lovers look for. They also point out that crisps are seen as part of everyday life and that people would not identify with a campaign which took itself too seriously.

Choose a personality to feature in your TV campaign and make up a twenty-second commercial in storyboard form featuring the character. Explain the thinking behind the storyboard and your choice of personality to the manufacturers.

Activity 4

Work out the most effective way to advertise an adventure holiday centre for teenagers. Your adverts should appear in the local press, and you need to decide placement and timing. You have a budget of £200,000. Your local paper charges the following rates:

- full colour page: £2000
- half page: £1200
- quarter page: £700.

Figures are halved if the advert appears in black and white. Add 10 per cent if the advert is to appear on a right-hand page, and 25 per cent for the back page or inside cover.

Decide where to place the adverts in the paper, taking into account the parts of the paper your target audience is likely to read and when you should advertise (which days and months) to make best use of your budget.

Present your proposals in chart form to your 'client'.

Activity 5

WOMEN'S MAGAZINES – TOTAL READERSHIP

	Sex				Social grade				Age			
	Male		Female		ABC1		C2DE		15-44		45+	
	000s	%	000s	%	000s	%	000s	%	000s	%	000s	%
Tops	–	–	2175	9.3	1111	9.9	1064	8.7	1435	12.2	740	6.3
Houseproud	–	–	2104	9.0	1481	13.2	622	5.1	1030	8.7	1074	9.2
Female	–	–	1805	7.7	1108	9.9	697	5.7	561	4.8	1244	10.6
Metro	–	–	1694	7.2	1114	10.2	550	4.5	1370	11.6	324	2.8
Family Way	–	–	1648	7.0	882	7.9	766	6.3	835	7.1	813	7.0
Homefire	–	–	1439	6.1	849	7.6	589	4.8	833	7.1	606	5.2
Trends	–	–	1375	5.9	913	8.1	463	3.8	958	8.1	418	3.6
Lunchbox	–	–	1374	5.9	974	8.7	400	3.3	773	6.6	601	5.1
Best Meal	–	–	1271	5.4	854	7.6	416	3.4	635	5.4	635	5.4

Look at the figures above. Which publication would you choose to advertise in to appeal to the highest number of women:

- regardless of age or social class
- in social classes ABC1
- in social classes C2DE
- aged 45 and over
- aged 15 to 44
- in social classes ABC1 and those aged 15 to 44
- ABC1 and those aged 45 and over
- C2DE and those aged 15 to 44
- C2DE and those aged 45 and over.

Activity 6

> ❝ *I hope critics of advertising will not misspend their energies by taking symbol for substance and believing that the analysis of advertising can substitute for an understanding of the economic, political, social and cultural forces that give rise to it and contribute to the social phenomena often attributed to it.* ❞
> Michael Schudson, 1993

Discuss.

Activity 7

Collect as many examples of men in contemporary adverts as you can. Divide the images into categories as follows:

- men as powerful figures (e.g. 'hunters' in sexual terms or bosses)
- men as weak figures (e.g. appearing foolish, undesirable or 'hunted')
- men as ambiguous figures who could be either powerful or weak
- heterosexual couples
- men in all-male groups.

Using this material, test the hypothesis that the portrayal of men in current advertising accurately reflects their roles in the real world as you experience it.

Activity 8

Collect a large sample of press and broadcast adverts for cars and try to classify them according to the types of image listed on page 184. Add other categories if you need to. If you find there is one type of image which occurs more frequently than the rest, try to account for this. If you can find car adverts from another decade, compare them with today's adverts and describe any differences which you notice in the sorts of images they present.

BIBLIOGRAPHY ▼

Duckworth, G (ed.), *Advertising Works 9*, NTC Publications Ltd, 1997

Dyer, G, *Advertising as Communication*, Routledge, 1982

Kemp Robertson, P, 'Clever Trevor', in *Media Guardian*, 27 January 1997

McDonald, C, and Monkman, M (eds), *The MRG Guide to Media Research*, Media Research Group, 1997

Lipman, M, and Phillips, R, *You Got an Ology?*, Robson Books, 1989

Packhard, V , *The Hidden Persuaders*, Penguin, 1960

Schudson, M, *Advertising: The Uneasy Persuasion*, Routledge, 1993

Wernick, A, *Promotional Culture*, SAGE, 1991

CHAPTER 15

Pre-production

Introduction

This chapter shows you how to prepare for a practical media project, providing guidance on the activities you need to carry out before producing a media product. The advice it provides is relevant whichever medium you decide to use for your final project.

You should read this chapter before going on to look at the following three chapters, which focus on how to produce:
- printed products (chapter 16)
- audio products (chapter 17)
- video products (chapter 18).

Preparing for a practical media project

When preparing to produce a media product, you need to work through the following key stages:
- coming up with ideas
- deciding what form your project will take
- deciding the purpose of your product
- identifying your target audience
- gathering the resources you will need
- outlining the content
- identifying the kinds of research you need to undertake
- drawing up a schedule for the project.

Coming up with ideas

Ideas for media products can come from various sources:
1 Inspiration – a bright idea that comes from your subconscious.
2 Recognising a need for a particular product. For example, you might hear people complaining that TV holiday programmes present glamorised images rather than telling the truth about destinations, and decide to produce a warts-and-all guide based on holidaymakers' actual experiences.
3 Market research – studying a cross-section of the population to find out what they would like to read, see or hear.
4 Brainstorming – pooling ideas, rejecting none, and discussing them with others before deciding which is the best and most practical.
5 Adapting other people's ideas. For example, you might see a fanzine for a particular band, performer or team, and use a similar format to produce your own fanzine.

Deciding on a form

Deciding on a form involves thinking through the nature of your media product and choosing the most appropriate medium.

To do this you need to ask yourself a number of questions. What would be the reasons for doing something in print rather than using video? Do you have the resources and skills to produce a video? Would you be better working in audio, where the technology is easier to master and the skills involved not so complex?

You also need to consider whether your choice of form matches the requirements of the examination specifications. Examination boards give advice about what is and is not acceptable, and if you are in any doubt about your choice of form, you should ask your exam board for advice.

In 1997, for instance, the Cambridge Board listed 'tasks which would be unlikely to meet the demands of the syllabus'. These included:
- leaflets, handouts and flyers
- brochures, town guides and school prospectuses
- photo exhibitions and albums
- stories and playscripts.

Tasks which should allow you to meet the requirements of the syllabus include:
- an advertising campaign for a product, using different media
- a trailer for a new film
- the opening sequence of a film from a particular genre
- a cover for a video or a film poster, featuring original photographs along with stills from the imaginary film
- a trailer for a new TV soap opera
- a title sequence for a new crime series
- an extract from a TV documentary
- an extract from a community radio show
- the opening of a radio play
- two or three pages from a new newspaper aimed at the teenage market
- two or three pages from a new magazine aimed at a specialised audience, such as people interested in a particular sport or hobby
- a community newspaper.

Describing your purpose

You need to be able to explain why you are producing your media product. This question is directly linked to the form you have chosen and will introduce the concept of genre.

Basically, media products do one or more of the following:
- inform
- entertain
- persuade.

You should be able to describe the key features of your product and how they will help you to achieve your purpose.

For example, if you decide to produce a community newspaper which will inform and entertain, you will need to decide what sorts of information the community needs and how to communicate this accurately and in a visually appealing way. This leads on to questions of design, such as page size, style of layout, use of photographs and illustrations, typography and suitability of language. How do you make your publication entertaining? Do readers want games, competitions, prizes, cartoons, witty stories?

Questions of representation should also be raised here. How will you portray particular social groups, for instance?

▶◀ *See Activity 1, page 195*

Identifying your target audience

You should have a clear idea of your audience before starting production. Whether your audience is real or imaginary, you need to be able to describe its:

- age range
- gender
- interests
- geography (where people live).

You should also have a clear idea of how you will try to appeal to this audience, and how it will affect the content and style of your product. For example, if you are preparing an educational video for a group of infant children you will need to make sure that your script can be understood, that the concepts are relevant to the age group, and that your style of presentation will sustain interest.

▶◀ *See Activity 2, page 195*

If you are producing a freelance article for a newspaper or a new idea for a TV quiz programme, your target audience could be a publisher or producer. In this case, you will need to think about the type of material the publisher or producer is looking for and make sure you understand the genre. If you are writing TV comedy sketches, for instance, you will need to know what type of comedy show you are writing for (is it family entertainment? alternative comedy? satire?).

You also need to know what your 'target' already publishes or broadcasts in terms of style, length and timing. If, for instance, you want to write a travel article for a colour magazine, you should make yourself familiar with the travel section of the publication, look at the kinds of locations covered, see whether there is a link between time of year and content, look at how long the articles are and what sorts of illustrations are used, and note the kind of language used by writers. You can find some guidance on these subjects in the yearbooks produced for writers and artists, but there is no substitute for a thorough knowledge of the publication or production you are aiming at.

Organising resources

Examination boards do not demand 'high-tech' products. They give credit for understanding the technology used and for using it in an imaginative and creative way. Don't attempt to be too ambitious; the technology should be your servant and not your master. On the other hand you are not a professional and you are expected to develop your skills during your media studies. The crucial thing at the planning stage is to recognise what equipment is at your disposal and what skills you need to develop to use it.

Printed products

For printed products, you should be able to use a word processor. This will allow you to produce columns of different widths, headlines and give you a choice of fonts. You should also have a 35 mm camera and ideally be able to scan pictures into your computer system. You should have the means of printing multiple copies of your product.

Video products

For video products, you need access to an editing suite which you can use effectively. If you do not know how to use an editing suite then make sure you build some training into your production schedule, working on small-scale projects. Student videos are often spoiled by having poor sound quality, so consider carefully the need for extra microphones and/or recording equipment rather than simply relying on a camcorder.

Audio products

For audio products, you need good quality tape recorders with a choice of microphones for different tasks and the means of editing either digitally (i.e. using a computer) or cutting and splicing. Although it is possible to edit from one tape recorder to another, the results are always crude.

Outlining content

At the planning stage you need to work out brief details of what will be in your final product.

Printed products

The following is a typical content outline for a publication. It shows what topics will be covered and gives ideas on how each will be approached.

Topic: Provision of local leisure facilities

Article one
An investigation of local residents' views on quality of what is provided and on what is missing.
Views of six people; male and female and a range of ages.

Article two
A guide to what's on in the area over the next few weeks. Information from playgroups and nurseries, sports organisations, local authority leisure services, church groups, voluntary groups, commercial leisure organisations, social clubs and pubs.

Article three
An interview with a local authority representative about future plans for the area.

Photos
Mugshots of individuals interviewed, plus two or three pictures illustrating current leisure activities.

Figure 15.1 Content outline

You could supplement this by preparing some rough plans for page layout, including details of:

- how many pages you have to produce
- whether they will include advertisements
- how many columns there will be
- roughly what space will be taken up by photographs
- how many words you need to fill the rest.

If you are planning a printed product, you also need to consider issues of representation and editorial stance at this stage. For the publication above, for instance, you would need to think about how to portray:

- the efforts of the local community to provide its own leisure activities
- the contributions made by commercial enterprises
- the provisions made by the local authority
- the attitudes of the local community.

This is a time to become aware of your own opinions and prejudices. Where do you stand on the question of private/commercial versus public service provision of facilities? Do you have a view about 'the dependency culture'? How do you feel about the politics of the local council? Do you feel that wealthier citizens should pay higher council taxes to provide better leisure facilities for the underprivileged? Is the word 'underprivileged' politically loaded?

Audio products

If you are planning an audio product, you need to be concerned with time rather than space. If you were tackling the topic above on a radio magazine programme, for instance, you would need to:

- allocate time for intros and outros
- decide roughly how much time to devote to each recorded piece
- think about sound effects and background noise (you might decide to make a separate tape of wildtrack sounds to edit into your final programme)
- decide whether to use music in your production, and choose which tracks to use so you can obtain permission to use them from the copyright holder.

These types of issues need to be thought through at the planning stage; not left until you start production.

If you are making a radio drama you need to produce a final script, a list of characters and a list of locations. You should also know how many seconds each page of dialogue will take to perform.

Video products

If you are planning a video product, you need to produce a script which indicates sound and vision.

Initially, the list of contents for the topic could be approached in the same way as for print, but as with radio you need to think in terms of time rather than space. As well as being concerned with recording wildtrack sound to edit into your final product, you need to think in terms of camera positioning. Think about what type of shot you need, whether you need to use a tripod so that you get a steady picture, what time of day your shots will be filmed and whether you need special lighting

(see pages 113–115). It can be useful to write a script as a storyboard, as in the example on page 225.

Researching content

Whatever type of product you are planning, you will need to do some research.

If you are producing a journalistic product, whether for broadcast or print media, your role is that of intermediary between those with expert knowledge or first-hand experience, and the reader, viewer or listener. You will probably carry out telephone or face-to-face interviews with people who have a story to tell or information to give. Sometimes you will also need to conduct desk research into written material, looking through cuttings files, on CD ROMs, on the Internet, in reference books or on audiotape. Journalists usually have to work under pressure of deadlines, so research has to be done quickly rather than in a leisurely way.

As an example of what research at this level involves, the author was asked to do a 500-word feature on the introduction of vouchers for nursery schooling. He had about three hours to find out the kinds of information needed by parents and had no prior knowledge of the topic.

By chance, a breakfast news programme on TV had organised a phone-in on vouchers. The author recorded this and so had access to two contrasting opinions about the scheme from headteachers of nursery schools which had been piloting the vouchers. There were also several questions from anxious parents which were answered by experts in the studio.

After studying the videotape, the author phoned a local authority education advisor with responsibility for early years learning. He arranged for a half-hour face-to-face interview on the topic, so that he could get a local angle on the story. At the interview the advisor handed over a government document explaining the scheme.

The scheme had implications for playgroups which seemed to be under threat of closure, so the next step was to ring the local playgroup association to find out their reactions and thoughts.

So the research for this story consisted of watching a videotape, skim-reading a government booklet, a face-to-face interview and a telephone interview.

▶◀ *See Activity 3, page 195*

Recces

If you are working on a film or video which needs location work, you will need to research the locations. This research is referred to as a recce (short for reconnaissance). You will need to check:

- that the locations fit the requirements of the script
- that permissions have been granted
- that the people who normally use the locations are aware of your plans
- technical details, such as what lighting you will need and the position of power points
- whether there are any potential health and safety problems, such as filming near busy roads.

This is a good time to look for cutaway opportunities. Cutaways are shots of backgrounds, places or details which can be used at the editing stage of production.

Drawing up a schedule

It is useful to draw up a detailed plan of action for every stage and every person involved in your production. If you work backwards from the distribution of your finished product, you can build up a timetable by asking what you have to do in order to complete each process.

The plan for a newspaper might be built up as follows.

Date	Activity	Personnel
April 1st	distribution of newspaper by door-to-door delivery	all
March 31st	newspaper printed	local newspaper contract
March 30th	final proofread	editor and deputy editor
March 29th	complete typesetting	all
March 28th	deadline for copy	all
March 27th	deadline for advertising	advertising manager
and so on...		

Figure 15.2

CASE ▼ STUDY

PLANNING A CHILDREN'S RADIO PROGRAMME

Rose Veitch, a media studies student at Sunderland University, planned her radio programme while on work experience at Sun City radio station. Her planning and thinking are shown in this case study, which has been only slightly adapted from work she produced as part of her degree course.

INITIAL CONCEPT

For the last three years I have been studying journalism at Sunderland University and hope to pursue a career in journalism. I have always been perplexed by the lack of news programmes for children in the mainstream media. Children cannot be expected to watch, listen to or read adult news and therefore do not have access to accurate information. I see this as a gap in the market.

Prompted by this, I decided to create a current affairs programme for children. Initially I wanted this programme to be a children's version of *Panorama*, focusing on issues which affect and interest children, with a view to educate, inform and entertain.

AUDIENCE RESEARCH

The programme has to be from children's point of view and I realised that talking to children to find their views was absolutely essential.

Last summer I spent two months teaching 6 to 16-year-olds at radio workshops. I discussed my programme plans extensively with them, and asked about 30 children what they were interested in. I issued a questionnaire to about 15 children (girls and boys) and I monitored children's media.

The questionnaire asked children to say how interested they were in the following topics: animals/pets; sport; science/technology; environmental issues; politics; the royal family; education/school; music; television; the Internet/computers. I asked them to rank each topic on a scale of one to ten, with ten being their most favourite.

As the following table shows, the four highest scoring topics were television, music, the environment and animals/pets. Politics and the royal family scored lowest.

Animals/pets	90
Sport	33
Science/technology	40
Environmental issues	99
Politics	19
Royal family	15
Education/school	68
Music	100
Television	118
The Internet/computers	73

Figure 15.3 Results from the questionnaire

I decided from the results that my programme had to include music, TV chat and environmental issues.

CONTENT

I decided that a ten-minute programme was ideal. Young listeners would get bored with anything longer, and a shorter programme would restrict the amount of information I could pack in. I decided on three packages of three minutes each, which would leave one minute for links. (A package is the term given to a mini-feature.) Most radio packages are between three and four minutes long. I decided to keep mine as short as possible, bearing in mind that kids aren't very good at concentrating. However, it is quite hard to explore an issue in much depth in under three minutes.

Once I got to this stage I had to choose three different packages.

Based on my previous research, I knew that one of these had to be about the environment. I knew that I couldn't use a topical news peg (e.g. the Newbury by-pass) to base my packages on, given children's lack of news knowledge, so I was looking for a new angle.

On 29 February 1996 the Brit Award Ceremony took place, and luckily for me there was a news story about Jarvis Cocker and Michael Jackson. This caused huge controversy in the music industry and among fans. I knew the children would want to hear an analysis of this, so I decided to cover it.

Although the Internet/computers only came fifth in the popularity ratings, I decided to do a package about the Internet as my final piece. Why? I was on the train, eavesdropping on a group of children. They were talking about the Internet which they had at school. I wasn't aware that schools were connected and they said that most schools weren't. However, I realised that a lot of kids' TV programmes have started broadcasting their E-mail numbers, which must reflect considerable interest in the Internet. Also this is a brand new issue which has not really been looked at, and one that could have a big impact on children.

PROPOSAL 1: THE ENVIRONMENT

Figure 15.4 Educating children about the environment

Angle

Although children are very interested in the environment, they don't seem to know much about it, so I decided to find out why they don't know and to look at ways they can get information.

Ideas

- Find out if environmental education is part of the National Curriculum.
- If not why not?
- How else can children get access to information?
- Once they have information, how can children protect the environment?

Interview ideas

- Speak to someone from the Department for Education and Employment involved in environmental education to find out to what extent children are taught about the environment. If they are not taught about it, speak to a politician and ask why not.
- Find out if pressure groups have youth departments.
- How do environmental charities help educate children?

Content research

Having no knowledge of this issue, I asked a teacher friend if environmental education is part of the National Curriculum. She told me that it wasn't really and that it depended on the interests of the teacher. I rang local education departments, was put in touch with someone who co-ordinates resources to enable teachers to spend more time on environmental education, and arranged an interview.

I then contacted three different pressure groups. Two did not have youth departments, but Animal Aid in London seemed very enthusiastic about educating children and I arranged a telephone interview with the head of its youth department.

I also arranged an interview with a representative from a local environmental charity, CEED.

PROPOSAL 2: THE BRITS

Figure 15.5 Jarvis Cocker of Pulp – hero or villain?

Angle

A dig at Michael Jackson's attempts to exonerate himself from the charges of child abuse by manipulating the media. A lot of people found Jackson's performance at the Brit awards sickening and Jarvis Cocker made a protest by storming Jackson's stage. Cocker was later arrested and charged.

This is quite a sensitive issue which could result in offending a lot of fans. However, every child I talked to who had seen the show was disgusted with Jackson's performance even if they didn't agree with Cocker. They were also fully aware of the previous charges made against Jackson and knew the meaning of child abuse.

This is not a news programme and I don't have to be impartial, so I decided to follow Cocker's side of the story.

Ideas

- What happened?
- What is the public reaction?
- What is Cocker's reaction to the incident?
- What is Jackson's reaction?
- Any evidence of hurt children to support charges?
- Expert opinion.

Interview ideas

- A vox pop amongst 7 to 12-year-olds – what do they think about the incident?
- An interview with Jarvis Cocker.
- An interview with Michael Jackson.
- An interview with a music journalist about the impact of the incident.

Research

I knew all about the incident. I had watched the show on TV. The next day I bought the *Sun* and the *Independent*, and the following week I bought the *Melody Maker* and the *NME*, all of which covered the incident in depth. The tabloids all came down heavily on Jackson's side, I suppose in anticipation of public opinion and a dislike of the rebellious teenage culture which Pulp represent. A lot of children, however, strive to be part of the subversive rather than the mainstream, and for this reason, I expected most children to support Cocker.

I asked 20 children their opinion, and they all criticised Jackson and most supported Cocker.

I knew I wouldn't get interviews with Cocker or Jackson, so after talking to my supervisor, we agreed that I could copy an interview from radio. The clip was originally recorded at a press conference.

Jackson didn't give any interviews, but his record company released a statement on his behalf. I wanted to use this statement but, instead of indirectly quoting him, I decided to get a child to say the statement for me. I stress this was not intended to be a parody of Jackson. It is serious.

My next move was to arrange an interview with an expert. I phoned the journalist who wrote the article about the Brits. He was very unhelpful and refused to speak to me. I phoned the editor of a local music magazine and he agreed to be interviewed.

I also looked through the files of a local newspaper and found a story about a few children who said they were hurt at the incident. I used this information.

PROPOSAL 3: THE INTERNET

Angle

I can't imagine many individuals having access to the Internet, so I decided to concentrate on the Internet at school.

Ideas

- What is the Internet?
- How many schools in the country are connected?
- If they are, why?
- How can the Internet transform education?
- If it can make education better and more fun, what is being done to install it?
- What are government policies concerning the Internet at school?
- What are the wider consequences of the Internet?

Interview ideas

- A computer expert to describe what the Internet is.
- A teacher to explain how the Internet can help learning.
- Some children at a school using the Internet to say what they do with it.
- Someone from the Department for Education and Employment to explain government policies.
- A science fiction nutter/genius to predict the future.

Research for the Internet package

I began with absolutely no knowledge about the Internet, so I talked to a friend who is studying media systems at the university. He told me what the Internet is and suggested I talk to one of his IT lecturers. I arranged an interview with him.

I then rang the local newspaper's education department to find out which schools in the area were connected to the Internet. I was given four leads and contacted the headteacher of Hill View Primary School who arranged an interview with the IT co-ordinator and with some pupils especially interested in the Internet.

I contacted the local Training and Enterprise Council and asked about government policy on the Internet. I was referred to the Department for Education and Employment in London. The press office gave me a rough estimate of how many schools are connected and suggested I should speak to John Birch from the department, but would not give me his telephone number. I wrote to him but received no reply.

Over the Easter period I worked at Sun City radio. One of the news bulletins included a story about the Internet. At a council meeting the head of the local education authority's IT service had suggested that all local schools should be connected. I rang him and arranged an interview.

▶◀   See Activity 4, page 196

▶◀   See page 214 for a continuation of this Case Study

Figure 15.6 Using the Internet at school

ACTIVITIES ▼

Activity 1

You have been asked to research an item about the difficulties which disabled people face in finding employment. Your item should be either for a broadcast, or for a newspaper or magazine feature.

Your task is to find out how disabled people wish to be portrayed and to identify particular areas of concern. You have been told that the programme's director (or the publication's editor) is especially wary of portraying people with disabilities as either 'brave heroes' or 'pitiable victims'.

Try to arrange a visit to a special school in your area to talk to some of the pupils. Alternatively, interview people with disabilities whom you know.

Find out which words cause offence (e.g. 'spastic', 'retarded' or 'defective').

How would you rephrase terms such as 'crippled with', 'victim of' and 'suffering from'?

What is the difference between 'learning difficulties' and 'mental illness'?

Find out the different terms that can be applied to degrees of deafness.

Do wheelchairs confine or liberate?

After your research, draw up a list of guidelines about how disability should be represented.

Activity 2

Choose a popular magazine aimed at your own age group. Photocopy the contents page and ask 30 people of your age to rate their interest in each item on a sliding scale. If possible, compare the opinions of regular readers of the title with non-readers.

Produce a chart to show your findings. What conclusions can you draw? How useful would these conclusions be to the magazine's publishers?

Activity 3

You are the editor of a community newspaper and the following piece of work has been submitted. You think there is a story lurking here somewhere, but the piece needs a better presentation of existing research findings and more research. It is also written more as editorial than a news item.

Ask for a rewrite and give the author some specific advice about how to improve the piece.

> Under-age drinking is a growing problem which is threatening to escalate out of control if something isn't done about it soon.
>
> Our school survey produced some worrying results which proves that the issue is closer to home than many people realise.
>
> There isn't a teenager in the country who doesn't either know someone who drinks or is an under-age drinker themselves, which shows how widespread the problem really is.
>
> Groups of teenagers swigging cider on street corners have become a common sight and one which most people have come to accept as normal. However, ignoring the problem doesn't solve it and people now need to face up to it in order for action to be taken.
>
> Despite frequent warnings about the dangers of alcohol, many teenagers continue to drink, either unaware or unconcerned about the possible consequences.
>
> Parents, shopkeepers and pubs are often blamed for the increasing popularity of alcohol among under-age drinkers, but it is a problem which society as a whole must deal with.

Activity 4

Analyse the case study on pages 192 to 194.

How effectively has Rose Veitch conducted her audience research? Consider the size of the sample and the validity of her conclusions. What about the categories listed? How helpful are they? Is it possible that although children may not give a high rating to sport in general, they may have a special interest in a particular sport? Why is the category 'The Internet/computers' not part of 'Science/technology'?

'I decided from the results that my programme had to include music, TV chat and environmental issues.' How far is Rose Veitch pursuing her own interests rather than the children's? Does this matter?

What do you think of her assertions that:

- 'Children cannot be expected to watch, listen to or read adult news and therefore do not have access to accurate information.'
- 'I decided that a ten-minute programme was ideal. Young listeners would get bored with anything longer.'
- 'I decided to keep mine as short as possible, bearing in mind that kids aren't very good at concentrating.'
- 'I knew that I couldn't use a topical news peg (e.g. the Newbury by-pass) to base my packages on, given children's lack of news knowledge.'
- 'Also this [The Internet] is a brand new issue which has not really been looked at...'
- 'This is not a news programme and I don't have to be impartial, so I decided to follow Cocker's side of the story.'
- 'A lot of children, however, strive to be part of the subversive rather than the mainstream.'
- 'Although children are very interested in the environment, they don't seem to know much about it.'

Try conducting the survey with a group of children using the same technique as Rose Veitch. Then try another piece of research with a similar group, asking them to list the things they like to read, view or listen to without prompting them. How different are your findings? Which are more reliable as a test of what the group will be interested in?

How effective is the student's content research? It seems thorough, but are there any other sources she could have contacted given time constraints?

BIBLIOGRAPHY ▼

Hoffman, A, *Research for Writers*, A & C Black, 1996

Writers' and Artists' Yearbook, A & C Black, Annual

The Writer's Handbook, Macmillan, Annual

CHAPTER 16

Print production

16

Introduction

This chapter shows you how to produce and edit a magazine or newspaper. The first half of the chapter looks at how to:

- write effective openings
- base your stories on people
- keep to the point
- write succinctly
- use photography well.

It also includes a case study of a fanzine directory produced by a student.

The second half of the chapter deals with the editing stage of production, providing advice on:

- page design
- making stories fit space
- proofreading.

Writing a magazine or newspaper article

Assuming you carried out research as described in Chapter 15, the next stage in producing a printed product is to shape your magazine or newspaper article and attract your readers' interest.

Writing an opening

The opening of any article has to demand attention. In a news story the most important information is usually placed at the beginning in a short first paragraph:

- 'A massive security operation is being mounted at Aintree race-course today, as preparations continue for the rescheduled Grand National.' *Scotsman*, 7 April 1997

Topicality is crucial in a news story and here the writer is mentioning something that is actually happening while the reader reads her morning paper. You can't be more topical than that!

The crispness of news openings like the following, all from the *Scotsman*, is not achieved without much practice:

- 'Thousands of theatregoers were forced to evacuate the Irish show *Riverdance* after a bomb alert.'
- 'Young people of the nineties have more in common with Swampy the road protester than with Kevin the obnoxious teenager created by the comedian, Harry Enfield, according to a survey published today.'
- 'Labour MPs are planning a £4 million rates raid on rich owners of Scottish sporting estates.'
- 'Muslim rebels have massacred more than 90 villagers in Algeria, slaughtering some with chainsaws and dousing others in burning petrol.'

▶◀ *See Activity 1, page 205*

There are other ways of attracting attention. You can arouse curiosity by mentioning unusual details and introducing some bizarre contrasts, as below:

- 'Glittering in a silver costume topped with a 3ft wig and a train of ostrich feathers borne by two semi-naked Adonis style attendants, Elton John set off for his 50th birthday celebrations in an office removal van.' *Scotsman*, 7 April 1997

This opening has the added bonus of mentioning a famous person.

You can introduce characters in unusual situations:

- 'The first child's name was José. He was an orphan and carried a Paddington Bear style note written by his father who had been killed in the fighting. It read, "This is José. I beg whoever finds my son to take care of him."'

You can begin with a mystery:

- 'Jane Searl was a success at everything she did – running a successful fashion business, riding for Britain in the Olympics, the first woman MP her town had ever elected, but one day she gave it all up and chose a life of poverty.'

You can ask a question:

- 'As the long drought continues, is Britain turning into a desert?'

Or you can tell a personal story:

- 'I was looking for an oasis in a desert of tourists – an empty pub on August Bank Holiday Monday. And I found it. But it's my secret.'

▶◀ *See Activity 2, page 205*

Having attracted the reader's attention, your next challenge is to keep it.

Personalising stories

Whatever your topic, think about personalising it. 'Hang your story on a person' is one of the conventions of journalism. At a simple level this might mean organising a vox pop (voice of the people), where you interview 'people in the street' about their views on a topical issue.

It is worth looking closely at magazines and newspapers to spot other examples. In 1997 one edition of *Bliss* contained the following treatments of astrology, lesbianism, incest, stalking and drugs:

- 'Horoscopes ruined my life' – which introduced the reader to 'Shilpa, 17', who 'believes she'll die before she's 22. Why shouldn't she? All her astrologer's other predictions have come true.' The article then begins in the first person:
  '"What's in store for me?" I asked eagerly.'

- 'My parents hired a private detective to find out if I was gay' – about Trish who announces in the first sentence, 'I've always known that I was gay'.
- 'I'm going out with my brother' – which is basically a love story about a girl and her stepbrother told in the first person.
- 'I was stalked' – about Claire who 'met a boy on holiday'. 'Little did she know that he'd never leave her alone.'
- 'I was the school drugs pusher' – about Tanya who 'knew that taking drugs was bad but then she started selling them too'.

▶◀   *See Activity 3, page 205*

Keeping focused

It must be clear to the reader what it is you are trying to communicate. It is easy to drift away from your main point, and readers will quickly become confused, lose interest and give up.

It is a good idea to write down the main point of your article before you start writing. Make sure that every sentence you write relates to this statement of intent. You might want to change the statement as you go along, which does not matter as long as everything you write is consistent with the revision. Be ruthless about discarding anything that strays from your main purpose.

Writing tight

When you write you should make language work hard for you. Once you have written a piece, read it over and see if you can use fewer words with the same effect. The care you take with language will tell your readers how much you care about them. Readers will quickly give up if they feel you are too casual, too pompous or too bored with your subject.

Clichés (over-used or hackneyed phrases) are a sure sign that a writer is not putting effort into making the subject interesting. They suggest laziness, lack of thought and lack of imagination. On the other hand, it is better to use a cliché than to use a phrase that doesn't work.

▶◀   *See Activity 4, page 206*

Keeping it brief

Succinct writing is difficult because you have to think carefully about each phrase and word. If you tried to do this from the outset your flow of thoughts would be impeded, so you need to rewrite everything you produce at least once.

Avoid using redundant words, for example:
- 'the flowers were purple in colour' (you could just say 'they were purple')
- 'she had a smile on her face' (where else would it be?)
- 'on the occasion when' (when is redundant).

▶◀   *See Activity 5, page 206*

Look out for unnecessary qualifying words, for example:
- 'very unique' (unique means the only one, so something is either unique or not)
- 'absolutely exhausted' (exhaustion is total loss of strength)

- 'completely destroyed' (destruction means ruining completely). Don't use unnecessary prepositions, for example:
- 'meet with'
- 'ascend up'
- 'connect up'.

▶◀   *See Activity 6, page 206*

The structure of a standard newspaper story

Parents are being urged not to panic about an outbreak of hand and mouth disease in local schools.	The lead paragraph is straight to the point and brief, saying **what** has happened.
There have been rumours that the disease is linked to foot and mouth disease which occurs in animals.	The second paragraph says **why** there has been concern.
But public health chief Dr Hannah Poole says that there is no cause for alarm.	This introduces an 'expert view'... which is quoted in direct speech.
"We have had several calls from parents who are worried," she said, "but there is no connection at all with animal diseases. Hand and mouth disease is a condition that occurs regularly at this time of year."	
What should parents look out for? The main symptoms are tiny blisters on hands and lips and inside the mouth. Children may not want to eat and there is a slight fever.	A question is posed to help involve the reader. Back to reported speech for variety.
"Unfortunately there is no treatment except painkillers to relieve the discomfort," says Dr Poole. "It is a virus and as with most viruses, it will pass within a few days."	Back to the expert telling the reader what they can, or perhaps can't, do.
Dr Poole says that the condition is quite common among young children and there are no public health implications.	Reassures readers who might be concerned about wider implications.
Worried parents should contact their family doctor if they need more information.	Don't call us! (Or the public health department.) Conclusions usually avoid using quotes, and sometimes anticipate how the story might develop – 'what happens next?'

Figure 16.1 The structure of a standard newspaper story

Using photographs

You should try to use photographs on every page of your publication to enhance its visual appeal. They should illustrate the text, so writer and photographer need to work together to make sure that the main purpose of the story or feature is clear. Don't print pictures regardless of their relevance or quality. In particular, be careful not to include 'firing squad' shots (where groups stand rigidly in a line facing the camera), shots of buildings without people and shots of poor technical quality (e.g. badly lit or out of focus.)

Figure 16.2 Children collecting for charity: an imaginative treatment of a standard local news photo opportunity

You should be able to produce pictures of the quality of Figure 16.2, which is a competent picture without being brilliant. It has several characteristics which you should try to learn from. The photographer could easily have done this as a 'firing squad' shot with the children standing in a straight line facing the camera. Instead she has organised a diagonal line which gives the picture depth. The diagonal line of coins is echoed by the line of children and the building, with the open door in the distance acting as a kind of full stop. It is important when you are framing a picture through the viewfinder that you make yourself aware of the background details and don't just concentrate on the foreground.

The photographer has chosen a low angle so that the children appear important. She is on their level. This enables her to fill the frame with faces instead of background. (Having too much background and not getting close enough to the subject are common faults of amateurs.) The children's faces are at a slight angle, which can produce a more interesting light and shade contrast than a full face shot.

The children are all doing something which relates to the story, which was about raising money for charity. The photographer usually has to work hard with a group this size to relax the subjects and produce the kind of mood relevant to the story. She has obviously asked the children not to smile broadly as they all have their lips together. This gives the picture a more natural quality and produces an interesting variety of expressions.

It is possible that the photographer was conscious of gender and ethnic mix when she took this shot, and probable that she picked out the most photogenic pupils to figure in the foreground. There are things that the photographer may not be completely pleased with, such as the fifth girl along being squeezed out. It is vital to take several shots when organising a picture like this so that you have alternatives if people stick out their tongues or make faces at the wrong time.

CASE ▼ STUDY

DONNA'S DIRECTORY

Donna's Directory (see Figure 16.3) was produced by a GNVQ Media Studies student while she was on work experience at the *Yorkshire Post* offices in Leeds. This is Donna Sheffield's account of how she produced it.

'In September 1994 I first started enjoying Suede's music. I saw an advertisement in the fan club magazine for a 'fanzine' being produced in aid of a cancer charity. I noticed adverts for other fanzines in the back pages. I began to collect them and wondered how many actually existed. Then I began to wonder why someone didn't compile a magazine of fanzines to let people know which ones were available and, more importantly, which ones were worth buying.

At the time I was visiting the *Yorkshire Post*'s classroom as part of my media course. I realised the facilities there were more than adequate to produce a magazine. I played around with the idea, produced a few simple pages and discussed the idea with Louisa Kerr, who was studying animation at Edinburgh University. She produced a mock advert for the 'Directory' and we sent it to the main fanzine writer at the time. He became the assistant manager for the band and he loved the idea. He said, "The kids have been needing something like this for a long time."

Figure 16.3 Donna Sheffield shows her work in the Yorkshire Post classroom

The fanclub published the advert for 'Donna's Directory' which was free for all those who sent in a stamped addressed envelope. I sent out over 70 copies world-wide. I then published DD2 which was advertised again in the fanclub magazine. This time it cost £1.

My target audience is Suede fans, a cult group of music followers. Suede are a London band, but they are very popular in Europe and the East. They also have a small following in America. The fanzines reflect this, as do the sales of my directory. Suede fans are both male and female, aged mostly 16–28. Of course, not every Suede fan likes fanzines. We try to persuade them otherwise.

I do all the writing, the typing, the page layout and the printing. Louisa does the cartoons that have given the Directory a corporate identity. At a gig in January fans approached us and remarked "You look just like your cartoons!" It has made us mini-celebrities in this area.

Everyone has only good things to say about the Directory. The lead singer of the band, Brett Anderson, viewed a copy and exclaimed, "This is excellent. Can I keep it?" Suede's management, two ex-ziners themselves, have been wonderfully supportive. I am in regular contact with them thanks to the Directory.

It has been a great experience and lots of fun. I have been offered a place at Preston University on a BA Journalism course and I feel sure that DD was instrumental in landing the place.'

Donna Sheffield produced the directory using QuarkXpress on an Apple Mac and printed it using a laser printer. It has 36 A4 pages. The first section has 14 reviews of different Suede fanzines with information about how to obtain them. In section two Donna reviews a selection of Indie fanzines, and in section three some variety fanzines. She calls section four 'Odds and Sods', and it includes cartoons, book reviews and an interview.

Figure 16.4 A page from Donna's Directory

Figure 16.5 Advert for Donna's Directory

Post-production

This section focuses on preparing the pages of a magazine or newspaper ready for printing.

The basic elements

On most printed pages there are four basic ingredients:

- text (the stories or articles)
- headlines (the large print that labels each story)
- photographs (the pictures that accompany the stories)
- captions (the words that accompany the photographs).

How well you arrange these four elements and how they relate to one another will determine how your page looks.

Designing the text

How you design the text will depend on the subject matter and your audience. Here are two contrasting magazine pages to illustrate the point.

The *Sugar* page, aimed at young, probably impatient readers who want colour and snappy information, is 'busy' with one theme but five separate pieces. Each piece has a different headline font. Punctuation is sometimes dramatic (as in the use of exclamation marks and question marks) and unconventional (omitting capital letters at the start of headlines). The word count is small. There are nine pictures and liberal use of colour. The layout does not rely on fixed columns but has a cut and paste look. Each box style is different. There are overlaps and cut outs. The overall effect is lively, easy-to-read, bright and anarchic.

The *Punch* page is much more formal and subdued, aimed at an educated, sophisticated, middle-aged audience. There is a three-column grid, just one font and a restrained headline. It contains a lengthy article and a single cartoon. The effect is easy on the eye, classy and ordered.

Figure 16.6 Contrasting approaches to page design from Sugar and Punch

Typography

You can use a wide range of typographic components to give different styles to your text.

First you can use different fonts or styles of typeface.

This paragraph is written in Helvetica, which is a sans serif font. This means that each letter is designed so it has no serifs (tiny cross-strokes). Sans serif fonts are often used in headlines because many people think they are clearer and easy to read.

This paragraph is written in Times, which is a font with serifs. Fonts like this are supposed to be easier on the eye if there is a lot of text.

Sometimes different fonts are used to provide variety, but beware using too many as this can make your publication look confused and badly planned.

The size of type you choose will depend on your audience.

Material printed for very young children usually needs different treatment...

... to material for a legal document which is not drawing attention to the 'small print'.

For most publications and audiences a font size of between 9 and 12 points is comfortable.

You can also adjust the leading (the space between lines of

print). In this paragraph the leading has been doubled – an

effect which might be useful in an advertisement, for instance.

Sometimes making slight adjustments to leading which the

reader will not notice can be a useful way to make text fit a

certain space.

If you can adjust the tracking on your word processor this will move the letters closer together. This is another way to fit text into limited space. This paragraph has been very tightly tracked.

There are *several* ways of **emphasising** words and PHRASES, three of which are used in the first part of this sentence.

> If you want to emphasise large blocks of texts, then you can put them in boxes, use a tinted background, or both.

You can break up text so that it seems easier to read by:
- using short paragraphs, as popular newspapers do
- missing lines so that there is a space between blocks of text
- using bullet points
- using crossheads or mini-headlines between paragraphs.

Making a page plan

Once you have all the ingredients of your publication – stories, photographs, other illustrations and possibly advertisements – you should draw up detailed page plans. You can do this freehand or electronically using a software package such as QuarkXpress or Aldus Pagemaker. Precise measurement is vital at this stage. The area of your plan should match exactly the area of your final printed page.

You need to decide whether to use columns, as in the *Punch* page, or a cut and paste technique, as in the *Sugar* page. If you use columns, they should be wide enough to accept an average of about eight words in the font size that you have chosen for the bulk of your text. Different publishing houses have different styles and conventions for page plans, but the one suggested here is commonly used.

Figure 16.7 A page plan from Campaign and the finished page

The story is given a catchline ('Cosmowoman'), which is a short label to identify it while it is stored in the computer. The font name and size are indicated. A wavy line shows where the text will go. Boxes are drawn with instructions identifying the picture, its size and any special requirements such as using cut outs (physically or electronically cutting round people or objects to give a silhouette appearance) and text wraps (flowing the text around the shape of the picture). The size of lines, such as the eyeline at the top of the page, is shown, along with colour instructions if necessary.

Design checklist

- Gather together all the material for your page and decide what is essential and what is optional. It is useful to have short pieces of writing ('fillers') to fill small gaps if necessary.
- Give each page a main (lead) story or a main picture which will attract the reader's eye to the page.
- Give your best picture a prominent position on the page, even if it does not go with your lead story.
- Scatter other pictures around the page so that they do not compete for interest with each other.
- Vary the shapes and sizes of your pictures.
- Check the eye movement around the page and make sure it is always clear to the reader where to go to next. Watch out for reverse 'L' shapes as these can make some eye movements awkward.
- Make sure every picture has a caption and every story a headline.
- Use lines and boxes sparingly, and only if they are needed to make separation clear.

▶◀ *See Activity 7, page 207*

Figure 16.8 Cropping a photograph can create an entirely different image and atmosphere

Making stories fit

If stories are too long, your options are to:

- cut the text – you can either drop a sentence or two or else find shorter ways of saying the same things
- trim or resize photographs – tight cropping (cutting) of pictures, especially head and shoulder shots, can make them much more dramatic
- shorten the headline
- alter the size or style of the font or change the leading or tracking
- move something else, such as an advertisement, off the page.

If your stories are too short, your options are to:

- add text
- enlarge a photo
- add an introduction (standfirst)
- alter the size or style of the font or change the leading or tracking
- put space between paragraphs
- add crossheads (mini-headlines) between paragraphs
- add a lift quote – take a quotation from the story, type it in a larger font, and draw attention to it by boxing it or giving it some white space
- add an advertisement or filler material.

Proofreading and style guides

In the excitement of wanting to see your work in print it is easy to overlook the vital process of checking for accuracy. When you proofread you should read text twice – once for meaning and once for literals (mistakes). A useful technique is to make a small window out of card and use this to focus on a word or phrase at a time, so you are looking carefully at the details. When you read for meaning, your brain 'corrects' what you see without you realising.

English is a living, changing language with many different varieties. For the purposes of most writing for the public, however, you need to restrict yourself to 'standard English'. Standard English is the variety described in dictionaries and grammar books and accepted by most educated people as 'correct'. There is more than one standard English, but in the UK British standard English is used rather than, say, American or Singapore standard English.

Many print media organisations such as newspaper offices produce their own guidelines on the 'correct' use of English. These are commonly known as style guides.

You may find it useful to produce your own guide to what mistakes to avoid. A brief style guide is given here for you to use as a starting point. It restricts itself to the type of standard, formal English which is used for most essays, reports and serious articles.

You can decide to depart from formal or standard English, but must be clear why you are doing so. You should always be sure that the way you are writing is acceptable to your audience and the context in which it is used. Words from a teenage slant (such as 'wicked' for good, or 'cheesy' for in bad taste) are appropriate in the context of a teenage magazine, but not in an essay for a teacher or examiner.

Areas for consideration in a style guide include:
- clichés and overused words and phrases from speech
- common misspellings
- common misuse of vocabulary
- punctuation and sentence construction
- non-standard grammar, or common grammatical errors.

Common misspellings

You should compile your own list of words which are commonly misspelt, or which you have particular difficulty with. A common mistake is to mix up words which sound the same but which are spelt differently (so-called 'homophones'):
- accept/except
- advise/advice (advise is the verb, advice is the noun)
- affect/effect (affect is the verb, effect is the noun)
- practise/practice (practise is the verb, practice is the noun)
- stationary/stationery
- there/their
- to/too
- your/you're ('you're' is two words).

English spelling is notoriously difficult. The following examples are the stuff of sophisticated spelling tests:
- accommodation
- comfortable
- liaison
- panicking
- necessarily.

Common misuse of vocabulary

This is a tricky area, because there is often no difference between misusing words and using them in a new way to reflect language change. For example:
- using 'less people' instead of *few people*
- using 'disinterested students' instead of *uninterested students*.

It was once clear that the expressions 'less people' and 'disinterested students' were incorrect if they were supposed to mean the same as the words in italics. As a result of language change, however, the uses given first are now widely accepted.

Here are some examples of words which are misused, and which you should try to use as indicated:
- If you *anticipate* rain you take steps to avoid getting wet, whereas if you *expect* rain you may simply regard it as likely.
- People are *injured* in accidents, but *wounded* deliberately.
- *Flaunt* means to display proudly, *flout* to disobey openly.
- *Lay* means to put something down, *lie* means to put your body into a position flat on the floor.

Punctuation and sentence construction

Punctuation and sentence construction are sometimes related. Long sentences broken up by repetitive punctuation are to be avoided. For example, if a writer is using long sentences with chains of commas, these should be broken up into a number of short sentences. The use of long, over-extended sentences is a common problem. It is much less common for short sentences to be a problem. The ideal pattern of sentences in a paragraph is an alternation between short and medium-length sentences.

Probably the most problematic punctuation mark is the apostrophe attached to an *s*. The apostrophe *s* is used to mark possession, for example:
- *Smith's* appeal
- my *horse's* name.

Apostrophes are also used to show that one or more letters are missing, as, in contractions such as I'm, you're, he'll. One common problem is mixing up 'it's' with 'its':
- *It's* is always a contraction of 'it is'.
- *Its* is the possessive form of 'it'. As a possessive pronoun it is one word, like 'his' and 'hers'.

A plural only needs an apostrophe if it is required to show possession or to show that something is missing. If a plural does need an apostrophe, the apostrophe is placed after the *s*, for example:
- *horses'* names.

As a general rule, if there is doubt about the need for an apostrophe leave it out. For example, you could argue that plurals such as 'photos' and 'autos' require apostrophes to show what has been missed out from 'photographs' and 'automobiles', but this is doubtful. It looks much clearer if the apostrophe is left out in such marginal cases, for example:
- *Michael's Autos* is much clearer than *Michael's Auto's*.

Non-standard grammar, or common grammatical errors

The most common cause of using non-standard grammar in an inappropriate context is writing as you speak or think. For example, when you are speaking or thinking you can change your mind about what you want to say halfway through a sentence, but in writing this is likely to result in non-standard grammar or 'errors'.

Here are some common deviations or errors.
- The 'double negative' describes the use of more than one marker of the negative, as in 'they never do nothing on a Saturday night'. It is acceptable in dialect, and was acceptable in Shakespeare's times, but has been banned from today's standard English.
- The 'double comparative' is another common error, as in 'she is more cleverer than any of the boys'.
- When we contract the verb have to – 've – it often sounds very much like 'of'. However, constructions such as 'would of' and 'should of' are not standard, and are errors in writing. It is better to write 'would have' and 'should have' in full.

▶◀ *See Activities 8, 9, 10 and 11, pages 207 and 208*

ACTIVITIES ▼

Activity 1

Write snappy opening paragraphs which capture the essence of the following stories. Use no more than 25 words for each.

1 There is a local rowing club which has had a male-only membership for over a hundred years. Recently it applied for money from the National Lottery. It wanted this money to buy a new boat and improve the club facilities. The club has been told that it can only have the money if it changes its rules to allow women to join. There has been a meeting of the members which has decided to change the rules in order to receive the money. Some members have decided to resign because of this.

2 Last year a woman who had taken a fertility drug was pregnant with eight babies. She signed a contract with a national newspaper to tell her story. She refused to have a selective abortion. All the babies died. There was much controversy about her decisions. She has just announced that she is pregnant again.

3 There has been a fire bomb attack on a livestock haulage firm. Three lorries were destroyed. The Animal Liberation Front has claimed responsibility for the attack. It says that this is the start of a new campaign to stop the transport of live animals. It says that fire bombs are a better way of attracting publicity than peaceful demonstrations. It plans more attacks in the next few weeks.

4 The British Medical Association (BMA) has called for a change in the law which prevents local authorities from promoting homosexuality. The BMA believes that it is only by teaching young people in schools about homosexuality that the risk of mental or physical health problems can be reduced. They also think that everybody needs to be educated about homosexuality in order to stop prejudice and stereotyping.

Activity 2

Make your own collection of opening paragraphs from newspapers and magazines and classify them according to the different techniques they illustrate.

Activity 3

Think about how you could personalise articles on the following topics:

- vegetarianism
- transsexualism
- werewolves
- friendship
- cars and the environment
- holiday romances
- contraception
- new hairstyles
- girls' violence
- spotting a 'rotter'
- divorce
- obesity
- cosmetic surgery
- swearing.

Refer to people you realistically have access to.

Activity 4

Think of fresh ways to express these clichés:

- back to square one
- the morning after the night before
- firing on all cylinders
- living in a dream world
- pull their socks up
- taste of their own medicine
- the writing is on the wall
- trouble flared
- spine-tingling
- costly blunder
- waltzed round his opponent
- in the final analysis
- at the end of the day
- when all's said and done
- sex monster
- mindless yob
- blanket of snow
- hard-hitting report
- government watchdogs
- tip of the iceberg
- tower of strength.

Activity 5

Replace the italicised words in the following sentences with single words.

The professor spoke *on the subject of* media imperialism.

He failed to find a university place *as a result* of his exam grades being too low.

Despite the fact that there was high rainfall in the spring, the south east faces a drought.

Owing to the fact that the IRA warning was too late the station was still crowded when the bomb exploded.

Activity 6

Rewrite this story in fewer than 80 words without changing the information.

A woman who was approaching her 80th birthday met a tragic end in the bedroom of the house where she lived which is in the town of Gobchester when a fire went raging through the building. A lot of people, who were very brave, tried to save her, but, try as they might, they could not do it.

The woman had a son who will be 40 next birthday and he made a lot of attempts to get to his mother and in the end people working for the fire service, which is based a few miles away in a place called Beesley, had to stop him from going into the raging inferno.

People who live in the adjacent house to where the fire was rang up the emergency services after the fire alarm in their house started to sound off. Their home and lots of things in it was very much damaged in the blaze. The fire must have probably spread through the loft.

People working for the fire service, who had on special equipment to help them breathe, found the person who had died in the bedroom at the front of the house.

The police think that the cause of the fire was most probably a cigarette which had not been put out properly.

Activity 7

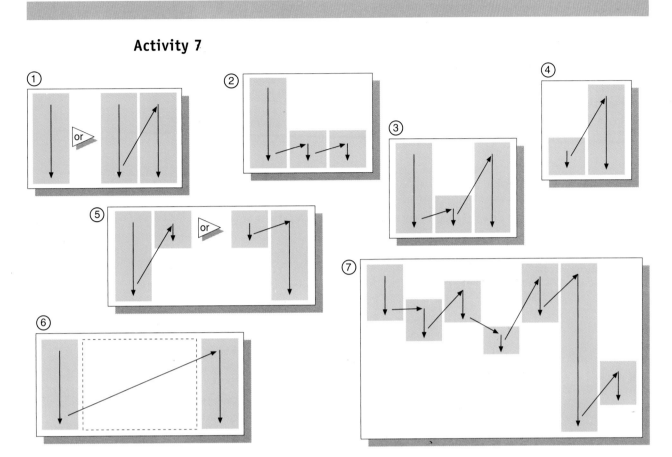

These shapes and arrows show the eye movements of readers trained in the Western culture of reading from left to right and top to bottom of a page. Comment on how convenient and helpful each pattern is for the reader.

Activity 8

Correct the mistakes in this letter from a problem page. However the letter has been written, the editor wants it to be printed in standard English.

"im 16 and Ill soon be taking my gcses. Im woried because my freinds and all the family exspect me to do well but Im not so sure. I spend most of my time worying instead of reviseing and Im just about craking up with the stress. My marks arent as good as they used to be and i do'nt even know what Im doing halve of the time. im just about ready to go mental what sholud i do.

Braking Point, herefordshire.

Activity 9

The guy who typed this into the system has been sent home for being drunk and you have to correct his work.

Moves by the govmernent to chang the larw on dagerus doggs has bean welcomd by the rspca. Under the 1991 Danrous dogs act, any classifeddog proved dangrous and not registered not registered. Would face a pelantuy of automtik death. But the charty has campaignd to have discretionover the fate of dogs who's owners are covicted.

It sports compululsory registration neutering and muzzling of breeds proved tobe dangrousbut wendy Lightfoot the rspcas pres ossifer said 'the rspca bleeves it is unfare to impose a death setnence on a dog becase thowner havee broked the law'

Activity 10

What is grammatically wrong with the following?

- Over one million boxes of Belgian chocolates is on offer to buyers of Slimlight margarine.
- Nottinghamshire Prison Service playing host to it's European neighbours.
- If you have something to moan about, laugh about, shout about or a complaint, let us know.
- It's us who helped change the system.
- Between you and I, the man's a fool.
- The only problem with foreigners are their strange eating habits.
- The time has come to once again decide which party to vote for.

Activity 11

Improve the following extracts, which were all taken from a university newspaper (honest!).

- Take a look at what this years Executive have done on pages 8 and 9.
- Chris was taken to hospital where his was kept overnight suffering from a broken nose, concussion and had stitches to the back of his head.
- The computing School gets through a lot of apre enabling the staff to raise £230 over the past year.
- Universities and Colleges Admissions Scheme (UCAS) have been called to allow Higher Education applicants to hold three offers for clearing rather than two, by school heads for 16-18 year olds.
- This has give me one or two ideas. If your having trouble with early morning lectures or assignments just say your therapist says your suffering from the debilitating Lorom-bov-Amorphsky syndrome, ie your a lazy bastard.
- The bus arrived at 1.00pm on Friday and after giving everybody a rousing welcome on the ferry we finally departed at 3.30.

BIBLIOGRAPHY ▼

Davis, A, *Magazine Journalism Today*, Heinemann, 1988

Dick, J, *Freelance Writing for Newspapers*, A & C Black, 1991

Freeborn, D, *Varieties of English*, Macmillan, 1986

Garcia, M, *Contemporary Newspaper Design*, Prentice Hall, 1993

Keeble, R, *The Newspapers Handbook*, Routledge, 1994

CHAPTER 17

Audio production

Introduction

Radio is the simplest electronic medium technically, which is one of its strengths. However, there is much more to producing a programme than just sticking someone in a studio and asking them to talk at the microphone. This chapter includes:

- a series of case studies on different types of programme, to help you decide what to produce

- practical advice on equipment, studios and recording techniques for actuality and dramas
- a continuation of the case study introduced in chapter 15, exploring the post-production of a radio magazine programme
- guidance on post-production techniques, including music reporting and tape editing.

What type of programme are you going to produce?

This section looks at a selection of the different types of programme which are broadcast on the radio. It includes case study material on:

- a studio drama
- a dramatised documentary
- a magazine programme
- an actuality feature
- a radio soap opera.

The case studies should give you an insight into how other people make programmes and may help you decide what type of programme you want to produce yourself.

Figure 17.1 Actors recording a studio drama

CASE ▼ STUDY

A studio drama

MAD DAN

Mad Dan was a 75-minute play broadcast on BBC Radio 4 about Dan Leno, the Victorian comedian who went mad.

PREPARING THE SCRIPT

A detailed proposal was sent to a drama producer, who had to sell the idea to the drama department and to the Controller of Radio 4. Only then was the play commissioned and the writer paid the first half of the fee.

Writing took a month or so, and the script went through several drafts before it was ready for studio. Because it was based on a real person, a great deal of research had to be done from books, and often copyright had to be paid even if the books were not quoted directly. Scripts used by Leno himself were usually out of copyright, but the writer had to prove that this was the case. The same was true of the many music-hall songs used. Directly quoted material is paid at a higher rate. Copyright fees are paid by the BBC, but the writer has to provide all the details.

When the final 'studio' script was agreed and the copyright cleared, the second half of the fee was paid to the writer. The producer then came up with a budget covering all aspects of the production, which had to be approved.

PREPARING FOR PRODUCTION

The play was cast from actors who could both act and sing the songs of the period in the proper style. They also had to be able to 'double' as the minor characters. Musicians were employed and the music was arranged to suit the instruments available. Leno would have had a full theatre orchestra at his disposal, but this was way beyond the programme's budget.

The producer and the studio manager (the chief sound technician) then discussed how to achieve background sounds and acoustics. For some of the time the action was supposed to take place on stage at the Drury Lane Theatre in London, and just the right amount of echo had to be found to make the studio sound like a theatre. Other scenes were in a church, which demanded a different type of echo. And of course the church had a congregation and the theatre an audience. The effect of an audience can be achieved by playing in a disc of a real audience, but this is never wholly satisfactory. Eventually it was decided that the half-dozen or so actors in the cast would be recorded over and over again clapping and cheering, to supplement the disc.

REHEARSING AND RECORDING

Only then was the producer ready to start the two days of rehearsing and recording. *Mad Dan* was recorded in sections, with some sounds added later to get the proper balance between voices and sounds. Dan Leno was a famous clog dancer, an early form of tap dancing. Sometimes the actor playing him, Chris Emmet, had to speak while he danced. But although he was puffing a bit and jogging about, the dancing steps were done by somebody else and put on during editing.

All in all it took several days of editing before the play was ready for broadcasting. Then the *Radio Times* billing had to be written, and trails prepared to advertise the show on air.

CASE ▼ STUDY

A dramatised documentary

MURDER MOST FOUL

This was a dramatised documentary series that the BBC decided to make about 'real-life' murders.

The department involved began by appointing a producer and a researcher. The researcher set to work in libraries, and came up with a list of about ten possible murders for the six-part series. A writer was then found and the six most suitable murders were chosen after discussions with the producer and researcher.

DECIDING A FORMAT

It was decided to personalise the programme by having a presenter talking to the audience rather than a simple narrator. The presenter would also have to link the dramatised scenes.

The dramatised scenes themselves were often taken from transcripts of the actual trials. These make good drama, are fact not fiction, and are also free of copyright as they are in 'the public domain'. At the time, Nick Ross was fronting the programme *Crimewatch* on television, and it was felt that his general style would make him an ideal presenter. Fortunately he agreed, and the writer watched *Crimewatch* and learnt to write in a way that suited his delivery. Meanwhile the leading actors (usually the murderers) were cast, and writing went ahead.

WRITING THE SERIES

The writer spent many hours in the British Library's newspaper section at Colindale tracking down reports of the crimes and, with luck, finding quotations from police officers involved. It also proved valuable to read other things in the papers which could be used to give the audience a sense of the period, including advertisements. Any reports used had to be noted down for copyright, as did any books (such as memoirs used for background). As with the play, if any sources were quoted directly a higher fee was payable.

Finally the supporting parts were cast, mainly from the BBC's resident Radio Drama Company, and the programmes

went into studio. They were relatively simple and took only one day in studio each, with minimal editing afterwards.

Figure 17.2 Nick Ross fronting Crimewatch

C A S E ▼ S T U D Y

A magazine programme

MERIDIAN

Meridian is a BBC World Service arts magazine programme broadcast live once a week to listeners all round the world.

A producer is usually given about a fortnight to prepare a show. Because the programme is broadcast to many different cultures and to people with a varying command of English, the subjects covered and the type of language used have to be chosen very carefully. Topical ideas will often come from the programme's office, but the producer also needs to check through newspapers and reviews. Ideas are then discussed with the senior producer and other producers who work on the show, to make sure the programme will fit in with what everybody else is doing.

ORGANISING ITEMS

The producer then has to contact:

- the presenter, who will write his or her own script and present it to the producer a day or two before the show is broadcast
- other people involved in the items being covered. For example, someone may be asked to review a book or play, and the author may be interviewed in the studio.

The producer may also ask the presenter to go out and pre-record some pieces: the general idea is to get a good mix of items.

People who are interviewed are not usually paid, as the programme is seen as good publicity. Short extracts taken from a play or book come within the legal definition of 'fair dealing', which means you don't have to pay anything to broadcast them. However, permission must be obtained if a chunk of a play is recorded, otherwise you may end up having to pay the actors and even the writer. People who review a play or book are paid.

BROADCASTING THE PROGRAMME

The programme should be a good mix of live and recorded items, often including a studio discussion. In case anything goes wrong, the producer needs a spare pre-recorded item in reserve. Playing this gives the producer and presenter a chance to have a quick crisis chat! The two are in touch via their headphones, but the producer must be careful not to waffle at the presenter while he or she is on air. The best time to talk is during pre-recorded items.

C A S E ▼ S T U D Y

An actuality feature

THE SQUARE MILE

This feature about the City of London was proposed by the BBC's economics correspondent at the time, Dominic Harrod. The idea was to make a sound portrait of the City using just unscripted voices of the people who worked there, recorded on location without any narration or linking material from the studio.

The programme was accepted by BBC Radio 3, and Dominic Harrod set about mobilising his contacts in the City. The final programme included the voices of the Chairman of Lloyds, the Governor of the Bank of England, the Warden of the Tower of London, Billingsgate fish porters, the choir of a city church and frenzied dealers on the stock exchange floor. Among the sounds that were used was the rattle of the Post Office's private unmanned underground railway as it carried letters and parcels across London. Although humans could not travel on it, a tape recorder and a microphone could.

AN UNSCRIPTED SCRIPT

As the programme was supposed to be unscripted, the idea was to link it together with a commentary from one of the tourist boats that travels along the River Thames.

Here the production team hit a snag: it was winter, and the boats weren't running. It decided to cheat.

Having borrowed a loud hailer and the Chairman of the Port of London Authority's launch, it contracted an actor (Ted

Kelsey, better known as Joe Grundy in *The Archers*). Where the contract usually printed the studio details, this was replaced with: 'Please be at Charing Cross Pier at 10 a.m. on...'.

Ted Kelsey arrived on time, somewhat bemused, and was handed a script hastily written overnight by Dominic Harrod. He spent a freezing winter's morning pretending it was summer, sailing up and down part of the Thames on the Chairman's launch saying through the loud hailer, 'On your right you can see the famous Tower of London, where...', and so on.

There were advantages to this deception. As this bit was actually scripted, the programme could be helped along by information such as 'The man in charge of the Tower is called the Warden...'.

The programme was then cut together later so the audience could hear the Warden's voice with ravens croaking in the background.

RECORDING THE PROGRAMME

The whole thing was recorded in a revolutionary form of stereo invented in Germany, in which microphones are set on a rubber head where the ears should be. This means that a listener using headphones hears things exactly as if they were actually where the head had been placed. This technique is called *binaural* (two-eared) stereo. Since the BBC didn't have a rubber head available it used an old paint tin full of sand, which worked just as well.

The programme was put up for an international award, but didn't win.

CASE ▼ STUDY

A soap opera

THE ARCHERS

The Archers is made at twice the speed of an ordinary drama: as much as an hour is recorded in a single day. The team carries out editing as it goes along. This is possible because the actors know their characters well and the same sound effects come up repeatedly, as our heroes and heroines work their way through yet another farming year.

Figure 17.3 A recording session for The Archers: an audio assistant recreates the sound of straw with old audio tape while Joe Grundy (played by Ted Kelsey) talks to Caroline Pemberton (Sara Coward)

PRE-PRODUCTION

Problems with *The Archers* come at the pre-production stage. The programme goes out every weekday on BBC Radio 4, which means that in any one month 20 shows go out. Each show lasts between 13 minutes 30 seconds and 13 minutes 45 seconds, and features 7 different characters.

At any one time:

- 20 scripts are being recorded
- 20 scripts are being written, checked, rewritten and sent out to the actors
- 20 scripts have been plotted in detail, and availability checks are being carried out on the actors required.

However, if something important happens in the farming world, a new scene has to be written quickly, recorded and squeezed into the programmes being broadcast that week (including the omnibus edition on Sunday).

Everything that goes into the show has to be totally accurate: someone will be sure to notice and write in if the two-week-old piglets sound like four-week-old piglets. And not only the farming details have to be checked. *The Archers* can call on a panel of over 20 experts, including a gynaecologist and a brain surgeon (remember when Brian was kicked in the head by a mad cow?). Huge, detailed files are kept on the past history of the 50 or so characters, sometimes stretching back over 40 years, because there is always the danger of a letter from a dedicated listener which goes something like this:

'Dear Sir or Madam,

I was surprised to find Phil eating turnips in last Tuesday's programme. I remember in 1957 he suffered severe indigestion as a result of eating turnips and was advised by the doctor never to touch them again...'

Making your own programmes

This section looks at some of the practical considerations when making your own radio programmes, including:

- equipment
- studios
- how to record actuality
- how to record dramas.

Equipment

If you have sophisticated digital editing and recording equipment, you will be able to record on DAT or mini-disc.

Otherwise, you'll need:

- at least one reel-to-reel tape machine. This uses reels of quarter-inch tape, rather than cassettes (cassettes cannot be edited accurately enough to make good programmes)
- a decent microphone, that doesn't need to be placed right against the mouth, can pick up more than one person at a time, and can also pick up some of the atmosphere of the room in which you are recording
- a microphone stand – either a table stand (if you are making a studio discussion) or a full-sized stand (for a play)
- sharp razor-blades for editing the show. These should be single-sided, not double-sided, unless you want to edit your fingers as well

- an editing block. This is a small block of metal with a groove to hold the quarter-inch tape and smaller grooves to make sure you cut the tape at the correct angle (see page 218).

With these few things and a bit of ingenuity, you can make a simple studio-based radio programme.

If you want to be a bit more sophisticated you will also need a mixer. This will enable you to:

- play in several microphones
- mix in music or sound effects from disc, cassette or reel-to-reel tape recorders, and record them all mixed together on a single tape.

The mixer will have faders, which are sliding knobs that you push up and down to make each sound softer or louder. Larger mixers may also have revolving knobs that allow you to change the pitch (make sounds higher and lower), and you may also be able to add echo (technically called 'reverberation').

The faders on your mixer will enable you to balance the sounds and ensure that they are all at the level you need them. In this way you can prevent one person speaking much louder than another, and make sure that your background music does not drown your speech. Of course to balance several voices, each person needs their own mike. This is normal practice in studio discussions, but not in plays where all the actors have to sound in the same acoustic.

If you are making a pop music show a mixer is essential. It will enable you to play in tracks and fade them down: you will find that you rarely want to play a number right through.

Figure 17.4 Radio recording equipment: microphones, reel-to-reel tape machine, sound mixing desk

Studios

For convenience, most radio shows originate from studios which are purpose-built for the job. But before you go out and hire a proper radio studio, think what you've got available.

The microphone will not only pick up the sounds spoken by your speakers, but also sounds bounced off the walls. So a room will sound very echoey if it has hard walls and, worst of all, a high ceiling and a lot of glass windows. This is fine if you are doing a play set in a church, but otherwise it's a disadvantage. Classrooms do not make ideal studios. But an ordinary living-room or bedroom, preferably at the back of the house to reduce traffic noise, can be fine. Draw the curtains (thick ones are best), to muffle the sound coming in through the windows and stop the voices of the speakers bouncing off the glass too much.

If you have your broadcasters sitting at a table, cover it with a blanket to stop the sound reverberating off the hard surface. Microphones vary, so you will have to experiment to work out the best distance from your speakers. If they are too close,

voices will sound very deep and the *plosives* ('Ps' and 'Bs') will make a nasty pop on words like 'pop' or 'bob'. If they are too far away, voices will sound echoey. Worst of all, if one speaker is close and the other distant, they will sound as though they are in two different rooms.

Recording actuality

If you are making a magazine programme, you will probably want to mix live studio discussions, interviews and reports with pre-recorded actuality made on location (e.g. interviews around the school or college, reports on events from where they are actually happening). Or you may decided to make a complete actuality feature, wholly recorded on location.

Since you will not want to lug around a big reel-to-reel machine, you will need a portable recording machine. These are usually cassette machines, so make sure you can re-record the material onto your reel-to-reel machine for editing afterwards. As your microphone will be hand-held, you will need a bit of practice before you make recordings for real. Our ears tend to shut out background sounds and it can easily happen that a recording made in a canteen, for instance, stars everything and everybody except the person who is supposed to be talking. Alternatively, you may try to block out the background by holding the microphone too close to the speaker or the sound source, causing distortion. Keep an eye on the recording level at all times. If it goes into the red section, it is distorting. Ideally you should wear headphones for outside recording, so you can hear what the microphone is actually picking up.

Figure 17.6 Recording an interview on location using the bare minimum of equipment

The trick with actuality is to plan your questions carefully so that you get the information you want, but to let the interviewees ramble on in case you get something unexpected. Record at least three times as much material as you need. When you have recorded it, listen to it while it is still fresh in your mind, and make notes on which bits you can use and how they will fit together. If it sounds dreadful you can always go back and try again. Many producers cheat with location recording. They record their speakers somewhere reasonably quiet and then go out and take a wildtrack of the background sounds. In this way they can edit the words down to the right length, then add the continuous background at a level that gives colour to the words without drowning them.

Figure 17.5 Press conference where a blanket is being used to cover the table to stop sound reverberating

Recording dramas

Dramas are usually recorded in a studio. It is possible to make a play on location (to actually record it where it is supposed to happen), but if you do this you have to accept the background sounds at their real-life level. If you then want to edit the tape, you may find that the background sounds do not match.

If you have background sounds, such as a disc of a railway station, it is generally best to add them after you have edited the voices. In this way you can balance the voices against the background more effectively. If you have background music, you must add this later. If someone makes a mistake and goes back to do it again, the music will sound very strange after editing.

On the other hand, things like footsteps and pouring drinks are best done live. As the person acting will be holding a script and can't move too much, someone else will have to walk for them or pour their drink in time with the actor's speech. These live effects are called 'spot effects' in radio and 'Foley effects' in the film industry.

If an actor makes a mistake, simply get them to go back and do it again. Somewhere in the middle of the second take you will find a chunk that will edit in seamlessly. But make sure they do more than just a word or two again, as the chances are they will say things differently and the edited section will sound peculiar.

Plenty of radio plays are published, so you should be able to find something to suit your needs. Methuen used to publish a collection of best radio plays every year. But why not try to write your own?

CASE ▼ STUDY

MAKING A CHILDREN'S RADIO PROGRAMME

You should already have read chapter 15 in preparation for carrying out your practical media project. This introduced the case study of Rose Veitch, a media studies student at Sunderland University, who planned a magazine programme for children while on work experience at Sun City radio station. Her planning and thinking were explored in chapter 15. Here we find out how she went about producing the programme. This case study has been only slightly adapted from work she produced as part of her degree course.

▶◀ *See page 192 for the first part of this Case Study*

INTERVIEW TECHNIQUES

When I conduct an interview, I'll begin with some idea of what I want the interviewee to say. However, a pre-interview chat is essential, so that I am completely aware and knowledgeable about the subject. This allows me to keep the interview as brief as possible, which keeps editing to a minimum. I first decide what I want the interviewee to say and then ask a question which allows her/him to answer as I anticipate.

Before I start I close the windows, take phones off the hook and do anything else to keep background noise to a minimum. I also ask the interviewees if they could pretend to be speaking to a nine-year-old child. I usually find it easier to ask questions twice, once without recording and again with recording. Doing it this way means I can listen to the answer, jot down any other questions that come up, or change the question if I don't get a sufficient reply.

PRODUCTION: THE INTERNET

For this story I interviewed Dr Bob Hogg (IT lecturer), Mark Lloyd (teacher), some pupils, and Ian Richardson (IT specialist).

Dr Hogg's and Ian Richardson's interviews were too long and needed editing down. The teacher was more succinct. I interviewed eight children who were keen 'surfers' of the Internet and then chose the best four voices and alternated boys and girls at the editing stage.

Music and presentation

I organised all the clips into a logical order and then chose the Shamen as a musical bed to be played through the package. I like the track I used because it has a fairly constant beat, melody and level. It is quite fast and this gives the feeling of action and excitement which complements the theme of the Internet.

I chose a drama student as presenter because he is overly dramatic, not patronising and can read well. I underlined the words in the script which I wanted him to emphasise. I then asked him to put more expression into his voice than he would usually.

PRODUCTION: THE BRITS

Interviews: vox pop, Jarvis Cocker, Michael Jackson and Steve Janes (editor of a music magazine).

Vox pop

To set the scene I really needed some display of public opinion (by public I mean 7 to 12-year-olds). In order to follow through my line of argument, I needed a vox pop criticising Jackson. I couldn't do this in the copy as directly pushing forward my opinion is not allowed. I interviewed about 12 children. I knew them all quite well, so they were not shy at all. One of the girls had a friend who she claims was hurt by Cocker. I tried very hard to get in touch with this girl but failed. I had to make do with the girl explaining how one of her friends got hurt.

Jarvis Cocker

A clip of Cocker explaining why he had acted the way he did would have been good. However, everyone already knew why he had done it and they wanted to know his reactions to the charges. The statement he gave wasn't very coherent, but I thought the fact that he was a big star would compensate for that.

Michael Jackson

I chose the same clip as the rest of the media, because it was brief and showed his feelings well.

Steve Janes

I had several choices of interviewees here. I thought about speaking to someone from the Brits committee, but I wanted an impartial, outside, expert opinion and a music magazine editor seemed perfect. Even though I would have preferred speaking to someone from a well-known magazine, the comparative anonymity of *Dissident* was offset by the fact that I could interview Steve Janes face to face rather than on the telephone.

Editing and music

When editing I chose the most coherent and opinionated voices, with an even mix of boys and girls in the vox pop. Even though Cocker's interview was incoherent I decided not to edit it as he is a big star and I wanted as much audio from him as possible. Steve Janes' interview was very concise and did not need much editing. He had the habit of pausing during his talk which did give the impression that he did not know what he was talking about, so I lightened it up to improve the flow.

For music I chose two tracks: 'Disco 2000' by Pulp and 'Earth Song' by Michael Jackson, because these people are the main protagonists of the story. I also started the piece with some actuality from the Brits ceremony to set the mood and give atmosphere.

PRODUCTION: THE ENVIRONMENT

Interviews: Mark White (Youth Co-ordinator for Animal Aid), David Lovie (Environmental Education Co-ordinator) and Judith Vardy (Development Officer for CEED).

Mark White

He is an expert in providing environmental knowledge for children and therefore a good interviewee. However, I'm not very good at interviewing people on the phone as I can't use my body language to encourage people and the quality of sound is dreadful. I asked him three questions: How important is it for children to learn about the environment? To what extent do schools have to rely on people like you for environmental education? What can the individual do to protect the environment?

I was not very impressed with the interview as it was too rambling, which was my fault for not being assertive enough. This needed quite a bit of editing.

David Lovie

I asked how important it is for children to learn about the environment, whether schools need to spend more time on the topic, and how schools could improve environmental education. His answers were very complicated and involved a lot of politics. I really wanted to avoid having to explain politics to children as their knowledge of politics is very limited.

Judith Vardy

When I went to see Judith she was helping children create a wildlife garden at a school. On that particular day firemen were filling the pond with water. I tried speaking to the children but they were very young and did not want to talk to me. I asked Judith just one question: What kind of things do CEED do in particular with children?

Editing and music

I decided to split Mr White's interview into three different clips. I wanted the first to set the tone of people being very worried about the environment, so I used his warning first. Then I wanted to follow that with 'but schools don't really take it seriously' so I used Mr Lovie's clip which explained that.

Mark White came next backing up Mr Lovie and describing the role of a pressure group. Next Ms Vardy explained the role of an environmental charity, and finally Mr White explained what individuals can do to protect the environment. I wanted to end on a hopeful note – I wanted to get across a serious message without it being depressing.

The music I chose was an African tribal chant which I think evokes environmental connotations.

LINKING THE PACKAGES

I now had to write the links and record it all with some music. I decided to call the programme BUZZ. I wanted a word that evoked feelings of action, youth, fun and 'happening things'. It is also a simple, trendy word that children can identify with.

A rule for radio programmes is that you should continue to remind the listeners what they are listening to, so once I had introduced the programme and the presenter, I summed up what was 'coming later' and then introduced the first package. After that I reminded the listener what was ahead and introduced the next package, while summing up what had just been broadcast (e.g. 'and let's hope the Internet comes to your school soon'). I thought this would give the presenter a more personal relationship with the listeners. It is important that the presenter acts as a mediator between the reporters and the listeners.

I thought carefully about the order of the packages. I knew the Brits had to come third because it was the most interesting and therefore would keep listeners listening. However, I wanted to follow the Brits with the environment to take advantage of the link between 'Earth Song' at the end of the Brits and the environment theme. So I decided to do this with a link: 'Now speaking about Earth songs is one thing, but doing something about the environment is another ...'.

The main presenter, Sarah Morrow, is a drama student at Sunderland University. I was very happy with her as she did not sound patronising and was very enthusiastic and informal.

I had a few problems with the signature tune. I wanted something newsy, but all the news sweeps in the library were much too serious. I came up with an old Carter tune, '1993', from *1992 The Love Album*. It starts with a fairly loud newsy intro and then fizzles out into just a few beats and a keyboard. I decided to use the intro as my theme tune and use the quieter bits to fill under Sarah's voice.

EXTRACTS FROM THE SCRIPT

The Buzz

Welcome to the Buzz, the show where you can get clued up about the bizz. I'm Sarah Morrow. Now unless you've been on cloud nine, you'll have heard about the row at last week's Brit awards. But what really happened? And are you worried about your environment and want to take action? All this will be coming up later.

But first if you've ever wanted to surf the net but don't know how, keep listening. We're going on line with a special report from Guy Rushworth...

IN   'Something big's happened'
OUT   'next millennium'
DUR   3.40

And let's hope the Internet comes to your school soon.

Still ahead, the environment. What can you do to take action? But first the Brit awards. Rose Veitch catches up on the gossip.

IN   'Jarvis Cocker's'
OUT   'to be seen'
DUR   3.50

Interesting stuff.

Now speaking about Earth songs is one thing, but doing something about the environment is another. Our environmental correspondent, John Green brings us this special report.

IN   'Do you care'
OUT   'Do something'
DUR   2.31

And if you want to get in touch with your local pressure groups give me a ring on 0191-510510.

That's all for this week's programme. Join me, Sarah Morrow on The Buzz same time next week.

The Brits report

Actuality
DUR   16 seconds

Jarvis Cocker's caused a storm of controversy with his attack on Michael Jackson's 'Earth Song' last week at the Brit awards. A lot of people agree with Jarvis and think that Jacko's performance was well over the top...

IN   'I thought Jarvis
OUT   'daft songs'
DUR   28 seconds

Jarvis was arrested and accused of hurting children who were on stage with Jackson. He was charged with actual bodily harm, but the charges have since been dropped. Jarvis says the

accusations have hurt him.

IN   'I think anyone'
OUT   'CV is it '
DUR   13 seconds

But Jackson and his record company are not happy. They were...

IN   'Sickened saddened'
OUT   'disrupt it'
DUR   15 seconds

Although Jarvis denies harming anyone, children performing with Jackson say they were hurt. 11-year-old Steven Webb's dad is taking legal action against Cocker. His lawyers say Steven got a bruised face and are calling for a massive fifty thousand pounds claim. When the case gets to court, a judge will decide if Cocker is guilty of hurting Steven Webb.

All other charges have been dropped, so there won't be an official judgement about whether Jarvis was right or wrong to lash out in the first place. The decision's now been left with the fans. A lot of people agree with Jarvis. Steve Janes, editor of music mag, *Dissident*, is just one of them...

IN   'I don't think Jarvis'
OUT   'Jarvis did'
DUR   27 seconds

Steve Janes thinks the row could have a big impact on the music industry...

IN   'I think in a '
OUT   'A lot stronger'
DUR   30 seconds

Jackson's private life is public once more with fresh rumours of child abuse. This plus the Brits fiasco has again put Jacko in the spotlight. Whether he survives it or not this time awaits to be seen.

Style guide for The Buzz

1   No clip should be longer than 40 seconds.
2   Copy should be as brief as possible and frequently interspersed with clips.
3   Interviews should be split into two or more shorter clips.
4   Audio should be inserted within the first 20 seconds of a package.
5   The first sentence of a package should grab the listeners' attention by being short, punchy and flashy.
6   The first paragraph should introduce the main idea or concept.
7   Sentences should be short, fast and punchy and the language basic.
8   Use as many trendy words as possible.
9   When introducing a clip give a brief summary and say the person's name and position.
10 Use as much actuality and sound effects as possible.
11 Have a bed of music at all times.
12 Except for the Brit awards package, use music that is not well known so as not to detract from the speech.
13 Try to get as many children's voices onto the programme as possible.
14 Always address one person.

▶ *See Activities 1, 2 and 3, page 219*

Post-production

One of radio's strengths is its spontaneity: people say what comes into their heads and it goes fresh, sparkling and, above all, live into our radio receivers. In this respect the post-production involved in radio may simply consist of an apology for something that was a bit too fresh and lively.

However, plenty of 'live' radio does include a pre-recorded element (DJs need discs, for example). All of these elements need some form of post-production.

Music reporting

Radio stations have agreements for playing music on air with:

- Phonographic Performance Limited, which collects royalties on behalf of record companies
- The Performing Rights Society
- The Mechanical Copyright Protection Society.

These bodies are known as 'collecting societies'. They collect money owed to copyright holders, whether these are composers, performers or publishers (recording companies).

Radio stations pay a set rate per hour rather than paying for individual discs played. They aren't expected to pay in advance; they simply have to make a note of the actual amount of music played. However, they do have to keep a detailed record of all music actually played, including length (often tracks are not played all the way through). And there is always the occasional maverick who turns out not to be a member of any of these societies.

Tape editing

Apart from music reporting, the most important aspect of post-production is tape editing. For example, many 'live' programmes contain pre-recorded interviews with people who cannot get to the studio for the actual broadcast.

Interviews

Pre-recorded interviews usually need to be cut down in order to:

- get them to a reasonable length
- cut out the boring bits
- get rid of fluffs and repetitions
- make a self-contained item with a beginning and a conclusion.

However, it is important to ensure that what is actually broadcast is fair to the person being interviewed – the edited version must reflect the interviewee's opinions accurately.

To take a very simple example: the word 'not' can easily be edited out, and it is perfectly possible to make someone who actually said 'I do not believe in capital punishment' sound as though they said 'I do believe in capital punishment'.

For this reason, you should always tell the person you are interviewing if an interview is going to be edited.

Montage

In contrast, it can be very effective to set a whole batch of snippets, perhaps reflecting conflicting opinions, against each other. Even sticking together the same basic idea said by different people in different ways can work well. This form of editing is called a 'montage', and it is often used to package together 'vox pop' recordings (short responses from people in the street).

For example, suppose your local team has lost a football match and you do a series of 'vox pop' interviews afterwards with spectators. You can then edit together the most striking phrases in a montage:

> ❝ "Load of rubbish!"
> "We was robbed. I blame the ref"
> "They should all be shot – and the manager should be hanged – slowly"
> "You can't blame them. The other side were simply the better team"
> "What a fiasco – the old folks home could've done better!"
> "Look it was a great game, surely that's what matters"
> "How did the goalie miss that. He must have taken a backhander, I reckon" ❞

Only don't include the last one. It's libellous, and even though your company didn't actually say it, you can be sued for publishing a libel.

Complicated pre-recorded programmes

Complex shows are usually completely pre-recorded. The most obvious example is drama, which is almost never broadcast live nowadays.

Drama

The technique of making radio drama is rather like film. You may well record one scene at a time and do several 'takes' until you get what you want. It is important that you mark up the script to indicate these different takes (most production assistants use different coloured pens and pencils to do this). If a take is dreadful you will normally wipe it, but you will probably keep two or three versions. Afterwards you can hear them back and, at editing, choose the best bits from each.

Most actors make mistakes. The good ones will realise this, and go back a sentence or so and do it again. This is called a 'fluff/repeat' and should be marked on the script for that take. If they don't notice they've made a mistake the best thing to do is to let them carry on and then repeat the section when the scene is finished (you can bracket this section on the script and write 'retaken at end'). Most producers will also indicate which of the takes they think is the best.

If actors have to do a retake, it is important that they go back a sentence or so rather than just repeating two or three words. Most actors will not necessarily do the second version in exactly the same way as the first, and you may need to experiment to find an 'edit point' (a point where the jump from one take to another won't be noticed). Experienced editors generally prefer to have edit points in the middle of sentences, rather than between sentences.

Finally, each take of each section has to be timed accurately, so that when the whole lot is added together you have the right overall length. Plays have to fit into specific slots of 30, 45, 60, 75 or 90 minutes. Comedy series and serials are usually in 25-minute slots. Often your completed recording will be a little long, and you'll have to agonise about which bits to take out. It pays to keep an eye on length as you are actually recording,

Figure 17.7 Complex radio dramas require input from producers and editors as well as actors

since it is easier to do minor rewrites to bring the length down at this stage. More seriously, if your recording looks like being too short, you will have to add lines. If you find your recording is too short at the editing stage, when the actors have gone home, all you can do is stick in tiresome chunks of music.

As this shows, successful post-production in drama requires an awful lot of care and attention when the play is being recorded.

Most producers will add background sounds after the play has been edited to length, so that they can balance sounds against speech. This is particularly important if background music is used. Editing speech when there is music in the background can do very nasty things to the continuity of the music.

Actuality features

Turning recordings made on location into whole programmes is the most creative form of editing. It involves:

- finding links or bridges between one recording and the next so that, in effect, you tell a story
- making sure that each of your separate recordings carries forward the story
- cutting down the material you have recorded (you will probably have recorded at least three times what you need)
- changing the order in which your speakers appear to say things, if their comments are rambling.

An extreme example of this was a programme on Pidgin English. An expert in Pidgin had about 30 hours of recording from all round the world. This was all listened to, and three hours of possible material was dubbed off. In consultation with the presenter, David Attenborough, these three hours were eventually reduced to just over half an hour of carefully selected material. With just under 15 minutes of David recorded in the studio, that half-hour of actuality recording produced an excellent 45-minute programme.

Editing is time-consuming, and editing actuality needs careful note-taking before you start.

How to edit

If you have the equipment to edit on mini-disc, then editing a radio programme is like editing video. You can either:

- copy the section you want from the original and place it against the next section you want to use
- copy from one disc or tape that has the speech and from another that has the background sounds or music, and mix them together onto a third recorder.

Even if you are using reel-to-reel machines you will still need three machines, or three tracks of multi-track tape if you want to put in backgrounds.

To carry out simple editing of speech recorded on open reels you need just one machine, an editing block, a razor-blade, a Chinagraph pencil, some editing tape – and a lot of patience. Work through the following steps:

1 Work out as exactly as possible where you want to cut.
2 With your fingers on both reels, wiggle the tape to and fro against the tape heads until you find a gap (a tiny silence).
3 Mark the gap with a dot (anything other than a China-graph pencil will leave a sound on the tape).
4 Cut the tape on the block using the 45 degree groove (assuming your tape is mono). Then do the same thing with the tape where you want to come back in.

5 Stick the two tapes firmly with a piece of the special editing tape (again, anything else will leave a noise).

With a lot of luck, and if you have done the whole thing carefully enough, your recording will now play through without anyone knowing there is an edit. But be warned: don't throw away the piece of tape you've cut out before you've heard the edited version. A lot of edits don't work first time, and you may want to stick it back and try again.

Figure 17.8 Radio tape being edited using a razor-blade and Chinagraph pencil

Once you have your whole tape edited together, it is a good idea to copy it onto another reel or onto a cassette, as edits can come apart. In the 1970s a distinguished producer from the 1950s was invited to do a guest production of a drama. She was used to producing plays live, and was horrified at the idea of pre-recording her production. She was a formidable lady and it took a lot of courage to insist that she pre-record the play. Tapes edited by professional sound technicians very rarely come apart – but her show did, while it was being broadcast on Radio 4. She wasn't terribly pleased.

Hints on editing

Two small but important points:

- People speaking 'off the cuff' tend to use a lot of 'ers' and 'ums', there are pauses while they think, and you can hear lots of little breaths. If all of these are left in, the speech can sound very broken up and clumsy. However, if they are all taken out, the speech sounds unreal. As a rule of thumb, most people leave in about one-third.
- At the end of a 'field recording', before you cut to the studio, copy off the final few seconds and fade down the end quickly on your mixer. Even if you have cut at the end of a sentence the background will still be there. Simply cutting to studio gives a rather jagged feel to the end of a recorded passage.

▶◀ *See Activity 4, page 220*

ACTIVITIES ▼

Activity 1

Rose Veitch, who produced the children's radio programme in the case study, says: 'directly pushing forward my opinion is not allowed'.

Having read the case study, how far do you think she has pushed her opinion indirectly?

Where do you stand on the question of partiality versus impartiality?

Activity 2

In the case study, Rose says: 'I knew the Brits had to come third because it was the most interesting and therefore would keep listeners listening'.

How far do you agree with this statement?

Activity 3

Write your own style guide for a radio magazine programme of your own design.

Activity 4

Working in a group, make a radio programme of your own. Each member of the group should have a particular responsibility – speaker, producer, sound technician, writer etc.

What sort of programme?

The programme can be whatever you like, for example:

- a play
- a magazine programme
- a scripted, dramatised historical feature
- an actuality feature about a topic or place
- a mixture of actuality and interviews, dramatised chunks and scripted narration
- a music feature (interviews and music cut together).

Don't try to do a phone-in – you need special equipment and permission from BT.

What should it be about?

The best ideas for programmes are original. No one said to Dylan Thomas, 'Would you write us a play about a day in the life of a dull little Welsh town in which nothing at all happens all day – oh, and why not do it in verse?' Yet *Under Milk Wood* is the most famous radio play ever written.

So don't copy existing shows. The most original ideas will probably come from your own unique experience. *Under Milk Wood* works because it was based on the place where Thomas lived, and he knew it inside out.

Make sure your show goes somewhere, not just round and round in circles. The best way to keep your audience interested is to make them eager to know what's going to happen next. Re-read chapter 15 on pre-production and the section in chapter 11 on writing for radio, and watch out for the pitfalls.

Your final programme should be 15 to 20 minutes long.

Good luck! It can be fun making radio programmes.

BIBLIOGRAPHY ▼

Best Radio Plays, Methuen, BBC Series 1978 to 1989

Chrisell, A, *Understanding Radio*, 2nd ed., Routledge, 1994

Horstmann, R, *Writing for Radio*, A & C Black, 1991

Mcleish, R, *Radio Production*, 3rd ed., Focal Press, 1994

McLoughlin, S, *Writing for Radio*, How To Books, 1998

Thomas, D, *Under Milk Wood*, Everyman, 1979

Wilby, P, and Conroy, A, *The Radio Handbook*, Routledge, 1994

Young Playwrights Festival 1988, BBC Radio Drama, 1988

CHAPTER 18

Video production

Introduction

This chapter shows you how to produce and edit a video. It does this through a case study of a student project, in which students evaluate the brief, production and editing of their video.

The case study is followed by practical advice on:
- what type of video to produce
- preparing for production
- editing.

Making a video

Making a video is a challenging task. Video production itself is a complex activity, and a finished video is likely to consist of images, sound, and text or graphics. In order to produce a soundtrack and credits, you will need to be able to use a fair amount of technical equipment.

Therefore if you are thinking of making a video for your media studies course, the first thing to remember is to keep it simple. More things can go wrong when producing a video than you'd care to imagine.

The following case study explores the experience of two students producing their own video as part of a media studies course.

C A S E ▼ S T U D Y

MAKING A STUDENT VIDEO

Between March and July 1997, two media studies GNVQ students at a Kent grammar school, John and Michael, planned, filmed and edited a video. Their English teacher then used the video to accompany a one-man show which he performed for Open University students at the University of Sussex throughout the summer.

Figure 18.1 Students filming for a video project

The finished video provided the students with evidence for three units of Advanced GNVQ Media: Communication and Production:
- Planning Audio Visual Products
- Producing Audio Visual Products
- Making a Narrative Video.

It could have been used as a practical project for A Level Media Studies coursework.

The following extracts from the students' evaluations give you an interesting insight into how (and how not) to go about producing and editing a video, especially if you are restricted in terms of equipment.

THE BRIEF

From Michael's evaluation:

The aim of our video was to visually represent the content of some of our English teacher's dramatic monologues about growing up in the South of England which form the basis for his one-man shows, one of which we were able to see during the 1997 Gillingham Arts Festival in May.

Having discussed the idea with him, we decided that we would attempt to represent visually on video the content of the three monologues which were set in locations close to our school. These places were Brighton in Sussex, Minnis Bay, near Margate on the Isle of Thanet, and Dungeness.

To prepare for the videos, we asked our teacher to look with us at a Brian Eno video called *Thursday Afternoon* which we had studied on our media studies course as an 'alternative' approach to the medium.

The Eno video, using his own ambient music, does not tell a story, but instead attempts to create a sort of video painting which can be playing on your television instead of hanging on a wall. Basically the video shows an image of a woman which has been slightly enhanced by computer effects and which changes ever so slightly as the tape plays. This sounds terribly boring but, in fact, the effect is rather hypnotic.

We thought that something like this could be played in the background whilst our teacher performed his monologues and could add a multi-media dimension to his performance without distracting the audience too much from what he was saying. He liked our idea.

In turn our teacher played us two videos which had inspired his work. The first, *Swimming to Cambodia*, was a filmed record of the American actor Spalding Gray's one-man shows about his experiences as a supporting actor in the film *The Killing Fields*. This had obviously inspired our teacher in terms of style.

The second was Derek Jarman's *Blue*, a film which only consists of a blue screen plus a recording of Jarman and friends musing about life and death. It was surprisingly moving. In addition we looked at a book by Jarman called *Derek Jarman's Garden*, which was all about Dungeness where he had lived, in the shadow of the nuclear power station, before his untimely death from AIDS.

These all helped us come up with the ideas for the video.

The idea was that we would go to the three locations, film about five to ten minutes' worth of footage at each using a camcorder and then edit this material into a short video which could be played to accompany the performance of each monologue using the school's editing facilities. We had not previously made a video or used the school video editing suite.

We arranged to go first to Dungeness, then Brighton and finally to Minnis Bay.

THE SHOOTS
From John's evaluation:

We did not storyboard as we had not visited any of the locations previously and therefore had little idea what to expect. We had sort of planned the content of the video with our teacher who gave us a copy of his show which we used as a script, of sorts. For example, in his piece about Dungeness, the steam railway was mentioned, along with the lighthouse and power station and Prospect Cottage, Jarman's home. All of these needed to feature in our video.

The Brighton shoot was to consist of a walk through the Lanes, a famous part of Brighton, where visitors and bargain hunters can find a bewildering array of shops, selling everything from bondage gear to Tibetan bells.

At Minnis Bay we would visualise the walk on the beach which concludes the performance.

In all three shoots we would attempt to capture the 'feel' of the places we visited.

The lighthouse from the 1960s is an architectural wonder. The light turns every eleven seconds from a tall black and white tower which shoots up from a spiral.

The old lighthouse for tourists who cross the marsh on the Dungeness light railway has an extraordinary room of glass prisms – an Aladdin's cave. From the top you can see that the Ness is made of waves of shingle fanning out to the sea.

Above: Lens room in the lighthouse

Opposite: Facing the lighthouse

Figure 18.2 Inspiration for videos can come from any source – in this case the book Derek Jarman's Garden

The Dungeness shoot

From John's evaluation:

Figure 18.3 Dungeness beach with the power station in the background

We arrived at 11.00 a.m. and found Dungeness to be as striking a place as we had imagined. There really is no other place like it. The hum of the power station plays like an out of tune radio permanently in the background. The sea is wild. The beach shacks are bizarre. The lighthouse stands sentinel. Our only real problem was that on the day of our visit it was not raining, which our teacher suggested it always did in his performance.

Nor was the light steam railway train running, which meant that we could not film these aspects of the monologue.

We decided that the best way to introduce the place on the video was to try to film a 360 degree pan from the centre of the beach which would show the sea, the beach shacks, the lighthouse and the power station and give the audience a chance to acclimatise itself.

We also decided that all shots for the video would be filmed using the camcorder's built-in letter-box format. This would then allow us the chance to add titles to the shots in the finished version, rather like the titles of paintings. We also thought that the letter-box format made our video look more professional.

The 360 degree shot was not as easy to achieve as we first thought it would be. There were two main problems: the first was that, although we had a tripod, rotating the camera steadily and without speeding up was very difficult. We did the shot three times before we got it right and even then the shot was not perfect. The second problem was, because we were filming on a shingly beach (shingle is special at Dungeness), the camcorder's built-in microphone picked up the noise we made as we walked round the tripod in order to film the shot. It would be necessary to remove all the original sound from the shot during the edit which then raised a problem with the soundtrack; after all, the 'feel' of Dungeness is created by sounds as well as sights.

The rest of the shoot was pretty straightforward. We took shots of all the obvious stuff: the lighthouse, the power station, the railway station café. The best shot was our last one. We wanted to close the Dungeness sequence with a shot suggesting departure. Our teacher's monologue ends with him leaving the place with his children on board the light steam railway train which, of course, wasn't running on the day we came to film.

Our solution was to film our own departure, rather dangerously but very effectively, by strapping ourselves into the back of the estate car we had borrowed to make our journey and, with the rear hatch open, film the village of Dungeness as we drove away from it. Our inspiration here was the 'road' movies we had looked at whilst studying genre for the Film unit, particularly a film called *Electra Glide In Blue* which ends with a similar shot which seems to go on forever.

The finished long take would not need much editing and lasted about five minutes: we drove out of Dungeness ever so slowly.

The Brighton shoot

From Michael's evaluation:

Figure 18.4 The Lanes in Brighton

A good day in Brighton today. We repeated our 'leaving Dungeness' approach and, with camcorder in hand, filmed a walk from the pier, through the Lanes, to the Duke of York's cinema, all in one take. It looks good on playback, apart from the trampy bloke who kept getting in the way on purpose – but we can edit him out.

The Minnis Bay shoot

From Michael's evaluation:

This was very straightforward. We had storyboarded this, working from our teacher's script. Before we got there we knew exactly what we wanted. We wanted a shot of the bay; a shot of a child's windmill on the beach; a shot of shoes on a beach and a shot of driftwood being thrown into the sky. Each shot would last about 3 minutes. All four 'captured' the content of our teacher's script. We would use the tripod for the first and last shot and an extremely low angle for the middle two: this basically consisted of putting the camcorder on the floor and letting it run. Once more we would use the letter-box format for all the shots.

On the day of filming, things went according to plan and we returned to school to edit the videos, confident that our footage would be sufficient for our brief.

THE EDIT

From Michael's evaluation:

Disaster: Brighton is entirely unusable and there's no hope of re-filming. We showed our footage to our teacher and it was almost unwatchable. The reason: we filmed it all by hand and the picture just wobbles far too much to make it at all usable. It's obvious really – you can't just walk about with a video camera in your hand and expect to record a steady image. Inevitably the picture jerks up and down as you move about.

The only way we could have achieved what we set out to do, would have been to have used something like a camera dolly – maybe a pushchair or wheelchair (in fact, now I come to think of it didn't Godard use a wheelchair when he filmed those famous tracking shots of Jean Seberg selling *New York Herald Tribune* in the Champs Elysées in his new wave classic *A Bout De Souffle*?).

Although the long tracking shot through the Lanes was a good idea, and if we had another chance to film in Brighton we could certainly come up with something usable, we all agreed that we would be better off trying to make use of our Dungeness and Minnis Bay footage than redoing the Brighton shoot.

Brighton was a wasted day.

The value of editing

From John's evaluation:

It is certainly true that editing material can make a massive difference to the finished product. This was my first time editing and I understand now that this process is not only very creative in itself, but it is also one of the most essential aspects of film-making. The auteur approach to film studies is all very well and good, but I'll be looking out for the names of editors from now on whenever I watch a movie. The editors really do put the finishing touches to a movie.

Having discovered that our Brighton stuff is no use to anyone, the aim is to put the Dungeness material and the Minnis Bay stuff into some sort of order; to add credits and titles to the shots (like the titles for paintings – we've already come up with simple, ambiguous titles: power, the house of Jarman, sea, shack etc. for the Dungeness material) and then to make two finished versions of the videos. The first can be used by our teacher during his performances and will be completely silent so that he can narrate his tales with the videos showing in the background in a relatively unobtrusive way.

The second version will be 'finished' and will include the credit sequence. We are even hoping that our teacher might record his monologues about both places onto the video and that we can use him as narrator. If we do this, then we will satisfy the evidence requirements of our GNVQ Media course and also make videos that can be used in a practical way.

Recording monologues

From Michael's evaluation:

Recording the monologues was another good idea which we found was not quite as simple as we'd imagined. Although the editing suite's Camlink audio mixer allowed you to record using a microphone directly onto the video; and although the mixer enables you to mix this with music from tape or CD and the original soundtrack recorded live on the video (replete with the conversations we were foolish enough to be having whilst filming which mean that much of our original soundtrack had to go); the problem was that there was no effects unit for the recording of voices on our school's editing suite.

Therefore, when we came to record our teacher's monologues, the sound was really dry, with no reverb or anything to make the voice sound professional. John said that he'd bring in his own graphic equaliser, but, after some discussion we decided that it would be simpler if we just went back to the local recording studio where we'd worked on our radio programme for the Audio units, and recorded the voice using professional recording equipment and the assistance of a studio engineer.

This we did last Friday and the results are excellent (although it cost the school £40 to hire the studio for a couple of hours).

I'm beginning to think that this video is going to be something to be really proud of – although sometimes I wonder if I wouldn't have been better off taking Physics!

Learning to use equipment

From John's evaluation:

The problem with the editing suite is that the more you run through the video in order to add effects or sound, the more quality you lose. We've assembled the Dungeness material and added the narration (plus some Eno music as a sort of tribute to *Thursday Afternoon*, Mike's going to write to EG Records to find out about copyright, although as we're only using the video for education purposes we don't think there'll be a problem) and, although all our edits are neat – they ought to be we did them about six or seven times each before we got them right – the visual quality of the final video is not really very good. Mike thinks we should start again, this time adding the credits and shot titles live. We can then audio dub on the monologue which means that we'll lose all our original sound, but most of this is unusable anyway because of our talking on it.

From Michael's evaluation:

I'm glad we started again on Dungeness. The finished video quality is much better. It'll be easy doing the Minnis Bay one now. I think that we're finally getting the hang of the equipment. It would have been a lot easier if we'd done some experiments before making this video. Every time we used it, until recently, I was convinced that we'd lose our original material and have to start again from scratch. Now I know that we won't and we're both a lot more confident.

The final product

From John's evaluation:

Minnis Bay is finished. The project is complete. Both videos are edited and the soundtrack added on. We've shown them to our teacher who is really impressed. I think that we should get distinctions for the work we've put in.

This really has been a high point of the GNVQ course. Not only have Mike and I made our first video, but we've also both mastered what can and cannot be done with the editing suite. In addition I think that I'll be paying particular attention in future to how films are edited, something I've never really noticed before now.

I'm pleased that the video project has resulted in something so professional and that everyone who's seen it is as impressed as I am, especially our teacher who's now using the video as part of his one-man show and advertising it as 'a multi-media event'.

▶◀ *See Activity 1, page 228*

What can you learn from the case study?

These extracts from Michael and John's evaluations give you a unique insight into the process of producing a student video. The circumstances surrounding the production are common for students making videos at schools or colleges with limited facilities. However, although the students only had the use of one camcorder and a tripod (both, incidentally, their own), and no lights or specific sound recording equipment, they still managed to experiment with the equipment available, and did not use lack of equipment as an excuse for not doing their best.

The students' naiveté is fairly obvious from the case study, but so is their enthusiasm, and this is probably the most important quality when it comes to working under these types of conditions. It is also apparent that the students kept their ideas fairly simple. This too is essential when attempting to work with limited resources.

It is interesting to note that, although the production was fraught with difficulties, the finished production was considered to be a success not only by Michael and John, but also by their assessors. Both students went on to receive distinctions for the quality of outcome of their final videos.

This case study is an excellent reminder to all prospective student video-makers of the need for thorough planning when preparing for both the production and the post-production of video products. It also underlines the need for flexibility when undertaking such a complex activity.

The real message here is that the production of a video is a very demanding activity which is likely to challenge you in ways you never considered at the outset. The following sections highlight some of the ways in which you can simplify the task, avoid mistakes and ensure final success.

Figure 18.5 Preparations for making a video should include producing a storyboard to help plan the shoot

Preparing for production

As you found out in chapter 15, coming up with ideas, planning, storyboarding, preparing schedules and so on are all essential elements in producing a video. The quality of your final product is likely to depend upon the success of these early stages. As you have seen from the case study, although it is possible to film with minimal planning, a haphazard approach to video production is likely to cause you problems in the long run, and may even make some of your work unusable.

Although everything you do should be scripted and storyboarded, and the logistics of your video shoot should be planned well in advance, remember to remain flexible. You never know, something that seemed a disaster at the time can sometimes be incorporated into your finished video to give it an innovative edge.

What type of video are you going to produce?

Successful video projects produced by media students include:

- pop videos (for their own music, or for songs by established artists)
- documentaries about a subject they are interested in (e.g. the cost of CDs, the impact of cable TV, the promotion of a local newsletter, opening a new sports centre)
- videos made in the style of a film director they have studied on their film courses (in the past, students have made excellent parodies of Hitchcock's *Psycho* and Eisenstein's *Battleship Potemkin*)
- advertisements or trailers for imaginary products, films or TV shows.

Students with access to studio facilities have sometimes attempted more ambitious projects, such as dramas, live chat shows, situation comedies and soaps. However, as in the case study, most students don't have access to a TV studio and produce videos using fairly basic equipment. This does not necessarily mean that your finished video has to be basic in either execution or design.

Even if students do have access to a studio, it is rare for them to produce videos which last longer than 20 minutes. You need to bear this in mind when producing your own video: more isn't necessarily better. Often short, punchy videos are preferable to lengthier, less well-organised ones.

The recce

It is important to visit your location before you start filming, in order to:

- check whether or not something you want to film will actually be there (in John and Michael's case they could have found out about the steam train)
- establish what shots you want to take when you film
- make notes about possible camera placement
- take some still shots of the types of picture you want to take when you start filming
- look out for cutaway shots that you can edit into the main part of the video to provide detail or atmosphere

- try to envisage things which might interfere with your film, such as the sudden intrusion of low-flying aircraft from a neighbouring airfield
- check whether you need to ask anyone for permission to make a film
- check the lighting conditions and locate any power points (if your location is indoors)
- check for potential safety hazards.

If you are working in a team, every member of the team should take part in the recce to think through the filming from different points of view.

The practice shoot

Organising a practice shoot can save you a lot of time, trouble and wasted material. John and Michael could certainly have saved themselves a great deal of trouble – and avoided losing one-third of their material – if they had organised a practice shoot in Brighton.

You should check all equipment before you start, making sure that you have:

- spare batteries
- numbered cassettes
- some way of labelling your shots (e.g. a clapperboard) and noting that they are practice shots.

Check the lighting by doing a white balance. Basically this means giving your camera a preview of ambient (surrounding) lighting, so that it can set its exposure level. This is done differently with different equipment, so you will need to consult your instruction book. With many cameras it simply means pointing the camera at a sheet of white paper. If the lighting changes during the shoot, you will need to reset the white balance.

At this stage you should also check your framing and mixing of close-ups with medium and long shots, so that you become accustomed to how the camera refocuses. If you intend to use panning and zooming (don't overdo it), check to see that you are doing these movements at a suitable speed.

Check that your in-built microphone is capable of capturing the sounds you want. You should have a tape recorder with you to record other sounds that you might want to insert during editing.

If you have to use artificial lighting, experiment with different intensities and positions, checking the images in your viewfinder. Try 'bouncing' lights off ceilings and walls to eliminate shadows. Make notes on your findings.

When you view your practice material, note any faults and work out how to prevent the same things happening again. If there are lots of problems, do another practice shoot.

Production roles

When producing videos in school or college, it is likely that you will be involved in all aspects of video production: from storyboarding to camera work, and from editing to credit writing. This is not the case in a professional video company, where different jobs are usually carried out by individuals who have developed expertise in a particular area (e.g. by taking a further or higher education course as camera people or graphic designers).

Your examiners will certainly understand that you will probably need to adopt a more basic, 'do-it-yourself' approach to producing video material. You will be rewarded for innovation and imagination as much as for 'professional finish'.

This is not a licence to do things in a sloppy way, but it does mean that when undertaking video production you must put as much effort as possible into all aspects of the project; from planning through to editing. In this way, your teachers and examiners will be able to make a more holistic evaluation of your contribution.

Your own evaluation of your work is important, because this can give your assessors a clear understanding of your intentions, why you made certain decisions, and how your team operated. Writing an evaluation can also help you to focus upon what you have learnt while producing a video. At this level, this is what the production of any media product is really about. Learning by doing is often the best starting point.

For more on actually carrying out a shoot, see the Case Study on page 221.

Post-production

As already mentioned, producing a video is a complex activity because it involves producing a soundtrack, text and graphics to support the final selection of images.

Video post-production is likely to be particularly time-consuming. Images, soundtrack, text and graphics all need careful editing in order to establish a continuity of shots. As John and Michael discovered, the production stages of making a video often seem relatively straightforward, but post-production may not be quite so simple.

Equipment

In the post-production stages, availability of equipment is a crucial factor. It is possible to film interesting material using a basic camcorder. However, in order to edit and add text to those images, certain equipment must be available.

The editing suite at John and Michael's school consists of a basic Panasonic set-up which allows you to manually edit material to professional standards. The suite is linked to a small audio Camlink mixer, which you can use to add audio material to finished videos from either cassette or CD. The suite is also linked to a text generator, which enables you to add text and basic graphics to the finished videos, and to an effects unit which you can use to add visual effects to the images created.

Essentially, the editing suite enabled the students to carry out basic post-production work. Including the two monitor screens, it cost about £5000 to buy.

John and Michael made the mistake of not using the system before editing their videos. As the case study shows, they encountered a number of difficulties as a result of this lack of experience.

Figure 18.6 A video production studio

Editing

John and Michael were lucky to have access to an editing suite for such a long time. In many schools and colleges you will not have that luxury, so the more preparation you can do in advance the better.

Practising editing

If you are not familiar with the editing equipment it is important that you practise on material which you do not want to use in your final video. It is probably best to keep things simple and not dabble with any special effects. Aim to be able to:

* place a cutaway into a sequence keeping the original sound
* have the cuts occurring exactly where you want them
* add commentary or soundtrack to pictures
* overlap sound so that the sound edit comes before or after the visual edit
* fade pictures and sound at different speeds.

Viewing raw material

You should look through everything you have filmed and make sure that each separate shot is listed:

> *Cassette 1; shot 1; take 1 becomes 1;1;1.*
> *1;1;1 Shot of steam train pulling into station. Slightly out of focus at beginning. Effective sound. 20 seconds.*

Assembling the material

Your next step is to determine which shots to use, in which order, for your final video:

> *Sequence A*
> *1;1;1 Long shot of train pulling into station.*
> *1;2;1 Medium shot of carriage door showing passenger.*
> *1;3;2 Close-up of passenger's face.*

You might want to add information about sound effects or voice-overs at this stage.

▶◀ *See Activity 2, page 228*

ACTIVITIES ▼

Activity 1

Read through John and Michael's evaluations of their video production and post-production experiences again (see page 221).

Where and why do you think they encountered most problems?

What do you think, if anything, they could have done to avoid the problems?

Activity 2

Imagine that you are to make a similar video to the one described in the case study, based upon your own feelings about a place you have visited.

Produce a treatment for the project, including a sample script and a plan of how you will go about filming your script.

Produce a storyboard for four sequences to be included in your video.

BIBLIOGRAPHY ▼

Daley, D, *Basic Film Technique*, Focal Press, 1980

Patterson, M, *A Quick Guide to Video Documentary Making*, BBC Television Training, 1993

Thompson, R, *Grammar of the Edit*, Focal Press, 1993

Watts, H, *Directing on Camera*, Aavo Media, 1992

CHAPTER 19

Media studies toolkit

Introduction

This toolkit provides detailed practical advice to help you organise your studies and prepare yourself for coping with the demands of examinations. It covers the following topics:
- study skills and effective planning
- research

- essays
- exams
- image analysis
- key skills
- knowing your syllabus.

Study skills and effective planning

Background preparation

There are few things as annoying as knowing that you could have done better in an essay, exam or coursework. Most of the time, marks are lost due to lack of information, lack of background reading and lack of confidence. This is not always laziness. More often than not, it is due to poor planning.

It is extremely useful to know what your work schedule is likely to be as far in advance as possible. In some instances schools and colleges will be able to supply a work schedule for the year ahead right at the beginning of the course. This is the perfect opportunity for you to plan ahead. If there is a list of books to read, you can order them or find out which libraries house them and set up an inter-library loan. If you are to study certain films or genres, you can begin to do some background reading or rent out relevant videos. Where schools or colleges cannot do this, it is worth finding out what background reading or research will be useful for your studies.

Towards the end of your course, you will find yourself spending more and more time:
- reading the newspaper (e.g. the *Media Guardian*, which is a supplement to the *Guardian*)
- reading magazines (e.g. *Sight and Sound* or *Screen International*)
- listening to the radio (e.g. programmes on Radio 4)
- watching out for relevant television programmes (e.g. behind-the-scenes documentaries or programmes on the BBC Learning Zone).

To start a step ahead, you can begin to look out for information which may be relevant to your course right from the start. Make notes if necessary, or simply broaden your knowledge base by purposefully keeping your eyes and ears open from the word go. Not only will this approach add to your knowledge base, but it will also add to your enjoyment of the course.

Responding to a task

You have been set a task; perhaps a complicated practical production, or simply an essay. Whatever the task, the most important moment is the point at which you sit down and sketch out a plan for your work. You will need to consider:
- which resources you need to borrow, hire, book or buy
- what notes you need to collect
- what research you need to undertake
- whether you need to book any interviews in advance
- how much time you are going to need for each stage of the process
- building in time to redraft work
- building in time in case things go really wrong, or in case more avenues for exploration emerge along the way

Planning a revision timetable

Advance planning is especially useful when exams are approaching. Make sure that you allow enough time to chase up any notes which you forgot to photocopy or to cover areas where you found it more difficult to assimilate the information.

Develop a revision timetable which works for you. A good revision schedule will include:
- time early on to catch up with notes and research
- clear study times for particular topics (e.g. Tuesday afternoon 2 p.m. to 4 p.m. and 4.30 p.m. to 8.30 p.m. – the rise of Hollywood)
- sketching out essay plans for exam questions
- doing timed essays
- discussing work with teachers and colleagues
- time off to relax.

Oral debate

Seizing the opportunity to discuss ideas – with colleagues studying media, teachers, friends and family – is a very important part of developing good study skills which is often forgotten.

Discussions like these give you a chance to hear other opinions, challenge ideas and put forward your own, argue a position and find evidence which supports that position. This is a key skill in the study of media. It is not simply about learning things, it is about using that information to have an opinion. And there is nothing like saying things out loud to an audience to test your active knowledge. In other words, what you come up with in a discussion you can rely on to be in your mind under exam conditions.

Commitment

Practical productions are an important lesson for us all. They teach us about the importance of planning, group work and good ideas supported by thorough research. They also remind us of the importance of commitment. It is no exaggeration to say that students who are committed to their work from the start will achieve one, if not two, grades higher than if their work progresses in spurts and pauses. All this means is maintaining a steady approach to work throughout the course.

Research

Research is generally divided into:

- Primary research. This is first-hand research. It may include interviews which you conduct (this is quite a useful avenue to explore if you have the time and access to relevant people). It also includes surveys or questionnaires which you organise and analyse. Be careful how you use information collected in a survey, however, as it is only a small sample and should not be used alone to validate arguments.
- Secondary research. This will form the majority of your research. It involves looking at information and texts already gathered, produced or published.

Research for practical production

You will need to carry out four types of research for a practical production:

- Background research – which involves finding out about and exploring similar types of products to the one which you will be producing. You will need to develop a sense of how the product is produced professionally, how audiences are targeted, what its particular codes and conventions are, and the relevant legal and ethical issues.
- Audience research – into the market for your product. Who will use the product? How? Why?
- Content research – information which you gather to inform the content of your media product. This may be facts and figures, interviewees and how to reach them, background information.
- Production research – information which you need to produce your product, such as locations, pictures, material, music, legal procedures, copyright.

Research for essays

Why do research? If you are to give the best possible answer to an essay question, you need to have:

- A broad overview of the area you are researching. This provides you with a solid context for discussing the media texts or issues in your essay. For example, if you are discussing the height of the Hollywood era, it would add to your overall understanding of the subject area, and therefore the quality of your work, if you had an insight into the political and social conditions of America in the 1930s and 1940s and if you knew two or three of the classic films produced at this time really well. You may not always use this information directly, but it influences the standard of your responses.
- Some knowledge of the work of theorists and debates which exist in that particular area. You need to make sure that you know the key books to read on the subject area. Your teacher or a specialist librarian can provide you with a list of the important books which you need to cover. This will ensure that you have a firm grasp of the relevant issues.

Planning your research

1 Target the areas which you need to research. It is useful to ask for some help with this. Otherwise you can overload yourself with work, some of which won't be absolutely necessary.

2 Target your potential sources. Phone around if necessary, as most libraries can tell you where to find appropriate information even if they do not have it themselves.

3 Plan a research schedule so that you limit the amount of time you spend gathering information. It is a process which has no natural end and could go on for years, so you need to be clear when to stop. If you have given yourself clear targets, this should be easy to do.

Organising and using your research

There is no point in regurgitating information or copying other people's work and ideas. The people marking your essay, whether at school, college or in exam conditions, will recognise that this is what you have done. In any case, it doesn't help you to develop your mind. Research is only useful where it broadens your knowledge, develops your arguments and supports or challenges your own position.

Notes made from research need to be organised so that you know where to go for a quote or to refer back to specific information (dates or names). It is advisable to categorise notes made during research, preferably using different colour marker pens to separate out areas. This will make them easier to use for revision purposes as well. For example, you may wish to gather notes under the following headings for the essay on Hollywood:

- the Hollywood studio system at its height
- films from the 1930s and 1940s
- the contemporary film industry
- contemporary films (studio and independent)
- post-modernism
- auteur
- genre.

This is by no means an exhaustive list, but it is a useful sample of the types of headings you could use to organise and use research more effectively.

Resources for research

You can use any or all of the following when researching:

- general libraries (a local library for example)
- specialist libraries (such as a film or newspaper library)
- CD-ROMs
- magazines
- newspapers
- radio
- television
- videos
- interviews (with industry professionals).

Referencing sources

Whenever you find useful material, make sure that you jot down where you found it and any details (such as date, time of transmission, issue number) so that the reference can be checked. You must always reference work used for research at the end of an essay. The work does not necessarily need to have featured within the essay itself. When referencing a book or CD-ROM note down:

- the author/s and/or editor/s
- the year of publication
- the title
- the publisher
- the page reference.

For example: Allen, J (ed.), *Channels of Discourse Reassembled*, Routledge, 1992, page 26.

Essays – a key to success

Responding to an essay question

You have been given the following question:

> ❛ *The structure of the American film industry today allows individual talent to flourish, whereas the Holly-wood studio system, even at its most successful, was a film factory – bound to turn out a mediocre product. Do you think that this is a fair judgement?* ❜

If you have studied this area, write some notes on what topics you would need to cover in the essay before reading on.

First of all you need to read the question to work out exactly what it is asking you to discuss. Some students consider this question and immediately think that they are simply being asked to compare Hollywood of the past with Hollywood today, recounting how the studio system worked and had a direct influence on the style and genre of all films produced. It is true that this information forms a large part of the question.

However, the title is also making a sweeping statement and inviting you to argue with its affirmations. Does the contemporary film industry really allow individual film talent to flourish? Isn't it still dominated by the majors? What about the rise of the independents and the fashion of alternative film-making styles? Does post-modernism affect the style of new film-makers (e.g. Tarantino) and the audiences who watch them? Could the old system have been considered a film factory? In what sense? Were they not simply at an earlier stage of development in terms of genre? What about the classic films from these years? There were not only one or two of them. Isn't there a notion of the popular being assumed to be mediocre? Isn't this too much of a value judgement? Should we simply be talking about an industry and audiences which have become more sophisticated and film literate? And so on...

If these questions seem too confusing, it is worthwhile breaking your answer down into segments, putting the facts and basics first, then the broader arguments, questions and considerations after.

Planning the outline of an essay

Once you have thought about the title and made notes on the basic and broader issues which you intend to cover, you will need to draw up an outline for your essay. Everybody does this slightly differently and there is no right way, but here are some suggestions:

1 Leave the introduction to begin with.
2 Number each paragraph 1, 2, 3 etc.
3 Each paragraph should have one key point. Write your points down alongside each number.
4 Write the first sentence for each paragraph. This should show the reader exactly what the paragraph is going to be about.
5 Check that you have covered the basics and broadened out your discussion further into the essay.
6 Once you have outlined the main body of your essay, write the introduction.
7 Once you have done this, write the conclusion.

This is all you need to do to outline your essay. It will probably take you a while to begin with, but you will soon be able to do it in under ten minutes.

Writing an introduction

An introduction should grab the reader's attention. You could do this by using a strong or interesting quote which is relevant to the points you go on to make. Or you could simply use an engaging and lively style. Then you need to outline briefly what the essay is going to go on to consider, particularly the complex issues which you will be tackling. Try to avoid sentences which begin 'I will then go on to look at...'. Instead use more dispassionate phrases, such as 'This raises questions about...' or 'It is therefore necessary to consider...'. The introduction is the gateway to your essay but it is not the essay itself, so avoid making it too long. A few clear sentences should do the trick.

Writing a conclusion

A conclusion summarises the arguments of the essay. Occasionally you will have vociferously argued a position and will wish to conclude that, while recognising alternative debates, your argument holds sway. More often, however, you will pull together the strands of discussion and consider the key issues or questions which the title of the essay raises. Again, the conclusion should not be too long. It is quite effective to end with a quote or comment which has not appeared in the essay so far. Perhaps it is even worth holding back a really good quote until the end.

Illustrating your argument

There is little point in arguing a position unless you can actually demonstrate how you reached your conclusions.

For example, two people are arguing about the health service being affected by political parties. One says: 'It's gone downhill since this party has been in power.' The other responds with: 'But 12 new hospitals have opened up, waiting lists have been cut by 15% and there has been a financial increase of 22%.' Which argument holds more sway?

The way to back up your argument is to use information to illustrate your point. This information can include research you have done into other media products. For example, if your answer to the essay question on page 231 referred to several key films from the 1930s and 1940s, as well as discussing contemporary films and film-makers in some detail, your position would look much stronger. The other essential way to illustrate your position is to refer to theorists, and if possible to quote them directly. This is very important as it demonstrates that you have researched the area, read theorists' arguments and have gone on to form your own opinion with this background knowledge.

Dos and don'ts for essays

Do:

- question the title of essays – do not accept them at face value. They are inviting you to argue with them in order to demonstrate your knowledge
- argue your position
- avoid absolutes
- develop your own opinion and certainly do not automatically accept the opinion of your teacher. You must be independent and come up with your own judgements
- show that you are au fait with key debates, ideas, contemporary issues and events in the media, particularly the one you are answering on.

Do not:

- simply regurgitate notes. Examiners recognise this a mile off and this isn't the point of what you are doing
- offer simple conclusions
- say 'I think'. Argue what you think within the body of your essay.

Exams

Preparing for an exam

Learning to write good exams is a technique which can be learned. If you have gathered detailed notes throughout the course, attended classes, written the essays which have been set and kept your eyes and ears open for issues in the media, then you are all set to write a good exam. Even if you haven't done all of the above there is no reason why you can't pull up a grade in the exam itself. The top tips for good exam preparation are:

- Plan a detailed, realistic revision schedule well in advance.
- Practise writing essay outlines and discuss them with colleagues and your teacher.
- Practise marking your own or colleagues' work as an examiner would. It should soon become apparent how an essay is read at top speed and what information stands out (the first sentences of paragraphs are crucial, underlining titles of books or media texts, using quotes).
- Practise writing single timed essays.

- Practise whole exams in timed conditions.
- Learn quotes which will be useful for a range of essays.
- Learn details which show that you have a grasp of the issues (dates, names, titles).

Writing the exam

If you have followed the exam tips you will be ready for the exam itself. Remind yourself of this checklist.

CHECKLIST FOR EXAMS

Always do all of the following for all answers:

1 Read the essay question carefully and think about what exactly it is asking you.
2 Plan the essay (in five to ten minutes).
3 State the basics first.
4 Consider the wider issues next.
5 Make sure that you have covered all concepts:
   - codes and conventions   • representation
   - institution   • audience.
6 Make sure that you refer to at least three media texts as examples to support your argument.
7 Quote at least one theorist to support your argument. Where you cannot remember an exact quote, at least refer to the theorist's argument.
8 Remember that there is more than one point of view – you are debating issues, not offering one answer.
9 Think for yourself. Remember that you are intelligent and confident – don't be afraid to offer more than the bare bones as you will not be penalised.

Image analysis

The process of analysing an image

The analysis of an image is a process which can be learned and then applied to the analysis of any other media product. It is simply a way of deconstructing a text which has previously been constructed for a purpose. By doing this, we unlock the details which often seem invisible to the eye at first glance. The process of deconstruction can, very crudely, be summarised as:

1 Denotation (describe what you see).
2 Connotation (describe what the things that you see may mean).
3 Anchorage (acknowledge any written text which helps to underline what is happening in the image or what its purpose is).
4 Treatment (describe how the image has been constructed using framing, lighting etc.).
5 Context (analyse who constructed the images and for what purpose).
6 Narratives (describe how the image suggests a storyline of which this is only one part).

An example of an image analysis

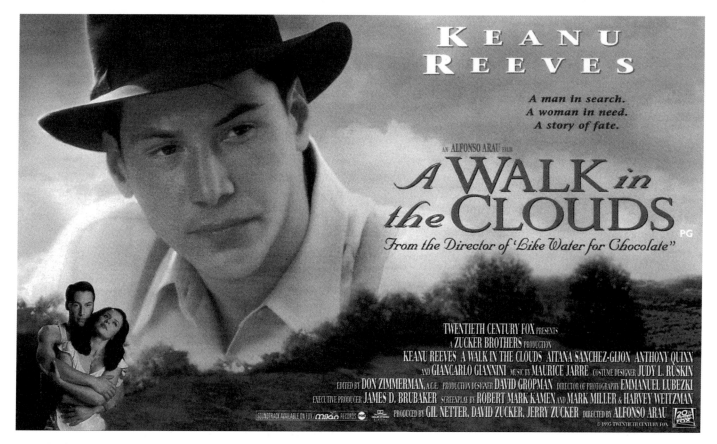

Figure 19.1

Denotation

Describe exactly what you see in the image.

There is a large photograph of a man wearing a brown hat. He is looking to the bottom right of the image. He is wearing a cream shirt with the top button undone. He is also wearing cream-coloured braces. In the bottom left-hand side of the image there is a smaller photograph of a male and female couple. It is the same man as in the main photograph. The man is standing behind the woman. He is standing up straight and has his arms around her. One hand is on her stomach and the other is holding her upper arm. He seems to be wearing a vest and no hat. The woman is bending to one side, her hair is long and loose. She is wearing a gold chain around her neck with a gold cross on it. She is also wearing a silky full-length underslip. Along the bottom of the image there is a brown landscape with trees and brush. The earth seems dusty but there seems to be some agriculture on the right-hand side and towards the distance. Behind the main photograph of the man there are clouds depicted in differing shades of brown. All of the writing is down the right-hand side of the image. There is bold writing in black and white along the bottom of the image.

Denotation and connotation

Extract the elements which you have described and briefly consider what meanings they suggest. Here are some examples:

Denotation (what you see)	Connotation (what it may mean)
Man wearing a brown hat	This is not a contemporary image. This is suggested by the fact that he is wearing a hat and by the sepia colours, which connote black and white photographs or films which have yellowed with time
Man wearing braces	The clothes worn in the image suggest an era such as the 1920s
Woman bending to one side	The stance suggests that she is weak in his arms, swept off her feet by his love, and needs to hold on to him for support

Why is it possible to work out many meanings from a few elements which have been put together to create one image? For example, there is a male and female couple in the image.

From the way that they have been dressed and the position in which they have been photographed we are able to understand much of their 'story'. How can we do this?

We have a bank of cultural information stored in our brains. When confronted with a new image, we refer to that bank to help us understand the meanings which an image offers. If we have lived in Britain for much of our lives, we will probably have watched old black and white films on a rainy Sunday afternoon from time to time. We will also have seen black and white photographs. We will know something of the era from these sources (i.e. what clothes were worn in different decades, social values). We are able to refer to that bank of knowledge and it helps us to scan an image such as this and, at the very least, to think 'that's old-fashioned – they are probably having an affair which they shouldn't be'. Our knowledge of romance novels and films also informs our reading of the film poster, as the image of the couple is borrowed in a sense from a history of romantic literature and film.

The producers are aware of this and use it as a shorthand to attract audiences used to and drawn in by this particular type of image. If you had lived on a remote island and were then faced with this image, your analysis would be based on different cultural experiences and might, therefore, be completely different.

Anchorage

If an image had no writing you could guess what it was intended for and what the meanings suggested were, but you could not be sure. Where there is writing, we say that this 'anchors' the meaning of the image. For example, here the writing anchors the fact that this is a film poster. It also helps to anchor the meanings suggested by the images alone. The words 'A man in search, A woman in need, A story of fate' reveal something of how the man and woman are brought together for this romance.

Treatment

You need to consider the treatment of the image. How has the image been constructed using framing, lighting, props and colours? In this instance, what effect does the use of browns have? How has the sepia tint affected the meanings of the image? How have the images been blurred in to each other? What effect does this have? What effect does the strong lighting from the left of the image on the man's face and shoulder have? How has the camera been positioned? What effect does this have on the overall effect of the image?

Who constructed the image and who is it for?

Who has produced the image? And how does this affect the image and the possible meanings suggested? For example, knowing that this has been produced to market a film, we need to be aware that Keanu Reeves is being used as a star vehicle for the film. In other words, he is the key element of the film which will pull in the crowds. Therefore, even if the story is equally about two people, his face has to be the most prominent on the poster. This is confirmed by the fact that his name is the most obvious wording on the poster. It is in white which contrasts sharply with the background, unlike the title which is in a shade of brown much like the rest of the poster. The reference to the fact that the director also directed *Like Water for Chocolate* confirms that this film will be attractive for audience who also saw that film. It will be in a similar genre.

Possible narratives around the images

A single still image suggests a narrative or story which surrounds the image. We are invited to imagine what that story might be. In this instance, of course, we are helped by the wording. However, we can still manufacture a whole scenario suggested by one image alone. For example, perhaps the man has returned from the First World War to find work on a farm. He meets the farmer's daughter and they fall in love. It is destiny, but theirs is a love that can never be...

Key skills

Media studies offers many opportunities to practise and improve key skills as an integral part of the course. You will find that you are able to prove your competency in certain skills over and over again. For example, you will use communication skills repeatedly in your study of media as you carry out research, undertake group work, make presentations and produce various types of written work. In other instances you will have the chance to learn a new skill (perhaps producing a particular type of computer-generated graph or animation).

Opportunities for covering key skills

Here are some examples of the types of areas where you might seek to cover key skills.

Communication

- research and note taking
- interviews
- phone calls for seeking information
- essay writing
- project compilation
- team production work
- making a presentation.

Numeracy

- the use and analysis of statistics from research
- tape logging, paper editing and time management in production work
- constructing a floor plan for studio work
- aperture and light meter readings and predictions
- budget allocation.

Information Technology

- compiling databases of information sources
- compiling a bibliography
- putting essays onto computer
- desktop publishing
- digital camera work and manipulation
- digital editing.

Knowing your syllabus

Media studies has several examining bodies which offer courses of study. They each offer similar types of assessment and content, and it is worth becoming familiar with the syllabus which you are studying. Although aimed primarily at teachers, a syllabus can offer you insight into the aims and objectives of that particular examining board. In other words, you can read about exactly what you will be studying and why. It will give you a sense of how important each component of the course is, the percentage of overall marks for each segment of the assessment procedure, and a breakdown of the key concepts which you need to be aware of. Beware reading this too near the start of your course, however, as it can seem quite intimidating.

Another useful tool is the report submitted each year by the chief examiners for each examination board. This includes the collected comments by the board in charge of assessing your work, and is worth reading and paying attention to. The report tends to comment on common mistakes made by candidates, examples of good work, and the strengths and weaknesses of students' (and centres') work.

Figure 19.2

Glossary

Actuality

Recording of real events, including film or sound recording of events as they happen. In theory, actuality events would happen whether the recording equipment was there or not. In practice, however, actuality has included staged events, particularly in early documentary films.

Aesthetics

The formal characteristics of a media text and how they relate to the intended audience. Also refers to relations between formal characteristics and what attracts, pleases or moves feeling in the reader/viewer.

Anchoring

Written text used to pin down the predominant meanings of a visual image.

Angle

The positioning of a camera or narrative 'I'. Also used to refer to a point of view.

Audience

Who uses the media and how. Who a media text is intended for.

Brief

Documents set out under headings such as 'audience' and 'outcome', used in the planning of media production. A brief can be a set of specifications handed out. It can also be used to 'sell' an approach to making a product.

Closure

This has two possible meanings:

1 It can refer to how far the outcome of a storyline is resolved. The death of a character is a 'closed' ending to their storyline. An accident in which it is not clear whether the character has survived or not indicates a lack of closure in the storyline. Soap storylines frequently end in an open manner (called 'cliffhangers').

2 It can refer to the way in which readers 'fill in' missing information. For example, a shot of someone falling off a cliff over a pool followed by a shot of bubbles rising in the water leads the reader or viewer to fill in that the person who fell has probably drowned.

Codes

Sets of signs which are understood by both the producer of a text and the audience. For example, the whistle of an approaching train in a film indicates an impending crisis or climax. The words 'and finally' towards the end of an ITN news broadcast tell the audience that the 'serious' news is over and some light relief will follow.

There are also particular kinds of codes. Technical codes in a visual image, for example, are about use of lighting, choice of lens, composition etc. Symbolic codes could be to do with gesture, clothing, props, background, setting, colour etc.

Connotation

Meanings which are suggested by the signs used to construct a media text.

Conventions

Uses and combinations of signs which are predictable in pattern and meaning. For example, the use of desks for newsreaders is a convention.

Decoding

Reading the codes of a media text to unravel its meanings and explore how and why it has been constructed.

Denotation

Describing what you see in a visual media text.

Discourse

A style of language which carries with it certain assumptions and expectations about what can and cannot be said. Institutions and social groupings can develop their own discourses which express their values. Discourse is closely connected with power and control. Bonney and Wilson use the example of the words 'police' and 'cops' to show how different discourses carry different assumptions:

> *Each [term] is associated with a whole range of words and phrases carrying the same opposed implications. Whereas the police restrain crowds, arrest suspects, protect citizens and detain criminals, the cops harass peaceful demonstrators, bash, push, shove, grab and threaten innocent bystanders. What we have here is a sharp distinction between two quite different ways of speaking and thinking about law enforcement.*
> Bonney and Wilson, *Australia's Commercial Media*, 1983

Grammar

Grammar is similar to code in that it refers to meaningful language patterns. Grammar was originally confined to describing meaningful patterns in verbal language. It is now sometimes extended to other patterns in communication, as in 'the grammar of television editing'.

Icon

This has two possible meanings:

1 It can be a sign which works through its resemblance to the thing it refers to. For example, a photograph is iconic.

2 It can be an image which is typical or representative of the ideology or whole area of activity it comes from. For example, Christ is iconic of Christianity.

Institution

A social, cultural and political structure within which the media operate. It includes the concrete (e.g. organisations which make, sell and distribute or regulate media products) and the abstract (e.g. the values and norms of media producers).

Jargon

Words which belong in form or meaning to a particular subject, activity, occupation or profession. For example, the recent phrase 'key skills' is now part of educational jargon. It is sometimes difficult to draw the line between where a word simply belongs to a variety of English and where it belongs to a special jargon. The word, 'swear', for example, can have a special meaning in the courtroom.

The term 'jargon' can be used negatively when its effects are confusing.

Language

Language is human behaviour with intended meaning which follows 'patterns' or rules. For example, verbal language follows patterns called 'grammar'. Language can be extended to describe more than just verbal language, as in the language of images, body language, the language of sound effects etc.

Metaphor

Metaphor describes when you talk about one thing in terms of another, making a link of common meaning. For example, if you say that the British press is a running sewer, you are talking about it metaphorically in terms of the dirt and unpleasantness of a sewer.

Mise en scene

Literally 'putting on the scene'. This is a term used in film-making that refers to what takes place on a set (e.g. the direction of actors, lighting, camera placement, choice of lenses). This process is distinct from 'montage' or editing, which happens after the film has been shot.

Negotiated reading

When a reader accepts some values and rejects others when reading a media text.

News values

The criteria used by news producers to select and prioritise news stories.

Oppositional reading

When a reader resists the dominant values of a media text.

Polysemic

'Poly' here means 'many'; 'semic' means 'of meaning'. When applied to an image, polysemic describes the many meanings the image contains or can be used for. For example, a cross without further information or context might mean a crossroads, a Christian cross, death, remembrance etc. In isolation, it would be polysemic.

Preferred reading

When a reader accepts the dominant values of a media text without any resistance.

Semiotics

The study of human activities as if they were languages, concentrating on signs, systems and meanings. Semiotics has its own jargon, as in 'connotation', 'denotation', 'sign', 'signifier' and 'signified'. A semiotic analysis of *Teletubbies*, for example, would look at all the signs and meanings in the programme as a text in order to analyse how it works and its messages.

Signified

The meaning of a sign.

Signifier

The physical form (visual, aural or smelt) of any sign. For words, the signifier might be the written form in letters, or the phonetic spoken form in sounds.

Synonym

Synonyms are words with the same denotation. For example, pail and bucket denote the same objects, although they have different connotations.

Text

A text is a collection of signs with a message. The term originally referred to a piece of writing, but it has been extended to refer to other pieces of language or communication which can stand as 'complete'. Media texts include pieces of writing such as articles, speech such as radio programmes, and visual texts such as advertising images.

Vocabulary

Vocabulary refers to the stock of words in a language. For example, the English has a large vocabulary for talking about the weather, and rain in particular, including 'downpour', 'drizzle', 'mizzle', 'monsoon', 'precipitation' etc.

Index